RUSSIAN SIDESHOW

Also by ROBERT L. WILLETT

One Day of the Civil War:
April 10, 1863

The Lightning Mule Brigade:
Abel Streight's 1863 Raid into Alabama

RUSSIAN SIDESHOW

AMERICA'S UNDECLARED WAR

1918–1920

ROBERT L. WILLETT

BRASSEY'S, INC.
Washington, D.C.

Library of Congress Cataloging-in-Publication Data

Willett, Robert L., 1926–
    Russian sideshow : America's undeclared war, 1918–1920 / Robert L. Willett—1st ed.
       p.   cm.
    ISBN 1-57488-429-8 (hardcover : alk. paper)
    1. Soviet Union—History—Allied intervention, 1918–1920.   2. Soviet Union—History—Revolution, 1917–1921—Participation, American.   3. Soviet Union—History—Revolution, 1917–1921—Personal narratives, American.   I. Title.
    DK265.42.U5W55   2003
    947.084′1—dc21   2003007949

Hardcover ISBN 1-57488-429-8
(alk. paper)

Printed in the United States of America on acid-free paper that meets the American National Standards Institute Z39-48 Standard.

Brassey's, Inc.
22841 Quicksilver Drive
Dulles, Virginia 20166

First Edition

10   9   8   7   6   5   4   3   2   1

Inspired by and dedicated to
the memory of
Golden Charles Bahr
Private, Company M, 339th Infantry Regiment
Eighty-fifth Division
March 5, 1887–March 12, 1919

Photo courtesy of Merlin Bahr

CONTENTS

MAPS

PREFACE

The purpose of this book is to give a realistic portrayal of the experiences of the two American forces that were sent to Russia in the fall of 1918. The American Expeditionary Force North Russia (AEFNR) was sent to Archangel, while the American Expeditionary Force Siberia (AEFS) went to Vladivostok in the Russian Far East. A detailed analysis of the events leading up to those interventions has been thoroughly covered in wonderfully researched volumes such as George F. Kennan's *The Decision to Intervene,* Betty Miller Unterberger's *America's Siberian Expedition, 1918–1920,* Norman Saul's *War and Revolution,* and many others. This book is not a discussion of the politics before and after intervention or of the parts played by other Allied forces involved. Mention is made briefly of the Navy and the 310th Engineers in North Russia, talented professionals who shared the same dangers and hardships as the infantry. Reference is also made to the Russian Railway Service Corps in Siberia and the Czech Legion; but the main focus is on the U.S. infantry, the doughboys, and how they fared.

My interest in the subject came from two sources. My wife Donna's uncle, Pvt. Golden Bahr, was a member of Company M, 339th Infantry; he landed with them in Archangel in September 1918 and fought on the railroad front. He became ill, probably with the flu, was sent home in December, discharged in February, and died at the age of thirty-two on March 12, 1919. Although he is not listed as a Polar Bear casualty, he is certainly deserving of that recognition. Golden's grave is in Marilla, Michigan.

A second spark was furnished when Donna and I spent the summer of 1998 as volunteers for Citizens Democracy Corps in the Russian Far East. We spent ten weeks in Magadan, Komsomolsk, Khabarovsk, and Vladivostok, where we first learned of the Siberian expedition. Until that time we had known of Golden's tour in Archangel from some old correspondence, but the Vladivostok effort was a surprise; thus began our research.

I went back to Vladivostok in December 1999 and visited the graves of the Allied dead in the Marine Cemetery on a bleak, wintry day. The little plot is virtually lost to visitors, surrounded by newer Russian graves. The Allied portion has new stones and plaques, but only old, almost unreadable stones identify the graves of the Czechs. The monument to the Allied dead is weather-beaten and pitted, but still stands tall and protective over its graves, much as it did on the day of the cemetery dedication, May 1, 1919. Some Americans were originally buried there, but all of the more than one hundred dead were returned to the United States during the expedition.

Vladivostok today is a sad city, suffering from severe political friction between various levels of government. The infrastructure is disintegrating, with water supplies available only 50 percent of the time, and in summer with virtually no hot water. Power outages are frequent and lengthy. The ancient trams still run along Svetlanskaya Prospekt, crammed with locals riding their free cars, much as they did in 1918. Still, the physical features of the city, the hills running down to the deep harbor, and the beaches on the lee side of the harbor gave some glimpse of Vladivostok's immense potential.

In July 2000 we took a White Sea cruise on the *Kristina Regina*, a Finnish ship, to Archangel, the Solovetski Islands, and Murmansk. As we left the White Sea and entered the Dvina River, the landscape was flat and forbidding, with swampy areas noticeable even from the river, with abandoned shacks and piers lying broken and desolate. But Economie Point, with its busy cranes and docks, seemed a busier and more prosperous area. The primary products of the local economy are still timber and fish. We saw vast areas of the Dvina covered by rafts of logs, ready for shipment overseas. The riverfront, dotted with occasional sawmills, and the docks at Solombola indicated more commercial activity. Bakharitza, across the river from Archangel, is still off limits, for reasons we never could fathom; the old Smolny Barracks of Archangel are long gone, and the grounds are now a rather overgrown public park.

The former American headquarters building, still an impressive riverfront structure, is now used mostly for offices. Two of the former buildings used as American hospitals are no longer medical facilities, but are well maintained. The Allied cemetery, still holding many graves, is overgrown and untended, although the headstones are straight and legible, and the memorial plaques in the rear of the cemetery looked clean and fresh. We met the commander of the Russian Army unit based at the old Alexandrovsky Barracks, site of a December 1918 mutiny. In contrast to a Russian military compound I visited in Khabarovsk, in the Far East, I found this compound to be active, neat, orderly, and freshly painted.

In Archangel we conferred with Vice Rector Vladislav Goldin of Pomor University, an expert on the Intervention period and author of a book on the subject. We found Archangel to be a relatively quiet city of four hundred thousand people, with its older, unique riverfront buildings providing a contrast to the background of high-rise Soviet-style apartments. Similar to Vladivostok, the free trolley still runs up Troitski Prospekt, the main street of the waterfront area, as it did in 1918.

Our brief visit to Murmansk was improved by bright sunshine, but its harbor area, particularly on the river to the sea, was marked by appalling numbers of rusting hulks, many already submerged, broken, and listing in all directions. Only weeks after we sailed past numbers of Russian naval craft, the Russian submarine *Kursk* sailed out of Murmansk harbor and tragically sank with all hands off the Kola coast.

My most recent visit to sites of the Intervention period was to Stoney Castle in Brookwood, England, where the 339th trained briefly before heading to Russia. The area is now a British military installation complete with rifle ranges and sturdy brick barracks. Nearby is the Brookwood American Military Cemetery, where two members of the AEFNR are buried. Pvt. Leslie Handy of the 310th Engineers died in an accident on August 22, 1918, only days after he arrived and is buried in the small American portion of the huge Allied cemetery. The other grave belongs to Cpl. Earl Collins, who was wounded and taken prisoner on March 18, 1919; later a captured YMCA worker found him badly wounded in a Bolshevik hospital. No further word was received.

It may be helpful to explain some of the labels that will be used to identify the various factions involved in the Intervention. The two basic forces involved in Russia's Civil War were the Reds, or Bolsheviks (Bolos), versus the Whites, or anti-Bolsheviks. In North Russia it was reasonably simple to distinguish the sides. The anti-Bolsheviks consisted of those who were former officials in the days of the tsar and those who were simply against the new Soviet government. The Whites were aided by the Allies—British, French, American, Canadians, and other smaller national groups. Russians who joined the Allies were anti-Soviets, referred to as White Russians, and occasionally as just Russians. Their enemy was the Soviet force fighting to control North Russia. The terms for these Soviet forces are used almost interchangeably: Reds, Soviets, Bolsheviks, or Communists.

In Siberia classifications were more complex. It was the Reds against the Whites, but the lines were blurred. During most of the Intervention period, the Whites were led by Adm. Alexander V. Kolchak, whose leadership was first ineffectual, and later brutal. U.S. Ambassador to Japan Roland S. Morris described Kolchak: "Admiral Kolchak is, in my judgment, an honest and courageous man of very limited experience in public affairs, of narrow views and small administrative ability. He is dictator in name but exercises little influence on the Council of Ministers."[1] He was primarily a Tsarist, but his authority was maintained to a large extent by ruthless Russian Cossacks and Japanese troops, part of the Allied presence. The anti-Bolshevik forces included the Allies—the Czech Legion, Japanese, Americans, Chinese, and some British and French—with two Russian Cossack tribes led by Gregorii Semenov and Ivan Kalmykof. Whenever the term Cossack is used in later chapters, it refers to these two bands. There also were White Russians, former Tsarists leftover from the days of royalty, military officers, and other Russians who were just anti-Bolshevik.

The distance from Moscow lessened the power of the Central Soviet with its communist philosophy, yet some ardent Bolsheviks recruited effectively in Siberia. Recruiting was made easy by the ruthless tactics of the Japanese and the Cossacks. Most of the Russians fighting under the Red flag were anti-Kolchak rather than pro-Bolshevik. While they are referred to as Bolsheviks and Soviets, their dedication to that cause was often minimal. A final group, which often joined the Reds, was the partisans. Usually, these were peasants who fought for the Reds when fighting came near their villages; however, they seldom stayed on with the Reds if the action moved on. They fought for their towns and their families, not for "the cause."

The majority of the Russians were apolitical citizens who only wanted to go on with their daily lives without interference, preoccupied with scratching out a precarious livelihood. With that underlying philosophy, it was easy to understand the frequency with which they switched allegiances.

In the text, names used without national identification are American. Also, the quotes used are in the style of the times and represent the educational level of the individual.

ACKNOWLEDGMENTS

Acknowledgments for this type of book are manifold. First, as always, thanks go to my wife, Donna, for her integral part in every stage of the project. As researcher, proofreader, fact checker, and mechanic of the English language, she was ever-present and ever-alert.

Col. Richard Sommers amazed us with his knowledge of the materials available at the U.S. Army Military Historical Institute (USAMHI) and pointed us in several new directions. His personal interest and attention were high points in our research activity. A generous grant from USAMHI made a return visit possible. The staff at the Bentley Historical Library at the University of Michigan was patient and most helpful in our use of their extensive North Russian collections. A grant from the Bentley Library was of invaluable assistance in allowing for repeat visits to Ann Arbor. At the National Archives in College Park, Maryland, Archivist Gibson Bell Smith assisted us with our initial research. Dr. Germaine Pavlova-O'Neill's help, during our visit to the Donovan Research Library at Fort Benning, Georgia, was also much appreciated.

Our two week-long trips to the Hoover Institution of War, Revolution and Peace at Stanford University, with its extensive Siberian collections, were memorable. Susan Lintelman at the United States Military Academy Museum provided copies of Colonel Stewart's papers and Siberian correspondence, as well as photographs of Academy graduates. The staff at the American Battle Monuments Commission helped us substantially in locating overseas graves and memorials. The Joint Archives at Hope College in Holland, Michigan, added more to our understanding of the Michigan contribution to the Polar Bears.

Stan Bozich at Michigan's Own Museum in Frankenmuth, Michigan, was one of my early sources; he provided a number of personal insights into the Polar Bears of Michigan. Stan, who knows more of the real story of the North Russian campaign that any single person we met, readily shared his knowledge. Barbara Martin at the Muskegon County Museum in Muskegon, Michigan, made museum papers available to us and pointed us to the Polar Bear monument on Muskegon's Memorial Causeway in that western Michigan city. An Internet contact, Jerry Richards, provided us with many documents on the Russian Railroad Service Corps, for which we are grateful. Steve Harold, director of Manistee Historical Museum in Manistee, Michigan, provided us with original materials about local veterans.

At Hoover and at the USAMHI we became aware of two individuals who were largely responsible for preserving the legacy of the Intervention. Edith Faulstich spent the last years of her life soliciting and compiling reminiscences from Siberian veterans; her materials are highly insightful. John Longuevan also spent decades collecting, assembling, and editing information from his fellow Siberian veterans. Both were extremely dedicated and provided valuable services.

A visit to the History Institute of the Army of the Czech Republic in Prague put us in touch with Jitka Zabloudilova, who provided not only insights into the Czech experience, but maps and photos, which have been extremely useful. Jana Hrstkova, an attorney in Prague, kindly translated and interpreted several of those documents.

And last, but not least, is a tribute to my friend in Komsomolsk, Nikolai Chaschin, who really gave me the idea that began this quest with a challenge: "You have written about your American Civil War, why don't you write about our Civil War?"

I need to say a special word of thanks to our excellent local library, the Cocoa Beach Public Library, Cocoa Beach, Florida. Director Ray Dickinson and his creative reference staff were able to find via interlibrary loan volumes that we had little hope of locating. All these people and institutions, plus many others, were key to gathering the hosts of documents used throughout the book. And to many, many others who offered materials, suggestions, or encouragement, I give a heartfelt thanks.

Thanks, too, to Dr. Thomas L. Graves, nephew of General William Graves, and David Roberts, descendant of Kenneth Roberts, for sharing family items and to Col. Richard R. Moore (Ret.), USMA class of 1945, for the use of academy texts and maps. Richard Goldhurst generously supplied original maps.

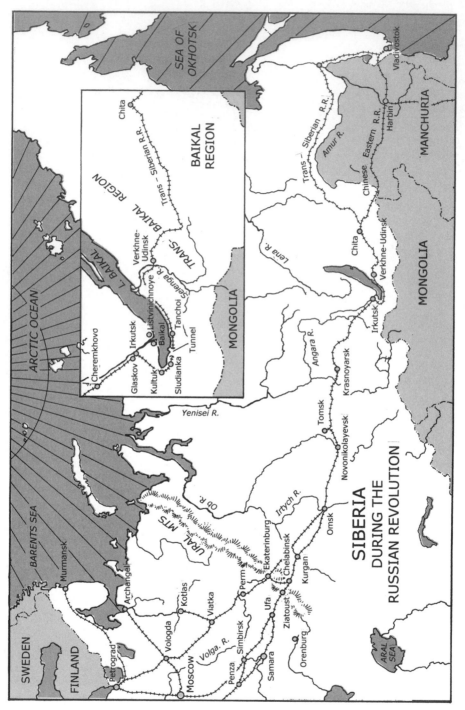

credit: Richard Barber

SIBERIA
DURING THE
RUSSIAN REVOLUTION

BAIKAL
REGION

INTRODUCTION

When World War I began in August 1914, the United States showed little interest in participating on either side. There were multitudes of Americans with recent German ancestry who had no enthusiasm for fighting Germany, and those Americans of French and British backgrounds felt no need to support the Allied cause. The Atlantic was a comfortable barrier between them and the war that was engulfing Europe. America's position was supported by President Woodrow Wilson, although he was not at all reluctant to send American troops to foreign lands when he felt it was the proper extension of the diplomatic process. In a recent book, *Between War and Peace, Woodrow Wilson and the American Expeditionary Force in Siberia, 1918–1921,* Carol Melton writes, "Throughout his presidency Wilson used the military in a new and untraditional manner; he used it not to wage war, but to restore peace. During his time as president he created a more benign role for the military while using it as a major agent of his foreign policy."[1]

In the first years of the war, Americans remained apathetic to the struggle in Europe, although they supplied large amounts of war goods to the Allies. However, aggressive German submarine warfare had a profound effect on both the American government and the American people. The sinking of the British passenger ship *Lusitania* in May 1915 and the loss of American lives brought submarine warfare to the fore of American consciousness, and, even though the German military called for temporary restrictions on submarine attacks, by early 1917 their submarines again ravaged ships in European and Atlantic waters. Finally, in March 1917 three U.S. ships were sunk by U-boats, and Wilson, with support of Congress, declared war on Germany.[2]

Another factor in Wilson's decision was the beginning of the Russian Revolution in that same month. This relieved President Wilson of entering the war on the side of the Allies and supporting the tyrannical tsar, Nicholas II. Recognizing the turmoil in his country, the tsar and his thirteen-year-old son, Alexis, abdicated on March 15, 1917, and a new provisional government was formed under Prince Lvov, and later Alexander Kerensky, favoring a democratic form of government. On March 20, the United States happily recognized the new government, and two days later, so did Britain, France, and Italy.[3]

Wilson was almost emotional in his April 2 speech as he talked about Russia: "Does not every American feel that assurance has been added to our hope for the future peace of the world by the wonderful and heartening things that have been happening in Russia?"[4] Wilson at that time was not an expert on Russian affairs, but had learned much from the most knowledgeable American available, Charles R. Crane, a prominent Democrat and Russophile.[5] In April 1916 Wilson had appointed David Francis as U.S. Ambassador to Russia, although he had little knowledge of that area. He, too, was counseled by Crane as he assumed his new responsibilities. Francis was a sixty-five-year-old Missouri Democrat, a former St. Louis mayor and state governor. He had a number of fine qualities, but his performance was clouded by a passion for whiskey, poker, and a friendship with a Russian woman, Mrs. Matilda de Cram, of suspicious background. The ambassador and the president were both learning as they became increasingly involved in Russia.

In the early months of the Russian provisional government, the United States pledged its economic and technical assistance and sent several missions to Russia. One was the Root Commission, tasked with bolstering Russian participation in the war and assuring the new government of U.S. support. The other was the Railway Advisory Commission, sent to Russia in May 1917 to study the condition of the railroads, particularly the Trans-Siberian Railroad that provided the only real link between European Russia and Siberia. It ran almost five thousand miles from St. Petersburg and Moscow across Siberia to Vladivostok and was a vital part of the Russian nation. The Railway Advisory Commission's successor organization, the Russian Railway Service Corps (RRSC), was later plagued by conflict with the Russians and with the Allies, most noticeably Japan. The Corps arrived in Vladivostok on December 15, 1917, in time to be confronted by the Bolshevik Revolution. Wisely, they retreated to Nagasaki, Japan, until things cooled down in Russia. The last elements of the RRSC did not find themselves in Russia until August 1918.[6]

The Root Commission was led by Elihu Root, a prominent Republican who had considerable prestige in Washington, both as a politician and as an international lawyer. The rest of the commission comprised eminent men from various walks of life and included the very knowledgeable Charles Crane. Their mission was to try to keep Russia in the war and to offer American support for the fledgling new government.

They arrived in Vladivostok at almost exactly the same time as the Railway Advisory Commission. Unfortunately, later events rendered their mission fruitless.

In addition to the government missions, U.S. charities added their enthusiastic support, including the American Red Cross, the YMCA, and others. Raymond Robins, part of the Red Cross mission, played an interesting role, loudly proclaiming his views, which clashed with most diplomats, including U.S. Consul General Maddin Summers. Robins took much notice of the rising left wing in Russia and strongly favored recognizing the Soviet government, which put him in confrontation with Summers and Ambassador Francis, both of whom were openly anti-Bolshevik.[7]

The Kerensky government pledged to continue the war against Germany, and on June 18, 1917, launched an ill-fated massive offensive against the Austro-Hungarian and German forces on the eastern front.[8] Initially successful, the drive stalled; then, the entire front collapsed as the German counteroffensive smashed the poorly armed Russians. It was the final straw for the Russian Army, which simply melted away in an orgy of mutiny and destruction. Officers were murdered for simply being officers, and soldier's committees made what few decisions were forthcoming. Russia was now out of the war, and there was no longer an eastern front. Unfortunately for the United States and its president, the provisional government under Alexander Kerensky was short-lived, and a successful October Revolution placed the Soviets in power.[9] The Soviet takeover was reasonably bloodless, with mutinied sailors and soldiers driving Kerensky out of power and out of the capital disguised as an ordinary seaman.[10] Led by the infamous Vladimir Lenin and Leon Trotsky, the Soviets began their oppressive rule as civil war raged in Russia.

The shift in power from the provisional government to the Soviets was extremely disappointing to the Allies. Under Soviet rule there was to be no continuation of the war, and to make certain of that, Lenin and Trotsky began negotiating a treaty with Germany. In December 1917 they signed an armistice with the Central Powers and also ceased fighting the Turks. The complicated negotiations kept on until February, when Germany tired of the process and once again invaded Russia. That was enough for the new Soviet government to swallow the unappetizing terms offered by Germany. In the Treaty of Brest-Litovsk, signed in mid-March 1918, Ukraine was given independence, as was Finland, and Russia lost control of part of Poland and the Baltic states.[11] One result of Germany's move into Russia was to move the Soviet seat of government from Petrograd to Moscow. Petrograd was considered too close to vulnerable Finland. The diplomats of the Allied nations decided to leave Petrograd, too, but decided going to Moscow could be interpreted as moving toward recognition of the new government. On February 27, Ambassador Francis led the Allied personnel to Vologda, located at the junction of the Trans-Siberian Railroad and the Archangel-Vologda Railroad.[12]

As the Soviets tried to consolidate their control, the United States maintained a state of confusion as to its position on Russia. Opinions and advice were available from any number of sources, but in most cases conflicted or offered no substantial information. The Allied nations were alarmed at Russia's treaty and its possible effects on the western front. With no eastern front to hold their divisions, Germany was in position to shift large numbers of troops to France. The western front stalemate was thought to be in grave danger. This concern was strengthened by the massive offensive launched by Germany against the Allies on the western front in March 1918. American troops were just coming on the line at that time, so the brunt of the attack was met by the depleted French and British forces. The Allies were desperate to bring Russia back into the war, and they now began discussions as to how best to accomplish that. The French had virtually exhausted their manpower in the carnage of western front warfare, and the British also were in no position to offer much in the way of manpower for any Allied intervention into Russia. The two countries that could afford to send men were Japan and the United States. Pressures began to mount on Wilson from Britain and France to agree to a Russian intervention. In fact, by May all the diplomats in Vologda, if not their governments, were ready to intervene.[13]

One of the more significant events took place in May 1918, not in Moscow or in Vladivostok, but in the town of Chelyabinsk. In any analysis of the American entrance into Russia in 1918, it is necessary to explain the presence of a military force known as the Czech Legion. Its history is legendary in itself and contributed significantly to Allied and American strategy and emotional justification for what became known as the Intervention.

When war was declared in 1914, there was no country called Czechoslovakia. What was to become that nation was part of the Austro-Hungarian Empire, one of the Central Powers aligned against the Allies. However, the people of the Czech region were more closely tied ethnically to Russia than to the European Austro-Hungarians and were a very unenthusiastic group fighting for the Central Powers. As the war progressed on the eastern front, the Czech soldiers found ways to surrender, sometimes en masse, to their Russian cousins.

The movement toward independence for the Czechs had not been encouraged by the tsar, but after the March revolution, the provisional government was sympathetic to the growing pressure for independence by leaders Thomas Masaryk and Eduard Benes. They had successfully lobbied for a Czech Corps to be made up of Russian Czechs and Czech prisoners of war to be used by the Allies. This was accomplished in the spring of 1917, and the corps fought effectively, but in vain, in the ill-fated offensive of Russian general Brusilov, which collapsed in the summer of 1917. With the collapse of the offensive, the Russian Army ceased fighting. That encouraged Masaryk to suggest that the very-much-intact Czech Corps be incorporated into the western front. In December 1917 the Allies officially accepted the idea, and the Czech Corps was placed under French command and assigned to the western front. However, there remained the slight problem of moving the fifty-thousand-man corps from the Ukraine to France across areas controlled by Germans and Austro-Hungarians. The solution was to go the other way, east, across Siberia.

In March 1918, the Soviet government unhappily agreed to the punitive German terms of the Brest-Litovsk treaty, giving up much of the Ukraine and the Baltic republics. At the same time, the Soviets, in a telegram from Joseph Stalin, gave hasty permission for the Czech Corps to move across Russia to Vladivostok on the Trans-Siberian Railroad without interruption by the Bolsheviks. "And so their echelons began their long pilgrimage of nearly 6,000 miles."[14]

As the trains began to roll toward Vladivostok, Stalin's authorization became increasingly meaningless. The trains moved from town to town, facing local Soviet governments and stationmasters who felt no need to obey a far-off official and who saw possibilities for payoffs. The payoffs were frequently made in the form of weapons, given up by the corps, now known as the Czech Legion, to insure safe passage. As the demands grew, any incident was used by either side to begin armed conflict. As would be expected, a complete break with the Reds came in May 1918. By that time the first trains were arriving in Vladivostok bringing about twelve thousand Czech soldiers.[15] By May, the legion was spread from Penza in the west to Vladivostok in the east, with one section in Chelyabinsk. In that city, one Czech on the eastbound train was killed by a piece of iron thrown by a Hungarian on a westbound trainload of returning prisoners. The Hungarian culprit was promptly identified by the Czechs and hanged. The situation degenerated into a series of retaliations. Finally, the Czechs left their train, stormed the railroad station and on May 17 seized the local armory, releasing the Czechs in custody. The action had repercussions in Moscow; a few days later the Czech National Council in Moscow was ordered to disarm the Czechs. The officers of the democratic Czech Legion met in Chelyabinsk as the Congress of the Czechoslovak Revolutionary Army and, when confronted with the National Council's order to disarm, published a resolution that included the legion's pledge to fight on to Vladivostok.[16] This was in spite of Masaryk's urgent pleas for the legion to maintain its neutrality as they crossed Siberia. Plainly, there would be no pretense of neutrality after the events of May 1918. From then on, every Czech train would find itself in some kind of confrontation with the Bolsheviks.[17]

Sadly, even as the relations between Czechs and Russians disintegrated, the Allies themselves were in a quandary as to the fate of the legion. In a series of meetings they had proposed that the legion be split, with those already east of Omsk to continue on to Vladivostok and those west of the city to be rerouted to Archangel. The British had hoped to divert the western portion of the legion to the Murmansk area to support their planned invasion. These discussions became moot when the Czechs issued their resolution and vowed to continue to fight their way east. The plan to split the legion was one more example of how the warring nations differed in their use of the valiant band of legionnaires.

After the open split with the Bolsheviks, fighting broke out all up and down the railroad, and the disciplined troops of the legion found the local Bolshevik troops no match for their skills. In three months the Czechs had established themselves along the railroad up to Irkutsk, but the Reds held Irkutsk and the road east of there through Khabarovsk and down to within forty miles of Vladivostok. The Czechs had even managed to establish anti-Bolshevik governments in areas they controlled. In Vladivostok, however, there was no word of the May resolution, and the Czechs there were confused by reports of fighting in the west. So those in Vladivostok took no action, partially because of Masaryk's explicit orders to remain neutral.

On the morning of June 28, 1918, the Czechs in Vladivostok learned that arms in Vladivostok were being sent for use against Czechs in the west, and they demanded that the Soviet government in Vladivostok surrender its arms. When the Reds refused there was a brief skirmish and the outmanned, outgunned government surrendered the city to Gen. Mikhail Dietrichs, a Russian then commanding Czech forces in Vladivostok. The next move was for Dietrichs to head west to aid Czech Gen. Rudolf Gaida's force, then doing battle for Irkutsk. Dietrichs left Vladivostok on the Trans-Siberian Railroad, turned off at Nikolsk to take the Chinese-Eastern Railroad to aid their comrades attacking Irkutsk, an attack that began July 11.

While some Czechs were on the move across Manchuria, others were moving west on the Ural front. This was the central force under General Voitsekhovskii, whose assignment was to take Ekaterinburg from his base in Chelyabinsk. The fighting was fierce as he moved north, probably due to the fact that the Bolsheviks held Nicholas II and his family in Ekaterinburg, and they feared his recapture. To prevent that happening, the tsar and his whole family were executed by the Bolsheviks on the night of July 17, 1918. General Gaida had planned to attack Irkutsk, then move on toward Lake Baikal to try to join friendly Ataman Semenov on the other side of the cliffs blocking the railroad. After taking Irkutsk, Gaida moved on to take Verkhne-Udinsk, which opened the railroad across Manchuria all the way from Vladivostok to Kazan in the east. Coinciding with the taking of Verkhne was the arrival of Dietrichs from Vladivostok who joined the western Czechs near Chita. The French high command gave command of the Czechs to Jan Syrovy, who had been a first lieutenant when the legion was first formed. The veteran Dietrichs, a Russian, was named Syrovy's chief of staff. With their combined forces, they moved back west to open a new front in the Urals. Historian Richard Goldhurst warned, "The vanguard of the Allied intervention was ready for the big push. Russia, however, is a place that swallows venturesome vanguards whole."[18]

The political climate was fast changing in the summer months of 1918. The French, in particular, favored using the Czechs as their elite force in Russia, instead of shipping them back to the western front. A well-trained and disciplined military unit with the experience of the Czechs was something to be sought after, and messages were sent out from the American diplomats and the French urging the legion to stay in Russia.

The reasons that persuaded the legion to move back to the west and begin a push against the Bolsheviks were simple. The representatives of both the French and American authorities had virtually promised that Allied forces would be coming to relieve the Czechs in the near future. Consul General DeWitt Poole was the American official who had most consistently promised the Czechs that Allied forces were committed to come to their aid. After the Intervention, Maj. Gen. William S. Graves, commander of the American Expeditionary Force Siberia (AEFS), wrote, "Mr. Poole by his communication led the Czechs, or helped lead them, to believe the United States and the Allies were going to intervene in Siberia."[19] Poole's comments, coupled with similar French remarks, incensed General Graves, who consistently tried to follow President Wilson's instructions to avoid any interference. The Czech leadership also felt that the legion's cooperation with the Allies would help insure the independence of Czechoslovakia, and there was a concern that Bolsheviks and Germans were plotting to stabilize Soviet control.

The Czech forces were successful on the eastern Ural campaign for a brief time, but they had reached their limit. On September 10,

1918, almost as the Americans were landing in Archangel and in Vladivostok, the Red Guard under Leon Trotsky attacked them in force, and their retreat began. The White Army in Siberia turned out to be as ruthless as the Bolsheviks, tolerating little opposition and committing countless atrocities with their own forces and their allied Cossack terrorists, Atamans Semenov and Kalmykof.

The Czech general Rudolph Gaida was a character out of a novel. Only twenty-six in 1918, he was young, rash, outspoken, adventuresome, and brave beyond question. But he was also highly political and temperamental. As the Czechs manned the Ural front in the fall of 1918, they tired of Allied promises of coming aid and were under increasing pressure from Bolsheviks. On October 28, 1918, two events illustrated the polar experiences of Czechs. First, the nation of Czechoslovakia was established with a bloodless coup in Prague. Second, a mutiny of legionnaires so discouraged their colonel, Josef Svec, that he shot himself. It was the first of many refusals by Czech soldiers to fight. Other mutinies followed; on October 20, the badly mauled Fourth Czech Division refused to fight as the Reds continued to advance. On October 24, the First Regiment mutinied, and the three young generals, Gaida, age twenty-six, Stanislav Cecek, age thirty-two, and Jan Syrovy, age thirty-three, who had tried to halt the Soviet advance, were left virtually without troops.[20]

The next blow to the legion was the coup that ousted a democratic Siberian government and installed Adm. Alexander Kolchak as Supreme Ruler of All Russia, in reality the dictator of the land. One legionnaire wrote, "Filled with indignation and bitter disappointment, the Legionaries lost the last of their enthusiasm for the anti-Bolshevik cause." This quote is from a chapter of a book written by Gustav Becvar of the Sixth Regiment in a chapter entitled, "To Hell with Intervention."[21]

The final blow to the legion was a visit from their revered Gen. Milan Stefanik, defense minister of the new Czech Republic. He told the weary legion officers:

> You must hold out here in Siberia until the end, until the victory is won, and this you must do relying only upon your own strength, for I can tell you authoritatively that no help from the Allies will come to this Front. It is useless our discussing the rights and wrongs of the case. The fact of importance is that help will not come. Now you know just how things stand, and also the extent of the task that lies ahead.[22]

At that point, the Czech Legion withdrew from the Ural fighting to take on their new role as guardian of the Amur section of the Trans-Siberian

Railroad. The legion was replaced on the Ural front by the increased armies of Admiral Kolchak, who had borrowed Czech leadership for his campaigns. Gaida was now the commanding general of the Kolchak forces, and Dietrichs and Voitsekhovskii, both Russian-born but with Czech ancestry, felt their place was to keep fighting the Bolsheviks.

The legionnaires had been away from their homes for four years, many for five, and now longed only for the orders to head for Vladivostok and ships to take them home. "Home to help in the building of our new State; home to the families who need us; home before all jobs are snapped up by those who stayed behind and did not raise a finger to secure the Independence," wrote Becvar.[23] But it would be almost eighteen months before the last of the legion would part company with the accursed Siberia.

The Czechs and their leaders were critical to the events of 1918, as Allied strategies developed, but their greatest contribution to the Intervention might have been their emotional tug on world opinion. As the United States struggled with the decision to intervene, logic could measure most of the factors involved. But emotion played a part as well. President Wilson's final moments of indecision were affected by his impression of the plight of the valiant legionnaires, caught in the vastness of Siberia, menaced by the Red Army and trying desperately to come to the aid of the Allies. The United States had thousands of Czechs who had emigrated to America, but still had ties to the old country, and their presence and voice were enough to tip the scales for intervention.

In the spring of 1918, much of the attention focused on the Russian Far East. The Japanese had been involved in discussions about their role in any Siberian venture and had one of their cruisers, the HIJMS *Asahi,* in Vladivostok where it had been joined by the U.S. cruiser *Brooklyn* and the British HMS *Suffolk.* Discussions centered around possible roles for the United States and Japan to take in the Russian situation. On April 4, four Japanese merchants were murdered in Vladivostok, and the Japanese cruiser sent a detail of *Asahi* marines ashore, ostensibly to protect the rather large number of Japanese citizens in the city. The British, alarmed by the Japanese marines, sent in their own contingent of marines to protect British interests. The sailors and Marines on board the *Brooklyn* went to general quarters, but stayed on board the vessel, held back by the Asiatic Fleet commander, Adm. Austin M. Knight, who was aboard.[24] Events stabilized as the two Allied marine forces went back to their respective ships, and the local Soviet government awaited the next development.

As the Czechs battled their way east and west in Siberia, the Allied heads of government had some vague consensus as to the plan of action for Russia. Britain and Japan had already established themselves in widely separated locations, Japan in Vladivostok and Britain in Murmansk. Even the uncommitted United States had sent warships to those two areas. The British and French were applying increased pressure on President Wilson to use American troops in Russia, but he remained stubbornly opposed. His advisors, Secretary of State Robert Lansing and Secretary of War Newton Baker, only confused the presidential dilemma. Lansing had begun as an opponent of intervention, even though his men on the scene, Ambassador Francis and Maddin Summers, pushed hard for American participation. However, by May, Lansing viewed the two expeditions more favorably, adding to the pressure on Wilson from Britain and France. The War Department and Baker consistently opposed the use of forces that they felt could be better used in France. The French hoped to replace their fallen with Americans and Russians. Both France and Britain believed that sending troops into Russia would excite the Russian people once again to fight the hated Germans, who, through the recent treaty, then controlled the Ukraine and most of the Baltic states. It seems difficult that anyone could believe token forces in the remote stretches of North Russia, and in far-off Vladivostok, could rekindle the flame of a war-weary nation bloodied by years of fighting. One of America's most prophetic diplomats, Felix Cole, vice consul at Archangel, who opposed intervention, wrote a long message to his superior, Ambassador David Francis, who favored intervention, on June 1, 1918. Cole said, among other things, "Intervention cannot reckon on active support from Russians. All the fight is out of Russia. . . . Every foreign invasion that has gone deep into Russia has been swallowed up."[25] Cole made many other cogent points that were never fully appreciated, probably because they were in disagreement with those of Ambassador Francis.

Under increasing pressure from the Allies, President Wilson weighed his decision. He had no moral objection to sending American troops into civil unrest in other parts of the world. In his years as president, he committed American armed forces in nineteen separate instances, from his September 1913 dispatching of Marines to Mexico to a landing of Marines in Vladivostok in February 1920. Haiti, the Dominican Republic, China, Cuba, Panama, Dalmatia, Turkey, and Guatemala all saw armed U.S. troops on their soil.[26] However, President Wilson opposed entry into the world war and was certainly hesitant to commit troops to Russia. Wilson was a very private person, and he seemed reluctant to heed advice from those around him. In this case it was probably wise, since his advisors were as split on the issue of intervention as he seemed to be. His military advisors urged him to stay out of Russia, while his diplomats were generally in favor of armed intervention.

With pressures mounting, on July 6 Wilson called a meeting of the head of the State Department, Robert Lansing; the head of the War Department, Newton Baker; the head of the Navy Department, Joseph Daniels; Chief of Staff of the Army, Peyton March; and Chief of Naval Operations, Adm. William Benson. The meeting resulted in several decisions:

1. Reestablishing an eastern front was impracticable.
2. Regardless of the situation, no Allies would proceed west of Irkutsk.
3. It was necessary to aid Czechs coming from Vladivostok to join their comrades in western Siberia.
4. Since no significant force could be sent from the United States, Americans would supply arms and supplies to the Czechs and land a force in Vladivostok made up of American and Japanese troops, each numbering about seven thousand, enough troops to hold Vladivostok in cooperation with the Czechs.
5. There would be no interference in internal Russian affairs.

The final resolution, however, was the most important; it was, "Await further developments before taking further steps."[27] There was still a debate concerning the Czechs and their use by the Allies. It would appear that U.S. help was not intended to evacuate the beleaguered Czechs, but to push them back to the west, where they could fight the Russian Soviets.

Wilson worried that a refusal to intervene would further aggravate the rift between him and the Allies. The U.S. delay in entering the war, Wilson's insistence on maintaining American control of American units, and his reluctance to send a representative to the Supreme War Council had jeopardized his relations with Britain and France.[28] He would need their support for his plans toward a unified approach to peace.

With the various views and opinions ringing in his ears, on the night of July 16, 1918, President Wilson, alone in his room, began typing. The result of his night's work reads as follows:

Aide Memoir
The whole heart of the people of the United States is in the winning of the war. The controlling purpose of the Government of the United States is to do everything that is necessary and effective to win it. It wishes to cooperate in every practicable way with the allied governments, and to cooperate ungrudgingly; for it has no ends of its own to serve and believes that the war can be won only by common council and

intimate concert of action. It has sought to study every proposed policy or action in which its cooperation has been asked in this spirit, and states the following conclusions in the confidence, that if it finds itself obliged to decline participation in any undertaking or course of action, it will be understood that it does so only because it deems itself precluded from participating by imperative considerations either of policy or fact.

In full agreement with the allied governments and upon the unanimous advice of the Supreme War Council, the Government of the United States adopted, upon its entrance into the war, a plan for taking part in the fighting on the western front into which all its resources of men and material were to be put, and put as rapidly as possible, and it has carried out this plan with energy and success, pressing its execution more and more rapidly forward and literally putting into it the entire energy and executive force of the nation. This was its response, its very willing and hearty response, to what was the unhesitating judgment alike of its own military advisers and of the advisers of the allied governments. It is now considering, at the suggestion of the Supreme War Council, the possibility of making very considerable additions even to this immense programme which, if they should prove feasible at all, will tax the industrial processes of the United States and the shipping facilities of the whole group of associated nations to the utmost. It has thus concentrated all its plans and all its resources upon this single absolutely necessary object.

In such circumstances it feels it to be its duty to say that it cannot, so long as the military situation on the western front remains critical, consent to break or slacken the force of its present effort by diverting any part of its military force to other points or objectives. The United States is at a great distance from the field of action on the western front; it is at a much greater distance from any other field of action. The instrumentalities by which it is to handle its armies and its stores have at great cost and with great difficulty been created in France. They do not exist elsewhere. It is practicable for her to do a great deal in France; it is not practicable for her to do anything of importance or on a large scale upon any other field. The American Government, therefore, very respectfully requested its Associates to accept its deliberate judgment that it should not dissipate its force by attempting important operations elsewhere.

It regards the Italian front as closely coordinated with the western front, however, and is willing to divert a portion of its military forces from France to Italy if it is the judgment and wish of the Supreme Command that it should do so. It wishes to defer to the decision of the commander in chief in this matter, as it would wish to deter in all others, particularly because it considers these two fronts so related as to be practically but separate parts of a single line and because it would be necessary that any American troops sent to Italy should be subtracted from the number used in France and be actually transported across French territory from the ports now used by armies of the United States.

It is the clear and fixed judgment of the Government of the United

States, arrived at after repeated and very searching reconsiderations of the whole situation in Russia, that military intervention there would add to the present sad confusion in Russia rather than cure it, injure her rather than help her, and that it would be of no advantage in the prosecution of our main design, to win the war against Germany. It cannot, therefore, take part in such intervention or sanction it in principle. Military intervention would, in its judgment, even supposing it to be efficacious in its immediate avowed object of delivering an attack upon Germany from the east, be merely a method of making use of Russia, not a method of serving her. Her people could not profit by it, if they profited by it at all, in time to save them from their present distresses, and their substance would be used to maintain foreign armies, not to reconstitute their own. Military action is admissible in Russia, as the Government of the United States sees the circumstances, only to help the Czecho-Slovaks consolidate their forces and get into successful cooperation with their Slavic kinsmen and to steady any efforts at self-government or self-defense in which the Russians themselves may be willing to accept assistance. Whether from Vladivostok or from Murmansk and Archangel, the only legitimate object for which American or allied troops can be employed, it submits, is to guard military stores which may be subsequently needed by Russian forces and to render such aid as may be acceptable to the Russians in the organization of their own self defense. For helping the Czecho-Slovaks there is immediate necessity and sufficient justification. Recent developments have made it evident that that is in the interest of what the Russian people themselves desire, and the Government of the United States is glad to contribute the small force at its disposal for that purpose. It yields, also, to the judgment of the Supreme Command in the matter of establishing a small force in Murmansk, to guard the military stores at Kola and to make it safe for Russian forces to come together in organized bodies in the north. But it owes it to frank counsel to say that it can go no further than these modest and experimental plans. It is not in a position, and has no expectation of being in a position, to take part in organized intervention in adequate force from either Vladivostok or Murmansk and Archangel. It feels that it ought to add, also, that it will feel at liberty to use the few troops it can spare only for the purposes here stated and shall feel obliged to withdraw these forces, in order to add them to the forces at the western front, if the plans in whose execution it is now intended that they should develop into others inconsistent with the policy to which the Government of the United States feels constrained to restrict itself.

At the same time the Government of the United States wishes to say with the utmost cordiality and good will that none of the conclusions here stated is meant to wear the least color of criticism of what the other governments associated against Germany may think it wise to undertake. It wishes in no way to embarrass their choices of policy. All that is intended here is a perfectly frank and definite statement of the policy which the United States feels obliged to adopt for herself and in the use of her military forces. The Government of the United States does not wish it to be understood that in so restricting its own activities it is seeking, even by implication, to set limits to the action or to define the policies of its Associates.

It hopes to carry out the plans for safeguarding the rear of the Czecho-Slovaks operating from Vladivostok in a way that will place it and keep it in close cooperation with a small military force like its own from Japan, and if necessary from the other Allies, and that will assure it of the cordial accord of all the allied powers; and it proposes to ask all associated in this course of action to unite in assuring the people of Russia in the most public and solemn manner that none of the governments uniting in action either in Siberia or in northern Russia contemplates any interference of any kind with the political sovereignty of Russia, any intervention in her internal affairs, or any impairment of her territorial integrity either now or hereafter, but that each of the associated powers has the single object of affording such aid as shall be acceptable, to the Russian people in their endeavor to regain control of their own affairs, their own territory, and their own destiny.

It is the hope and purpose of the Government of the United States to take advantage of the earliest opportunity to send to Siberia a commission of merchants, agricultural experts, labour advisors, Red Cross Representatives and agents of the Young Men's Christian Association accustomed to organizing the best methods of spreading useful information and rendering educational help of a modest sort, in order in some systematic manner to relieve the immediate economic necessities of the people there in every way for which opportunity may be open. The execution of this plan will follow and will not be permitted to embarrass the military assistance rendered in the rear of the westward-moving forces of the Czecho-Slovaks.

Department of State
July 17, 1918[24]

The strange document, which was not signed by the president, became the basis for the two Russian expeditions. It was a rambling, misguided document based on false assumptions and misinformation and was virtually impossible to comply with, particularly the paragraph that announced that a military intervention was probably justified, but it would be carried out without "any interference of any kind with the political sovereignty of Russia, any intervention in her internal affairs." It began with the reasons for not sending troops to Russia, but ended with the statement that a token force could be sent purely for the purpose of guarding military supplies. Equally puzzling was the reference to the westward movement of the Czechs, which indicated an acceptance of the Czechs' not leaving Russia, but being prepared to reenter the fighting in the Urals. Without national support or a clear understanding of their purpose, the two American expeditions entered Russia in late summer 1918, and, confused and unhappy, many stayed there until early in 1920, long after their brothers-in-arms on the western front had paraded in victory back in the United States.

The Allied expeditions to Russia were classic demonstrations of an isolated and uninformed military subject to irrational government decisions. While these were Allied efforts, this book deals primarily with the American involvement with the Archangel and Siberian expeditions in their regrettable campaigns. It is a tale of heroism, hardship, cowardice, and comradeship under conditions that rival those of Valley Forge and the Chosin Reservoir. While most of the men returned home to lead normal civilian lives, over four hundred of them never returned, but paid with their lives for the ill-fated Allied campaigns.

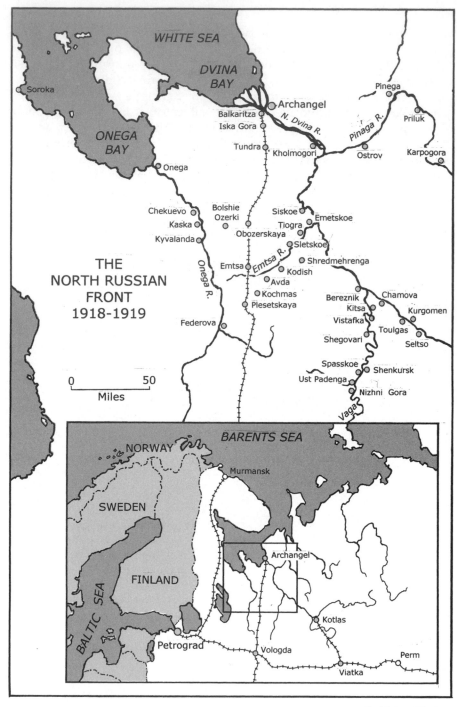

THE
NORTH RUSSIAN
FRONT
1918-1919

WHITE SEA

DVINA
BAY

ONEGA
BAY

Soroka

Pinega

Archangel

Balkaritza
Iska Gora

N. Dvina R.

Pinaga R.

Priluk

Onega

Tundra
Kholmogori

Ostrov

Karpogora

Chekuevo
Kaska
Kyvalanda

Bolshie
Ozerki

Siskoe
Tiogra
Obozerskaya

Emetskoe

Sletskoe

Onega R.

Emtsa
Emtsa R.

Shredmehrenga

Kodish
Avda
Kochmas
Plesetskaya

Bereznik
Kitsa
Vistafka
Shegovari

Chamova

Kurgomen

Toulgas

Seltso

Federova

Spasskoe
Ust Padenga

Shenkursk

Nizhni Gora

Vaga

0   50
Miles

BARENTS SEA

NORWAY

Murmansk

SWEDEN

Archangel

FINLAND

BALTIC SEA

Kotlas

Petrograd

Vologda

Perm

Viatka

credit: Richard Barber

PART I

North Russia

*The American Expeditionary Force
North Russia, 1918–1919*

The Early Days in Murmansk

On the Murmansk Railway, which they have seized, the Anglo-French bandits are already shooting Soviet workers.

—Soviet document, August 1918

WHEN the first gunfire of World War I sounded in August 1914, Murmansk did not exist. The only town of any size in that remote area was Kola, named for its geographic territory, the Kola Peninsula. Any description of the area, miles above the Arctic Circle, was a combination of unpleasant terms: winters featuring unrecordably low temperatures; bleak, snow-covered stretches of frozen tundra; settlements that possessed no sanitary facilities; and near inaccessibility to the Russian capital of Petrograd, eight hundred miles away. The summers proved almost as difficult as the winters: swampy surfaces of the soil covered permanently frozen subsurfaces that harbored mosquitoes of huge proportions. It did have one advantage: it was an ice-free port, unlike Archangel well to its south, which was usable only five or six months a year. The Gulf Stream currents in the Barents Sea kept the Murmansk port from freezing.

In 1915 the Allies and Russia determined that a new port was needed to receive the goods being shipped to Russia for its war effort.

Although iced in half the year, Archangel, six hundred land miles away, was the only existing port for even limited Allied use. The British entered the waters off the Kola Peninsula to protect the area from potential threats from the Finnish border, only a few miles away, and to safeguard the waters from the German Navy. Since Russia was an ally, it was logical to have the powerful British Navy as the area defender. As the 1915 winter season began to close in on Archangel, the British ships, which had patrolled there in the summer, moved up to Murmansk. There were eight ships: the battleship HMS *Glory*, the cruiser HMS *Vindictive,* and six smaller ships.

The British ships provided not only defense, but also some funds and expertise for building a town. Construction of Murmansk was begun in September 1915; at the same time, construction of a railway south to Petrograd was also begun under British supervision with Russian prisoners and German prisoners of war (POWs) providing the labor. In some ways the construction of this railroad was comparable to the construction of the Trans-Siberian Railroad. The difficulties were enormous. "Twenty-five percent of the line had to be laid through marshland. There were severe technical problems connected with permanently frozen subsoil. To avoid an even higher percentage of swampy foundation, forty percent of the line had to be laid out on curves."[1] Then there were the waterways that required bridging, the long Arctic winter nights, and the required transporting of all supplies across hundreds of miles from Petrograd, factors which made its completion in the spring of 1917 a construction miracle.

As the railroad progressed, buildings sprang to life in the city. Warehouses, barracks, and other structures were completed in record time. Soon Murmansk became a thriving port; tons of supplies, furnished by the Allies, began piling up in new warehouses near the docks.[2]

But its utility was short-lived. The October 1917 Revolution shut down the railroad, and Murmansk was virtually cut off from the rest of Russia, dependent on shipments and supplies from the Barents Sea. The Bolshevik influence in Russia was then primarily confined to the central European areas, and its philosophies, although spreading, had not reached many of the outer edges of the huge country. With British ships off the coast, French and British diplomats in the city, and little contact with the Petrograd Central Soviet, it appeared that Murmansk needed Allied help. However, that was not a universal opinion in the city. Russian sailors and railroad men had harbored communist leanings for years, and the city had recently formed its own Murmansk Soviet, led by Aleksei Yuryev. The local Soviet was technically allied with Petrograd, but since they were so isolated and communications were so poor, there was considerable disagreement with the Central Government. The railroad workers and rebellious sailors, in port without ships, opposed the local Soviet. Murmansk was a seething mass with no real governing body with the strength to enforce itself.

Then came a change: in February 1918, Germany reattacked Russia in the Ukraine, although Germany was still in negotiations with the Bolshevik Soviet. In Murmansk there was concern that the nearby Finnish border would offer Germany a haven from which it could launch a North Russian offensive. The threat of German attack brought some harmony to the three diverse Murmansk groups—the government, rebellious military, and allies—as they recognized the need for British defense and supply. At this time, an American, Lt. Hugh Martin, a passport control officer, was the senior U.S. representative on the scene. A few other Americans were also there: Allen Wardell of the Red Cross had made his second appearance in the new city, while YMCA official Reverend Jesse Halsey was a more recent arrival.

With this new spirit of cooperation among the three Murmansk groups, the area faced a new concern: a civil war had begun in Finland, and it was feared that Germany would aid the White (anti-Bolshevik) side, possibly invading Murmansk with a combined force. In retrospect, we know that both Germany and Finland had their hands full and gave little thought to any additional fronts. However, anticipation provided fuel for those who saw the possibilities of a German threat. Historian George Kennan wrote, "In March and April there was no serious danger of attack on Murmansk by Finns under German command; but by the time the British and the French had spent some weeks acting as though there were such a danger, they succeeded in conjuring it into real existence."[3] As tensions heightened, the British sent another cruiser, HMS *Cochrane*, and the French sent the heavy cruiser *Amiral Aube*. At last pleas to Wilson finally caught his attention. Rumors flew about, all indicating German-Finnish forces heading toward Murmansk or its railroad.

Eventually, in April 1918, Wilson relented and reluctantly made a step toward intervention by sending the USS *Olympia*, Admiral Dewey's old flagship, Capt. Bion B. Bierer commanding. However, Wilson cabled, "to caution him [Bierer] not to be drawn in further than the present action there without first seeking and obtaining instructions from home."[4] With Bierer's instructions was the added information that he would be under the command of the British naval commander Adm. Thomas W. Kemp. Admiral Kemp had telegraphed earlier:

I beg USS *Olympia* may have orders to come to Murmansk and that she be put definitely and fully under my orders the same as the French cruiser *Amiral Aube*. There can be only one Allied head here and I consider this step indispensable for both military and political reasons.[5]

The decision to have American forces commanded by British officers would lead to a host of problems in coming months.

By mid-April the USS *Olympia* was steaming from Charleston, South Carolina, toward Murmansk, stopping several times en route, with Captain Bierer on a collision course with the president's cautionary advice. With him on the *Olympia* was the new Allied commander, British major general Frederick C. Poole, who took command of all Allied forces in North Russia on his arrival in Murmansk on May 24, 1918.

With mounting concern over threats of German or Finnish invasion, the Murmansk Soviet telegraphed the Central Soviet on May 18, 1918, "The representatives of the friendly powers, the French, American and British missions currently at Murmansk, continue to show themselves inalterably well-inclined toward us and prepared to render us assistance, running all the way from food supply to armed aid, inclusive."[6]

An immediate answer on the same day was an important piece of the Murmansk story. It came from People's Commissar Leon Trotsky, who warned:

> The Germans are advancing in small detachments. Resistance is possible and obligatory. Abandon nothing to the enemy. Evacuate anything that has any value; if this is impossible, destroy it. You must accept any and all assistance from the Allied missions and use every means to obstruct the advance of the plunderers.[7]

Threats of invasion by German and Finnish troops worried even Petrograd Soviets, so the telegram opened the door for cooperation between the Murmansk Soviet and the Allies, even if it eventually antagonized the Central Soviets. The wire would also haunt Trotsky in years to come, as he fell from favor.

From this point on, the Allies began a gradual buildup. The French already had a Slavic command of a few soldiers in the town of Kola. Admiral Kemp had landed about 130 Marines from his ship HMS *Glory* on March 6, 1918; they had quietly housed themselves in barracks and awaited developments. These British marines were the first purely military troops to take part in the Allied Intervention.[8]

On June 8, apparently at British request, but with the blessing of U.S. ambassador David Francis, Captain Bierer was ordered to land a shore party to help garrison Murmansk. Captain Bierer sent Lt. H. C. Floyd with eight officers and one hundred men and their equipment to

Murmansk. Murmansk was under Soviet control, but already some Allied troops were in the city; the local Soviet anticipated a break with the Central Bolsheviks in Petrograd, so the landing was not contested. The American sailors also kept busy, assisting British and French marines in capturing the Russian cruiser *Askold* and other smaller ships, whose Bolshevik-sympathizing crews had mutinied.

On June 23, a six-hundred-man force under British major general Sir C. Maynard was put ashore with its equipment. Major General Maynard's writings after the war indicated that the goal of these and subsequent troops was to protect Murmansk and Archangel and the southbound railway, but he also stated, "When ready to take the field, the whole force was to endeavor to join hands with the pro-Ally forces in Siberia, and then to assist in opening up a new front against Germany."[9] The misinformation and lack of understanding of the situation was evident in this stated goal of the expedition.

As General Maynard's task force landed, his commander was already in Murmansk. Major General Frederick C. Poole had been an honored guest on the USS *Olympia* when it sailed into the Russian harbor on May 24. He was the overall commander of the Allied North Russian land forces. Poole was noted for his colonial approach to Russians: he patronized them, scolded them, misunderstood them, looked down on them, and generally made himself heartily disliked by those hapless souls he was preparing to liberate. His first contingent of British soldiers was not impressive; most of them were veterans of the western front who were classified as unfit for active service, yet they were expected to conduct themselves with typical British stoicism in an utterly hostile climate and topography.

Poole and Maynard conferred for hours as the contingent arrived. George Kennan says, "From his initial discussions with Poole, Maynard, as will be seen in his memoirs, derived a wildly distorted picture of the situation, including the impression that 15,000 White Finns, in German service, were already on the march against the Murmansk Railway."[10] Maynard set out on a mission to strengthen his defenses, traveling south on a locomotive with several cars full of troops. His reception by the Russian railway workers and stationmasters as he rode south was decidedly antagonistic, to the point of open rebellion. Later Maynard explained, "Bolshevik Russia was a recognized enemy, and I had a free hand to take such military measures as were possible to combat a Bolshevik–White Finn combination."[11] South of Murmansk in the town of Kandalaksha, he was confronted by a northbound train filled with Red troops. Maynard's unfortunate response was to mount machine guns covering the Bolsheviks and order the Red trains to turn around and return south. He called for reinforcements from the port and visited a nearby Allied base at Kem, where he forcibly disarmed two more Red trains and sent them back south. His high-handed actions opened armed hostilities between Allies and Bolsheviks, the first real signal of the conflicts to come.

Even before Maynard's railroad journey, the relations between the Murmansk Soviet and Central Soviet in Moscow had soured. Murmansk, concerned with its daily survival, depended almost entirely on Allied supplies. The Central Soviet in Petrograd saw things very differently. Trotsky's invitation had disappeared; the Petrograd government now issued a decree to the Murmansk government to throw the Allies out. The tone of a June 26, 1918, telegraph from Petrograd grew even more critical: "If you still refuse to understand Soviet policy equally hostile to English and to Germans, blame it on yourselves."[12] Murmansk fired right back in the same tone, "It is all very well for you to talk that way, sitting there in Moscow."[13] Lenin could not tolerate that kind of behavior and promptly called the party members of the port city Soviet traitors and declared them outcasts, subject to execution. "The President of the Murmansk Soviet Yuriev (Yuryev) having gone over to the side of the Anglo-French imperialists and participating in inimical actions directed against the Soviet Republic, is hereby proclaimed an enemy of the people and outlawed." The telegram was signed by Lenin and Trotsky.[14]

In an action which completely frustrated the Soviets in the capital, the Murmansk Soviet signed an accord with the Allies, British, French and even American. This agreement pledged the Allies to defend Murmansk and recognize the Murmansk Regional Soviet as the acknowledged government of the area. Captain Bierer of the *Olympia* signed on behalf of the American government, even though he had no authority to do so. It is interesting to note that this document was executed several days before Wilson's *Aide Memoire,* which authorized intervention in Russia. The Murmansk agreement was completely unauthorized by the U.S. government, yet it was finally approved in October 1918.[15] While it was a stroke of luck for the Allies to have the tie-in with a Russian government, even an out-of-favor one, the Allies pledged to protect those individuals who had faced the wrath of their own people by separating themselves from the Central Soviet. From then on, only Allied strength would keep the North Russians in Murmansk from the typical Soviet purges. Sadly, this was a pledge that the Allies could not fulfill in the disastrous months ahead. The U.S. government recognized the serious position these loyal governments would be in if Allied support were withdrawn. American colonel J. A. Ruggles voiced his concern: "This act [the break with the Moscow Soviet] of the newly organized government and of all who actively supported it was equivalent to a death sentence should the Bolshevik government return here.''[16] This prediction would prove tragically true in coming months.

Maynard's memoirs show the anger he felt toward the Americans as he viewed their role in the Great War and the Intervention.

> This lack of effective co-operation on the part of the United States can, I think, be ascribed almost wholly to the attitude adopted by President Wilson, who, totally devoid of strategic insight, refused to be guided by those who had been responsible during four tumultuous years for the conduct of a world-wide conflict. . . . One thing was now abundantly clear. America was determined to avoid pulling her weight in Russia. . . . But if America failed the Allies in North Russia, the British Empire did not.[17]

Maynard, throughout his months in Murmansk, was convinced that German forces would wipe out his small garrison. Even as late as 1928, he wrote in his memoirs, "Had Germany been left to carry out her designs unimpeded, it may be assumed fairly that, by early autumn at latest, Murmansk would have been in her hands, and her submarines stealing down the Kola Inlet." Citing the movement of German divisions from the eastern to the western front, he added:

> But the stream [of German divisions] ceased abruptly with the first landing of the Allies at Murmansk. During June, July, and August no single unit was sent from east to west. For these three months the Murmansk force tied down the whole German army in Finland, and put a stop to the transfer to France of the probable equivalent of from three to four enemy divisions.[18]

That was a considerable exaggeration; most sources state that few German troops actually served in Finland.

On July 30, 1918, the Archangel invasion fleet left the Murmansk harbor, sailing into the Barents Sea, down the White Sea toward the mouth of the Dvina River. Led by General Poole, these fifteen hundred troops were the initial forces of the Archangel campaign; Major General Maynard was left to his own devices in Murmansk with very few men.

The invasion force, code-named ELOPE, would involve many Allies, but few Americans. Some of those Americans would find danger, excitement, and adventure as they took part in the Allied Force B.

Force B—Archangel

My arm was raised near my face when shrapnel from one of the enemy rounds struck my arm. If my arm hadn't been raised, the shrapnel would have killed me.

—Seaman George Perschke, USS *Olympia*

THE Allied fleet was impressive for that era: two subchasers, several armed trawlers, the HMS *Nairana* with its seaplanes, the light cruiser HMS *Attentive,* the HMS *Salvator,* and the French *Amiral Aube.* The landing forces were on transports *Stephans, Asurian, Westborough,* and *Kassala.*[1] The senior U.S. navy commander, Capt. Bion B. Bierer, with two officers and a detachment of fifty men joined the Archangel invasion fleet on the British transport HMT *Stephans.* Leaving the *Olympia* in Murmansk, they took part in the landings and occupation of Archangel, in spite of Wilson's warnings to avoid conflict.[2]

The fleet set out on July 30 at 10:40 P.M. from Murmansk into the White Sea, seeking the mouth of the Dvina River and the upriver city of Archangel. At 3:00 A.M. July 31, in dense fog, the *Amiral Aube* went aground off Intzi Point, close to the river's mouth. The fleet waited there until the fog cleared and the *Aube* could be refloated. The crews of the small boats launched from the *Attentive* captured a Russian light-ship and two trawlers; from the lightship they telephoned the Bolshe-vik shore battery defending the river, requesting their surrender, emphasizing the "massive" force opposite the battery.

Without waiting for their decision, the Allies began a bombard-ment and sent two seaplanes from HMS *Nairana* over the enemy guns, strafing and bombing the Reds. The shore battery fired a few shots, one breaking the smokestack of the *Attentive*, causing no casualties and lit-tle harm. As the fleet came into sight of the battery, the Soviet gunners made a hasty evacuation, leaving their undamaged guns intact.[3] Later that day, August 1, two small ships were sunk in the channel by the Bolsheviks to keep the Allied fleet from going further; later a third ship was sunk, which delayed, but did not stop, the Allies. The following day the Allied ships cleared the sunken Red boats and sailed up to Eco-nomie, just north of Archangel. There the Allies were given a royal wel-come by the townspeople; the fleet then sailed on up to Archangel, where they learned a new government was in place.

On August 2, a coup, instigated by the British, removed the Bol-shevik government and replaced it with a Socialist revolutionary gov-ernment headed by an old Russian socialist named N. V. Chaikovsky. The entire invasion was neatly orchestrated. The British had employed several revolutionaries in Archangel to stage the coup as the Allied mil-itary expedition moved toward the city. The coup, led by George E. Chaplin, a mysterious former Imperial Russian Navy commander who sometimes posed as a British naval officer, was a smashing success. When the Red government and its loyal supporters heard the gunfire from the fleet attacking the shore batteries and saw the strafing by Al-lied seaplanes, they headed south in panic.[4]

The Allied flotilla sailed upriver on the winding, sprawling Dvina River, some twenty-five miles from its mouth on the White Sea, past islands and shore batteries, to Archangel, arriving as the successful coup ended. Both the coup and the invasion were synchronized per-fectly to affect an almost bloodless landing. According to Captain Bierer, "when the *Salvator* anchored, river craft, tugs and steamers blew their whistles and the other officers landed by General Poole; Ad-miral Kemp, myself and other officers landed by invitation. . . . The people went simply wild with joy to an extent almost beyond imagina-tion."[5]

General Poole, the officer commanding this expedition, wired London in an undated message: "I occupied Archangel today with Al-lied troops—American-British, French, Serbian and Czechs. Moduski battery offered slight resistance which was quickly overcome by sea-plane and (attentive). Two ice breakers and mine layers had been sunk in Channel but we were able to pass with little difficulty."[6] Records indicate the date was August 2, 1918.

A. L. Lawes, a British civilian working for the Russo-Britain Shipping Company in Archangel, wrote to Mr. W. A. H. Hulton in London on July 27, 1918:

> The general feeling amongst the population of Archangel is of a most panicky nature. All the bourgeoisie is being called up for service and being sent to Moudinga to dig trenches. The "Anglichani" [English] are expected any day now and everyone is in a state of excitement. . . . All the Allied Diplomatic Corps is here and is expected to leave tomorrow, for Murmansk. What will be the ultimate outcome of everything is impossible to say. We may be arrested and sent to the interior of Russia, or a thousand and one other developments may take place. "Wait and see" is the only policy available.[7]

Less than two weeks later, he wrote to his mother:

> At last I am able to write you freely and, I hope, regularly. You will probably have learnt from the English newspapers that the Allies have entered Archangel & the power of the Bolsheviks has been overthrown. . . . For a week or two before the change, the position of Britishers here was more or less uncomfortable, not to say dangerous, as the Bolsheviks wanted to arrest us and send us as prisoners to Moscow. However, when the time came the Bolsheviks ran away like hares, taking with them all the money from the banks & large stocks of foodstuffs.[8]

Captain Bierer of the *Olympia* reported America's first entry into Archangel: "Two officers and 25 men landed with the landing force and 25 men at Archangel. They were divided due to the desires of Admiral Kemp [British invading fleet commander], who felt the great desirability of having American forces here." Bierer went on to say, "Admiral Kemp also wanted the Olympia's band ashore to be used in recruiting Russians."[9] The twenty-two-member band joined the Allies in Archangel on August 7.

The August 10, 1918, entry of the ship's war diary stated:

> Ensign [Donald M.] Hicks, U.S.N.R.F., with one French soldier and one U.S. Seamna [sic], brought into Archangel 54 Bolsheviki soldiers who had voluntarily come in and surrendered at Tundra on the railroad about 30 miles south of Archangel, where a part of the *Olympia* landing force, together with a few French, are at present.[10]

At that point Ensign Hicks and his twenty-five men became part of the Allied Force B, the only part of Poole's southward movement to include

Americans. These were their orders: "August 11—Force under Lt. Col. Haselden, Called Force B. 100 French, 25 American seamen, 35 Rus. [Slavo-British Allied Legion], 27 Poles, to go up river to CISKOYE and then by road to PLESESKAYA to outflank Bolos at OBOZERSKAYA."[11] Haselden also added a few British soldiers, even a few Australians. This same document designates Force A as the Railroad Force under Lieutenant Colonel Guard, and Force C, the River Force under Colonel Josselyn, both British officers. These units were made up of British, French, and Russian troops.

The Slavo Battalion Allied Legion (SBAL), formed early in the campaign, was composed primarily of deserters from the Red Army, and later prisoners from the overcrowded jails of Archangel. Although General Poole mentions that he started the legion in the early days of the Intervention, Poole's replacement, Gen. Edmund Ironside, took it a step further when he accepted prisoners from the jails and determined to make them soldiers. The battalion formed by these prisoners was named Dyer's Battalion, after a young Canadian officer who died in the early days of their formation. The legion was commanded by British officers and British noncoms. Both Poole and Ironside were convinced that British training, uniforms, and discipline would turn these conscripts into fighting men, but it was faulty logic, as future events would prove. As the tide turned against the Allies, desertions would become frequent. One of General Poole's officers later explained:

> He was carrying on an experiment that had been forced on him by a combination of circumstances: the time was coming when he would have to leave the Archangel Russian Forces to its own device and it was essential so to encourage them that they would not feel any sense of desertion.[12]

These aggressive movements into the Russian interior were the result of General Poole's determination to conduct offensive warfare and to pursue his dream of linking with the Czechs at Vologda or Viatka, the nearest points on the Trans-Siberian Railroad.

Force B left Archangel on barges, towed by tugs against the Dvina River current; they lived on the barges for two days, then disembarked to head westward toward the railroad. As they moved inland they found their reception friendly and were even given lunch and tea in the tiny town of Vaimacku. On August 15 at 3:00 A.M., they entered Tiagra and learned that a Bolo force was in the next town, Seletskoye, about nine versts away.[13] At 5:00 P.M. Force B found itself facing 250 Soviets with machine guns and an armored car. By 7:30 P.M., the Allies had bombed the car, blown up one of the Red machine guns, and taken the town. There they suffered some of the first Allied casualties—seven

killed and six wounded, including Seaman Dewey Perschke, who took
a bullet in the arm to become the first American casualty of the Russian
Intervention.[14] The dead included British captain Dennis Garstin, who
had wangled passage to Archangel from Kem to join Force B. He had
been decorated for his part in an Onega expedition in August, but never
lived to receive his medal. "Photographs show him as a big, laughing
young man mounted on a shaggy pony."[15] While the surgeon took the
six wounded back to Archangel, the remainder of the men rested in Seletskoye for a week, waiting for the surgeon's return and sending scouting parties ahead. They learned that the Soviets held the next town
with a large force.

By this time, Force B had been found by the Reds. They faced five
hundred Bolshevik in their front, while three hundred vicious Russian
Baltic Sea sailors were getting in place behind them. The Allies sent a
flanking party of seven Poles and twenty Russians to get behind the Soviets, four miles west of the village called Verst 19. Ensign Hicks, with
eight American machine guns manned by his sailors, was to join the
frontal attack, which was to begin at noon August 22. They moved
toward the Bolos, taking the #19 village without any opposition. That
night an airplane dropped a message from Poole ordering Force B to
break off its move on #19 and to move west toward Obozerskaya,
where Force A was planning to attack at 6:00 A.M. on August 31. Hicks
and his group moved back to Tiagra and were reinforced by fifty Russians with three officers and two machine guns. These reinforcements
were sent to Seletskoye to hold that town and protect the left flank of
Force B as it moved toward Obozerskaya.

The Allies remained in Tiagra, training with their rifles and machine guns, apparently in no hurry to move on Obozerskaya. Finally,
on August 27 they advanced, covering twenty-five versts, then camped
for the night. The next day they pushed forward another twenty versts,
and camped again, this time about twenty versts from their objective.
On August 30, they found the advance outposts of Soviets and drove
them toward Obozerskaya, with the fighting escalating as the Bolos fell
back on their reserves.

The Allies had almost sixty carts of ammunition and supplies
with them, which slowed their movements. As the fighting grew more
intense, these carts were abandoned. Early on August 30, a telegram
was intercepted announcing that four hundred Bolo sailors would arrive in Obozerskaya from Petrograd that night. At 6:00 A.M. on August
31, Hicks and the Allies attacked the city. They met with stiff resistance
and found advance impossible. There the American sailors took their
second casualty, Seaman Charlie B. Ringgenberg, who was hit in the
left elbow, causing a compound fracture. That night the bluejackets

took over the front line, replacing French troops. There Seaman Bert Gerrish sprained his left leg as he dived for cover when a Bolshevik machine gunner found him.

On September 1, the fighting resumed with heavy enemy casualties. Ten Red soldiers were killed, caught in the crossfire of British Lewis guns, but the pressure on the Allies was too great, so they began to withdraw. In the meantime, they received word that Red sailors had taken both Tiagra and Seletskoye, mainly because "the [Allied] Russian force of 50 men, 3 officers, 2 machine guns sent to Seletskoye from Tiagra fired three shots at the [Bolshevik] sailors and then sought salvation in flight."[16] At 6:00 A.M. on September 2, the Reds attacked again, but the Americans, French, and British with their machine guns broke up the assault. The French and Americans were left to hold the line and await the expected Bolshevik charge. Inexplicably, at 5:00 P.M. there was a lull in the firing; not a shot was fired again for two hours.[17]

The expected attack by the Bolsheviks came on September 2, when three hundred newly arrived Red sailors from Tiagra converged on the trenches to the east of Force B. With ammunition exhausted and supplies virtually gone, the men of Force B, numbed by fatigue, had lost their fighting spirit. Colonel Haselden ordered the force to cross the swamps to their west, toward the Archangel-Vologda Railroad, and a general withdrawal began. The Americans were the last to retreat, joining the rest of the Allies at about 10:30 P.M. after Hicks had blown up the abandoned machine guns and ammunition.[18] As they fell back, they found that the Russians and Poles in reserve had helped themselves to the supplies in the abandoned wagons, leaving the rest of Force B without rations or equipment.

In the darkness they made their way across unfamiliar swamps and bogs to the railroad.[19] According to Seaman Harold Gunness:

> They left through the swamps for Col. Guard and the Vologda Railway, after turning all the horses loose and destroying supplies, what little was left. Our food was also used up. The rest of us stayed on the line until 10:30 p.m. when we also left through the swamps and headed for the railroad.[20]

He described his escape, walking through waist deep water, through rain and mud, noting, "The dead were buried along the way, right in the road, as marsh was everywhere. I have often wondered if the bodies were ever recovered. They were buried just as they fell with no box of any kind."[21] Gunness reached the railroad on September 5 and arrived safely in Archangel September 6; his last mission was to guard 123 Bolo prisoners being taken to Archangel.[22]

A terse entry in the British War Diary on September 6 simply states, "Force B turns up at Kholmogorskaya after being surrounded and forced to take to woods."[23] With that notation, Force B ceased to be. However, their casualties were not as heavy as might be expected. There were eight killed and twelve wounded, but, sadly their efforts accomplished little.[24]

It was the first of numerous futile expeditions in North Russia.[25]

Force B's raid was only the beginning of the ground war in North Russia. Already a regiment had formed and was on its way to rescue the various elements of Poole's overly ambitious plan. The regiment that would bear the heavy burden of winter infantry combat near the Arctic Circle was the U.S. Army's 339th Infantry Regiment, forever after known as the Polar Bears.

The 339th Takes Shape

Members of the June draft are already part of the 85th Division and undergo rapid-fire training.

—*Trench and Camp*, Camp Custer, Michigan, newspaper, July 4, 1918

THE *Trench and Camp,* a Camp Custer, Michigan, weekly paper dated July 4, 1918, reported:

The recruits who came to Camp Custer in the June draft have received a hurry-up introduction to the National army. . . . Most of the men have been completely outfitted, thousands have received gas mask instruction and a similar number have been to the range for their first work with the soldier's best friend, his rifle. . . . a tremendous amount of training must be crowded into the next few weeks.[1]

The Eighty-fifth Division, the principal unit in formation at Camp Custer, then commanded by Maj. Gen. Joseph Dickman, was destined for the western front as soon as its full complement of soldiers could be outfitted. The division became known as the Custer Division, and one of its regiments, the 339th, became known as Detroit's Own. The division was activated on August 25, 1917, at virtually the same time that Camp Custer opened. The June 1918 draft brought new recruits from

17

various parts of the Midwest, particularly Michigan, and especially from Detroit. The Detroiters included a large number of men who were immigrants or first-generation Americans from Eastern European nations; their language capabilities would be helpful in the coming months.

Many of the recruits were assigned first to the permanent brigade at Custer, the 160th Depot Brigade, for outfitting, but most ended up in one of the infantry regiments being formed, the 337th, 338th, 339th, and 340th Infantry Regiments. Those with some special skills wound up in specialty units, the 310th Engineers, or the 310th Sanitary Train, made up of the 337th Field Hospital and the 337th Ambulance Company. The draft included men eighteen to thirty years old; most of the Custer recruits were in the upper range of the age brackets.[2]

While in camp they were provided some forms of entertainment: movies, girl's quartets, bell ringers, lectures, impersonators, and some tips on what to expect in France. Fortunately, the division left Custer before the Spanish flu epidemic hit. In October 1918 the camp was hit with the flu; 533 died of the disease.[3]

For most of the men, it was a fleeting visit to the Battle Creek camp. On July 14, after only three weeks of army life, the men in the four regiments boarded the Michigan Central Railroad for the trip east, passing through Detroit, then into Canada to Buffalo, and on to Camp Mills on New York's Long Island. According to Gordon Smith, assigned to Company D of the 339th, their train from Buffalo pulled into New York City at 1:00 P.M. They transferred to a ferryboat for the ride across to Long Island. From there they boarded another train, arriving at Camp Mills late on the night of July 15, where they were housed in tents. The few days they spent at the New York camp were pleasant enough. During the day they drew overseas equipment and endured the constant army physicals. Most of them took the opportunity, with authorized or unauthorized leave, to see New York City.[4] The few nights they spent in Camp Mills, on wooden cots in canvas tents, made them appreciate the wooden barracks and steel bunks most of them had been assigned at Custer. Those who had grumbled about the accommodations at Custer grumbled more at Mills and would find, in most cases, that they had experienced luxury in their first army days. The troopships and their future duties in Russia would provide them with living conditions that were far worse.

On Sunday, July 21, fully convinced that they were headed for France, the 339th left Camp Mills on trains, then transferred to ferryboats, which sailed under the Brooklyn Bridge toward their transports, the SS *Plattsburg* and the HMT *Northumberland*. The Red Cross was waiting for them in the huge warehouses in which the companies assembled, dishing out welcome ice cream on the hot Sunday morning. Each man filled out a card addressed to his family, assuring them of his safe arrival in Europe; these cards would be mailed after their actual arrival. Then the doughboys mounted the narrow gangplank; the embarking officer called out each last name, and the soldier responded with first name and middle initial as he boarded. The *Plattsburg*, an American ship, appeared to have better conditions than the British *Northumberland*, according to several diaries, but all troopships are designed for utility, not comfort. The ships sailed out of New York on July 22 in a convoy of eleven to eighteen ships, depending on the view of the individual involved. One diary mentions eleven ships, one fifteen ships, and another eighteen; ships in convoys are difficult to count, but it can safely be said that the ships left in convoy, accompanied by a variety of naval warships and at least one dirigible.[5]

The voyage passed with some discomfort; the troops were occupied with the usual boat drills, reading, mess duty, and letter writing, but with little excitement as the convoy sailed through the Atlantic waters still patrolled by German U-boats. Some members of the expedition, the Engineers and the medical units, sailed on other ships at different times. Charles Simpson of the 337th Ambulance Company wrote that on August 2 their ship attacked a U-boat and sank her. He mentioned in his diary, "Friday August 2d a submarine was sighted, and our sub-chasers opened fire, giving 16 large boatloads of 'Green Yankees' their first experience with the 'Big Noise.'"[6] Some soldiers reported submarine encounters, and depending on their position in the convoy, others may have been unaware of any submarine contact. James Siplon of Company I, 339th, noted in his diary that there were duels with the U-boats on both July 23 and August 2, the same day he sighted land.[7]

The Atlantic seas took their toll on the traveling troops; seasickness affected many in their crowded quarters. But soon land was sighted, and the troopships slowly entered the waterways leading to the docks at Liverpool, England. It was a welcome sight as the Midwesterners lined the rails, drinking in the green lands of England. They disembarked, some on August 3 and some on August 4, happy to be on land again, still believing they were headed for France and the western front. Again, the Red Cross met them, and gave them their first taste of English cakes. There was another train to ride; some went to Camp Cowshot, and others went to Camp Stoney Castle in Brookwood, some twenty-five miles southwest of London. They found more tents, but no bunks, so many slept on the cold, soggy ground. There they had their first taste of mutton, which would become one of their least favorite, but most plentiful, meats. Companies E and H were bivouacked on an old country estate once occupied by an African explorer, Sir Henry Stanley. Pvt. Donald Carey was moved by the beauty of the countryside: "Though depressed and tired upon arrival I soon appreciated the natural beauty of the place with its grass, excellent drinking water, and rolling country."[8]

The 339th Regiment was given the rest of its abbreviated training in the English countryside at Camp Stoney Castle, while the other three regiments of the Eighty-fifth went to other sites, and soon after, to France. The Engineers and the hospital units were sent to different English locations that provided their own training. They often spent their days in long marches toting full packs and rifles, sometimes wearing their gas masks.[9] This took place during a hot summer season, complete with English rain and fog.

In the evenings, passes were available, and nearby London kept them busy with its theaters, saloons, restaurants, and sightseeing. It was an exciting time for most of the men, despite their rather rigorous training schedule. Company D's Pvt. Frank Duoma noted in his almost daily journal how impressed he was with his several visits to London. He did all the tourist things imaginable, making good use of his spare moments. A nighttime visit to London was an eye-opener: "The bartenders were all girls. The women drink in the saloons the same as men and also smoke a great deal."[10]

It was while in training that some of the men and officers first learned that the decision had been made to send them on an "intervention" into North Russia. In England Lowell Thomas, a famous author, lecturer, and broadcaster, was one of the first to inform the recently arrived doughboys they would not be going to France as they all expected, but to Russia.[11]

Gen. John J. Pershing, the American commander of all forces in Europe, selected the 339th to make the Russian expedition. There were several reasons for his choice. Their commander, George Evans Stewart, was a forty-six-year-old, experienced Regular Army major with the temporary rank of lieutenant colonel. He had served in the Philippines for a number of years where he won the Medal of Honor for the river rescue of an enlisted man in November 1899. Since that time he had been in the Engineers, served two years in Alaska, and most recently was in the Quartermaster Corps.[12] His service in Arctic Alaska made him a good choice to lead men from the colder northern states. Besides, the regiment was conveniently stationed near London and readily available.[13]

The 339th Infantry, joined by the First Battalion 310th Engineers, 337th Field Hospital, and 337th Ambulance Company, was identified as the American Expeditionary Force North Russia (AEFNR). They would be under British command; in addition, they were issued British clothing and winter equipment. Most significantly, they had to trade in their familiar Enfield rifles for older and more cumbersome Moison-Nagant 7.62mm Russian rifles, long, clumsy weapons with corkscrew bayonets. Even though these rifles were American-made weapons, they had been manufactured specifically for the Russian Imperial Army and were far from popular with the Americans. Pvt. Donald Carey of Company E was amazed when he was issued his new weapon: "It was a Russian rifle! No wonder they lost the war. What was the object of equipping American troops with such a rifle? Were we to fight alongside the Russians against the Huns on the broken-down Eastern Front? Certainly no troops would go to France with these worthless weapons."[14]

Not only were rifles exchanged, but the machine guns on which the 339th had trained at Custer and in England were taken away and replaced with the British Lewis and Vickers machine guns. The Vickers was a water-cooled gun that took two hands to fire. Russell Hershberger, a machine gunner, wrote that they had no training on these guns before being sent to the front. He added with disgust:

> And at night, many times it was three of us slept together, and we'd take them guns between us in the bed to keep them from freezing. . . . Can you imagine using a water-cooled up in that climate where for twelve straight weeks it never got above fifty below zero. And using a water-cooled gun![15]

Maj. J. Brooks Nichols, Second Battalion commander, commented on the exchange of rifles. "No two weapons shot the same ammunition and not one shot American ammunition, or was in anywise related to the character of the weapons the men had been trained to use before they reached Russia."[16] The explanation given was that a large cache of ammunition fitting the Russian rifle awaited the troops in Archangel; however, those cartridges had long since been confiscated by the Bolsheviks. The weapons provided were a source of great resentment with the troops; that resentment would be fueled later by the issue of British food rations. It was to be a truly British show.

Since England was suffering through one of its hottest summers in years, the newly issued wool uniforms became an itchy nuisance.[17] Another annoyance was the infamous Shackleton boot, a bulky piece of footwear designed by the famous Antarctic explorer Sir Ernest Shackleton and totally unfit for use by an infantry force. It would come to be as universally hated as the British rations.

Perhaps the lack of enthusiasm for the Intervention by senior U.S. Army officers led to the equipment exchange. Army chief of staff Gen. Peyton March related:

The President, on July 17, decided to authorize the sending of an American force as part of the proposed North Russian Expedition, and I then
washed my hands of the whole matter. I told the Secretary that we could
furnish from America neither transportation nor supplies for the proposed expedition.[18]

On the whole the men enjoyed England and they were reluctant
to leave. Nevertheless, on August 25, amid persistent rumors concerning their destination—back to the United States to fight Mexico or to
Italy, India via the Suez, or Siberia—the regiment marched in orderly
ranks from their various locations to the trains in London. There they
took a ten-hour ride to the docks at Newcastle-on-Tyne, 270 miles north
of London, for the final leg of their overseas journey. While they traveled across England, they were sometimes cheered and stared at by the
women and older men left in the English countryside, but sometimes
jeered at by Britishers saying, "You're finally here—what took you so
long?" The recent citizens-turned-soldiers from the American Midwest
were less than enthusiastic as they entrained for the docks at Newcastle.

On their way to the docks one of the Yanks, a lumberjack from
northern Michigan, had a problem. He had been severely constipated
for days and finally went to the medics, who obliged him with a supply of #9 pills, which in some cases had the same effect as an internal
hand grenade. On a troop train, without sanitary facilities, the Michi-
gander began to feel the effects of the medication, growing more and
more panicky as the train moved slowly north, meandering through,
and stopping frequently at, the little towns dotting the landscape. Finally, as the train paused in a tiny station, panic overtook pride and
he jumped off the train, dropped his olive-drab pants and squatted on
the platform. "People looked disgusted and shocked. He didn't look
right or left. His face was red, as he was busy making a big pancake
that almost touched his shoes. We yelled at him, 'Mac, your shoes,
your shoes!' He looked down and moved his feet farther apart."[19] His
traveling companions, all of Company G, helped him back in the car,
but were having a hard time, watching Mac with his pants still at half
mast, trying to get through the tiny door. After he was safely aboard,
he reached in his pocket and pulled out the welcome card from King
George issued to them as they landed in England. Mac read the card,
then said, "I wasn't going to shit in my pants for no King George." His
bunkmate John Toornman, writing about the incident, said, "I wonder
what the English people thought of us, and what you or I would have
done in this predicament."[20]

On the docks at Newcastle, just south of the Scottish border, waited four British troopships whose mission it was to carry the Americans, plus a contingent of Italian infantry, to Murmansk, Russia. Tragically, these ships carried more than their assigned troops to the northern Russian port. They also carried the deadly Spanish influenza.

The Americans Land
in Archangel

Down the gangplank we went and I stepped on the blood-cursed soil of the despotic Tsars.

—Donald E. Carey

WITH their training in England finished, on August 27, 1918, the American troops were marched down to the Newcastle dock to greet their transports. Three British transport ships waited for the Americans, the *Nagoya*, the *Somali*, and the *Tydeus*, while the *Tsar* boarded Italian troops also headed north. The voyage was reasonably pleasant, although the weather became increasingly colder as they moved north. The barracks bags that held their winter clothing were stowed in the holds, unavailable to the doughboys, who wished they had the warm gear as they headed up the Norwegian coast into the Barents and White Seas. Originally, the plan was to send the Americans to Murmansk, but as they sailed north, the word went out to the little fleet to go directly to Archangel to rescue the endangered Force B with its American sailors, lost in the Russian interior.

As there was still concern about roaming German U-boats, the ships steered a zigzag course, hoping to elude any lurking submarines, but there was no mention of submarine sightings. The northern waters had been heavily mined, too, so there was a constant watch for mines that might have broken loose from charted mine fields. On the ships, long lines formed at the canteens, which opened to sell chocolate and sweets to the men, who had recently been paid.[1] Several escort vessels busied themselves around the troopships, and their presence was both reassuring and entertaining. At night there was the midnight sun, a strange experience for the Midwesterners; the sun would barely dip below the horizon, and there was daylight almost twenty-four hours a day.

Somehow, the killer Spanish Flu had been brought aboard the vessels; the incubation period ended four days out of Newcastle, and the men began to drop like flies. (The deadly Spanish influenza epidemic of 1918 turned out to be a killer of more citizens worldwide than the Great War itself.[2]) The *Tsar*, carrying the Italians, was especially hard hit. Several soldiers reported seeing burials at sea taking place on the *Tsar*; it left the little convoy to dock in Murmansk. In the cramped quarters of the ship, unsanitary conditions prevailed and the disease took hold in its worst form. Men slept in hammocks, virtually touching each other; there was little ventilation due to the increasingly cold weather; and the ships themselves were disgusting. One description of the *Nagoya* read, "She had formerly been employed as a Pacific and Oriental trade ship and since that time had not been properly cleaned. The ever-present cootie, and a number of other species of vermin repellant to men were present in force."[3] Descriptions of the other ships were no more flattering.

A few of the men were seasick on the nine-day boat trip, but that condition was mild compared with the flu epidemic. Of the three remaining ships, the flu hit the men on the *Somali* the hardest. The official medical report listed no deaths at sea on board the three American troopships; however, some soldiers wrote of burials at sea. Charles Simpson wrote that he witnessed burials at sea on his ship, the *Somali*: "The large plank is raised to the side-rail, your Buddy, draped in the American flag, slides from the plank into the ocean and the ship sails on. . . . Thank goodness there were but few funerals at sea."[4] That vivid description seems a rather strong indication of shipboard deaths, yet the official medical reports and records of bodies brought back after the expedition, state that this was not the case.

The city of Archangel lies on the Dvina River some twenty-five miles south of its mouth. It flows north, carrying silt and fallings hundreds of miles, broadening and turning as it swings by Archangel. It finally empties into the White Sea, a sea named not for its clarity, but for its winter coating of snow and ice. The Dvina is roughly one mile wide at its widest point at Archangel.

On September 4, the transport fleet moved into the harbor area, passing Economie Point, a number of lumber mills, Solombola, then Archangel itself, docking at Bakharitza on the west side of the river.

The city normally housed about forty thousand people, but the war had doubled its size with refugees and military. The first impression was of masts and boats, docks and warehouses lining the river, but beyond the riverfront areas were scores of multistory buildings with chimneys and church spires with their colorful domes. The city itself was only a few blocks wide, running along the crescent-shaped harbor, from the Bakharitza area on the south end with its warehouses and docks, up to Economie in the north with its industry, sawmills, and shipyards, where there was a huge split in the river. While it was generally referred to as gray and dismal, some saw it in a better light. Capt. Joel Moore wrote:

> Prominently rises the impressive magnitudinous structure of the reverenced cathedral there, its dome of the hue of heaven's blue and set with stars of solid gold. And when all else in the landscape is bathed in morning purple or evening gloaming-grey, the leveled rays of the coming or departing sun with a brilliantly striking effect glisten these white and gold structures.[5]

Unfortunately, closer inspection revealed some basic flaws: streets were unpaved and always churned into foot-sucking mud; sidewalks were planks laid endwise and constantly in need of repair; sanitation was almost nonexistent, so that any fresh air that appeared was almost immediately fouled; and a distressing poverty was everywhere.

As soon as the regiment landed, the first priority was the treatment of the sick. Commander of American medical personnel Maj. Dr. Jonas Longley reported:

> On the 5th day of September, 1918, arrived at Archangel, with more than one hundred cases of Influenza on the S.S. *Somali,* seventy-five cases on the S.S. *Nagoya,* and on the S.S. *Tideus* [sic], none. The Deputy Director of Medical Services of the British Army was immediately notified of our epidemic and we attempted to obtain accommodations for the patients at the 53d Stationary Hospital (British) but they were able to take only about twenty-five; and then their consent to accommodate this number was not received until the transports had moved up the river to Bakharitza, some five versts distance. For want of better hospital treatment and under great difficulties, as the mode of transportation was very poor, the worst cases were transferred.[6]

The official report indicated that the first flu-related death, Pvt. Albert F. Rickert of Mt. Clemens, Michigan, took place only hours after the ships docked in Archangel.[7]

Diaries written during those early days in Archangel, particularly of the Second Battalion assigned to the city, tell of an almost daily funeral detail. Charles Lewis, adjutant of the regiment, wrote of the death of Pvt. Joseph Brieve of Company E on September 8, then on September 9, of funerals for one American and two French, on September 10, of funerals for nine Americans, and the same on September 11, and so on.[8]

The British hospital was the only hospital open at the time; the lack of concern by British medics for the dangerously ill Americans was one reason British-American relations began badly and grew steadily worse during the expedition. As rudimentary medical housing was made available using sailors' housing—old, filthy barracks—American men of the 337th Field Hospital strained their capacities to the limit. There were few supplies and virtually no medication. Medicine had been forgotten, according to some reports, or replaced with British whiskey rations, forty thousand cases of it.[9] G. J. Anderson, of the 337th Field Hospital, wrote:

> They lay on stretchers without mattress or pillow, lying in their O.D. uniforms, with only a simple blanket for covering. The place was a bedlam of sinister sounds of rasping, stertorous breathing, coughings, hackings, moans, and incoherent cries. All we could do was stand and watch some poor fellow gasping, burning with fever and dripping with sweat, then a sudden rigidity, a silence, and the staring eyes becoming fixed. . . . Whenever a patient died one of us would wake the other [orderly] and together would carry out the corpse and store him in the hallway.[10]

Major Longley was at Bakharitza where the sick were unloaded. He sought help from the Red Cross who willingly shared what expertise and supplies they had. The British felt that the Americans should not set up a hospital in Archangel since it was deemed that they were lacking in equipment and experienced personnel. But Major Longley, with Red Cross help, scrubbed and cleaned space in an available warehouse to administer to his sick, and when he was finished, he raised the American flag at his new hospital. The British orders were to fly only the Union Jack; it took two armed sentries on twenty-four-hour watches to keep the Stars and Stripes flying.

Despite the care offered the sick, many succumbed to the deadly flu. So one of the first assignments for the 310th Engineers was the layout of an American cemetery in Archangel. By September 30, it would have sixty-three American graves, all flu victims. Miraculously, only four more would die of disease during the rest of their stay in Russia.[11] That was the good news: death by disease was controlled; the bad news was that death in combat was not.

As the ships tied up at their various docks in Bakharitza and Smolny Quay in Archangel, the disembarking companies of 4,344 men and 143 officers were ordered to take part in a parade through the streets of the city. It was a gloomy September day, with drenching rain; with the immediate concerns for the sick and the dying, the parade was called off. It gave the regiment a chance to unload the sick, to transfer them to quarters that were barely habitable, let alone hospitable, and to seek medical supplies and assistance. So the American soldiers of the 339th Infantry patiently waited for the next move, some on the docks, some still on ships, and some in sick quarters.

Because of the effects of the epidemic, some men found themselves on ships back to England without really spending much time in Russia. Many of the sick who recovered were still not fit for field duty, and a slow trickle of men began to be evacuated to England, then to the United States. Pvt. John Oudemuller of Holland, Michigan, was one of the first to leave. He was hospitalized on September 6, the day he arrived, and was taken to Murmansk by ship on October 27. After several delays, he boarded the busy U.S. cruiser *Olympia* with Ambassador Francis and the wounded Seaman Perschke, late of Force B. He was taken off in Scotland, then made the rounds of hospitals in Britain before being shipped home and discharged January 13, 1919, just seven months after he enlisted.[12] Many of those who died from the flu in September had been in the army less than ninety days. On November 26, fifty-two men were ordered back to England from the Archangel hospitals, including Golden C. Bahr of Marilla, Michigan.[13]

The 339th was commanded by Lt. Col. George Evans Stewart, who had replaced the regiment's popular commander Col. John Craig at Camp Custer. According to Army chief of staff General March, Stewart was sent a copy of Wilson's *Aide Memoire* to make sure he understood the government's position; however, it is doubtful that Stewart ever received his copy. As soon as his troops were ashore, he virtually lost control of the regiment. Stewart had been instructed to report to British general Poole for orders, and Poole lost no time in rushing two American battalions into the Russian interior.[14] As soon as the troops disembarked, they were ordered south. Some thought the situation might have been different if the 339th had been led by their old commander, Colonel Craig. Lt. Harry Costello later wrote, "Col. Craig would not have stood supinely by while his outfit was stolen. . . . Today in Detroit's Own Regiment Colonel Craig's name is revered, the man himself is worshipped by all those he ever came in contact with."[15]

The whole North Russian expedition was engulfed in confusion—miscommunications, misunderstandings, and blatant misuse of the Americans. For this, President Wilson was primarily responsible. After he circulated his *Aide Memoire*, he had little more to say to the Allies, despite his knowledge of actions that flagrantly violated his whole concept of the Intervention. As Americans were drawn into battle with Bolsheviks, word was transmitted to Washington on a regular basis. Ambassador Francis, who had been one of the strongest advocates of actually fighting the Bolsheviks, was the senior American official in Archangel. One historian described the conflict: "Indeed, the government record of cable communications between the [State] Department and Ambassador Francis during the month of September gives somewhat of the impression of two deaf persons carrying on a conversation while their hearing aids operate only intermittently."[16] On September 11, 1918, Francis cabled Washington that Poole had already sent two American battalions into action. However, on September 13, a State Department cable to Francis repeated the instructions that activity was to be only defensive, guarding stores in Archangel and surrounding areas. A covering message also repeated that Stewart was under Poole's command. Faced with conflicting instructions, Francis interpreted these instructions according to his own philosophy. In those early days, he was in complete agreement with the ambitious British general Poole in his attacks on Bolsheviks.

Poole's plan was to send Force A four hundred miles down the railroad to Vologda before winter set in. Force C would also go south, three hundred miles up the Dvina River as far as Kotlas, from there to move south to meet with the Czech forces, which would presumably be arriving from the east. The ill-fated Force B would go up the Dvina, disembark and cross to attack Obozerskaya, while a small force would be sent to Onega to protect the Murmansk-Archangel line and Force A.

All of these strategies were totally unrealistic. Vologda was already heavily occupied by Bolshevik troops, as was Plesetskaya, north of Vologda. On the Dvina, shallow-draft Red gunboats were able to pass over the shallows of the upper Dvina, while Allied boats, with a deeper draft, were unable to navigate those shallows. In addition, the Czechs never intended to move north to join Archangel forces, even had the Supreme War Council advised the legion to make that effort. And Force B was routed before the other campaigns could get fully underway.

Poole's optimism, plus a lack of knowledge of true conditions, led him to make these aggressive, but totally unrealistic, moves. As the two forces moved south, they were getting farther and farther away from each other; had they been successful in their missions, they would have found themselves separated by three hundred miles of Red-controlled territory.

Another weak link in Poole's plan, and other Allied plans as well, was the expectation that the Russians themselves would support Allied movements into the interior, even supplying troops to fight with an Allied force. Experience soon taught them that Russian peasants had no inclination to join any such operations.

Eventually, the British High Command in London learned of the ineptitude of the Archangel commander; Poole was allowed to take leave and returned to London on October 14. He was replaced by Maj. Gen. Sir Edmund Ironside, a giant of a man who turned out to be more popular, and more conservative, than his predecessor. Surprisingly, Ironside was told that the Supreme War Council had decided to conduct a winter campaign in North Russia even if Germany surrendered.[17] This information had not been communicated to the Allied officers in the Archangel area. While Poole briefed Ironside on the situation before he left, Ironside was puzzled by two facts: (1) that Poole was convinced that his forces would be substantially strengthened soon, and (2) that all of Poole's orders had been verbal and there was virtually no record or knowledge of Poole's troop placements. However, Ironside took up his duties with vigor, visiting his fronts frequently, a routine that Poole had ignored.

On September 5, 1918, with Poole still firmly in control, the Third Battalion of the 339th, Companies I, K, L, and M under Maj. Charles Young walked down the gangplank and off the troopship. Immediately, they boarded ferries for the cross-river trip to the train depot at Bakharitza and filed into the tiny Russian railway cars. The Second Battalion debarked at Smolny Quay, headed for barracks and duty in Archangel as security forces. First Battalion, Companies A, B, C, and D stayed on the ships until September 7, when they debarked and headed up the Dvina River on barges. Some of the companies would not see each other again until they departed Russia nine months later.

Action began almost immediately on the railroad front as the Third Battalion moved to support embattled French forces and attempted to rescue the lost Force B, silent since late August and supposedly lost in the bogs of North Russia.

The Railroad Front

Somewhere deep in the forest beyond that skyline of pine tree tops a handful of French and Scots and Americans were battling the Bolos for their lives.

—Joel E. Moore

A S the American Third Battalion headed south down the Vologda-Archangel Railroad, rattling along in their Russian version of the French "40&8s," they stopped at a small village, waiting for a northbound train to pass. There they saw their first Bolos, guarded by sailors. The sailors were most likely part of the Force B *Olympia* contingent, en route back to their ship, although they were not recognized as such at the time.

General Poole's Railroad Force, Force A, was vulnerable, tied as it was to the tracks. Poole soon placed two flanking forces on either side of the railroad, the Onega Force to the west and the Seletskoye Force on the Emtsa River to the east. The three forces were designed to operate together, but seldom did.

Just outside Obozerskaya, recently captured by Force A, the Reds had blown a bridge with artillery fire. Here the American battalion detrained from their "side-door Pullmans" and formed up in column of twos. They were tired and hungry from poor food at sea and on the dingy train cars; many were still sick from the flu, but afraid to be hospitalized; and worst of all, they were virtually untrained in the art of warfare. Yet, they plunged into their strange war prepared to do their very best.

American battalion commander Maj. Charles Young was not one of the favorites of the regiment; he had a reputation as a stickler for regulations and had a great concern for his own personal safety. As the column of men from I and L Companies stood in ranks near the rail station, Major Young called for an officers' meeting. As they congregated, a French officer approached excitedly, gesturing and shouting in French. Finally it dawned on the major that the shell holes and destroyed bridge indicated the place had been under Red artillery fire recently:

> [He] shooed the platoons off into the woods. The area was one big swamp, and as the men dispersed, they wound up in water knee deep. When the Americans met their French guides, they noticed the poilus had built fires to dry their soggy clothes, but Major Young stuck to the book. There would be no fires for the doughboys on their first night under combat conditions.[1]

In Obozerskaya, Poole's original Force A was made up of French poilus, with some Russian Slavo Battalion Allied Legion (SBAL) troops, all led by British colonel Guard, who was later replaced by Colonel Sutherland. Their objective was to take Vologda, three hundred miles away from Archangel. Companies I and L were immediately sent into Obozerskaya to relieve the French who had been fighting steadily since August 31. Then began a significant buildup of the Allied defensive position. There were British armored cars, which proved to be almost useless, breaking through bridges and burying themselves in mud, and an armored train with naval guns, sandbagged and protected by a collection of machine guns. There were even a few western front airplanes flown by the Royal Air Force (RAF).[2] Part of the work done by the engineers was the leveling of a primitive landing strip for these aircraft, which were sometimes as dangerous to Allied troops as to the Reds. The airplanes played a role on the railroad front, but their bombing was inaccurate. Frequent mention was made of aircraft involvements, but weather and equipment combined to keep them from being a major factor.

As the defenses improved, Railroad Force commander British colonel Sutherland gave his instructions, "We are fighting an offensive war, and not a defensive one, although for the time being it is the duty of everybody to get the present area in a sound state of defense."[3] The men kept busy doing just that, with only patrol action forcing any contact with the Reds.

Units of the Third Battalion were separated further on September 7, when Colonel Sutherland ordered Company K to drive east to look for Force B. Company K left Obozerskaya and moved toward the town of Seletskoye. On the way they discovered carts, supplies, weapons and even fresh graves, evidences of Force B, but no sign of the men. (Actually, by this time Force B was located in Kholmogorskaya, some twenty miles north of Obozerskaya.) Later, on September 11, two platoons of Company L led by 1st Lt. Charles Lennon left Obozerskaya to join Company K, leaving one platoon of Company L still near Archangel and one platoon in Obozerskaya.[4]

Inevitably, fighting began. On September 11 at about 9:30 A.M., a two-platoon patrol from Company M, working its way south from Obozerskaya, ran into a sizeable Bolshevik patrol. After some skirmishing, the Bolos withdrew, leaving the Yanks in possession of the tracks as far as the bridge at Verst 464.[5] The action was brief but intense; there were no known American casualties.[6]

Major Young was involved in another episode on September 15 outside Obozerskaya. A unit of Company I had been ordered to shoot at any airplane that approached the area. When a plane appeared, Lt. Albert May gave the command to fire. Major Young became upset when the plane was hit and crashed nearby. Young ran toward the downed aircraft, yelling, "Don't shoot, we're Americans!" The Bolshevik pilot blasted away with his machine gun and Young dived headfirst into the mud while the pilots escaped into nearby woods. Afterward, in the ranks, men would occasionally call out, "Don't shoot, we're Americans!" which always brought a chuckle.[7]

Clashes increased between Third Battalion and the Bolsheviks. On September 16, the Reds launched their first real attack on the American positions, against the line held by Companies I and L near Verst 464. Their offensive was made with fierce artillery and machine gun fire, but both American companies held firm, and the initial attacks were beaten off. In the action, however, two platoons of Company I under Lt. Gordon B. Reese became separated from the fight in the heavy woods where they were attacked by a Red unit. The doughboys fought until they virtually ran out of ammunition. Reese surprised even himself by ordering a bayonet charge reminiscent of the trench warfare of the western front. His surprise charge confused the Bolsheviks, who suddenly broke and ran.[8]

The little battle was a victory of sorts for the Americans. The official report was brief:

On morning of September 16th the enemy attacked our outpost position at VERST 464 with machine gun and shrapnel, and was beaten off by "L" Company, supported by two platoons of "I" Company, and artillery of Allied armoured train.

Casualties—Americans—   3 Killed
                         2 wounded[9]

Those three killed were mechanic Ignacy H. Kwasniewski and Pvt. Anthony Soczkoski, both of Company I, and Pvt. Philip Sokol of Company L. They were buried in a little cemetery in Obozerskaya beneath wooden crosses fashioned by their solemn comrades. Since there was no chaplain on the front, services were performed by a local Russian Orthodox priest. It was a moving final service:

> With the long-haired, wonderfully robed priest came his choir and many villagers, who occupied one side of the square made by the soldiers standing there in the dusk to do last honors to their dead comrades. With chantings and doleful chorus the choir answered his solemn oratory and devotional intercessions. He swung his sacred censor pot over each body and though we understood no word we knew he was doing reverence to the spirit of sacrifice shown by our fallen comrades. There in the darkness by the edge of the forest, the priest and his ceremony, the firing squad's volley, and the bugler's last call, all united to make that an allied funeral.[10]

Colonel Stewart was in Obozerskaya on one of his infrequent visits to the front at that time. Several versions of his behavior were recorded: one says he was at the site, but read a magazine during the service; another says he left hurriedly before the service began.[11] It appears he could have attended, but chose not to. This caused deep resentment among the Third Battalion soldiers.

For the next two weeks, reports indicate only intermittent shelling by Bolshevik armored trains and limited patrolling. Unexpectedly, on September 28, British general R. G. Finlayson, Poole's field commander of both the Dvina River Force and the Railroad Force, appeared in Obozerskaya. Finlayson ordered Colonel Sutherland to prepare for an attack toward Plesetskaya, beginning immediately. The charge was to be launched on Bolsheviks at Versts 458 and 455. The order caught Sutherland by surprise, but it was Sutherland's task to prepare and execute the order.

One of the problems facing the force was a lack of knowledge of the area and a shortage of maps. Sutherland's hastily contrived plan was simple on paper, but was doomed from the start. He ordered Major Young to make two flanking movements: Company M and half of Com-

pany I under Capt. Joel Moore were to take the woods on the west side
of the tracks, while the other two platoons of Company I, plus half the
Headquarters Mortar Battery took the other flank on the east side under
Lt. Albert May.[12] But there were no knowledgeable guides for either
force and no maps, except very sketchy outlines of the terrain. Off the
tracks on either side of the railroad, heavy woods and swamp covered
almost every inch of the ground. Between the two flanking units, the
French with one section of American machine gunners and the rest of
Headquarters Company (lately and hastily trained on the French Stokes
mortars) were to move down the railroad tracks.

The attack was scheduled for 5 A.M. on September 29; the larger
flanking units under Captain Moore left around 5 P.M. on September 28
to get into position. Their instructions were:

> We must follow the blazed trail of an east-west forest line till we came to
> a certain broad north-and-south cutting, down which we were to march
> so many verst posts till we were past the enemy's flank and then attack
> him in the rear. Lt. Chantrill, the pleasant British interpreter, was to act
> as guide, although he himself had no acquaintance with the area.[13]

Company M immediately found itself in trouble; they encountered swamp and forest, and darkness fell as they left on their march.
Platoons became separated, and men strayed, forcing the column to
pause to keep men together. Getting lost was a death sentence in that
hostile bog.

Meanwhile, the two platoons of I Company on the other flank
under Lieutenant May were having more problems. Lieutenant May
had asked for maps but was told that two British officers would lead
him, so maps were not necessary. May wrote, "About 2 A.M. the two
British officers left us out in the woods, stating they had to get back,
and handed me this map and said, 'Go this many paces straight ahead
and this many paces to the right and you will be in position.'"[14]

The mortar crews, carrying their heavy weapons, stumbled and
crashed through the swamp, trying to keep up with May, but he was
soon out of sight. Instead the mortars found one line of the Bolshevik
entrenchments and fired away at them, driving them back. May's platoons of I Company managed to get back to the original line of departure as the mortars wound up in their own little skirmish. The
mortarmen were not only forced to abandon their position under heavy
Bolo fire, but they also left their three mortars, base plates, elevating
stand, and six shells. Lieutenant Keith, the battery commander, reported, "The mortars in this event would have proved themselves very

valuable. They are, however, with their excessive loads of both mortars and shells rather immobile in a swampy country."[15]

May summed up his venture: "Well, we ended up in a swamp, knee-deep in water. We found no positions. When the artillery opened up, we were in front of their barrage. The whole thing was a debacle of the worst kind."[16]

While these two columns were facing their soggy trails, a deadlier fate lay ahead for the French and Americans ordered to storm the Bolo camp, moving straight down the tracks. The artillery barrage failed to dislodge the Reds, so it was up to the attackers to rout them out of their defensive works. The French led off, taking the bridge and the first trench line; then, supported by the heavy American weapons, but without the supporting flank attacks, their momentum slowed. Gradually, the heavy Bolo fire drove them from the trenches, back to the bridge.

The flanking party of Company M had returned to the railroad by then, having been lost, found, then lost again, and finally rescued by two stalwart north-Michigan woodsmen, who managed to find the return path.[17] They were tired, soaking wet, hungry, and disgusted. The rough, sketchy map that Colonel Sutherland furnished Captain Moore made no mention of a lake or of the depth and current of a stream or swamp. Still, when the men were asked to charge up the tracks to the bridge where the French and Americans were in trouble, fifty-eight volunteers stepped forward. Although they were exhausted, the thought of their friends and bunkmates in trouble enabled them to forget their own condition.

The Bolsheviks in a counterattack tried to take the bridge, but the combined Allied force with their automatic weapons and mortars intimidated them enough that they concentrated only on artillery fire to keep the Allies pinned down. As the day wore on, the bridge stayed in the hands of the weary, dirty, American and French soldiers. However, Colonel Sutherland, convinced that the bridge would fall to the Communists, ordered his artillery to fire on the bridge. The shells landed in the midst of Company M, taking a heavy toll: nine were wounded, two mortally. Pvt. Schliomi Dyment died at the bridge and Pvt. Matthew Niemi died en route to the hospital. Privates Drews, Jarrain, Karapuz, Yasas, and Smaglich were severely wounded, as was Lt. James Donovan. Several others were slightly wounded and one man wandered in a daze, the first victim of shell shock.[18] It was a bitter fact that these early casualties were from friendly fire.

The Americans were unsure whether the friendly fire was a mistake or a reckless order. This was further questioned when an American soldier in Sutherland's headquarters reported, "When Col. Sutherland was informed that his artillery was getting his own troops, he first asked on one telephone for another quart of whisky and later called up his artillery officer and ordered the deadly fire to lengthen range."[19] That brief, deadly barrage was another wedge in the American-British relationship.

As this action was taking place, the unpopular Maj. Charles Young was relieved of command and summoned to Archangel to command the Second Battalion, and Maj. J. Brooks Nichols became commander of Third Battalion. Major Nichols decided to keep the bridge at Verst 458. Colonel Sutherland ordered the troops to withdraw, but Nichols, knowing the price that had been paid for that ground, stayed in spite of Sutherland's orders. Cpl. Cleo M. Coburn kept a terse diary: "Sept 29—At 6 bells, started artillery fire, and started attack at 6:25. Under enemy artillery fire for two hours. Several Americans wounded, 7 French killed. Stopped fighting with the Bolsheviks, retreated about five versts."[20]

The Bolos never did press their attack on the bridge, and the Americans counted their losses. From September 28 to October 2, two had been killed, fourteen wounded, and five were missing. Of the five missing, two were from Machine Gun Company, Pvt. Simon Kieffer and Pvt. Arthur Frank; three were from Headquarters Company, Cpl. William R. Babinger, Cpl. Perry C. Scott, and Pvt. James Carter. The bodies of these five were never found; they were later declared killed in action. One of the medics, Godfrey Anderson, wrote in his diary, "Cpl. Babinger and Cpl. Scott were killed as well as Privates Center [Carter] and Couch. At least we have to believe that they were killed for their bodies were not found."[21]

Private Couch did turn up later, but not the others. Babinger, whose brother was in the same Headquarters Company, wrote a letter home which was published in the *Detroit News*: "Do not worry unnecessarily about brother Bill, we will bring him back with us Providence allowing although the poor kid and two of his 'buddies' who were also severely wounded in the same battle September 29 are still missing."[22] When Cpl. Joseph Babinger returned to his home in Detroit, he returned alone. Brother Bill was never found.

The next two weeks saw limited patrolling and almost continuous Bolshevik artillery fire. The battalion had no casualties and even managed some rest. Companies I and M took turns relieving the French in the forward positions, most days living under gray skies and a cold rain. Their rest was short-lived, however; orders came to try again to advance toward Plesetskaya. General Poole was in the process of being relieved, but his final effort against the Bolos would begin October 14, the day he sailed off to England.

On October 13, in another nasty rain, two platoons of Company M with two French platoons and the American Machine Gun Company set off toward their objective, a Red armored train. As they entered woods on their way to Verst 457 and the Red train, they came under artillery fire from the train. There were no casualties as they passed a sleepless night in the woods waiting for H hour, 5:00 A.M. But again the plan rapidly fell apart. The lead platoon moved too far in front, so their surprise attack was spoiled. The attack was made from the woods, across an open field, into heavy, but fortunately inaccurate, fire.

After the brief skirmish, the Bolo train escaped, but with heavy casualties. The Americans suffered one fatality, Company M's Pvt. Walter Merrick. Four others were wounded and sent back to Archangel.[23] Later in the day Americans hit forward positions of the Bolos at Verst 457 and drove them south. During the day, they were reasonably successful, gaining ground to Verst 455 and killing many of the Red infantry, but they still failed in their objective, the armored train. As the day ended, Company I was still pushing the Soviets down the tracks, clearing the area all the way to Verst 445, and the enemy "was on the run."[24] Company I, led by Capt. Horatio Winslow, suffered another fatality that day. Pvt. Frank S. McLaughlin of Sandusky, Michigan, was killed by more friendly fire as they pushed their way south, and four more were wounded by the British armored train artillery. Cpl. Cleo Coburn noted, "Chased enemy all day. Heavy artillery fire. Spent night at front. Frank McLaughlin killed by English shrapnel."[25]

The battalion was now down to little more than a full company. Company K and half of L were still off to the east, in Seletskoye on the north bank of the Emtsa River; Company L had a platoon in Isaaka Gorka, near Archangel; Companies M and I had suffered several casualties and the sick had been evacuated. Those who were left led a new attack on Plesetskaya on October 17. There was no flanking, just a simple straight-down-the-tracks charge, straight at the enemy. The tracks were bordered by heavy woods; any units sent into them might suffer the fate of Company M in their first attack, finding themselves lost and disoriented. The charge was a huge success: nine Bolsheviks dead, no Americans hit, and a chance to dig in a good defensive perimeter.

A few American replacements from France showed up at that time, part of the 510 men sent from the other regiments of the Eighty-fifth Division.[26] A French company in Archangel had been expected to join the Americans on the front lines, but, having heard rumors of a western front armistice, they considered that their war was over, too. Their commander, Major Alabernarde, shamed them for deserting their American comrades, and the poilus came smiling into the newly fortified area at Verst 445.[27] But they were never again quite the aggressive fighters that they had been; slowly, confidence in them waned, and in the spring, they were pulled off the line and sent back to France.

On October 20, the first snow fell, and the men began building log huts for shelter, which would be badly needed when the temperature dropped to between 40 and 60 degrees below zero, weather that would plague the regiment throughout the winter.

The clearing at Verst 445, with woods on either side and swampy, water-filled lands beyond, was to mark the end of the Allied penetration on the railroad front. It was still three hundred miles from Vologda, Poole's ambitious target. The men from Companies I and M, plus the reluctant French and one section of American machine gunners, dug in for the winter, building wooden blockhouses with the help of the 310th Engineers, digging, or blasting, through the permafrost soil for their primitive trenches. The need for blockhouses, built above the ground, was strong, since the frozen ground and high water table made digging deep trenches and dugouts almost impossible. There the engineers proved invaluable. The Reds made sporadic efforts to move them back, mostly with heavy and demoralizing artillery, but no infantry assaults. In time, the British armored train with its artillery pieces came up within range and provided some protection. On November 3, Pvt. George Albers of Company I was captured while he was on a remote observation post. (He was released, in good condition, in Stockholm on April 25, 1919.)

The First Battalion 310th Engineers consisted of three companies, A, B, and C. While many were at work in Archangel, other units were far afield, building blockhouses, repairing railroad, constructing (and destroying) bridges, and generally trying to make life easier for the infantry. One platoon of the 310th, under 1st Lt. William Giffels, served with the Railroad Force and performed remarkable work throughout the campaign. They strengthened the front-line positions with blockhouses, barbed wire, and trenches. At the same time, using some Russian labor, they built the permanent buildings in Obozerskaya. They built barracks, latrines, warehouses, repair shops, mess halls, washhouses, stables, and other installations. They were an outstanding group of talented, hard-working young men.

The most serious Red attack came on November 4, when they struck with strength against the forward positions of I Company, who were ready for them. The Americans were helped by the accurate fire of the White Russian artillery, and, again, the Reds lost heavily, but the attack also cost the life of Pvt. Leo Ellis of I Company.[28] Against the well-entrenched defenders, the Soviets struck, were repulsed, then retreated, and throughout the 1918–1919 winter, they seemed content to let the artillery do their fighting, as action slowed.

On December 6, Company M lost another man when British airplanes mistakenly bombed the trench line, killing Pvt. Floyd Sickles. "[W]e picked up our popular company barber, Floyd Sickles, in a blanket and buried him in the bomb crater." The same bomb left Private Lachacke disabled for life with a foot injury.[29] So far, Company M had lost seven men: two killed by the Bolsheviks, three by friendly fire, and two by disease. Shortly afterwards, on December 18, two platoons of M Company were selected to leave the railroad front and journey east to Pinega, 150 miles from Archangel. Their place was taken by two platoons of Company C.[30]

What had been an offensive posture of the Allies turned into a defensive position on the railroad front. The new commander, General Ironside, had orders to halt offensive operations and set up winter defenses. The British Headquarters War Diary on October 16 noted their own explanation for the change in strategy: "Offensive operations on the railway abandoned owing to attitude of French and American troops."[31]

One of Ironside's first visits to the fronts, while he waited for Poole's departure, was to Obozerskaya. Poole had left him virtually no maps, no copies of orders, and little information on the location of troops, so he determined to find out. As a result of his trip, he suggested to Poole, who was still commanding, that the railroad and Dvina fronts be separated and placed under separate commanders. He also requested permission to replace British colonel Sutherland on the railroad front because of his inept handling of the move toward Plesetskaya. Colonel Stewart was suggested for the railroad front, while Finlayson, also British, was to keep command of the Dvina. Ironside approached Stewart with his new assignment and was surprised when Stewart petulantly refused. Ironside reported, "He then refused, saying it would be exceeding his instructions if he left Archangel, and although I pressed him hard he would not change his mind."[32] So French colonel Lucas replaced Sutherland on November 3.[33]

Ironside's first impression of American soldiers was not the best, as he viewed the railroad troops and talked to Stewart. But he conceded that they would be valuable as their experience grew. Ironside had served in France and was used to the heavy bombardments on the western front. When he saw a group of Americans near Obozerskaya being held at the ready while a few Red artillery shells fell some distance off, the general cautioned the American captain that his men would need rest. The captain was astounded; "What! Rest in the midst of this hellish bombardment!" Ironside was also confused sometimes by American speech. When he dressed down an American officer, the officer held out his hand and said, "General, I'm with you." Ironside wrote in

1953, "To this day I am not quite certain whether he meant to say that he agreed with me, or merely had heard what I said."[34]

Life on the railroad became more bearable as winter set in. There was occasional shellfire, but troops frequently were quartered in railway cars, which had heat and other conveniences. Later, the YMCA came down with movies, snacks, and books, and relief stretches in Archangel broke the monotony.

Despite Ironside's decree halting offensive actions after October, in late December he directed Colonel Lucas to structure an attack to the south to find better winter quarters. Lucas ordered the Onega, Railroad, and Seletskoye units to take the rail city of Emtsa, some thirty miles south of Obozerskaya.

Again, the objectives for the attack were unrealistic. In September the Railroad Force's attempt to take Emtsa and Plesetskaya had met with disaster, when flanking units became disoriented and floundered in swamps and bogs. Lucas's plan was to have the Onega Force move toward the railroad, capture the town of Turchesova, move to support the flank of the Railroad Force, and finish at a bridge twelve kilometers south of Plesetskaya. The Seletskoye Force, split into a right wing under Major Donoghue and a left wing under another British officer, Colonel Haselden (of Force B fame), was to take Kodish, then Avda, Kochmas, and Plesetskaya. The three forces would then join up and be in control of Plesetskaya.[35]

The Railroad Force concentrated its forces south of Obozerskaya in preparation for the move on December 30. One of the early movements was to be made by a unit of French-led Russians who had been specially trained on snowshoes. These troops, the Coureurs de Bois, were to skirt the railroad through heavy forest, move south, and strike Emtsa from the east, then move with other forces toward Plesetskaya. Russians, French, and Americans, supported by machine gun companies, trench mortars, and the Allied armored train, were to move out on December 30, take Emtsa, and move through Plesetskaya on December 31. They never came close.

First, the snowshoes supplied to the Coureurs de Bois were not to their liking, and they made little progress in the heavy snows of December. Second, the Seletskoye Force reached Kodish, but advanced no further. Third, the Onega column could not take Turchesova. The campaign was methodically planned, with intricate timetables covering each unit. Originally scheduled to begin December 30, it was delayed one day, until December 31, because of problems getting troops into position. With his own troops floundering and the two flanking forces stymied, Lucas called off the battle plan late on December 31.[36]

According to Ironside, Lucas bore much of the responsibility for the failure:

> I found out that he had not been out to see his left column commander, who was to have carried out the most important part of the operations, but had arranged everything by letter and telephone. This was a gross piece of disobedience, and I told him so, as I had given him a direct order to arrange the plan on the spot.[37]

Lucas sent out one patrol, a dozen men, who advanced fewer than five hundred yards, found nothing, and returned. By January 2, the Onega Force was back in Chekuevo, the Railroad Force was still at Verst 445, and the Seletskoye units once again had evacuated Kodish.

Lucas himself had done little to make his presence known to the forces under his control, much to General Ironside's disgust.[38] When Lucas called off his offensive, he failed to notify Companies E and K on the Seletskoye front, so they continued their attempts to take Kodish. The American troops led, expecting support from Russian troops who failed in their flank attack; British machine gunners never followed their orders; their commander was caught up in the holiday spirit and overcome with other spirits.[39] The Americans, by themselves, had taken the town.

Not only was the effort thwarted by Allied ineptness, but the Bolsheviks were now showing some decided improvements in their effectiveness. "In this whole action we have found that the bolsheviks are now well organized and offer stubborn resistance. Their artillery fire has greatly improved in quality and often their guns outrange ours and they do not spare ammunition."[40] However, as cold weather came on, interest waned in offensive action, and winter became the enemy.

By mid February, the railroad front was static; the troops were still the French, parts of the American Third Battalion, and the British armored artillery train. Because the Allies were tied to the railroad, the support forces and the fighting units stretched out from Verst 466, nearest Archangel, to the front lines at Versts 444 and 445. The units had developed a series of fortifications and improvements from Obozerskaya down to Verst 445. Verst 466, just north of Obozerskaya, was considered a reserve area, and served as a training site to keep troops occupied when they were off the front line. Housing was provided in railway cars that were lined and insulated and furnished with stoves and bunks. The cars also transported the units to and from the front and, occasionally, to Archangel. The support troops lived in barracks and warehouses, so there was little need for blockhouses or dugouts. The area was miles from the front, and any attack during the winter would be through the unfriendly terrain of swamps, deep snow, and heavy forest.

A report by Capt. H. Prince of the American Military Mission in Archangel indicated that by February 1919 the railroad-front units lived almost as well as those in Archangel. They had modernized train cars and homey blockhouses/dugouts, well protected from Bolo artillery. The YMCA established a canteen in Obozerskaya, movies became routine, and rum rations were issued, despite some YMCA protests. The dark days of December and January were gone, and it was getting lighter every day, a significant factor for front-line troops. For those behind the line, there were classes in the proper use of weapons, drills, and even occasional parades. The French and British conducted several much appreciated awards ceremonies, presenting medals to the Americans for their heroism in combat.[41] Additional troops were coming into the railroad front: the British Liverpool Regiment and platoons from C and G Companies of the 339th Regiment.

Throughout the winter, companies of Americans and French exchanged front-line duties on a regular basis, until the French finally refused to continue to fight. In March 1919, most were sent back to France.[42]

Farther south, the headquarters of the Railway Force was at Verst 455, where the armored train was kept most of the time. One platoon of the 310th Engineers lived there, as did the medical staff for the Allies. Even though there was little chance of a Bolshevik attack, the camp was well fortified with barbed wire, blockhouses, and outposts manned by infantry units. By February, there was an observation tower that could be used to keep a watchful eye out for any movements. In return the Bolos had a tethered balloon that spied on Allied movements, helping to keep the stalemate.

Even farther south at Verst 448, defensive positions were serious and thorough. Barbed wire, blockhouses, trenches, and dugouts, manned by a small infantry force, supported artillery pieces located in woods by the tracks. The Allied armored train chugged its way up to this outpost when Soviet artillery needed some response. But the front line was at Verst 445, where one American company traded places each month with a French company, both supported by one platoon of the 339th Machine Gun section. For several months infantry and engineers had built a series of interconnecting trenches with communications linked to all outposts and dugouts. Barbed wire and blockhouses were key parts of the defense. All of the works were well-heated, and even in the bitterest cold, the men were comfortable.[43] All installations were linked by a single set of railroad tracks, but south of Obozerskaya, Allied influence generally ended only a few yards on either side of the tracks.

Several episodes indicated the erosion of American morale on that front. On January 31, an American soldier fired at and killed a British officer at Verst 445. There were several versions of the killing. Lt. Albert May was required to make a complete investigation and report the results to Major Nichols. According to May, "The American either just went nuts or mistook the officer for the enemy. When the Britisher stuck his head out his dugout he was shot and killed. There was an investigation. I gave testimony but there was no court martial."[44]

Capt. Eugene Prince, on a fact-finding trip for the American Military Mission, wrote a report which brought up several factors that affected the declining morale of the Americans. First, he said, the men felt that the American headquarters in Archangel, particularly the 339th Supply Company, was unconcerned about the men in the field. They felt that their welfare had been handed over to British officers who were disinclined to supply anything but basic, unpalatable, British rations and the hated Shackleton boots. Until the YMCA brought some added rations, their fare consisted of the highly unpopular "M& V" (meat and vegetables), and hardtack, hardly sufficient for troops required to be outdoors, training or patrolling. On an inspection trip to the front, sanitation officer Lt. F. J. Funk, found that sanitary conditions were unsatisfactory and a real threat to health. "The whole place was in frightfully unsanitary condition. Nothing in my experience compares with what I saw there." Next, he went farther forward to Verst 446 where he found more shocking conditions.[45]

However, the lack of any clear purpose for the expedition was the most prevailing complaint; on all fronts, Why are we here? was the unanswered question that plagued the men, not just Americans, but British and French as well. The later loss of Shenkursk and the gradual retreat on that front shook both the American and other Allied forces, as the dominance of Bolshevism began to show. The unrest was taking tangible form.

One battalion of the Thirteenth Yorkshire Regiment[46] had replaced American units on the railroad, having marched all the way from Onega, almost one hundred miles. They were good men, in excellent physical condition, unlike many of the other British veterans who had been classified as unfit for combat when they were sent to Russia. The Yorkshires stayed only briefly in Obozerskaya and then were sent on to Seletskoye. There they met Americans who told them of their bitter winter campaign in and around Kodish and of their losses. The newly arrived Brits were unnerved.

On February 26, when they were ordered to form up to march to the front lines, the Yorkshire battalion refused to budge. Their commander, Colonel Lavoi, went into their barracks and ordered the men to fall in without rifles, which they promptly did. After they were formed, two sergeants stepped forward and stated that the battalion would do no more fighting. Lavoi promptly ordered a corporal to take a few men to retrieve rifles from the barracks; when they returned, he ordered them to escort the sergeants to the guardhouse. The rest of the battalion, he sent on an exhausting march to wear out their resistance. After their return, they armed themselves and dutifully marched off to the front.

The incident brought General Ironside to Seletskoye. He said, "I interviewed the two sergeants in the guard room, where I found them very nervous and crestfallen. I told them of the gravity of the crime they had committed and that they would be brought before a court martial as soon as one could be assembled."[47]

Word of the Yorkshires' revolt circulated around the various fronts, and was the cause of the next mutiny by a company of French resting in Archangel. When ordered to the trains to go back to Obozerskaya on March 1, they flatly refused to go, despite the threats of Ironside and the pleadings of the French Military Attaché. While no individuals were punished, the unit was confined on board the French ship *Guedon* under guard and sent back to France.[48]

Ironside noted that there were no incidents among American troops, but, in late March, there was a reported American "mutiny." When Company I, resting in Archangel, was ordered to load their sleds for a return to the front, they refused. Colonel Stewart, showing rare wisdom and restraint, immediately went to Smolny Barracks where the company was quartered and had the men assembled in the YMCA hut. He talked to them for thirty to forty minutes, explaining the consequences of their actions; after his talk, he asked if there were questions. One question, which is not mentioned in Stewart's report, but appears in soldiers' diaries, was, Why are we fighting here in Russia? He responded that he "had never been supplied with an answer as to why they were there, but that the Reds were trying to push them into the White Sea, and that they were fighting for their lives."[49] That seemed to ease their discontent, and they entrained for Obozerskaya.[50]

Company I proved their mettle two days later when a blockhouse at Verst 445 was attacked. Machine Gunner Cleo Coburn found himself under fire once again:

April 1—First Bolo spied by Private Stempczyk at 7:40. Directly Private Kronkie shouted, 'Oh, God. Here comes a million!' I ordered windows raised, Gunner Menteer, on Lewis gun, opens first, then I cut loose with

'Old Vic'. Steady exchange of fire for 1 1/2 hours straight. During our firing, Private Becker and I about kissed ourselves goodby. Becker's pill
passed just over his head and went through our back door, and mine hit
my tripod directly in front of me.[51]

The railroad front diminished in importance as the winter wore
on. Two other fronts were established to give protection to the railroad
flanks, the Onega front to the west and the Seletskoye front to the east.
These two flanking forces, however, took on lives of their own as winter
made communications between the three areas difficult, if not impossible. The Seletskoye Force battled continuously through the winter, and
the Onega front was in action as well with its last, bitter battle to keep
the Soviets from driving through the Bolshe-Ozerkiye village, splitting
the Onega and Railroad Forces. This battle in late March and early
April brought some of the widely separated forces together in one of
the most dramatic fights of the Intervention.

As the Railroad Forces gathered to hold back the Bolsheviks at Bolshe-Ozerkiye in April 1919, several attempts were made to exchange
prisoners. The American Red Cross was instrumental in arranging several exchange meetings, although the meetings had limited success. At
the first meeting, Lt. Alfred May and Lt. Dwight Fistler, both of Company
I, met with three Reds.[52] They reported that the Allies had five hundred
Bolshevik prisoners, and the Reds had seven Allies.[53] Fistler wrote,
"They traded us two of the seven Americans for the five hundred Russian soldiers, and we had to toss in a round of cigarettes to seal the bar-
gain."[54]

Later the Soviets invited Allied representatives to discuss an exchange of prisoners. A group of three Allied officers, Capt. A. Barbier
from France, Capt. J. A. Hartfield of the United States, and Capt. E. M.
White of the British Army, went through the Bolo lines in late April and
sat down with a series of Bolshevik leaders. By May 1, they had arrived
at no real solution, the Soviets claiming they had authority to release no
more than twenty-two Allied prisoners, although there were fifty more
estimated to be in Moscow. The twenty-two in question were being held
in Vologda and were readily available for exchange. Records indicate
that the Allied officers informed the Reds that they were appalled that
the exchange discussions were being conducted by Bolshevik leaders
who really had no authorization to conclude any trade. On May 1, they
requested transportation back through the lines to their headquarters at
Verst 445, with little to show for their efforts. The Allied officers protested loudly when they found that the Soviets had no authority to negotiate swaps. In fact, the Americans themselves lacked that authority as
well. In typical bureaucratic fashion, the State Department notified the

AEFNR that no one could negotiate anything with the Soviets, because the United States did not recognize the new Russian government.[55]

The Onega Force was the west wing of the Railroad Force, and although separated from the Railroad Force by many miles, it was a significant factor in the later stages of the expedition as the Bolos made their move through Bolshe-Ozerkiye.

The Onega Front

Fighting their way through the untracked forest and deep snow, American soldiers of the 339th Regiment, with the Polish Legion, Russian volunteers, and their French allies, have advanced fifteen miles up the Onega River on the extreme west of the Archangel sector.

—*Detroit Free Press*, January 1, 1919

THE Onega front was established before the American forces landed. A small British party landed in Onega without much opposition on July 31, 1918, even before they took Archangel, believing Onega to be a strategic base to protect a Murmansk-Archangel connection. A Russian warship, manned by British sailors, fired several full broadsides into the dock area while a British infantry unit came in from Kem, miles to the west, and the Bolos left town in a hurry.[1] The Allied goal at that time was to move from Onega to Obozerskaya to join Colonel Guard's Railroad Force; however, the little detachment found the going too rough and retreated back to Onega, arriving August 6. Part of the expedition evacuated the area by ship, arriving in Archangel on August 9.[2]

Two of the British officers were decorated for their Onega expedition toward Obozerskaya: Col. C. J. N. Thornhill won a bar on his Distinguished Service Order, and Capt. Dennis Garstin (later killed with Force B), a new arrival who had literally walked the five hundred miles from Petrograd to Kem to join British forces there, was awarded the Military Cross. An expedition headed by these two officers started from Kem, on the Murmansk Railroad, and marched all the way to Onega, where they remained as a garrison.[3] The British were later replaced by sailors from the USS *Olympia*, who in turn were replaced by two platoons of Company H of the 339th Infantry on September 15.

Soon after they debarked in Archangel, first and third platoons of Company H, under Lt. C. H. Phillips and Lt. H. H. Pellegrom, boarded the steamer *Michael Kace,* headed for Onega, where they arrived about 5:00 P.M. on September 15. Onega itself was secure with the occupation by Allied troops, but the countryside between Onega and Archangel, and Onega and Obozerskaya, was not. Obozerskaya was almost ninety miles away from Onega across marshy lands and heavy forest with only the roughest of roads. Archangel was equally far and even harder to reach.

Almost as soon as Company H arrived, British lieutenant colonel W. J. Clarke, commanding at Onega, sent Lieutenant Pellegrom's fifty-eight man third platoon fifty miles upriver to Chekuevo. Pellegrom left Onega on a barge towed by the little steamer *Juniis* and arrived late on September 19. On September 22, Colonel Clarke ordered Lieutenant Phillips and his first platoon to join Pellegrom in Chekuevo to assume command there. With their arrival on September 23, there were 115 Americans and 93 Russian volunteers in the Chekuevo town.[4] For a few days, they concentrated on settling into their new quarters, which were adequate, but they had to sleep "on the soft of the boards."[5]

On September 24 at 5:00 A.M., the Americans received their baptism by fire. Under rainy skies, 350 Reds attacked Chekuevo from three sides of the Allied position. The third platoon was on outpost duty when the attack began, and quickly withdrew to the city. The Americans were able to beat off the attackers. The Allied Russians, placed on the right bank of the Onega River, were driven back by the Reds, allowing Soviet machine guns to fire at the Company H platoons. However, the enemy guns were quickly located and as quickly silenced by the American Lewis machine gunners. After the Soviet commander Major Shiskin was killed by machine gun fire, the attackers lost their spirit and departed. They were followed closely by an American combat patrol for more than five miles, the victors picking up a variety of abandoned equipment. The battle report stated, "Russians—Killed 3, Wounded 7; Americans—Killed none, seriously wounded one; slightly wounded—1."[6]

The next few days in Chekuevo were uneventful, but on September 30, Lieutenant Phillips received a report that enemy activity was increasing. Colonel Clark in Onega ordered Phillips to join a friendly Cossack unit coming from Obozerskaya and head south to cut off a Bolshevik force that was planning to attack Obozerskaya. Phillips promptly moved out with his two platoons about 2:30 A.M. on October 1. His objective was Kasca, eight miles up river from Chekuevo, where there were reported to be some 500 to 750 Red troops. Only eighteen Cossacks showed up to join Phillips, and as soon as the firing began at 5:00 A.M., they hightailed it back to Chekuevo.

British captain Burton, with two Company H squads and fifty Russians, was to cross the river and attack Wazentia on the opposite side of the river from Kasca. Lieutenant Phillips would make a frontal assault as Burton held the Soviets' attention with his flanking movement. Phillips's two platoons advanced, but were pinned down as they dug in opposite the town. Meanwhile Burton's Russians deserted and his attack failed, but Phillips was unaware that he had no diversion. He stayed in an exposed, improvised shelter, unable to move forward or back:

> It was found impossible to either advance farther to reach the enemy trenches or retire, to try any flanking movement, owing to the fact, that by the time that the men had themselves dug in, the enemy sweeping all the ground by this time with heavy machine gun fire. Men who volunteered to take messages from one platoon to the other, paid with their lives for the attempt.[7]

Evidence of the collapse of the entire mission is found in noting times of the various units' returning to Chekuevo. The Cossacks appeared as early as 6:00 A.M.; Captain Burton's two American squads, minus their absent Russians, returned at 10:30 A.M.; but Phillips, unable to get his men out until darkness fell, arrived in Chekuevo at 7:30 P.M., after taking punishment for fourteen hours. Phillips's casualties were six killed and three wounded.[8] The bodies of Pvt. John Boreson, Pvt. Claus Graham, Pvt. Eugene Richardson, Pvt. Frank Silkaitis, Pvt. Edward Ritcher, and Pvt. Harley Avery were left where they died, but the wounded were taken back to Chekuevo. One of the attackers, Pvt. Roy Rasmussen, noted in his diary:

> Then we rushed across the swamp, getting all wet. In a few minutes we were on a hill where we lay on the frozen ground fighting Bolsheviki until 4 P.M. when we returned through the woods to Chekuva. At the battle we kept low all the time listening to the bullets flying over. We lost six men and four wounded. We killed thirty and wounded fifty of their men.[9]

This abortive foray was designed to be one of the three prongs of Poole's October plan to move rapidly down the railroad to the railhead at Plesetskaya. The push south from Obozerskaya failed, as did this attempt by the Onega Force. There were no easy victories for any of the Allied units, and so far, the American doughboys were doing the biggest share of the fighting, along with their French companions-in-arms. This was increasingly noticed by the doughboy and the poilu.

The Onega front was quiet for a few weeks, with limited patrolling in all directions to stay on the alert. The only details worthy of note were the increasing strength of the Onega Force and a new commander, British lieutenant colonel Edwards, who replaced Colonel Clarke. Two platoons of Company H, which had been left in Archangel, rejoined the first and third platoons on the front with twenty-five French troops and more Russian volunteers.

On October 19, virtually the entire Onega Force moved up both sides of the Onega River, having heard that the Soviets had abandoned much of their territory, including their stronghold at Kasca. Patrols sent out in advance of the columns reported that the Bolsheviks had consolidated in Turchesova in a solid defensive position. The column moved past Kasca finding no opposition. However, with snow falling and winter fast approaching, Colonel Edwards ordered a return to Chekuevo on October 24. No one wanted to be in the frozen wastes of the valley in a blinding snowstorm. As they passed through Kasca, the Americans found the graves of the six privates killed on October 1; they had been buried by sympathetic townspeople. They were reburied with proper military honors and their gravesites marked.[10]

During the rest of October and November, patrolling was constant with occasional brushes with Red patrols, but no casualties. By mid-December, the units were spread out from Onega all the way to Kylavenga on the river, still with only limited activity. Platoons were shifted back to Onega from the front-line positions, Chekuevo and south, to give them some relief from conditions at the front. Pvt. Ray Rasmussen was happy in Onega, where a YMCA had set up a canteen: "Here we have a Y and a canteen where we can get most anything we want. On Thanksgiving Day we certainly had a great feast."[11] But they were on constant alert for an attack, all up and down the river. On December 20, a large Allied patrol ran into a Bolo patrol, and the Allies drove them from a village with no casualties. The next day, a patrol led by Lt. Harry Ketcham left on a combat-reconnaissance patrol with twenty men and a British naval section; they met resistance from a Red patrol, which retreated toward Turchesova. On December 23, Lt. Arthur Carlson's platoon took on a Bolo patrol, killing several and taking five prisoners.

On Christmas Day, Rasmussen received word that his sister, Fannie, an army nurse, had died from the flu at Fort Sheridan, Illinois. "A bleak Christmas Day for me."[12]

In concert with the anticipated railroad advance, the British commander ordered Lt. Edmund R. Collins to take the second and fourth platoons and flank the Reds entrenched up-river at Turchesova. Collins left at 4:00 A.M. on December 29 in miserable weather with zero and subzero temperatures and waist-deep snow. When Collins found he was unable to get close to Turchesova because of the conditions, he was sent to reinforce some Polish infantry that had just captured the little town of Goglova one mile outside Turchesova. The Polish and the American infantry fired and took fire all day. Early on December 30, the Soviets attacked Goglova, but the reinforced Polish section held its ground. The following day Collins was ordered to take Lieutenant Ketcham and his platoon to attack Zeleyese, a small town in the rear of Allied forces that was considered a threat. The doughboys took the town, but Red reinforcements from Turchesova almost immediately assaulted the town. The defensive position of the Americans was excellent; they inflicted numerous casualties on the Bolsheviks, suffering only three wounded on December 31 and New Years Day 1919.[13]

By January 2 the Allied attack on the railroad front had been called off. Colonel Edwards issued orders for all his troops to fall back to the town of Kleshevo, farther down the river. The retreat upset Captain Ballensinger, commander of Company H, who reported:

> Indications pointed toward an inclination on the enemy's part to evacuate Turchesova. Therefore a message received by Lt. Collins about 5:00 P.M. Jan 1/19 from O.C. Onega River Det. to withdraw all troops to KLESHOVO within two hours, came somewhat as a surprise. Much ammunition, equipment and supplies were lost, during this hurried retreat, considerable confusion arising among the carts, horses and drivers being injured.[14]

Fortunately, the Reds chose not to follow.

During the rest of January and until early February, little happened along the Onega. On February 10, Lieutenant Ketcham took a patrol out from the base at Kleshevo at 7:00 A.M., heading toward Khala, three miles away, where Bolsheviks were reported. Ketcham met heavy machine gun fire as he approached the village, but his brisk rifle fire and accurate Lewis gun enfilade fire drove the Reds from the town, and Ketcham settled in. He eventually returned to Kleshevo with no casualties, reporting Bolo casualties as one killed, two wounded.[15]

By the end of February, the Allied force in North Russia consisted of forty-five hundred Americans, five thousand British, seven hundred French, and seven hundred Poles.[16] Ironside also had five thousand Russians of whom he was fairly confident, plus twelve hundred he considered unreliable. Opposing these various elements of Ironside's scattered forces were 16,800 soldiers of the Bolshevik Sixth Army under Gen. Boris Kuzmin, spread over three hundred miles from the Dvina to Turchesova. About 3,200 more were in position on the Pinega front, and another seventeen thousand waited as reserves in Kotlas and Vologda.[17] These were not the untrained, disorganized mobs of the fall, but well-led, disciplined troops supported by artillery larger, and with more range, than Allied guns.

A major Allied concern was the mutinies of the French, British, and Russians; by February, there was general discontent among almost all forces. Americans sometimes proved reluctant to go back to the line, and Ironside himself said, "We were drawing terribly near to the end of our tether as an efficient fighting force."[18] As the buildup of Soviets continued, the British general "waited for the offensive that would make him draw the entire force into Archangel, there to be smashed to pieces against the ice."[19] With the White Sea frozen, there was no escape by sea. Had the Russians driven a threatening wedge between the Allied positions on the Onega and their positions on the railroad front, disaster could have followed. Joel Moore later wrote, "Success at this point would probably have resulted in the [Bolshevik] capture of Archangel itself and the possible annihilation of the entire North Russian Expedition."[20]

On March 16, Captain Ballensinger relocated Company H headquarters from Onega to Chekuevo in order to keep in close touch with the Railroad Force at Obozerskaya. To do this, Ballensinger sent regular patrols from Chekuevo east to Bolshe-Ozerkiye, only sixteen miles from the railroad headquarters at Obozerskaya. This little village would prove to be the site of the final battle of the North Russian campaign.

General Ironside had no firm knowledge of a plan by Siberian Allied forces to link with the North Russian forces; however, the Soviets feared that Kolchak forces under Czech General Gaida were moving toward Viatka on the Trans-Siberian Railroad for a possible linkup with the North Russian Allies. While this was far-fetched in hindsight, it was a possible reason for a Bolo offensive in Bolshe-Ozerkiye.

While a diversionary assault took place by the Soviets against Vistafka on the Vaga River, the offensive which Ironside had feared started when the Bolos moved in force out of Plesetskaya, moving between Onega and the Vologda Railroad, headed for Bolshe-Ozerkiye. Some twelve hundred Reds on skis moved silently toward the few French who were on outpost duty there, taking them by surprise on March 17,

1919. The French were quickly and quietly wiped out; the Bolos had driven a large wedge between the Onega Force and the Railroad Force in Obozerskaya. With the Reds in Bolshe-Ozerkiye unopposed, Soviet general Kuzmin could then move on Obozerskaya and cut off the units below, then move straight on to Archangel. It was the most vulnerable position for the Allies during the North Russian campaign.

The Onega force in Chekuevo had no knowledge that the Soviets had captured Bolshe-Ozerkiye when they sent a routine patrol east toward the village, a two-day trek. The six-man patrol disappeared; after they failed to report back, searchers were sent out.[21]

The ill-fated American patrol arrived at Bolshe-Ozerkiye just after the Reds occupied the town. One of those subsequently captured, Pvt. Earl Fulcher, reported that he had joined the French detachment in the village as the Bolsheviks attacked on March 16, then fought with the Allied group of French, Russians, and Americans who were surrendered by the French commander. "The engagement continued all day Tuesday, and until about Wednesday noon, when the enemy artillery reached our position, and the French officer in command went out with a white flag and surrendered the entire detachment, consisting of about 50 French, Americans and Russians."[22]

By a stroke of luck, Colonel Lucas, the commander of the Railroad Force, just missed being taken with the French defenders, having passed through the area a few hours before the Red attack. He was with the Onega Force in Chenova several miles west of Bolshe-Ozerkiye, still unaware that a large Soviet force was between him and his Railroad Force command. Lucas had seldom left the comfort of his railroad car in Obozerskaya; this visit was largely due to the pressure put on him by Ironside to visit his two flanking forces, Onega and Seletskoye.

As word sifted back to Chekuevo that the Reds were in force and had cut the Allies off by their occupation of Bolshe-Ozerkiye on March 17, British lieutenant colonel N. A. Lawrie dispatched a patrol of thirty Americans led by Lieutenant Collins. Traveling by sleigh east out of Chekuevo, they had orders to report enemy strength in the village. The patrol reached the outskirts of Bolshe-Ozerkiye, accompanied by Colonel Lucas, who was hoping to find a way back to Obozerskaya. Still unaware of the large number of Bolos in the town, they came under heavy machine gun fire one verst west of town. The patrol lost one man killed, Cpl. Nathan Redmund; they were able to escape only by crawling through waist-deep snow to stay out of sight.[23] They saw that the town was occupied in force. Lucas eventually returned to Obozerskaya under mysterious circumstances and was relieved of his command by General Ironside, who came immediately to Obozerskaya to take personal command of the railroad front and the Bolshe-Ozerkiye situation.[24]

The actual battle at Bolshe-Ozerkiye was the only time when the Onega Force and the Railroad Force combined forces in the same battle. Company H prepared to attack Bolshe-Ozerkiye from the west, while Company E, recently arrived from Archangel, attacked with other Allied troops from the east.

In reality the battle of Bolshe-Ozerkiye was two separate battles. Phase one was two-pronged: First, the Onega Force attacked the Reds in the village from the west while Americans from the railroad front struck the same target from the east. Second, the Soviets attempted to drive the Americans from their defensive positions, especially the Railroad Force at Verst 18.

The battle began March 23, 1919. Colonel Lawrie, directing the western attack, sent Lt. Clifford Phillips with two platoons of Company H to rendezvous with three companies of the Sixth Battalion Royal Yorkshires, commanded by Major Monday.[25] The British, en route from Murmansk to Obozerskaya, arrived in Chenova just in time to join the assault forces.[26] Phillips and Lieutenant Collins then had seventy Americans and three hundred British for the assault on the roughly twelve hundred Soviets in town.[27] There was also a four-man American medical team under Lt. Ralph Springer, who would be called on for yeoman's service.[28]

The start time for the western attack was set for 2 A.M. on March 23, and the team moved out of Chenova on schedule. The snow was deep, and the weather was cold; advancing was not only dangerous, but extremely exhausting. The Yorkshires were assigned both left and right flanks, while the Americans went down the middle. The popular Lieutenant Collins was one of the first casualties, shot by a sniper. As the day progressed, the Allied troops made some progress, but never came close to the town. The heavy enemy fire, lack of ammunition and reinforcements, and the bitter cold played key roles in making the decision to retire back to Chenova. The Americans had lost two men killed, Pvt. Edward McConville and Lieutenant Collins, who died on the way back. Eight others were wounded. The Yorkshires lost two officers and two men, with eight wounded.[29] American captain Ballensinger withdrew Company H to Usolia and Chenova to heal frostbitten hands and feet and wait for replacements from Onega.

At the same time, an Allied force from Obozerskaya under British colonel Card was trying to attack Bolshe-Ozerkiye from the east side of town. This force included Company E and one platoon of Company L, a company from the Russian Archangel Regiment, and one half a company of the French-led, Russian-manned French Foreign Legion. The Russians advanced into machine gun fire, took heavy casualties, and withdrew, so British commander Colonel Card called off any other efforts to move forward.[30]

.Company E was not in the mood for combat; the night before the scheduled attack, all the corporals of the company held a meeting. Pvt. Donald Carey wrote, "Every corporal attended. It bordered on mutiny. The men—privates and corporals—were satiated with fighting and did not relish a similar experience. The feasibility of refusing to leave for the front was thoroughly discussed. . . . As no one would accept responsibility for leading the mutiny it came to naught."[31] Company E's performance was less than enthusiastic as they were ordered to attack through the deep snow, bitter cold, and gloom of the Arctic winter. Carey complained about his Shackleton boots, the cold, and the scanty British rations and derided his officers. On March 23, he wrote, "About 0400—a propitious moment for zero hour, as our spirits were equally low—we were ordered to 'Push off,' as Lt. Baker casually phrased it. With two of our lieutenants stupefied with liquor, we started toward the Bolo stronghold."[32]

Progress was slow through waist-deep snow; Carey noted that no one was in a real hurry to find the Reds. "A repetition of the Kodish fiasco and hours of fighting in the snow and cold appealed to no one."[33] Company E was happy to receive Colonel Card's orders to return to their prepared defenses at Verst 18 on the Onega-Obozerskaya line and break off any attempt to advance, so they did no fighting that morning. Company H's Lieutenant Pellegrom, in Archangel on assignment, had been assigned recently to Company E, which was very short of officers. He reported, "The company arrived back in camp at about 11:30 A.M. in a very exhausted condition. Outposts were immediately established and tents pitched."[34] Pellegrom returned to Archangel and shortly after rejoined Company H.

Both Allied forces remained on opposite sides of the town, shelling the area steadily, guided by airplanes from the nearby Allied airbase at Obozerskaya. On March 28, Company E was relieved by Company M, which would take the main part in the next series of battles on the east side of Bolshe-Ozerkiye. The men of Company M had recently arrived from the Pinega front with little rest. As they moved into the barricades and protection at Verst 18, the engineers from the 310th continued to strengthen and improve the defenses. It turned out well that they did such good work.

On the morning of March 31, 1919, at 9:00 A.M. the Bolsheviks attacked the rear of the Obozerskaya forces in strength. Machine gun crews drove off the Bolos. The infantry was in the rear protecting the Russian artillery, which wheeled its 75mm guns 180 degrees, firing

point blank into the densely packed Red infantry. The cannons broke
the back of that Red attack.

Then, at 10:00 A.M. Company M was hit by three Red battalions in
a frontal charge as the Allied forces dug in on the Obozerskaya-Bolshe-
Ozerkiye Road. According to Company M's commanding officer, the
Reds used the Second Moscow Regiment, the Ninety-seventh Saratov
Regiment, and the Second Kazan Regiment in their two attacks.[35] The
Soviets killed Company M's Pvt. Charles Dial and took Sgt. Glenn Leit-
zel, Pvt. Freeman Hogan, and mechanic Jens Laursen prisoner.[36] A non-
combatant, YMCA worker, Mr. Ryal, was taken as well, one of several
Y men captured during the campaign.[37] Finally, Russian artillery
caught the Bolos in the open, and the Soviet assault was broken.

On April 1, Company H, west of Bolshe-Ozerkiye, was ordered to
attack the town, relieving some of the pressure felt by Company M and
the others on the east side. But most of the work that day fell on the
Obozerskaya Force, which received its attack at daybreak, 3:30 A.M.
Three waves of Bolsheviks came in and were beaten off, leaving Soviet
dead and dying on the frozen white surface in front of the American
lines. The American fortifications, most of them constructed by Company C, 310th Engineers, were mainly responsible for the successful defense. Another Red attack in the rear, similar to that of the previous day,
was smashed, causing more Bolo casualties. Company M lost Pvt. Alva
Crook and Cpl. Frank Sapp, both killed that day.

On the following day, the Allies rushed the Bolsheviks from the
west as Captain Ballensinger sent Company H with British support.
Company A of the Yorkshires was to draw first fire from the northern-
most Reds. As they approached the Bolo lines through the woods, dogs
tied to trees gave away the Allied approach with a chorus of yelps,
barks, and howls. British captain Bailey, leading his men toward the
enemy lines, was killed by machine gun fire; a second officer was severely wounded, and the Allied attack was stopped dead in its tracks.

Shortly afterward, the enemy counterattacked, and early in the
morning, British commander Lund ordered Phillips's platoon to support Company A. One company of Polish soldiers came up, but they
were hit so heavily, they quit after twenty minutes. Company C of the
Yorkshires was to attack the other flank, but inept guides had lost them
in the woods, so they failed to arrive on time. The Yorkshires Company
A had withdrawn, its Company C was lost, the Poles were decimated,
and Lieutenant Phillips was left with twelve men and one officer of
Company B Yorkshires to stop the Red counterattack. Ballensinger
wrote in his report:

> Lt. Phillips through his superior control over his men and personal con-
> spicuous conduct, kept every one of his men in their places, keeping his

two Lewis guns constantly in action, and his rifle men kept up a steady fire. Altho' the enemy's counter attack was extremely heavy, and all of his fire swept the road continuously, this officer gave ground only very slowly, in spite of heavy casualties, until he was himself very seriously wounded.[38]

When the lost Yorkshire Company C finally arrived about 9:00 A.M., and Lieutenant Pellegrom arrived with his platoon, the exhausted troops had the support needed to drive off the attackers. The skittish Polish gunners, however, were content to fire their weapons over the heads of the American-British front line, instead of joining them up front. Company H lost two men: Pvt. Floyd Auslander, killed, and Pvt. Mattios Koslousky, who died later of his wounds. Lieutenant Phillips was hospitalized and seemed to be recovering, but infection set in, and under the primitive medical conditions existing on the expedition, Phillips died on May 10, 1919, just before some of the first troops were boarding ships to return home.[39]

On April 2, the Reds made their last attempt to break the Allies at Bolshe-Ozerkiye. Company M took several half-hearted enemy charges and beat them off handily. In his book *M Company*, Captain Moore describes the Red attack: "The third days fight was soon over. The enemy was repulsed. His artillery put over gas shells among the rest of the 'pineapples' he sent."[40]

The Soviets attacked several more times, using heavy artillery barrages, but very light infantry assaults. They seemed worn out by the weather and their heavy casualties, but finally picked up their dead and wounded, and by April 5 they had withdrawn.

Finally, the weeklong series of battles was over, and it appeared that Archangel was safe.

Just five days later, Company H was ordered back to Onega, where they drilled and paraded until they were sent back to Archangel for transportation home. On April 17, Captain Ballensinger heard that Bolshe-Ozerkiye had been evacuated and sent Lieutenant Carlson to search for bodies. The captain reported that at the time of writing of his report, April 25, 1919, two bodies had been recovered.

On April 29, Pvt. William Negake drowned while crossing the Onega River. Ray Rasmussen was a pallbearer at Negake's funeral on May 7: "Pvt. Negaki of Hart [Michigan] was buried at Onega cemetery at 11 A.M. I was one of the pallbearers (Mauritz, too). Carried wooden casket 1/4 mile and then had to cover grave."[41] Rasmussen was from the same little town. On April 5, Company M was relieved by a mixed Russian-British force and sent back to Archangel. Their most recent front-line assignment had lasted only eight days, but they were probably the most difficult days of their tour. Neither Company M nor Company H would see further combat. To the men of Company M, the clash in early April 1919 was known as the Battle of Verst 18, the verst marker on the Onega-Obozerskaya railroad at Bolshe-Ozerkiye.

The battle at Bolshe-Ozerkiye was certainly not a victory; however, it kept a sizeable Soviet force from the railroad front and possibly from cutting off the troops in Obozerskaya and sections farther south. It also prevented a Red push on through to Archangel.

On April 17, to everyone's surprise, American brigadier general Wilds P. Richardson arrived without announcement to become the new regimental commander of the 339th, replacing Colonel Stewart, as the regiment prepared to leave the Russians to their own affairs.

Meanwhile, the two platoons from Company K that had left the Railroad Force in early September to form the Kodish, or Seletskoye, front, the railroad front's flank protection, were joined by other Allied forces and made up a very respectable concentration. Their mission was to protect the Plesetskaya-Archangel Road and keep the Bolos away from Archangel. It was a flank protection of the important, but stagnant, railroad front. Miles to the east of the railroad, the bloody Seletskoye Force found itself in almost constant combat, but during the winter, it held its ground before the overwhelming Soviet Sixth Army.

The Emtsa/Seletskoye Front

[I]t seemed that the only fitting epitaph for them was the saddest that can ever be written above the graves of fallen soldiers. They died in vain.

—E. M. Halliday, *The Ignorant Armies*

THE Emtsa front on the Emtsa River developed as a result of the disappearance of Force B. Since the sailors of the *Olympia* were considered to be in danger, the newly arrived doughboys were sent to rescue their missing brothers-in-arms.

As Third Battalion rolled down the rails from Archangel in the early days in September, Companies I, K, L, and M were anticipating their first action as American fighting men. Companies I, M, and L remained with the Railroad Column, but Company K was ordered to Seletskoye on the Emtsa River on September 7. On the way, they were to find and attempt to rescue Allied Force B.[1] After passing stacks of abandoned equipment, ammunition, and supplies, as well as freshly dug graves, they arrived in Seletskoye.[2]

Company K was led by one of the AEFNR's toughest leaders, Capt. Mike Donoghue, nicknamed "Iron Mike" by his men. Iron Mike and his troops headed east from Obozerskaya on September 7, but unfortunately, became lost in the swampy forests of the area and floundered for days before they were rescued. On the fifth day of their adventure, battalion adjutant Lt. Clarence Gardner found them and directed them toward their assignment in Seletskoye. Shortly after leaving Obozerskaya, one of the men of Company K found a diary with the last entry August 30. The diary belonged to the daring Ens. Donald Hicks of the *Olympia;* he had lost it as Force B fought its way toward Obozerskaya.[3]

The details of the arrival of the first American forces on this front are conflicting. Stewart's report shows two platoons of Company L joining Donoghue en route to Seletskoye; other sources indicate that L came later. On September 14, Company K and two platoons of Company L arrived at Seletskoye to join the British and French of the newly designated Force D. That force consisted of troops previously on the Dvina that were quickly routed to the Seletskoye-Kodish area to protect Kodish's critical position on the Plesetskaya-Kodish-Sisko Road. It was feared that on this main route ending just south of Archangel, large numbers of Red troops in Plesetskaya could be funneled north to threaten Archangel.

The headquarters for Force D was Seletskoye, a small village located not far from the Emtsa River; it became the supply base for the troops that would be fighting across the river and down the road to Kodish, the key village. Seletskoye, a small, unimpressive village, would house hundreds of troops coming and going during the coming months. It was typical of many of the towns in which the doughboys would find themselves quartered. Its five to six hundred villagers lived in houses stretched on either side of the road.

One feature of the Russian house was the absence of a "privy." Harold Weimeister, a wagoner with the 337th Ambulance Company, wrote of his stay in Seletskoye. Although he spent many months in a variety of homes at four different fronts, he remembered his home in Seletskoye best:

> Every house was built in conjunction with the barn for convenience in the extreme cold and prevalent throughout central Europe. The toilet was on the second floor and was only a hole in the floor with the sewage dropping to the cattle stalls below. When used a turd would freeze before it hit the floor below with the consequences that in time it formed a tower about the diameter of a telephone pole. When the Russians started asking us when we were going to leave, we humorously answered, "When we fill up the privy." This turned out not to be so humorous. We filled two up to the time we left Seletskoye in February. This tower of shit would grow steadily until it came abo[v]e the second floor too high to squat over—THEN WE MOVED.[4]

With the arrival of the Americans, Force D numbered 380 men, including the Royal Scots, French machine gunners, and Royal Marines.[5] A sudden attack by the Bolsheviks on September 16 tested the force, but the many automatic weapons and determined resistance of the Allies threw it back. Surprisingly, the British force commander Captain Scott decided to withdraw.[6] Americans lost one man, Pvt. Glenn Staley of Company K, killed on September 17, and two wounded.[7]

This fight had some embarrassing aftermaths. Captain Scott, convinced that more Red attacks would come, retreated north from Seletskoye to Tiagra (Tegra), while the Soviets retreated south to Kodish, fearing more Allied attacks. As the Allies withdrew, they burned several bridges to prevent enemy advances, not realizing that their opponents were heading in the opposite direction, also burning bridges. Finally, a British patrol from Tiagra determined that Seletskoye was deserted. As the patrol returned to their main force, to their surprise they discovered Yanks burning a bridge. Puzzled, one Brit called out, "I say, old chaps, what's the bloody gaime?"[8] They finally got things sorted out; the Allies did some bridge repair, then walked back into Seletskoye on September 19, while the Reds remained in Kodish.

As the capture of Kodish was considered vital to the three-pronged attack planned by Allied headquarters and to the area defense, reinforcements were sent to Seletskoye from Archangel. The other two platoons of Company L arrived with the Machine Gun Company of the 339th, forty-seven men under Lt. Clifford Ballard. The new commander of the force was, of course, a British officer, Colonel Henderson, who lasted five days before he was relieved and returned to England.[9]

Late in September, Captain Donoghue was ordered to take Company K, Company L and Machine Gun Company to board rafts made by the 310th Engineers and assault the Bolo position on the east bank of the Emtsa River. It would have been virtually a suicide move, throwing the three companies against heavily fortified Bolo strongholds defended with a fierce tenacity. The Yanks refused to wade across the river, but found a half-destroyed bridge and started across. The Reds defended the bridge with everything they had. Lieutenant Ryan of Company K wrote on September 27:

> Started out about 5 A.M. and was with the main body at the bridge 3 versts outside of Kadish [sic] ran into something this proved to be a regular battle there must be 1000 of them. I was on the right flank. The left caught it the heaviest. Lt. Chappel was killed and I guess also Sgt. Agnew. Sgt. Pease, Sgt. Nykus, Cpl. Dickey were all wounded . . . spent the night in the woods, walking around in water up to my knees.[10]

Company K mechanic Percy Walker wrote:

[T]he machine guns are popping to beat the band and big shells are bursting all around we have no big guns. . . . Commons [Lieutenant John] puts a sgt. in charge and takes me with him to do a little scouting so we started out in front of our lines and go about 5 rods when I get a rifle bullet through my right leg just below the hip.[11]

By that time they had been bloodied, as well as battered. Killed were Lt. Charles F. Chappel, Sgt. John Agnew, and Pvt. Charles Vojta from Company K; Cpl. Edward Mertens and Cpl. Edward Kreizinger of Company L; and Cpl. Harley Hester and Sgt. Emanuel Meister from the Machine Gun Company. In addition there were twenty-four wounded.[12]

During the next two weeks, Force D had numerous skirmishes in the frigid swamps near Kodish; low on supplies, with feet and legs soaked and swollen, they were unable to gain an inch of ground. British colonel Gavin relieved Colonel Henderson on September 29, the third Seletskoye commander in less than a week. Official reports indicate on October 7, Colonel Gavin relieved parts of the three American companies and sent them north to Mejnodskaya, out of harms' way.[13] Lieutenant Ryan's diary indicated that Company K was relieved on October 3, but returned to the front lines on October 5; however, Company L remained on the line. A very welcome addition to the complement was a two-gun section of the awesome Canadian artillery, which arrived on October 8, fresh for the fight, along with Company D of the 339th.[14]

Orders came for a new push on Kodish. Colonel Gavin ordered a ferry to be built some three versts south of Mejnodskaya; his plan was to cross to the east side of the Emtsa River, then push south along the river toward Kodish. On October 12, Companies K and L paddled across the river without opposition and advanced toward Kodish. That night they slept in the marshy woodlands, cold and hungry. The next morning Captain Cherry of Company L took his four platoons, plus two Company K platoons, in a move to cut off the Bolsheviks in their rear, while the rest of Company K attacked the Bolo line at the river. The frontal attack was supported by Canadian artillery, the machine guns of the Machine Gun Company, and the Royal Marines.

But all to no avail; once again the terrain was their worst enemy, and Cherry never found the Soviet rear. Lieutenant Ryan, who was in the column, wrote in his diary:

10/13—We started at 7:30 The woods and swamp are so thick that one cant see 20 feet ahead. Moved in squad column as best we could . . . just at dark about 5 P.M. they attacked our flank, we had no MG but 15 rifles, stood them off. We lost Pvt. Cromm [Louis Cronin] and Sgt. Scheunerman wounded. C [Lt. John Commons] and myself stayed on the ridge all night. Mean night.[15]

October 14 would be no better. Gerrit Knoll of Company D wrote, though, that things were not all bad. "We moved up to Kadish and crossed the Ymsa River and lived in dugouts made by the Bolshevikies and they were good ones as they intended them for winter quarters."[16]

Patrols sent out the night of October 13 indicated that the Reds had fallen back south of Kodish, so Companies K and L, with two platoons of Company D, began moving cautiously down the road toward town. The Bolos had left a rear guard that opened on the Americans, killing Pvt. Joseph Ozdarski and Pvt. Arthur Christian of Company L and wounding several, including one from Company D, but by 2:30 P.M. on October 15, Kodish was in Allied hands.

The next city on the road to the elusive Plesetskaya was Avda, about 20 versts south of Kodish. The British officers thought that they should continue the offensive, take Avda and move on to capture the railroad center, Plesetskaya. The two American companies, reinforced by forty Royal Marines, set out after a brief rest in Kodish, moving along the Avda Road, sending out their point men to locate any problems. But soon after they had rendezvoused with the other two American platoons, the Bolo artillery opened with their heavy guns, killing the point man, Pvt. Otto Taylor of Company K, and stopping the advance. That night the doughboys rested in the woods, waiting for daylight in the water-filled swamps that surrounded Kodish. At daybreak on October 17, the Allies attacked again, but the heavy Red artillery fire and the impassable swamps held them fixed to the road south of Kodish. The determined assaults that kept up for three days finally forced the Bolos to retreat south, leaving the town of Avda abandoned. On October 18, Ryan wrote, "This P.M. Dave Cromberger walked down the road and found their position deserted. L Company has gone up there."[17]

The next day, patrols moved through Avda and into positions two versts south of town. The situation stabilized for the moment as the Soviets dug in at Verst 16 between the towns of Kochmas and Avda. Both sides were content to find defensive positions and send out patrols in a number of directions. Three platoons of Company D were released as the action quieted down for the first time since late September. A force made up of Royal Scots and some SBAL troops, along with a number of Russian Officer Training Corps gunners and forty Lewis Machine Gunners, seized Tarasevo and Shred Makharenga east of Kodish.[18] Rumors and prisoner reports told of desertions and unrest in the forces at Plesetskaya; it appeared that the prize, Plesetskaya, could be theirs with a final push. That was not to be the case.

Back in Archangel, however, General Ironside had just replaced General Poole as the new British commander and attitudes were changing. No longer was the word "offensive" used for the campaign; the word now was "defensive." General Ironside ordered all forward movement to cease and the various fronts to prepare to settle in for a winter stalemate. With snow in many places hip-deep, temperatures seldom rising above zero and often dropping to 50 degrees below zero, it was felt that neither men nor equipment were prepared for any aggressive combat. The front line for the Seletskoye force at that point was at Verst 17 (Kodish was at Verst 11), held by Company K with one platoon of Machine Gun Company. Miles away in reserve were two platoons of Company L and some Russian artillery in Seletskoye, the Canadian artillery having been sent to the Dvina Force. Captain Donoghue had his headquarters in Kodish with a British medical unit; he had no more than 180 men, including thirty sick or wounded. Seletskoye was about eighteen miles north of the Kodish contingent. Some added support came from several Vickers machine guns, which were dug in along the road behind the front lines.[19] In view of the fact that Plesetskaya was just as important to the Reds as it was to the Allies, the Allied defensive force left outside Avda was hardly an impressive one.

Apparently the Soviets detected the change in posture, and began moves to retake Kodish on November 1. They succeeded in driving out the Americans at Verst 17 with heavy artillery fire on November 3 and kept up the pressure, so that on November 4, the Yanks retired from Verst 16, still under heavy attack. In those four days, four men were wounded.[20] (On November 1, the Kodish/Seletskoye Force acquired yet another new commander, this time Colonel Haselden of Force B fame, while Gavin was sent to the railroad front to replace the incompetent Colonel Sutherland.)

Fighting continued for the next several days, with Red forces pounding away at every dugout, house, or hole that contained the men of Company K and the Machine Gun Company. These embattled troops of the front line, exhausted, cold, filthy, and half-starved, were in imminent danger of being cut off as Red troops worked their way down the Emtsa River, trying to get in the Allied rear. The objective was the one remaining whole bridge, the Americans' only means of withdrawal to their old entrenchments on the other side of the river. Donoghue described the action:

> For half an hour there raged a fight as intense as was the bitter reality of the emergency for the forty Americans with Lieutenant Clarence Gardner in those dugouts. By almost miraculous luck in directing their fire through the screen of trees that shielded the Reds from view, Sgt. Cromberger's Vickers gun and Cpl. Wilkie's Lewis gun inflicted terrible losses upon this fresh battalion just getting into action against the Americanskis.[21]

With that effort, on November 7, the Yanks were able to leave Kodish, cross the bridge and man their fortifications on the American side
of the Emtsa. Donoghue recorded, "The bridge was occupied by the
enemy at 10:30 A.M. November 9."[22] Engineers from the 310th joined
the doughboys to build blockhouses and lay wire to strengthen the little
fortress, and artillery came down from Seletskoye with the reserves
from Company L and some fresh replacements from Archangel. In spite
of the reported ferocity of the fight, American losses were only seven
wounded from November 1 to November 9, although the reported Soviet casualties were two to three hundred.[23]

As the Kodish/Seletskoye front settled down to a kind of trench
warfare, Major Nichols, commanding Third Battalion on the railroad
front, visited the remnants of the original Force D. He sent Company K
back to Archangel on November 20 and forwarded Company E from its
Archangel area guard duty to Kodish. The Royal Scots had gone back
to Dvina, the Royal Marines had been sent to other fronts, Lieutenant
Ballard's machine gun platoon had been relieved by fresh Yankee gunners, and only Company L remained of the original Force D.

Pvt. Donald Carey with Company E said Seletskoye impressed him
more favorably than other Russian towns and seemed to him to be an
agricultural community. "The land, cleared for a considerable distance
and crudely fenced into fields, appeared to have been farmed for many
years."[24] As Company E arrived, a detail of American and British were
building a line of zigzagging trenches and other fortifications as a defensive position for the protection of the vital road. Quarters for Allied soldiers were uncomfortable, but warm. And bugs were definitely a
problem. Cockroaches, lice, even flies in the bitter cold, were part of
the average Russian house. The smell often was the hardest thing to
stomach. There was little bathing during the winter, and much of the
soap was a derivative of some fish products.

As Company E arrived on the line, they discovered that their barracks bags, which had been held by the supply company in Archangel,
had been rifled. Pvt. Fred Krooyer seemed resigned to that fact:

> We went back to Missinowski [Mejnodskaya] for warmer clothing. It had
> now got so cold some of the boys were freezeing their fingers or feet
> nearly every night. When we went back to get our warmer clothing out of
> our barracks bags we found that supply sergeant Patton who had been
> taking care of our barracks bags had sold about all that he could sell so
> we didn't get much warmer clothing to go back to the front.[25]

There was always some kind of diversion, and some of it involved
liquor. Fred Krooyer's diary on November 28 noted that he was at the

Emtsa River front line in the bitter cold, hoping for a quiet tour on the line. "Major Donohue came in drunk that night and began throwing grenades in the Bolo line, this didn't go far before the Bolo's opened up machine guns on us, they kept a firing until nearly morning."[26]

During the next month, the weekly reports showed, "Routine patrolling and outpost duties at bridge position with intermittent sniping and shelling without major operations or American casualties."[27] In fact, Krooyer mentioned that a limited truce took place near Kodish in December. A Red officer had communicated to Lieutenant Baker that a British officer had died in a Bolshevik hospital, and they had found seven hundred rubles on him, which they wanted to return to the Allies. "Dec 20—Bolo officer comes over and [hands] in the seven hundred rubles he took off the British officer to J.J. Baker and invited him over to dinner. He also said as long as we didn't fire they wouldn't."[28]

Donald Carey wrote home shortly after Christmas:

> The most unexpected thing happened Christmas Eve. I received your box and eight letters. They came at just the proper time, and the best part was that I never expected the box. Believe me I appreciated everything you sent and all of it comes in handy. Many thanks. Others also got boxes and we all acted like kids. That maple sugar couldn't have been better. I crave sweets more than anything else in the way of eatables. Altogether I thought it a pretty good Christmas—considering the circumstances.[29]

The British High Command decided to order the Railroad Force, including the Seletskoye and Onega units, to make another attempt to capture Emtsa and Plesetskaya in late December. Despite their defensive posture, it was felt that much better winter quarters would be found further south in Emtsa. By then, strong Bolshevik forces were in place between Kodish and Plesetskaya, unlike the November situation where the Reds were in a state of confusion. War Minister Leon Trotsky had moved seasoned troops from South Russia to bolster the sometimes ineffective conscripts of the north; these all were consolidated into the Sixth Bolshevik Army, with headquarters in Vologda.

Late one night a Bolshevik officer came to the center of the Emtsa Bridge in full view of a number of American outposts and began a harangue about the Americans being pawns of the British, and repeatedly asked why Americans were fighting Russians. He closed by saying, "Poor Americans dying in the swamps of Russia."[30] Donald Carey, new on the line, felt no one was taken in by the talk, but it brought to mind once again, that simple question: why?

Just before the Americans were to attack there was a strange interruption. A group of Russians appeared on the Emtsa Bridge with a flag of truce carried by a Soviet commander, accompanied by a Russian journalist named Bernstein and Bolshevik soldiers, all escorting an American prisoner, Pfc. George Albers, Company I.[31] The Reds proposed to exchange prisoners, but Lt. Charles Lennon wanted clearance from above before he made any commitments and told them it would three or four days before he could give an answer:

> Bernstein, the Bolsheviki Newspaper Correspondent got angry and notified 1st Lieut. Lennon that if the allied forces did not vacate the River position in course of two or three days, they were going to drive them into the White Sea, and he answered that it was pretty cold at the present time, so the Bolsheviki commander and his escort left, taking Prisoner Albers Co "I," 339th Inf. Back to KODISH Village.[32]

The inept assaults of the Railroad Force and the strong Bolo opposition on the Onega front caused Colonel Lucas to call off his three-pronged December offensive; however, news about the cancellation did not reach the Kodish Force. Force D had been split into two commands, with Captain Donoghue named as the leader of the right wing, consisting of the recently returned Company K, Company E, two platoons of Company L, one section of machine guns, one section of Canadian artillery, and supporting medical and engineer continents.[33] On December 30, the Americans jumped off, to be supported by the left wing under British colonel Haselden, commanding the Russian Archangel Regiment, along with elements of the British King's Liverpool Regiment, supplied with numerous machine guns.

The battle orders called for the right wing to make the frontal assault and meet with supporting forces under Capt. Bernard Heil of Company E on the other side of the river, while Haselden was to use his forces for side flanking and diversionary attacks. There were a British machine gun unit, one platoon of the Archangel Regiment, and thirty White Guards who would leave Shred Makharenga by sleigh under British captain Gilbey and attack Kodish from the southeast at 6:30 A.M. Then another task force, fifty White Guards under Lieutenant Fedrov, would attack Avda from the east at 6:30 A.M. to create distractions for the Americans.

Departure time was 6:00 A.M. on December 30; Donoghue had his men ready despite the fact that the main Railroad move had been delayed a day, then called off. Promptly at 6:00 A.M., his men moved out with supporting artillery and, according to Major Donoghue,[34] "Attack on River position was promptly made simultaneously from all points of assembly, maintaining a heavy fire, forcing enemy to withdraw from River positions."[35]

Lieutenant Baker, leading the assault with elements of Companies E and K, trench mortars, and machine guns, had run into heavy Soviet fire early in the morning and was stalled between tenth and eleventh versts in Kodish. Baker's report explained:

> The two platoons of K Company were lost in the woods in our rear and slightly to our left. . . . The terrain through which we were moving was almost impassible. The snow was two and three feet deep in places, the swamps slightly covered with snow and an abundance of underbrush along with numerous windfalls made our progress very slow and also accounted for the loss of the two platoons of K Company.[36]

And it was eerie with the Arctic darkness that lingered late in the morning and began again in the afternoon.

By 10:00 A.M., there was still no word of the diversions by the British and Russian left wing, but the Americans, pushing flanking attacks and frontal assaults, again took Kodish. Passing through the town, they found more Bolo resistance and were forced to stop and dig in. They had no sooner found a defensive position than the Reds counterattacked in force. With trench mortars, machine guns, and rifles, the Americans beat off at least two attempts to force them back. By 4:00 P.M. action had subsided to artillery fire and occasional sniping, but in the battle, the 339th had lost nine men killed and thirty-two wounded.[37] One of the dead was Harold Wagner of Manistee, Michigan. On June 2, 1919, the local paper ran a short article that ended, "Information of this [his death] was received through the return of a letter mailed to him by the Red Cross. It was returned here with the notation that the addressee was killed in action on December 19, 1918. Efforts are now being made to reach his parents."[38] Almost six months had passed without an official notification.

After the fighting had lessened, at 9:30 P.M. Donoghue received the same orders he had received six weeks before: halt your advance and defend Kodish.[39] Word had finally been received that the major offensive to the west had collapsed, and with the exception of the Seletskoye right wing, no units had come close to capturing its objective. Donoghue's December 31 report reads, "Col. Haselden relieved from command of SELETSKOYE Det by Col. Pitts, 17 Kings Liverpool Regiment." The next entry was, "Col. Haselden makes a visit to front line position and while there was wounded across the back by a sniper." In a memoir written after the war, Harold Weimeister, an American medic, remembered Haselden making derogatory remarks about American draftees; "Immediately an American rifle cracked and Hazelteen got it in the back of the neck. Needless to say, I did not ease his sleigh over the rough spots. I hoped the son-of-a-bitch had a pain in the neck the rest of his life."[40]

Another story that surfaced was of two sergeants from Machine Gun Company, who, weary from the fighting, sat down to rest on a log in the deep snow outside Kodish:

> Both sergeants approached the log and sat down. It made a comfortable seat, but soon it started to move. The two 'non-coms' were puzzled when suddenly an arm appeared followed by a colonel of the British army, who was demanding to know what was on him. Both 'non-coms' were thunderstruck to find that it was the commanding officer of the Kadish front.[41]

They also discovered that he was full of "influenza cure" and would likely remember little of his experience.[42]

As December 30 ended, platoons of Company E and Company K were holding a front some two versts south of Kodish and extending into heavy woods on both sides. Kodish, though, was a hellish place to defend. In a hollow, surrounded by hills and rocks, it offered attackers the advantage of simply lobbing shells into the American lines with little need for accuracy. During that night, the Reds, now more disciplined and effective, kept up steady fire from machine guns, mortars, and heavy artillery, heavier than that of the Canadians. It was some comfort just after midnight on December 30 when Donoghue received a wire from general headquarters (GHQ): "Convey to O.C. [Officer Commanding] Right Wing and American troops under him the warmest congratulations of Commanding General on their splendid efforts so gallantly and successfully carried out."[43]

December 31 was occupied by fortifying and strengthening Kodish until shortly after noon when heavy Soviet artillery fell on the town and the Yankee lines, but there were no casualties. By 4:30 P.M., Donoghue had posted strong outpost lines and continued patrolling east and west. By 5:00 P.M., he reported the situation normal, and the same on January 1. His report concluded with some testy remarks about his lack of support from the left wing. "Capt. Gibley [British Machine Gun commander] informed O.C. that they were exhausted, which was a poor excuse. . . . Lieut. Fedrov attacking AVDA from the east at 6:30 A.M. Dec 30 and to cooperate with Right Wing Force advancing south, states that it was not the right kind of day to make the attack."[44] Ironside himself found much fault with the left wing; he traveled from the Vologda front, where he had been chastising Colonel Lucas for his lack of success, to join the Seletskoye detachment on December 31. First, he sacked British colonel Haselden in charge of the machine gun attack, replaced him with Colonel Pitts, and ordered Donoghue to pull back into Kodish.

That night, New Years Eve 1918, Ironside stayed with an American company in a blockhouse in Kodish. He later gave an account of his stay:

> I saw some faint figures moving in front of us as if they were floating in air above the snow. Several of our machine guns opened fire and a Stokes mortar let off half a dozen rounds. After five minutes there was complete silence. The captain decided he would go out and see what had happened, and when he left with his orderly I followed with Piskoff [Ironside's orderly] at my heels. Some hundred yards beyond the wire we came across six bodies lying in the snow. They were dressed in long white smocks and were on short skis, which were bound with rough skins to keep them from slipping. All were quite dead and frozen stiff in the intense cold. Two had been wounded in the legs and had died of exhaustion and loss of blood. They must have died within moments of being hit.[45]

Ironside left the next morning, ordering the detachment to hold Kodish. Although Donoghue reported the situation normal on January 1, other reports indicate heavy shelling during the day, making the holding of the town a nightmare, and Donoghue decided to withdraw six hundred yards to a position more defensible on the Emtsa River. Private Krooyer's diary reported that on January 5, Company K returned briefly to Kodish and burned the town, then returned to its defensive position. On January 6, Krooyer says:

> Major Donohue got rummed again came over to our quarters asked our captain for a few men to reinforce the river front. Ours was also drunk and told him to take what men he wanted. . . . Started for the Mosyic [Emtsa] River but didn't stop untill we got within a mile of Kadish. There we had to chase the Bolo's away from the fire and we captured the city.[46]

GHQ reported on January 6, "KODISH evacuated and partly burned yesterday 'without good reason.'"[47]

In that same British headquarters report was a copy of a telegram from Ironside to Colonel Lucas in Vologda in reference to Colonel Pitts, commanding the Seletskoye detachment. "If he does not feel he is capable of running Allied troops I shall have no option but to replace him and give the command to someone who can run a column made up as his is." Ironside had not solved his command problem on the railroad or its supporting fronts.

Although the British headquarters reported Kodish evacuated on

January 6, Colonel Stewart recorded the evacuation on January 2, with Donoghue's drunken reoccupation taking place, as Carey noted, on January 6. Stewart wrote, "O.C. Right Wing re-occupied KODISH village as an outpost position with one platoon 'E' Company and two Lewis gun crews 'K' Company, 339th Infantry." That gave a certain official sanction to the major's raid.[48]

While Company E was in the defensive position north of the Emtsa, the men had a chance to review their personal situations. Donald Carey found, for the first time, cooties (lice) in his clothing. Cooties were an AEFNR plague, attacking all who were quartered in Russian houses. The bugs flourished in the crude huts in the Russian interior and were delighted to find the fresh pickings of American doughboys. Almost every diary contained references to, even pictures of, the nasty creatures. Carey summed up the typical experience of virtually every AEFNR field officer or enlisted man:

> Opening my undershirt at the neck, I found it well occupied by a colony of small cooties. Some men had acquired them a month before, but I failed to find any while at Mejovskayia.
>
> Since entering Kodish my body had itched incessantly. I doubt if any man who slept in that foul, dirty, lice-ridden village escaped the physical torture. . . . The mental and physical discomfort was terrible. They used the belt-line and seams of clothing as runways. When cold they were not so active, but when warmed became extremely annoying. They were typical gray backs—body lice. Some men mailed specimens home.[49]

With the exception of a late-night false alarm on January 12, when new British troops opened fire on a snowy tree, there was little action, but the men of Companies E and K periodically returned to Kodish to man listening posts in the totally destroyed village. Ryan was fed up with the logic and when ordered back to Kodish on the January 10, wrote in his diary, "We, K Company, are ordered to go back to Kadish. This is a farce, there is no more Kadish, its all burned down, we will have to build shelters for the men. The Colonel is doing this for spite, I think."[50] Ryan indicated that Colonel Pitts was a boy colonel whose permanent rank was lieutenant, having received an instant battlefield promotion.

This was the last gasp for the American doughboys in Kodish. On January 13, Companies E, K, and L were relieved from the Seletskoye front and began their journey back to Archangel. They did leave one machine gun section on the front, and the feisty Major Donoghue remained in command of the right wing. His command now consisted of one company of King's Liverpools and one company of SBAL Russians, the American gunners, and Canadian artillery. A description of the SBAL's makeup was furnished by one of the 339th officers: "These . . . were an uncertain lot of change-of-heart Bolshevik prisoners and deserters and accused spies and so forth, together with Russian youths from the streets of Archangel, who, for the uniform with its brass buttons and the near-British rations of food and tobacco volunteered to 'help Save Russia' "[51] As has been seen, their loyalties were difficult to determine, as was their reliability.

Finally, all outpost positions were abandoned in Kodish, and the Allies withdrew to their defensive positions three versts north of the burned out town on January 21.

The British could not accept the fact that Kodish was the limit of their advance on Plestskaya, so another advance was ordered for February 7. The reports of events within the troops involved in that effort indicated that the whole front was fraught with dissension. Troops refused to attack and became lost and confused; orders issued by commanders were in violent disagreement; supplies were abandoned and lost to the Bolos; and the whole advance became chaotic. The Americans involved in the two-day assault were the machine gun section under Lieutenant Ballard and a section of trench mortars under Lt. E. A. Tessin. Lieutenant Ballard became the last American fatality on the front when he was killed on February 7. Ballard's death was a shattering blow to the 339th. He was killed as he aided a Russian machine gun platoon that had been isolated, surrounded, and abandoned by the Russians and King's Liverpools as they battled toward their rear. The lone survivor of the gunners trapped in the blockhouse told of the heroic death of his Russian bunkmates and the brave Ballard, killed, as he said, "at the point of the Bolshevik bayonets."[52] Two more Americans were wounded on February 9.

This virtually ended the American participation along the Kodish line. On February 12, when the British headquarters learned that during the previous few days, the British and Russian forces had been forced to abandon positions in Tarasevo and Gora, and Shred Makharenga had been attacked heavily, Colonel Pitts was relieved of command and replaced by Colonel Levy. On February 15, Iron Mike Donoghue ended his command of the right wing in favor of British major Holmes. On February 22, the section of machine gunners was relieved, leaving only one section of trench mortars as the American support of the front. The trench mortar men of the Headquarters Company were sent up to the front to act as instructors for the newly recruited Russians. Their role turned out to be more than that, as they participated in more than a month of combat duty in the Shred Makharenga sector.[53]

Stewart's report on March 12 closed that chapter of the AEFNR:

"Trench mortar platoon carried out usual routine without casualties until March 11 when the platoon was relieved by Russian troops and left for rest at Archangel leaving no American troops on this front."[54]

There are no further references to the Seletskoye/Kodish front in American reports.

While the railroad front was concentrating on the narrow confines of the double track and its two protecting fronts were fulfilling their missions, the other major force, the Dvina River Force, was finding its path to Kotlas blocked by increasing numbers of Red troops.

The Dvina Front

March 4, 1919—Drew up Resulution to request reason Why We are fighting Boloes and Why We haven't any Big Guns and Why the English run us and Why we haven't enough to eat and Why our men can't get proper medical and mail.

—Sgt. Silver Parrish

THE Dvina River front was one of the major fronts devised by Gen. F. C. Poole. It was his plan to take his few troops up the Dvina River as far as Kotlas, then at Viatka to connect with the Czech troops, who supposedly would be routed through to Archangel.[1] Early on, General Poole wrote of his goal:

> I hope with this force I may be able to bring off a coup which will sink or capture the enemy [river] fleet annihilate the force and capture the guns. If I can bring this off successfully at an early date I do not think I shall meet with any more serious opposition before reaching Kotlas which I am reckoning on being able to occupy by September 20th and push on toward Viatka during the winter.[2]

It would cost a number of Allied lives to realize the errors in that plan. As late as July 1919, that same proposal was again put forth by Poole's successor, General Ironside, but with requests for seasoned troops, adequate gunboat support, and other qualifications.

It all began with great expectations. The Bolsheviks had quickly departed Archangel as the Allied invaders swept in with their fleet covered by seaplanes, appearing to be a powerful fleet. With the American sailors, some Polish troops, and the Royal Scots chasing the enemy up the river with little opposition, and another of Poole's task forces headed south on the railroad, there was reason for optimism. Force B was the first to realize that Bolos could fight; it was virtually destroyed trying to cut off the Reds near Obozerskaya. By early September 1918, the Allies had occupied both Bereznik on the Dvina River and Obozerskaya on the railroad. But gradually the Reds discovered that the invaders were only a small expedition, not nearly sufficient to make any incursion into the vast interior of Russia.

As the First Battalion lay on their *Nagoya* bunks in the harbor near Archangel, they knew nothing of the Dvina Force or the role they themselves would play. On September 7, they debarked at the Bakharitza dock across the river from Archangel and headed straight for a fleet of coal-carrying barges. These clumsy, filthy, uncomfortable conveyances were to be their home for the next five days. There were many concerns as they filed off the ship and loaded onto their transports. One sergeant expressed his thoughts:

> On a coal barge going up Dvina River to face many hardships & trying times in pursuit of the Bolo as they are called. But as I know beter they are working men trying to through off the yoke of Capitalism & gain for their selves and family nessicaties of life & a few pleasures.[3]

On the barges, the sick mingled with the well, and the flu continued to riddle the ranks. On September 8, the little convoy stopped by the riverbank to bury one of the flu victims, Pvt. Joseph Gresser, Company C. Another private from the same company wrote, "Today another man died named Dresser [sic] from Wyandotte, Michigan. He was on guard and told the corporal he was sick but was not relieved."[4] Another diary entry notes, "Man from Company C [Private Gresser] dies on barge. Left in improvised coffin on open front of barge. Blood from underneath coffin trickles across floor of barge while we eat our hard tack and black tea."[5]

The next day Sgt. Henry Gariepy from Company C succumbed and was buried in the little riverside village of Armorge on September 11.[6] Still on the barges, Pvt. Carl Jordan of Company B died quietly, and a military funeral was held over another riverside grave. Finally, on September 12, the string of barges arrived at Bereznik at the junction of the

Vaga and Dvina Rivers, more than 150 miles from Archangel. Death had taken one more on the barge, Pvt. John T. Westerhof of Company B; many others would join him in the little cemetery near the Bereznik church.

Poole decided that Bereznik would be his supply base as he moved his eight-hundred-man force farther up the river: Royal Scots, Russians, Serbs, Poles, and Americans were all poised to move south. Bereznik was a more prosperous city than Archangel, and there was evidence of some cultural activities. One of the late tsar's hunting lodges was located there, which had attracted some of the Royalist elite. Shortly after Company A set up camp, the men were awakened by gunfire. The Scots had spotted a boat coming up river and waded out to greet it; however, it held Bolos instead of Scots. Three Scots were picked up by the boat and stripped of weapons and clothes, then turned loose. When the Scots got about fifty yards from the boat, the Red sailors opened fire, killing two and wounding one.[7] The doughboys, watching the affair, anxious to get their first taste of combat, immediately opened fire on the riverboat. The gunboat then moved out of range and began shelling the shore. At that point, a British patrol boat rounded the bend and, with three shells, set the Red boat on fire.

The Royal Scots, mostly category B1 men unfit for field duty, performed well throughout their stay in North Russia. On the Dvina front, they were assigned the east side of the riverbank, with the Americans on the west. In September the Scots moved rapidly through the towns of Pless, Turgomin, and Topsa and got as far as Nizhni-Tiomski, even farther upriver than the Americans from B, C, and D companies.

The conditions on both sides of the river were miserable: swamp and forests, few houses of any kind between villages, and winter fast approaching. Leaving Company A in Bereznik, the rest of the battalion moved farther south on September 15, up the Dvina River to Chamova, replacing some Royal Scots.

On September 18, two platoons of Company A, left at Bereznik, marched along the scenic Vaga River to Shenkursk, joining thirty Russians of the SBAL already in the village. Company A was to be the vanguard of the second river front, the Vaga front, moving almost due south along the river. Their units would establish outposts farther from Archangel than any other Allied post during the entire expedition.

Meanwhile, Companies B, C, and D continued south on the west bank of the Dvina, and on September 18, approached the village of Seltso. So far, the Bolsheviks had just kept retreating, giving the Yanks a false sense of superiority. The Bolos decided Seltso was the place to stop their retreat.

The Dvina River in that area is a sprawling, slow-moving river that overflows its ill-defined banks on many of its courses. Consequently, flooding leaves swamp and marsh for a considerable distance inland from the river. Such was the case with Seltso, a village on the river virtually surrounded by waist-high water. On September 19, Company D easily took the village of Yakovslevskaya, one mile north of Seltso, separated from it by a mile of open swamp. They moved slowly through the muck and water toward Seltso in a skirmish line, getting only part way across an open field before they were stopped by a hail of Soviet gunfire. They dug in as best they could, waiting for darkness, and for their battalion commander, Maj. James Corbley (later lieutenant colonel), to give them directions. He had been held up by Bolo artillery as he helped push forward the guns of the Russian artillerists. Fortunately for the battalion, the artillery was on the way, while the men, weary and soaking wet, tried to keep from slipping into the swamp waters as they endured the night of September 19 with no supporting artillery. During the night Companies B and C were brought up to dig in and pass the wet and rainy night in the woods on the right flank.

On September 20, Major Corbley joined them, bringing Russian artillery that had been mired in hub-deep mud, delaying its arrival. The newly arrived guns softened up the town and intimidated the Red boats that had been shelling the Allies. Then Corbley ordered Company B's Lt. Walter Dressing with Sgt. Simon Davis's squad to scout the area. They came upon Bolo trenches and were scattered by Soviet fire. On this patrol, Cpl. Herbert Schroeder disappeared. At noon, another advance was ordered, partly to escape the steady Red artillery fire that plagued the dug-in troops. Corbley sent two platoons on the assault, but after three men were killed and eight men wounded, the attack bogged down.

Finally, Corbley ordered a barrage on the town by the Allied Russian artillery, which was highly effective; the three companies advanced without further loss, taking the town about 5:00 P.M.[8] The two-day fight, however, was costly: Pvt. John Van Herwynen of Company D was killed, and Cpl. Morris Foley, Pvt. John Van Der Meer, and Pvt. Peter Kudzba, all of Company B, died there too.[9] Lt. Albert Smith was wounded, shot in the side, and Archie Perry was hit at the same time.[10]

Before the attack, after their soggy night, Corporal Foley shared breakfast, a British can of bully beef, with his buddy Bill Henkelman. Henkelman said to Foley, "Hey, Morris, let's save some for after awhile." Foley's response was prophetic as he ate the last of the beef: "There might not be no after while."[11] Unfortunately, Foley was right.

The Dvina casualties came just four days after the Railroad Force had its first battle deaths. Pvt. Edwin Arkins wrote in his journal, "The sight of that first casualty I'll never forget: the lower part of the face a bloody mass; the eyelids swollen and blue and the head resting on the inside of the upturned helmet."[12] Sgt. Silver Parrish held the right flank for one period, mounting his machine guns to flank the Soviets. When he found and rejoined his company, Company B, he wrote with tongue in cheek, "But we should worry we had Lewis Guns now, and all the enemy had was gun-boats, Pom _____ Me Guns [Machine guns] rifles and field pieces and trenches but orders were to keep on for about 52 hours."[13]

As the doughboys entered Seltso, the Bolsheviks were actually re-treating once again, but with a purpose. With their dominant artillery, the Reds needed no troops to hold the Allies at bay. The Allied infantry units no sooner entered Seltso than they found themselves under artil-lery fire from the long-range Red guns and from gunboats on the river. Allied artillery was unable to cross the swamplands to give the support necessary to offset the enemy guns, so Corbley ordered the men to with-draw to Yakovlevskaya. They managed the retreat without casualties, struggling through the waist-deep water, wondering what their previ-ous day's work had been all about.

With their first combat behind them, the three companies rested and tried to dry out and get warm. Their barracks bags with winter clothing had not yet arrived at the front, and nights were turning cold. A few days later, September 26, all three companies made a fifteen-mile march farther upriver to the town of Puchuga. They slogged through mud up to their ankles in a drizzling cold rain, arriving about 7:00 P.M.[14] Moore's book said:

> [T]he rest of the company was scattered in billets all over the village, being so tired that they flopped in the first place where there was floor space to spread a blanket. Then came an order to march to the main vil-lage and join Major Corbley. At least a dozen of the men could not get their shoes on by reason of their feet being swollen, but we finally set out on a pitch black night through the thick black mud. We staggered on, every man falling full length in the mud innumerable times, and finally reached our destination.[15]

On September 27, Allied GHQ in Archangel issued orders to cease active operations on the Dvina and dig in for winter. The Americans of First Battalion were then detached from the Dvina River front and sent to the Vaga River, where increased enemy activity troubled Allied headquarters. With the new organization of the fronts, Companies B and C of First Battalion moved by barge up the Vaga River to Shenkursk, arriving on September 28, with First Battalion headquarters following on October 2. On September 28, Company D went even farther up the

Dvina River to Kodima, which would be the end of the southward movement of the Allies on the Dvina.[16] Later, on October 2, Company D was pulled out, put on barges, and sent north to the Emtsa River to join Force D in Seletskoye.[17]

Throughout all of the campaigns on the various fronts, the 310th Engineers were a part of each battalion. Companies B and C of the 310th stayed in the Archangel area during most of the fall and winter, constructing all the different kinds of buildings required by the Allied command. The Engineers' Company A was split up and sent to the three infantry forces. Although they were few in number, they were vital to the defenses of the outposts, building and repairing blockhouses, dugouts, railroad bridges, and anything else that was needed. Their efforts were not without cost. On October 8, 1918, while they were working with the Americans and British on the Dvina River, Lt. C. B. (Doc) Hill, Sgt. Elmer Bloom, and Pvt. Arthur Dargan of Company A were drowned in the Dvina River. They were trying to free a boat stuck on a sandbar when they were fired on by the Bolsheviks. The three decided to swim for it, leaving three others on board. Lt. Ray Mc-Curdy of the 310th wrote, "They were all husky men and good swimmers. . . . Strong swimmers though they were, the cold water of the Dvina was too much for them and none of them made it to shore."[18] Engineer Thomas Hancock's diary noted:

> Routed out at 4 A.M. to go to rescue of Leut & party in river aground. Caldwell and I in rowboat took off survivors—3 were rescued by Caldwell and I under heavy shell fire. They were Privates Munich, Thompson and Kury. Lt & 1st Sgt and cook all reported drowned. Gloom over all.[19]

While the regiment's reports show no other casualties that day, the AEFNR casualty list indicates Cpl. Lloyd Connor, Company A, 310th, was also drowned that same day, presumably in the same incident. However, individuals of his unit wrote that he died on June 8, 1919, while working on a bridge on the railroad front.[20] October proved to be the worst month in terms of engineer casualties. Bloom, Dargan, and Hill were lost on October 8, and perhaps Corporal Connor. Cpl. William Ziegenbein died on October 16 of wounds suffered in Seletskoye; John Morris also died of his wounds on October 16; Myron Assire of Company A was killed in action on October 26; and Alfred Lyttle died of wounds on October 31.[21]

In November parts of the RAF moved up to an advance field on the Dvina front to man a primitive airstrip and to offer some support to the Allied troops on the river. Using sleds and ponies to manhandle the Nieuport 17s, the Sopwith Strutters, and their old DH. 4s, they arrived at the strip in time to begin limited strafing and reconnaissance flights against the Bolos. One of their squadrons was led by a loyal Russian, Capt. Alexander Kozakov, who was the first to shoot down a Bolshevik plane in January 1919 and was Russian's leading ace from the eastern front, credited with shooting down twenty German planes. He was a veteran of the eastern front, flying frequently, and a favorite of all the Allies.[22] The tiny air force played a small part in the Dvina campaign, but as the weather turned colder, planes were less effective.

Despite being sent to other sectors, the 339th First Battalion was not finished with the Dvina Force. As the Bolos moved northward toward Seltso after their earlier retreat, B Company was ordered back to Seltso on October 7, arriving there on October 10, just in time to attack the Bolo trenches south of Seltso. Sergeant Parrish was in the forefront "in a scurmish line through Woods and in Water up over our Knees and lots of places up to our Hips and over them." Parrish volunteered to lead a platoon across a road to clear some enemy lean-tos. He crossed the road while his men waited, drawing fire to locate the Bolos. "I wanted to draw the enemys fire and see Where they Were and I damd soon found out for they Were every Where."[23] He added, "I had a personal incounter with a Officer and took his Saber from him and he is now asleep." American losses were only two wounded.

The next day was a repeat performance, charging the Bolos, but this time Sergeant Parrish and Company B ran into an ambush and were driven back to Seltso. Again they had light casualties, just one wounded. " My friend Tom Downs got his Eye Shot Out and after he got it he Walked through Swamps and timber to Camp Without kicking."[24] Only three days later Company B found itself being pounded by Red artillery and snipers. The Soviets attacked late in the afternoon on October 14, and the British commander ordered Seltso abandoned that night. The evacuation was completed without casualties, as the Americans, the Royal Scots, and the Canadian artillerymen left their positions and retreated to Toulgas. That same day, Capt. Robert Boyd was designated commander of the so-called Left Bank Force.[25]

While the evacuation was without casualties, it was not without danger. Capt. (Doctor) John Hall of the 339th Medical Corps was assigned to take a hospital ship, the *Vologjohnin*, up the river to evacuate wounded from Seltso. He tried to find wounded Royal Scots, but could not locate anyone in the area to give any information, so on the night of October 10, he sailed back to Toulgas. Doctor Hall, not ready to give up, went back up to Seltso, braving more artillery fire. The Russian crew was very unenthusiastic about a return to the fighting zone, but Hall convinced them (with a drawn revolver) that it was necessary to make the trip. He found the wounded and several female Russian nurses and headed back to Toulgas. "On this night [October 12] medical supplies were handed over to Captain Griffiths, R.A.M.C., and casualties were safely placed on board. The *Vologjohnin* proceeded to Beresnik, where all casualties, totaling forty-three, were handed over to the 337th Field Hospital."[26]

During the next month Dr. Hall spent time caring for the Allied wounded, but, in accordance with his medical creed, he found time to minister to the Russians, who had contracted the influenza that had so devastated the Americans. Hall's diary mentions his ministrations to the peasants, "among whom the ravages of Spanish influenza and pneumonia were heartrending to behold."[27]

By that time, First Battalion was almost completely split. Company B remained with the British forces on the Dvina, Company A was the farthest away at Ust Padenga on the Vaga River, Company C was at Shenkursk, and Company D was farther north at Seletskoye. Since the Allied instructions were to cease any offensive movement, the offensive shifted to the Bolsheviks, who were becoming more organized, more aggressive, and more proficient. However, the masses of men they could provide to any front at any time proved their greatest advantage. Their losses, while heavy, scarcely dented their manpower pools. The Allies had few replacements for the fallen. On September 30, a shipment of replacements had arrived, bringing some three thousand additional British troops with 510 Americans.[28]

By October 17, the Allied Left Bank Force was entrenched in Toulgas, frantically digging in both for defense and for winter quarters with the professional help of a squad of Company A, 310th Engineers. On October 20, both Americans and Royal Scots received replacements, including Lt. John Cudahy, who joined Company B. Cudahy was so shocked by the poor rations that he paid for additional provisions out of his own pocket.[29]

The replacements were just in time to beat off an attack from increasingly aggressive Bolshevik units. Parrish commented on October 21, "Snow and Cold and laying out in Coald Wet Rifel Pits."[30] The weather was definitely becoming a factor, and barracks bags with winter clothing were still somewhere on the docks. The restless Bolos attacked the upper Toulgas area on October 23, but were easily beaten off, sustaining but one American wounded.[31] With the increasing activity against Toulgas, two platoons of Company D, then at Chamova, were ordered to hike to Toulgas to bolster the Scots, Canadians, and Americans. They arrived barely in time.

Red gunboats had retreated because of cold weather and ice in the river. A brief thaw brought them back on November 7 after a week's absence, and they began firing shells into Toulgas. Enemy patrols became more aggressive, civilians became less friendly, and all signs pointed to an imminent attack. British gunboats had long since retreated to friendlier shores, with no orders, just their own instincts for self-preservation. The Allied boats were sorely missed during the renewed Red attacks, and the failure to leave any of the British rifled artillery created a major hole in the Toulgas defenses. While the Bolos could bring their ships from upriver during the thaw, the ice freed by the thaw served as a plug in the narrow lower Dvina, preventing any Allied ships from coming upriver to support the men in Toulgas.

Toulgas was a river town, split by a creek that ran east-west through the village. It was really three villages in one. Upper Toulgas, south of the creek, had some sixty homes, as well as two American outpost locations manned by Company B. The central village housed the local church and priest's house, with several other houses in a level, cleared plot just north of the bridge over the creek. The northern, or lower, area included the hospital and quarters for the Sixty-seventh Battery, Canadian Field Artillery's fifty-seven men. The north-end hospital was three miles from the outposts in upper Toulgas and virtually unprotected. Just south of the hospital, the two Canadian field pieces, eighteen-pounders, faced south, from which a Red attack would most likely come. To the west of the town, heavy forest formed a semi-circle from the southern end to the northern end; the ground sloped fairly steeply to the river, with a shallow ravine running through the lower village to the Dvina. Most of the homes were in the central and north sections of the village, which also housed a newly constructed blockhouse near the creek bridge. The doughboys were billeted in various houses in the three areas, as well as in outposts at the edge of the woods.

Early in the morning on November 11, as the western front grew silent, all hell broke loose at Toulgas. During the night the Reds had brought up two of their most powerful gunboats, landed a battery of artillery in the woods, and opened fire on the outposts and blockhouses in upper Toulgas. Simultaneously five hundred Red infantry poured out of the woods to the west, and a like force appeared suddenly from the woods to the south. As the attack came, the exposed men in the outposts ran frantically for the blockhouse, all but one making it safely. Lt. Henry Dennis made a brief attempt to slow the Soviets at the outposts, but he was unsuccessful.

The first American to fall was Pvt. Leo Gasper, who fell just short of the bridge. The gunboats continued to fire at the blockhouse guarding the bridge on the creek, as the doughboys began their defense. Their Lewis and Vickers machine guns cut into the swarms of attackers coming across the bridge; at the same time the Reds sent their infantry into action coming down the ravine, sweeping almost everything before it. Had it not been for the bravery of the Canadian artillerymen, with their small, but deadly, eighteen-pounders, and the stubborn Yanks, the three sections of Toulgas would have fallen quickly. But the Canadians fired their eighteen-pounder guns point-blank into the masses of Bolos, causing them to stumble back up the ravine and regroup. Lt. John Cudahy wrote of the Canadians:

> They swore fine, full chested Canadian blasphemies that were a glory to hear, crammed shrapnel into their guns, and turned terrible blasts into the incoming masses, that exploded among them and shattered them into ghastly, dismembered corpses and hurled blood and human flesh wide in the air in sickening, splattering atoms.[32]

The Bolsheviks, however, had captured the hospital filled with wounded Scots, Canadians, and Americans. There, a legend was born:

> One of the leading commanders was an extremely powerful giant of a man, named Melochofski, who first led his troops into the village hospital in the rear of the gun positions. He strode into the hospital wearing a huge black fur hat, which accentuated his extraordinary height, and singled out all the wounded American and English troops for execution, and this undoubtedly would have been their fate, had it not been for the interference of a most remarkable woman, who was christened by the soldiers "Lady Olga." . . . She had fallen in love with Melochofski and had accompanied him with his troops through the trackless woods, sharing the lot of the common soldiers and enduring hardships that would have shaken the most vigorous man. With all her hardihood, however, there still was the touch of eternal feminine, and when Melochofski issued the orders for slaughter of the invalided soldiers, she rushed forward and in no uncertain tones demanded that the order be countermanded and threatened to shoot the first Bolo that entered the hospital.[33]

Melochofski left and took his men back into the fight, but the close-up cannon fire by the Canadians forced them back, and the hospital stayed intact, with the lovely Lady Olga as a welcome addition. The Bolo commander went out to join the fight against the Canadian gunners and within minutes was brought back mortally wounded to die in the arms of his lover.[34]

At the bridge, the fire from the blockhouse kept the Bolos on the south side of the creek. With only seven doughboys in the blockhouse, it was a test of their bravery and marksmanship that no Soviet soldier made it all the way across the eighty-foot bridge. Sgt. Fred Marriott was the noncom in charge, supervising the Vickers and machine gun fire.

The Reds turned their artillery and gunboat fire on the little block-house, but by some miracle, at the end of the day the blockhouse still stood. As the shells burst all around the post, debris blocked some firing ports. Sgt. Floyd Wallace was one of those in the stronghold. Twice, Wallace went outside to clear the ports; the second time, his luck ran out and he was hit in the arm. After almost a full day of attacking the bridge, the Reds retreated with extensive casualties.

Late in the day, Lieutenant Dennis took a squad to wipe out Soviet snipers, who had inflicted a number of casualties during the day. Despite the savagery of the Red attacks, and the enormous casualties inflicted by the defenders, the U.S. loss was small. Pfc. Jake Anderson, Pvt. Leo Gasper, and Pvt. Alek Pilanski died, and several others were wounded.

The battle, begun on Armistice Day, continued the following day as the Soviet land batteries and enemy gunboats opened fire, trying to drive out the Yanks without using infantry. All day the shells rained down on buildings and on the blockhouse. Sgt. Fred Marriott left the protection of the log blockhouse to clear a firing port, but was killed as he stepped outside. The Canadian gunners continued to pour their fire at the Bolo land artillery and into the woods, where the Soviet infantry waited. The only other American casualty that day, Pvt. John Zajaczkowski, was killed in the hail of artillery fire.

The shelling continued on November 13, with the blockhouse miraculously still intact. Finally, a shell hit it directly and collapsed the log roof, killing two of the gunners inside, Pvt. John Angove and Cpl. John Savada, and wounding five others. One of the wounded, Pvt. Charles Bell, was severely hit in the face and blinded in one eye, but covered the withdrawal of the other wounded from the ruined blockhouse until dark, when he was evacuated.[35] As the Bolos kept up their attempts to cross the bridge, an American Yankee, Stanley Karan, set up another machine gun in a rifle pit across the road from the rubble of the blockhouse; he kept up his fire, maintaining control of the bridge.[36] During the day, the Royal Scots counterattacked in lower Toulgas, taking back the hospital and buildings there.[37] That night found the doughboys still in central Toulgas. The weather continued to be bitterly cold with temperatures dipping to almost 30 degrees below zero.

The Allied forces at Toulgas were really on two sides of the Dvina River, which was some two hundred yards wide at the village. The first day the communications cables were mangled, and contact could only be maintained by signals. At first, the Royal Scots on the right bank, many of whom were Russian volunteers, had been kept out of the fight, which took place on the left bank. The situation changed on November 14 when the Bolsheviks sent 140 men against the by then jittery Scots.

Their commander, Lieutenant Dalziel, attempted to hold his men in their defenses, but early in the fight, he was wounded in the neck. His men were tired of fighting and, without hesitation, fled the scene, leaving the wounded lieutenant to the Reds. A woman observer reported that he tried to reach for his holstered revolver, but was immediately set upon by two Soviet soldiers, who smashed his head and face with their rifles, killing him instantly. General Finlayson's report verified this: "His body was recovered later and its appearance helps bear out this statement."[38]

In Toulgas Captain Boyd decided to risk an attack on the Bolos in the woods. Using Lieutenant Cudahy's platoon and parts of Company D, newly arrived from Chamova, the doughboys jumped off early on November 14 and headed west toward the woods, sending parts of their force south to cut off snipers. During the night the river began to freeze, so the Soviet gunships left to go south. Boyd's attack was a success; the demoralized Bolos fled the scene. Private Henkelman, with Cudahy's platoon, while resting after the attack, was handed a letter from his father. "It said my brother Carl had been killed in France in October. There was also a picture inside of his grave and a cross. Poor Carl. My only brother."[39]

The assault was enough to break the enemy; on November 15, patrols found the Bolshevik positions abandoned and the Toulgas fight was at an end. The American casualties were listed as seven killed and twenty-three wounded.[40] By November 15, two of the wounded had died, Pfc. Elbert Ball and Pvt. Allick Detzler. The Scots' casualties were the heaviest of the Toulgas force; the total Allied loss was twenty-eight killed and seventy wounded.[41] The enemy losses were significantly higher in terms of men, but possibly the greatest impact was in the leaders killed. Not only were Generals Melochofski and Murafski killed, but the expedition leader, Foukes, died in the final American attack.[42] The civilians suffered as well. The village priest had barricaded his family in his church, which gave little protection from the fury of the artillery. After the Bolos fled, he was found in the church with his son and daughter, all dead.

Late on November 15 the order was given to burn upper Toulgas to protect the forces in the central and lower villages. Sergeant Parrish was sympathetic, yet a loyal soldier:

> Nov. 15th made a Counter atact on Bolo and Routed him and was Ordered to Burn Small village where Enemy Could do efective sniping. Women opened fire on us and we had to advance Without firing on them But we took 16 Enemy prisoners and Killed 2—then We Burned the Village and my heart ached to have the Women fall down at my feet and grab my legs

to Kiss my hand and Beg me not to do it. But orders are orders—and I Was in comand of the 15 men Who Went across that field So I done my dutie.[43]

Several honors were bestowed on the Toulgas defenders: Private Bell, Sgt. William Bowman, and Cpl. Robert Green (Company D) all were awarded the Distinguished Service Cross (DSC). On March 11, Sergeant Parrish was decorated by the British with the Military Medal. General Finlayson's report commends "the actual leaders, British Col. Skiel 2/10 R. S. Com. Rvr. Column and Captain R. P. Boyd, U.S.A. Inf. Com. Left Bank Col."[44] Finlayson closes his report as follows: "I think the above covers practically the whole of the operations unless it is that I have not sufficiently commended the staunch work done by 'B' and 'D' Cos., U.S.A. Inf. Whose bearing throughout hardly ever gave the commander, Capt. Boyd, any anxiety."[45] What part Finlayson himself played in the battle is uncertain. Ironside reports that Finlayson was on the left bank and in charge throughout the battle, yet Finlayson's words in his report indicate he was not the leader, and none of the other reports mention him.

From then until March 1919, Toulgas was held by Company B, with Company D relieving periodically, supported by Royal Scots. There were periodic attacks by the Bolsheviks, which kept the Allies from sending their troops to other fronts, but there was little real activity other than normal patrolling and scouting. However, on March 1, 1919, one of these patrols found the Soviets in force. Cpl. Arthur Prince led a patrol out of Toulgas, walking single file in an open field approaching the woods. As they neared the woods, the air rang with rifle fire, and the patrol took cover in the deep snow. Three men were killed outright, Pvt. Joseph Pawlak, Pvt. Daniel Robbins, and Pvt. Frank Ruth, with Corporal Prince missing.[46] Two more men died later that day, Sgt. William Bowman (who had won the DSC in November) and Pvt. Frank Clish. In his report, Lt. Albert M. Smith showed that he was troubled by the incident: "The affair was most unfortunate, but one which had been expected for some time, as daily patrols over established routes, which it is necessary to follow owing to depth of snow, could only lead to an ambush sooner or later."[47]

On the same day, while entering a blockhouse in central Toulgas, Pvt. Dale Wilson accidentally shot himself in the leg and was bleeding badly. He was brought to the British hospital in Toulgas, and his leg amputated on about March 4 by a young British surgeon. He was transported to Bereznik on March 15, but appeared to be suffering from severe bedsores. Captain Boyd complained to the chief medical officer in Archangel about Wilson's treatment by the British. Finally, on June 9, 1919, a report was given to Boyd stating that Wilson's treatment had been adequate.[48] That was small consolation to the men of Company B; Wilson had died on April 3.[49]

Following the ambush of the patrol, the discontent that had been present ever since the Armistice in France surfaced in Company B. On March 15, 1919, four members of the company issued a proclamation:

> To the Commanding Officer of Archangel District
> We the undersigned firmly resolve that we demand relief not later than MARCH 15th 1919
>
> And after this date we positively refuse to advance on the Bolo lines including patrols and in view of the fact that our object in Russia has been accomplished & having duly acquited ourselves by doing everything that was in our power to win—and was asked of us, we after 6 months of diligent and uncomplaining sacrifice after serious debate arrive at this conclusion and it is not considered unpatriotic to the U.S.
> In view of this be it that the interests and the honor of the U.S.A. are not at stake, and that we have accomplished the defeat of the Germans which was our mission—and whereas find our activity means interfearance in the affairs of the Russian people with whom we have no quarrel—we do solemnly pledge ourselves to uphold the principles herein stated and to ceace all activities on and after above mentioned date.[50]

The petition was signed with the initials H. P. D. K. Two of the signers were Pvt. Bill Henkelman and the heroic Sgt. Silver Parrish. Parrish was brought before Colonel Stewart, who read him the Articles of War, reciting the punishment for mutiny, which was death. Parrish, who had been recommended for a commission by Captain Boyd, wrote in his diary, "But I knew it anyhow and should worry I won't get my Commission Now (more Luck)."[51] In spite of the severity of the warning, no official action followed. On February 2, Captain Prince of the American Military Mission verified that the mood indicated by the petition was the feeling of most of the company: "Regarding the present operations, the men feel that they are contrary to the policy announced when the A.N.R.E.F was sent to Russia." That fact, plus lack of enthusiasm and lack of spirit among officers and inadequate artillery, kept morale at a low point after the Armistice.[52] The Company B petition came only two weeks before Company I on the railroad front made their protest. The Allies—British, French, Russian, and Americans—had all reached their limit. Only the Canadians seemed to be impervious to the morale decline felt by the others.

The ambush of Corporal Prince's patrol marked the end of any action at Toulgas. The Bolsheviks made no real effort to take the town, content to just harass the Yanks and Scots. Still, it was unnerving to the patrols. "Remembering their comrades who had been ambushed before, it took the sturdiest brand of courage for small parties to go out day and night on the hard packed trails, to pass like deer along a marked runway with hunter ready with cocked rifle."[53] Happily, though, their days in Toulgas were numbered; in early April the Yanks were ordered back to Archangel, as Ironside began his preparations for evacuating the Americans. Toulgas was turned over to the Third North Russian Rifle Regiment. On April 25, the Russian regiment mutinied, murdered their officers, and handed the town over to the Bolsheviks. The Canadian and loyal Russian artillery responded in May with devastating fire, and the Scot infantry retook the town in mid May.

The partners who spared the doughboys much death and destruction at Toulgas were the Canadians of the Sixty-seventh Battery, Sixteenth Brigade, Canadian Field Artillery. They had literally saved Company B from total destruction. One of these Canadians was nineteen-year-old Frank Frape, who won the British Military Medal for his efforts at Toulgas. The Canadians were universally popular with the Allied troops, and they had a definite aversion to the British, but a strong liking for the Americans. Another friend-in-need was the 337th Field Hospital and its medical personnel. They were on the scene whenever a doughboy was hit, getting him to the Toulgas hospital and quickly on down to Brezenik. Sometimes there was tension between British and American medical personnel, but the Yanks had front-line American medics to look out for them. While they could not save all the wounded, it was not because of lack of concern or effort.

In all, it had been a team effort to hold Toulgas through the miserable winter months with temperatures often 30 degrees below zero. Winter clothing finally arrived on November 18; from then on, there was less frostbite and fewer frozen fingers. The real tragedy of Toulgas and the lower Dvina campaign is that the goals, capturing Kotlas and joining the Czechs, were totally impossible and should have been recognized as such by Poole. Ironside recognized the futility of the plan and ordered a holding action with no attempt to move south, so Toulgas became the dismal end of that mission. The Dvina expedition and the Vologda Railroad action were to have been the two most significant advances of the North Russian campaign. Their failure was not due to poor troop performance, but to inept planning.

As winter waned and spring approached, enthusiasm for the campaign dimmed noticeably. Rumblings were heard, petitions passed, and open mutiny took place in Russian, French, and even British troops. The failure of the expedition became obvious to even the most ardent supporters of intervention.

While the campaign had been difficult for the Dvina units, it was even worse for its offspring, the Vaga front.

The Vaga Front

The snow was terrible, being waist deep, and at every other step a comrade fell wounded or dead. It was impossible to assist them as each man was fighting for his life.

—Dorothea York, *The Romance of Company A*

ON September 16, 1918, General Poole concluded that while the Dvina River was important, it was vulnerable to Bolshevik movements from the Vaga River, which flowed into the Dvina. Consequently, he ordered elements of the First Battalion, already on the Dvina, to divert to his new force on the Vaga River. The Vaga Force would be led by Company A, commanded by one of the best company commanders of the regiment, Capt. Otto Odjard.

The First Battalion had been confined to its barges for days, stopping periodically to bury the dead flu victims; it finally arrived at the Vaga River where the troops disembarked. The battalion moved into Berezenik, near the junction of the Vaga and Dvina Rivers. Berezenik, a rather nice town with fashionable ladies, was a welcome sight to the barge-weary Yanks. The men of Company A expected a better life here in Berezenik; they remained in town as their First Battalion mates in Companies B, C, and D moved on up the Dvina. Those hopes were soon dashed; new orders from Poole stated that the British staff was coming to stay in the town, and outposts were needed farther up the Vaga River. Company A was ordered to move south along the Vaga to man the new posts.

Before Company A moved out, the men performed the full military burial rites for the first officer to die, 2d Lt. Marcus Casey of Company C, another flu victim. Then two platoons of Company A, under Captain Odjard and Lt. Harry Meade, boarded the old side-wheeler *Tolstoy* and sailed quietly, but swiftly, up the river with a few Slavo Battalion Allied Legion (SBAL) Russians, searching for the enemy. They took Shenkursk on September 18 without firing a shot and bivouacked there.[1] A pretty city of about two thousand people, Shenkursk was set up high on the east bank of the river.

The Vaga was far different from the Dvina. The Dvina crawled slowly over its courses, overrunning its banks on a regular basis. Following the Dvina was an assignment in misery. The Vaga's banks were high, sometimes steep, and the scenery was more to the men's liking. But like the Dvina, the banks were dotted with little villages of log huts and the most primitive of conditions. Their toilet facilities were basic: "The villagers had no toilets but utilized a railing just outside their door. The excrement would become a pyramid and the peak would be knocked over when interfering with sitting. In the spring all would be cleaned up to put in a mix with soil."[2] This was the procedure even in winter temperatures, which reached 50 degrees below zero.

On September 21, about 4:00 A.M., Captain Odjard and his two platoons of Company A left Shenkursk and reboarded the *Tolstoy* to go up river. After five hours of comfortable travel, they received their first enemy fire, which came from the banks of the river. Their orders were to clear the area, so the doughboys made their first amphibious landing. The Bolos retreated after wounding four men, including Sgt. John Komasrek and Pvt. Floyd Stevens, the first casualties of the company.[3] The Americans continued up river for the next several days, passing through a number of villages, finally locating in Rodvinskaya, some 90 versts beyond Shenkursk. They were joined there by the other two platoons of the company under Lieutenants MacPhail and Saari.[4]

By this time, Company A was completely out of touch with the Railroad and the Dvina Forces and miles beyond any other Allied units. Odjard continued to move upriver, capturing Puiya on October 8, but Bolos got between Company A and Rodvinskaya, so they retreated to Rodvinskaya, carrying their wounded. Their short stay in Puiya marked the furthest penetration of the Allied troops into North Russia.

During the next few weeks, Company A patrolled, scouted, and kept its eyes open for Bolshevik activity, while Company C came over from the Dvina front to headquarter at Shenkursk.

As winter approached, the railroad drive to Plesetskaya had failed; Force A was entrenched just south of Obozerskaya with its flanks protected by the Onega and Seletskoye Forces; and Force C on the Dvina was stymied at Toulgas. That left the smallest force, the Vaga Force with its Americans, SBAL, and Royal Scots, in the most exposed position, with Company A by far the most remote unit, located at Rodvinskaya.

The men at Rodvinskaya ate well, dining especially on fresh game—duck, fish, rabbit, and even venison.[5] With hard freezes every night, the roads, formerly muddy, were now passable, making Bolshevik movement easier. It was time to send Company A back to the supposedly safer Ust Padenga. They arrived there on October 24; on November 2, 1918, Company A was relieved by Company C, with 75 Russians, 35 SBAL, and one Russian eighteen-pounder. It was not a very significant force for its isolated position. Orders were to hold positions two versts north of Ust Padenga, positions critical for Shenkursk defense.

On November 13, a patrol set out from Ust Padenga on horseback. Lt. Glen Weeks of Wisconsin wrote in his diary, "They fell into a trap and one got away. The three were killed, then mutilated badly."[6] One American, Pvt. Adolf Schmann of Company C, and two Canadians of the Sixty-eighth Canadian Battery, D. Fraser and F. H. Russell, were killed.[7] Probably because of anger over that mutilation episode, on Sunday November 17, "We caught two spies trying to find out our position, outpost strength, etc. Lt. Cuff, Lt. Winslow and myself took one of them out in the woods and shot him."[8] Sgt. Robert Ray's diary noted on November 14, "Well, we caught a couple of spies who we found had told about the patrol going out. Took one of them out and shot him let him lay 2 days so the people could see it & tell the Bolos."[9] Another death occurred when Pvt. Louis Szymanski was accidentally shot by Private Blass on Thanksgiving Day.[10]

For the next three weeks, until December 2, Company C patrolled the Ust Padenga sector while Company A relaxed in Shenkursk, drawing occasional patrol and scouting duty, but the rest of the time making use of the city's hospitality and culture.

Company C noticed in late November that Bolsheviks were using new tactics, scouting in snow camouflage suits. Up until then, the Reds had given way almost any time they had faced well-organized, aggressive enemies. Now, new troops, veterans of fighting in the south and on other fronts, were being freed up to join their less-well-trained northern comrades. Instead of poorly armed, untrained, and ill-equipped youngsters, the Allies were finding a more experienced and better-equipped enemy.

Just after Thanksgiving, Lt. Francis Cuff and Lt. Harry Steele of Company C led a sixty-man patrol out of Ust Padenga toward Bresenik (not to be confused with far off Berezenik), nine miles south of Ust Padenga. Within a mile of the town, they were heavily ambushed, and Cuff ordered a fighting retreat. While the lieutenant and four men fought as rearguard, protecting the others, they were surrounded and killed. Steele managed to get back with the survivors. Lt. Glenn Weeks led a rescue party. "I took out all available men, but in the meantime our casualties were many. Lt. Cuff was killed after he was almost out of enemy territory. I got the main body out without any additional casualties. Total 15 killed or missing, one wounded. We evacuated 5 bodies."[11] The bodies of Cuff, Cpl. John Bosel, Cpl. John Cheeney, Pvt. Raymond Clemens, Pvt. Thurman Kissick, and Pvt. Irvin Wenger were recovered, but had been badly mutilated.[12] Lieutenant Cuff's arms and legs had been severed.[13]

On December 1, five of the men killed with Cuff were buried in the local cemetery in Shenkursk. Cuff was especially mourned. The lieutenant from Wisconsin was both popular and competent, so he was sent off with full military honors. His casket, mounted on a caisson, was taken to the cemetery with his steel helmet atop the coffin, and he "was given every military honor possible to bestow."[14]

Others on that patrol, Pvt. Henry Weitzel, Pvt. Nicholas Jonker, Pvt. Elmer Hodge, Pvt. Boleslaw Gutowski, and Pvt. Johnnie Triplett, disappeared during that action, but the search for their bodies was fruitless. Eventually, they were declared killed in action.

One happy event occurred on December 2. After Cuff's funeral, two men missing from the patrol stumbled into camp. One was Pvt. Roy Clemens, brother of the slain Ray Clemens, and with him Private Greenlund. For almost four days they had outwitted the Reds by hiding in deep snow and moving constantly to avoid succumbing to the twenty-below temperatures. They were ragged and half-starved, with badly frostbitten fingers and feet, but alive.

By that time, it was obvious that there was trouble ahead for isolated Vaga forces. They were supposed to be protected by the advances of the Railroad and Dvina Forces by early January 1919. With the failure of these movements, the southernmost Allied position at Ust Padenga was badly overextended, with Shenkursk almost as vulnerable.

Ust Padenga was a typical village with clusters of huts and cabins stretched along the Vaga River. Besides the central village of Ust Padenga itself, slightly south of it, closer to the woods, were the few houses of Nizhni Gora, and to the north was the cluster of buildings known as Visorka Gora, separated from the central village by a stream that circled to the south.

After the patrol ambush, Company C remained in Ust Padenga, alert and anxious. Meanwhile, Company A was in Shenkursk patrolling and scouting outside town and in nearby Shegovari. In mid-December, Company A moved back to Ust Padenga, and Company C went back to Shenkursk. The Ust Padenga routine was to establish one platoon on the hill at Nizhni Gora, rotating that duty each week. The rest of the company was in Ust Padenga itself with a company of Cossacks. Captain Odjard's headquarters was in Visorka Gora, with one Russian artillery section and a platoon of engineers. Odjard's position was on a high bluff, almost a mile from his other platoons. The snow was almost thirty inches deep, and the Vaga was frozen solid by mid-January. The increased Bolshevik activity was evidenced by a white-clad Bolo shot by one of the doughboys only fifteen feet from the American outpost.

On January 19, Lt. Harry Meade, with forty-four men of his fourth platoon, relieved Lieutenant MacPhail's second platoon in Nizhni Gora, with orders from the British to hold at all costs. He woke to hear artillery landing near his cabin. Adjusting his field glasses, Meade saw swarms of Soviets, dressed in white, moving across the plains in the distance. As the heavy Red bombardment continued, Meade's men readied for the attack. Suddenly, the barrage lifted. Facing the Americans were not the distant Reds, but hundreds of Soviets barely one hundred yards down the hill from the doughboys. They had crawled forward during the night and covered themselves with snow. When the artillery stopped, the snow-covered Soviet infantry could spring into action. The Americans opened fire and slowed the charging Soviets, but they swept on, despite their losses. The Allied Cossacks, to their credit, came up to support the defenders, and even though their commander was killed as they approached, they accomplished some relief in the day's fight. Cpl. Victor Stier picked up a Cossack machine gun and laid down a withering fire, but was hit in the jaw.

Lieutenant Meade saw his embattled force caught in a hopeless vise and ordered a fast retreat. It was a desperate time for Meade's little group as they struggled through deep snow, downhill, exposed, and taking casualties as they went. The hard-packed road was being swept by Soviet fire, so the Yanks were forced to flounder through the heavy snows in the village on their retreat. The subzero temperature made breathing painful and movement exhausting. As they retreated, they waited in vain for supporting artillery fire from the Russian artillerymen in Visorka Gora.

Finally, the pitiful few who survived passed through Ust Padenga, at last getting the supporting rifle, machine gun, and artillery fire they so urgently needed. Captain Odjard was running to the artillery camp when he met the Russian gunners, panicked and deserting. Pulling his pistol, he forced them back to their guns to begin their supporting fire.

The price was high. By the time they reached Visorka Gora, Meade's forty-five-member platoon numbered seven unwounded fighting men. The three-hour retreat turned Meade's hair completely white.[15] Meade remembered later, "One by one men fell either wounded or dead in the snow, either to die from his wounds or from the terrible exposure."[16] Of his original platoon, Meade lost twenty-one killed, including four who died of wounds later, and fifteen wounded, plus three cases of shell shock.[17] Only four bodies were recovered; seventeen were listed as missing, and none of that seventeen was ever located. It was not only the worst battle in terms of casualties, but it began a series of retreats that ended with the American withdrawal from North Russia several months later.

Heroism was routine during the fight. When Lieutenant McPhail saw Corporal Stier signal weakly from the bloody snow near Ust Padenga, he took Odjard's horse into heavy fire to bring back the corporal, who died the next day.[18] Cpl. Giussepe De Amicis, trying to stop a Bolo charge with his Lewis gun, died refusing to leave his gun. McPhail, Sergeants Trombley, Nees, and Rapp, and Private Kuna went after the wounded. "The five set out along that death strewn road, back into the relentless rain of shell and fire, back into the valley where the wounded and dying lay among the dead awaiting they knew not what."[19] As darkness fell on the first day, it was as if a sudden curtain had fallen on a great tragedy.

On January 20, two survivors of the Nizhni Gora massacre returned to Visorka Gora. Pvt. Peter Wierenga and Cpl. James Burbridge had lost touch with the platoon and found themselves trapped inside the Red lines. They found refuge in a closet provided by a friendly villager, killed two captors, and floundered through the snowy woods until they arrived at the Allied camp, half frozen and starved. That day was also marked by the deaths of Victor Stier and Pvt. George Smith, both of whom had been badly wounded on the retreat.

Wagons from Shenkursk, loaded with supplies and ready to carry wounded doughboys back to safety, arrived with a small amount of mail bringing news from peaceful little Michigan towns, news that contrasted sharply with the horrors of the day.[20]

The Nizhni Gora rout was not the end of the Ust Padenga nightmare. As the forces withdrew from Nizhni Gora and Ust Padenga to the bluffs of Visorka Gora, the Bolsheviks continued their attacks with massed artillery, causing extensive damage to the few buildings on the bluff. Realizing his exposed position and the overwhelming numbers of Soviets, Odjard waited for orders to withdraw. But the British high command was silent.

A wagon driven by Wagoner Carl Berger of Headquarters Company arrived from Shenkursk on January 19. It was part of an almost endless train of ambulances taking the wounded to Shenkursk. While Berger was resting in one of the houses waiting to take more wounded, a dud shell came through the roof and decapitated him.[21] Canadian artillery under Lt. Douglas Winslow also arrived that day, a relief for the Americans, who trusted their Canadian neighbors with their lives, and they immediately launched counterbattery fire. At daybreak the following day, the Bolos launched a vicious attack on the deserted Ust Padenga, not realizing that the Americans were then all on the hilltop of Visorka Gora. From the bluff, the Canadians fired grapeshot at point-blank range, decimating the Reds. All that day, Red artillery poured shell after shell into the now vacant village. They finally took the village, finding nothing but rubble.

To support the beleaguered Allies, the RAF sent up the best planes they had to strafe and bomb the Soviet forces, doing their best to keep the village of Visorka Gora out of Bolo hands. Their efforts were helpful but could not stem the mass of Red soldiers, who continued to sweep across the fields despite heavy Canadian artillery fire and the automatic weapons of the Americans.[22]

Throughout the attacks and bombardments, Lt. Ralph Powers, medical officer of Company A, had been treating the wounded. He first set up operations in a dressing station, which was bombed out. Then, he moved to Lieutenant MacPhail's quarters; when that was hit several times, he moved on to the sergeant's quarters. There, while he was treating an amputee, a shell went through the wall, bursting just outside the room. It not only mortally wounded the doctor, but killed Sgt. Yates Rogers, Cpl. Milton Gottschalk, and Pvt. Elmer Cole. Sergeant Rogers had been one of the platoon favorites, joking and keeping spirits up; his death hit everyone hard.

> Corp. Boren hastily entering the room, lifted Sgt. Rodgers [sic] from the floor where he had been thrown by the shell concussion. No flesh was torn, no blood flowed, but he lay limp and motionless. As though even fate had dealt gently with so much life and youth there was not a mark or bruise on the length of his big body, but 'Curly' too was dead. His jokes would never set the barracks in a roar again. His unquenchable spirit of laughter would never again relieve the tension and calm the raw nerves of an outgoing guard or patrol. Curly was dead.[23]

The orders to leave finally came at 11:00 P.M. on January 22; by 1:10 A.M. the entire force was moving out toward Shenkursk, covered by darkness, but still harassed by shell fire. The Canadians were upset because they had to leave one of their guns, since the horses that pulled the piece had been killed. The gun was stripped, the block removed, and it was left disabled by the side of the road.[24] An intelligence officer in Shenkursk wrote on January 22:

> They are sure out there in force right enough. The clans are rapidly gathering for the big prize—Shenkursk. Later—Orders from British Headquarters for troops at Ust Padenga to withdraw tonight. 10:00 P.M.—There is a red glare in the sky in the direction of Ust Padenga and the flames of burning buildings are plain to be seen.[25]

Although the retreat was not a rout, it was a disheartened lot of Allies who trudged wearily out of Visorka Gora, bitter at the loss of life and the feeling of abandonment. The artillery had failed them until Canadians arrived; the order to withdraw was issued only after all had been lost; and although the massive number of Soviets facing them was known, little had been done to protect the troops from the crushing defeat.

The order to retreat was delayed so long that the Reds were able to get behind the forces at Ust Padenga, occupying towns on both sides of the Vaga River. There had been a brief rest in Shalosha on their way to their next destination, Spasskoye, but there were few fires, little warm food, and scanty shelter. The men were exhausted, frozen, hungry and demoralized. Once they got to Spasskoye in the early hours of January 23, there was little relief. Lieutenant Mead found a house with a bed after they arrived; he almost made it to the bed, but fell asleep in a rocking chair before he reached it. Lieutenant MacPhail found him and remarked, "I thought, my gosh, just three more steps and he could have fallen on the only bed I saw in Russia."[26] By MacPhail's count, he had slept ten hours in six days.

As they entered Spasskoye, Canadian gunnery captain Ollie Mowatt and Lieutenant Mead climbed a church tower on the village square, only to discover hordes of enemy infantry and artillery on all the roads leading into town. A battle began once again. To make the most of their small artillery pieces, the Canadians moved one gun in plain sight on the crest of a hill, but one of the first casualties was to that gun crew and the officers closest to the Bolo lines. A shell made a direct hit on one piece, wounding both Captain Odjard and Captain Mowatt; Mowatt later died of his wound.

The battle in Spasskoye was summarized in Pvt. John Crissman's diary:

We left here at 1:15 A.M. and hiked to Spasska where we put up for the night. Canadians are here with one piece of artillery. We slept until 9 A.M. About noon the enemy attacked and a battle was on for all day and guns from Shenkursk fired on our enemy. Enemy guns opened on us and nearly destroyed the town. Captain Odjard was wounded and several others also. About 3 P.M. received orders to retreat. Retreated under heavy fire and arrived at Shenkursk safely about 5 P.M., Had supper and went to bed. About 11 P.M. we were told to get ready to leave, carrying nothing but overcoat, rations, gun and belt. We hiked all night single file through woods without noise or smoking. Hike was very tiresome.[27]

Soon after the survivors of Ust Padenga staggered into Shenkursk, there was a funeral procession for twelve of the dead whose bodies had been recovered. It was a solemn procession that moved through the streets of Shenkursk, which was no longer a rear area. "Preparations for the funeral were hurried to make way for what must be done for the living but in spite of the impending crisis everything was done that conditions would allow and care could suggest."[28] Since there was no chaplain in the town, the ceremony was led by Lt. Charles Warner; three volleys and taps ended the solemn service. The grave markers were never placed because the Soviet bombardment began again, driving everyone to shelter.

British commanders were finally absorbing the full impact of the Bolshevik offensive. Between Shenkursk and the main Allied base at Bereznik on the Dvina River, more than one hundred miles away, were two Allied-occupied positions. The closest was Shegovari, forty-four miles away, then Kitsa, twenty miles beyond. These were weak positions, with only three platoons between them. With the massive Red Army approaching Shenkursk, there was little choice: the British headquarters in Bereznik ordered a further retreat. It was easier ordered than achieved, because the Soviets had sent strong raiding parties to cut off Allied withdrawal. That meant that all main routes north were in enemy hands. The local Russians told of one old trail that was sometimes used for travel to Shegovari. After scouts had determined that it was open, the route was chosen, and the whole Shenkursk Allied force stole silently out of town, single file, followed by Russian Tsarists, more afraid of the Bolos than the dark, hostile woods and subzero temperatures. Before they left, an RAF plane traveled the route flying at three hundred feet, seeing no sign of the Reds, a minor miracle.[29]

The British officers ordered the troops to retreat, but to leave the wounded behind. The American officers refused to leave without their injured and found sleds and carts to move them out, although it meant abandoning virtually everything else, including ammunition, rations, equipment, and medical supplies. The reasoning for not burning the town was that it would alert the Reds to the Allied withdrawal and cause ambushes on the road. It was a humiliating decision.

Ambushes were not the primary concern, however, as the march began. The Shackleton boots were fine boots for certain conditions, but they were not made for marching long distances. They were long and wide, allowing for several pair of socks, but were ungainly and awkward for walking. Shackleton himself was in Murmansk at the time, and the Yanks fervently wished he were along for their hike. It was not long before almost all the men had thrown their boots in the snow and marched in their socks. Lieutenant MacPhail had eleven pair of socks, plus overshoes, and when they had a rest stop, one of his men said that Coon Dog Williams feet were freezing because he had only three pair of socks. "So I gave Coon Dog my overshoes, a good snort of rum and a cigar to chew and the never-down-hearted rascal said, 'Let's go. I can march to Archangel now!'"[30] Many tales developed, even some poetry, concerning the footwear, such as the one described in *The Ignorant Armies:* "It required the development of a new gait altogether—a kind of half-waddle, half-dance step which soon became known as the Shackleton Walk. (One step forward and two steps back—a sideslip down with a hell of a whack)."[31]

Moving the wounded was an agonizing process. To keep them from freezing, the wounded were stuffed into sleeping bags, their only means of keeping warm. One of the medics of the 337th Ambulance Company, Pvt. Godfrey Johnson, wrote, "Some of these were so badly injured that the slightest touch would cause excruciating agony. But there was need for urgent haste and we had no alternative but to stuff the patient in the bag as best we could despite his agonized screams."[32]

The march was done with minimum light; daylight lasted at most six hours with temperatures conservatively recorded as twenty to forty below zero. As the column moved slowly out of Shenkursk, unknown troubles lay in store. Canteens froze solid, so there was little to drink; the road soon turned into a rutted, pitted trail that tripped and bruised the troops and accompanying Russian civilians. Even with the cold, they began to sweat inside their layered clothes, and they soon had icicles forming on their noses and mouths. With poor boots, rutted, frozen roads, pitch-black darkness, frostbitten extremities, and the possibility of a Bolo attack at any moment, the march resembled a frozen hell.

The guns of the Canadian artillery led the march, followed by some one hundred sleds of wounded, then the troops, and finally the Russian civilians who chose to risk the trip. Gradually, possessions were dropped—packs, rations, even overcoats—as fatigue took over. By the time the column reached Shegovari, the Canadians had lost four guns, and the rest of the men were down to absolutely minimum weight. During the march, the Russian Allied troops found the route too risky and fled for safer areas, probably to the Bolo lines.

At Shegovari, elements of Companies C and D held off a Soviet attack on January 23. Actually, it was local partisans who attacked, rather than the Bolsheviks. They were mostly peasants who were slated for conscription into the Allied army, but preferred to join the Reds. As the partisans approached Shegovari from the south, they captured the lone sentry, Pvt. Anton J. Vanis, without raising the alarm.[33] The next sentry, positioned just north of Vanis's post, was Pvt. Frank Syska, whom they killed with a blow to the head. They crept closer, still undiscovered, and were almost at the guardhouse when they were detected. They attacked by throwing grenades through the window, but few actually exploded. One did detonate, wounding the unit commander Lt. Harry Steele, but the attack was driven off. Only one dead attacker was found; he was a native of a neighboring town.[34]

With the arrival of the retreating column in Shegovari, the force was still no match for the Reds, so the retreat continued. Eventually, they arrived at Vistafka, where they made an attempt to fortify and defend the town, letting the main column pass through to the next village, Kitsa. The nighttime retreats were described by Godfrey Johnson: "Travelling in the nighttime as we did, that forest became a gloomy, sinister, ominous wilderness, fraught with hidden menace."[35] Companies A and C stayed on outpost in Vistafka and found themselves under constant pressure from the Reds. The Reds could probably have launched a major assault and wiped out the Allied command, but were content to harass and shell the defenders. Occasionally, they launched infantry attacks, but most of their damage was done by artillery. On January 29, they launched a furious bombardment, according to Pvt. Gus Grossa of Company C: "One awful day, if we get out of here alive it will be a miracle. At 3:00 A.M. Bolos get range on our billets, poured it on us."[36] Sgt. Wilbur Smith of Company C was killed that morning; Pvt. Isiador Dunaetz died two days later; and Thomas Keefe was killed, but his body never found.

The story of Isiador Dunaetz was a sordid example of the experiences of the wounded in that long, cold evacuation. The medic assigned to unload the wounded was Private Johnson. As Dunaetz was being taken off the sled, his hair was frozen to the straw, and he complained that they were pulling his hair. Johnson said, "Taking a closer look we noticed he had been creased by a bullet along the left side of the skull and the brains had oozed out and were frozen to the straw, and in moving him we were actually pulling out his brains."[37] The surgeon worked on him that night, but to no avail. The other passenger on Dunaetz's sled had been hit with machine gun bullets in both thighs; the Bolos were using dum-dum bullets that broke up on contact with a body and caused massive exit wounds. As he was having his wounds dressed and packed with gauze, he was asked if it hurt much. He truthfully said, "If it don't nothin' ever did."[38] Eventually, the sleds with the wounded made it back to the relatively safe city of Berezenik, where the 337th had set up a field hospital and more adequate treatment could be given to those who survived the trip.

On January 29, Company D was sent back to the Dvina River column, and Company A, relieved by Scots, rested in Kitsa. Private Grossa of Company C reported his misery on February 1, 1919. "It will be a gift of providence if we ever get out of here. Tedichi accidentally shot in hand. Have not washed, shaved, or changed clothes since Jan 22. Am loaded with cooties and they never seem to get tired or fed up."[39]

Another Bolo infantry attack on February 4 surprised the outposts at Vistafka, and Company C lost three more men killed: Pvt. Nikodem Ladovich, Pvt. Joshua Clark, and the cook Elmer Speicher. The front then remained quiet until March 9. Company A had taken over the outpost at Vistafka. There the Soviets massed an artillery and infantry assault on March 9, with reportedly four thousand troops.[40] Fighting was brief, but took the lives of Sgt. Albert Moore, Cpl. Bernard Kenney, Pvt. Earl Sweet, Pvt. Dausie Trammell, and Pvt. Walter Welstead. Pvt. Benny Rose lived for two days with wounds that almost severed both legs, dying on March 11. With Vistafka a smoking ruin from the shelling and fighting, the Americans and Canadians withdrew on the night of March 9 to a line of defense some three versts in front of Kitsa. It was a poor place to defend, mostly in the open, but fortunately, the Soviets were unable to bring artillery fire to bear. Here parts of Company F joined Company D, who had relieved the battered Company A. The doughboys alternated duty with the Royal Scots for two months, until it was time to go home.[41]

That was the story of the Vaga Force; in fulfilling their original mission to protect the Dvina units, they suffered the most casualties of any of the AEFNR units. Their orders put them in untenable positions with but a few men pitted against mounting numbers of effective Red soldiers. They had inadequate artillery support and were using unfamiliar equipment, which had replaced their regulation issue. These men, perhaps more than most, had reasons to be both bitter and critical.

Finally, in May 1919 the weather warmed, the ice broke up, and boats could once again bring the doughboys back to the Archangel area. Company F, however, would remain until June.

The Pinega Front

The Reds certainly had plenty of courage. They came deliberately up and fired at us. You could see they were experienced soldiers, for they attacked us from every available point of shelter.

—Pvt. John Toornman, Company G

IN the Allied strategy, the Pinega front was probably the last planned and the least significant. Its purpose was the protection of the more important forces to its west; there was no plan to advance toward a major objective.

The railroad front, with its protective elements in Onega and in Seletskoye was optimistically assigned to move not only to Plesetskaya with its railway significance, but on to Vologda for possible merging with other Allied or loyal Russian troops. The Dvina Force, with its auxiliary Vaga Force, was to head for Kotlas and then on to Viatka to join with Czech units trying to reach the western front through Archangel.

Although Pinega was not as strategic a location as the other fronts, it was equally remote. Pinega sat at the apex of a huge split in the Pinega River, one hundred miles east of Archangel. As a city it was reasonably prosperous, with three thousand citizens and a local government that was a curious mix of White and Red Russians. As the revolution swept Russia, the city accepted some of the Red influence, but tempered the Communist presence with trusted old citizen-leaders who were more anti-Tsarist than pro-Red.

A primary need in Pinega was flour. Towns in the area, needing flour for the coming winter, found a source by buying from the stockpile of military stores and provisions supplied by the Allies. Shipments had arrived in Archangel for months, but were gradually confiscated by the Reds before the Allied arrival. Actually, little remained of the mountains of war goods shipped for Russia's use against Germany. But during one of the windows of opportunity, the Pinega district was able to acquire substantial quantities of flour.

In October 1918, the mixed Red-White government, ignoring ideological differences, requested military assistance from Allied headquarters in Archangel, hoping to protect their source of flour. Capt. John Conway and two platoons of Company G were sent on this mission of mercy. On October 20, 1918, Conway's little unit left their comfortable Archangel quarters, boarded a fast steamer towing one barge, and three days and two nights later took up their new duties in Pinega.[1] For the most part, the Americans were well received. These were new faces, speaking new languages, wearing new uniforms, bringing plenty of cigarettes, candy, and other scarce items.

Almost as soon as Company G arrived, pressures began to mount from Archangel headquarters to clear the Reds from the Pinega Valley. Finally, British GHQ ordered Conway to send a force up the valley to Karpogora, 90 versts from Pinega. The expedition planned by Captain Conway included support by Russians under the command of Colonel Shaposhnikoff. The Russians would attack the Bolshevik rear as Conway's men made the frontal assault. On November 15, Lieutenant Higgins took 35 men and 210 Russian volunteers up the Pinega Valley. For ten days they found no sign of the Reds, but light resistance began soon after; still, they took Karpogora on November 28, Thanksgiving Day, and the Bolos moved out to nearby Verkola, where they had strong fortifications.

One of the men on that expedition, Pvt. John Toornman, later wrote of his experiences:

> All the way from Pinega to Kopogora we did not have a doctor or a nurse or any medical help. The white Russians had one man with a satchel with some first-aid. I saw him only once with the White Russians. I think that later they talked about a hospital in Pinega but I never saw it. No newspapers, no magazines, no toilet paper, no writing paper, and not enough food once we were away from Pinega.[2]

Their stay in Karpogora was brief; such a small force in an isolated area was a perfect target for growing Soviet forces.

During the Allied occupation of the town, the quarters were cold and drafty. One of the larger members of the platoon was bitter and not at all reluctant about expressing his displeasure.

> This fellow was a farmer and really hated the army. He would start cussing, "The son of a bitch, President Wilson," through the "S.O.B., General Pershing," then would begin on our officers from the top down. In between the fellows would tease him, asking how he would like a steak with all the trimmings, etc. . . . But he would keep on cussing. Then the door opened and Lieutenant Higgins stood there. The big fellow had his knees under his chin trying to cover himself with his too-short overcoat. The coats were sheep-skin lined and warm, had a large collar. Barkel had it turned up over his face, but because everyone stopped laughing and teasing him, he turned the collar down and saw the lieutenant, but kept cussing and said to the lieutenant, "And you, too, you son of a bitch. This damn army. If there was a place to run to, I'd be out of here so damn quick. But there is no place to run to." Lt. Higgins was not a bad officer, I thought. He smiled at us, never said a word and went out.[3]

Lieutenant Higgins reported to Captain Conway, and Conway to Archangel, that he needed artillery and reinforcements to take Verkola, the next objective. Headquarters had no intention of sending valuable artillery to Pinega, and reinforcements were not available at the moment, so Higgins remained in Karpogora. Meanwhile, he awaited Colonel Shaposhnikoff and his three hundred or so loyal Russians, who were to join him in his next move. The Russian commander sent word that he had lost track of his troops somehow. Captain Conway, in Pinega, wired Higgins that he really should not depend too much on the newly recruited Russians. On December 2, after having been ordered to hold Karpogora, Conway was told by Archangel headquarters to keep in mind that his primary mission was the defense of Pinega.[4]

On December 4, the Reds attacked Karpogora in force and were beaten off with heavy losses; Company G lost two men killed and four wounded.[5] Private Toornman was in the middle of the battle as a machine gunner. He and his gun section under Sgt. Mike Burke were dug in on one side of the main road leading into town; Sgt. Edward Young, with his gun, was across the road. Toornman and Pvt. Clarence Malm were walking toward the mess hall in town when heavy shelling began. They were always hungry and hated to miss even their meager breakfast, but as shells began dropping closer, they scurried back to their hole. The shelling was the beginning, followed by brief glimpses of infantry forming in the woods. The Bolos were experienced and daring;

they began a series of short forty-yard rushes, after which they flopped in the snow out of sight. Early in the fight, Young's gun was knocked out, then Toornman's gun jammed.

> The Reds certainly had plenty of courage. They came deliberately up and fired at us. You could see they were experienced soldiers, for they attacked us from every available point of shelter. They came to within thirty yards of our line. Their was no mistaking their nerve. About this time our machine gun went on the bum.[6]

Just before the gun jammed, Clarence Malm was hit by a bullet in the head, killing him instantly. About ten minutes later, Pvt. Jay Pitts was killed, and Private Stark wounded.[7] The firing kept up until 8:00 P.M., but the Reds never came closer than their early charge.

After the smoke cleared from the December 4 battle, Colonel Stewart said, "it was decided that the occupation of Karpogora was inadvisable and the attacking force withdrew after the engagement of December 4 to Pinega, leaving detachments (of Russian troops) at Trufangora, Visokogor and Priluka."[8] It is not clear who made the decision, but it certainly seemed logical. In fact, Toornman's memoirs indicate that shortly after the Reds ceased firing at 8:00 P.M., orders were received to move out toward Pinega, leaving another mound of military equipment and provisions to the Bolsheviks.

As the Americans and Russians beat their hasty retreat, horses and sleds were used to transport what they could take of the equipment, as well as the wounded, and the bodies of Malm and Pitts. Toornman remembered the bitter cold. "I remember walking beside our horse and every once in awhile sticking my face into his long thick hair and remembering how good it felt."[9] Later, a report said:

> It is proposed at an early date to relieve Capt. Conway, and the two platoons now at Pinega by an American company which will be under the command of a more senior and more experienced officer who it is hoped will be able to take hold of the situation and reorganize where necessary and stabilize the situation on this front.[10]

On Thanksgiving Day Capt. Joel Moore, commanding Company M, shared a fine roast beef dinner with Major Nichols, French Major Albernarde, and a Miss Ogden of the YMCA at Verst 455. The next day he returned to his unit at the front line at Verst 445. Eight days later, he was surprised to learn that his unit was ordered to the Pinega front. On December 11, he divided the company in two sections; first and fourth platoons and Headquarters Company with Lieutenants Stoner and Wright would leave for Pinega with Captain Moore. Lieutenants Primm

and Wieczorek with their second and third platoons, all under Lieutenant Donovan, were to stay in Obozerskaya and follow later. These last
two platoons were kept to be part of Colonel Lucas's December plan to
capture Plesetskaya.[11] Moore remembered later, "One of the most memorable events in the history of our company in Russia was the march
from Archangel to Pinega in dead of winter."[12] They knew that a march
when daylight hours were shortest was risky, but they knew that Company G needed help.

The men left on December 18, finally reaching Pinega on December 27. This was not at all like Company G's easy three-day boat trip.
The second day, they marched only from 8:40 A.M. to 12:15 P.M., when
light disappeared in the heavy forest and there was no way to see the
many obstacles in the road. The men were exhausted, and the temperatures plunged well below zero, but fortunately, they found quarters
with the villagers. The march continued with stops in Liavla, Koskogar,
Kholmogori, the monastery, Ust Pinega, Verkhne Palenga—each was a
memory filled with cold and hunger. The troops rested in a monastery
for one whole day, but exhaustion and illness took its toll, and five men
were left at Ust Pinega to recover.

Besides the stress of the travel, there was the overwhelming gloom
of the Arctic dark. One soldier wrote, "Harbinger of hope, oh you red
sky line! Shall we see the sun today?"[13] The Shackleton boots reappeared as the curse of mankind, making walking even more difficult
than ever; finally, orders were passed down the line to discard them
and put on the less protective, but more mobile, field boot. The rugged
Russian ponies, seemingly oblivious to cold or the challenge of the
trail, dominated their caravan, and the Yankees' admiration for the little
animals grew with each passing day.

As the column moved along, requiring quarters with the villagers
at night, the mood changed in the homes of their hosts. On Christmas
Day, the column halted overnight in Leunova, and here the people were
described as "lukewarm" toward the Allies. That seemed to be the exception, as other villagers saw these foreigners as a break in their rather
humdrum existence.

The weary column reached Pinega on December 27, ragged but
ready to assume its duties. On the same day, the Allied Russian troops,
left behind by Lieutenant Higgins in the towns of Trufangora, Visogora,
and Priluka, abandoned them after weak Red assaults.

Captain Moore had explained to the men of Company M the purpose of the Pinega effort, which he repeated in his February 20 report
to Ironside:

> I really think, sir, that I have two missions here. One is to make the de-
> fenses of PINEGA so formidable as to discourage further advances of Reds

in this area. And their burning of the villages around themselves makes it look as though they were assuming the defensive. Second, I am to inspire and develop self-reliance among Russian troops. I believe I am getting results.[14]

Stewart's report noted that Company M's other two platoons arrived in Pinega in good order on January 14 "after marching most of the distance of two hundred and four versts [approximately 135 miles] with temperatures of 40 degrees below zero Fahrenheit."[15]

Two Soviet commanders in charge of the Pinega area, Comrades Smelkoff and Kulikoff, were both committed to driving out these foreign troops. Company M, the platoons of Company G, and the new loyal Russian commander, Captain Akutin, were charged with Pinega's defense. Moore reported on several occasions that he was getting on well with Akutin, and his diplomatic relations with the strangely mixed Pinega government seemed to be harmonious. Although things seemed quiet inside the Pinega perimeter, however, the Reds were conscripting, propagandizing, and using other tactics to turn the peasants (*muzhiks*) against the Americans, who were considered by many to be pro-Monarchist. The defense of the area was borne mostly by the loyal Russian Allied troops. The Americans were held in reserve in the city, while the Russian troops manned the outer defenses, taking periodic casualties, but learning the arts of war and defense. So far, the only American casualties were those taken by Company G on their excursion to the valley. On January 31, one last Allied offensive effort was made to keep the Soviets off balance. Russian troops, with Americans in support, scouted the Bolos in Sayola, but with the discovery of forces outnumbering them two to one, the expedition retreated to Pinega without American casualties.[16]

By the end of January, the Reds had learned of the successes on other fronts, and their aggression was fueled by the impotence of the Allies. What the Soviets had originally believed to be a massive Allied invasion had proved to be a collection of highly vulnerable, small units in isolated posts. While the Allies could inflict heavy casualties, there was not much doubt about the ultimate success of an all-out Soviet attack. To some Allies, it seemed as if the Bolos were reluctant to press for complete victory, a drive to the White Sea, but preferred to keep pressure on in the various limited offensives that made up the North Russian campaign of the winter of 1918–1919.

The major task of Americans in Pinega was instruction: training machine gunners, mortar men, artillerists, even medics, so the Russian troops could fend for themselves after the Americans returned to Archangel. There were hosts of experiences in Pinega: a firing squad executing a Russian officer for desertion in the face of the enemy; the coldest day of the winter, with a temperature of 52 degrees below zero; the fire that burned the high school used as a barracks; and the frustration of fighting in such bitter weather. Moore wrote:

> Did you have any trouble keeping the crowd away from the fire the night of January 4th when your barracks burned? Not hardly any. The grenades bursting in that building drove all but the firefighters away. . . . it was Private Sapp who was killed later at Bolsheozerke road, who distinguished himself fighting the fire that night.[17]

One unhappy event included the selection of Burke's machine gun section to participate in the execution of a Russian. Burke's section stopped in sight of an open grave with a Russian officer standing in front of it. Private Toornman described the procedure:

> A row of Russian soldiers lined up facing the officer. Then we lined up behind them, covering them with our machine gun. More than one of them looked back, wondering what we were going to do behind them. Someone up front read Russian from a paper. The officer was blindfolded but he pulled it off and threw it on the ground. Then he crossed himself. The firing squad raised their rifles and fired. He went down like his legs were putty.[18]

Toornman wrote that the only time he spoke to Captain Conway was shortly after the execution. The captain asked Toornman how he liked the execution.

> I told him I did not like it because I did not know why, or what he was shot for. Then he told me he had visited the Russian officer where he was kept under guard, then said "And when I left him I left my gun on the table." I asked him, "What for?" He said "so he could shoot himself." That was something I couldn't understand.[19]

He saw other evidences of the savagery of that war:

> The English had intelligence officers with red bands around their caps. When they wanted to arrest someone, they would ask for a squad of Americans to go along. I went on two trips. We would go on a couple of sleighs, mostly at night, surround the house so no one could get away, as there were no locks on the doors. Someone would then go inside and get a light and get the family out of bed. By this time all of us would be inside to get out of the cold. Grandma, mother and the children would all be crying by this time. The husband was told to get dressed. His wife gave him a couple of coins and we took him along. A few days later a fellow

whom I knew from Kalamazoo told me that they had taken the husband to the river, then stuck him with bayonets until he had backed into a hole in the ice. This was the place where everyone came to get water every day. The man who was killed had been suspected of being a Bolo.[20]

Later, Toornman was a witness to the Bolo slaying of a White Russian patrol. They had been captured and killed and their bodies left in a village. The Yanks found the frozen corpses and discovered that they had been brutally butchered. Toorman visited the hospital in Pinega, which had been a gymnasium before the war. Most of the patients were Russian soldiers, wounded in the constant skirmishes in outlying outposts.

> The wounded were sitting on the floor with their backs against the wall. The only person I saw there in this large room was an old woman with a large pan in her hands and a wooden spoon, walking from one to another wounded offering them a few spoons of food. Some would shake their heads. Others would take some. The smell was horrible.[21]

Through the months of January and February, the Reds continued to build up their forces, threatening the villages outside Pinega, constantly pressuring the front-line Russian troops. Inside the city, the remaining Red sympathizers appeared again, hoping the Soviet advance would capture the city and install a Red government. But, at the last minute, the Bolsheviks would always withdraw, and the city would regain its life. The Allies were getting the message that the Reds really wanted only to continue applying pressure, not to gain decisive victories. The Reds burned their advance bases and pulled back to their strongholds and waited. Captain Moore puzzled about it: "Why? Americans here at Pinega, like the vastly more desperate and shattered American forces on the Vaga and at Kodish at the same time, had seen their fate sealed, and then seen the Reds unaccountably withhold the final blow."[22]

The Russian Red Cross was a vital part of the entertainment that was so helpful during the long dark days of January and February. They put on plays, concerts, ballet, folk dancing, all followed by great Russian food. American Red Cross major Williams made a fast trip to dispense Red Cross parcels and Christmas packages in December. He passed Company M on its way to the new Pinega front.

> Up on the Pinega River, many miles from any place we passed a considerable body of American soldiers headed for the front. Every man was the picture of health, cheeks aglow, head up and on the job. These same men were on the Railroad front—four hundred miles in another direction—

when I had seen them last. . . . From our sled supply every man was given a package of Red Cross cigarettes, and every man was asked if he had received his Christmas stocking. They all had.[23]

Even on the isolated outposts of North Russia, the doughboys received and welcomed this kind of attention.

The success of the Pinega front was that it embodied the program that had been set out from the beginning: Allied troops were to train and prepare Russian troops to man the front lines and bear the brunt of the Red attacks. Throughout the American stay, the relations between Yanks, *muzhiks*, and the local government were harmonious, if they were not always in total agreement. It became evident by mid-March, after weeks of such reports as "Routine garrison and outpost duties and patrolling without casualties during above period," that the doughboys could be used to better advantage on other fronts.[24] On March 4, Company M received the order to return to Archangel, and on March 10, Captain Moore was officially replaced by Russian lieutenant colonel Delatorski as Officer Commanding Allied Troops in Pinega.

The two platoons of Company G stayed on.[25] Their job was to keep the telegraph lines open between Archangel and Pinega. To do this, it was necessary to keep small garrisons on the road between the two cities. One garrison of eight men was sent to the town of Gabach, where they could patrol in either direction to keep wires repaired and communications open. Pvt. John Toornman was one of the men in Gabach. According to him, they never had it so good. Billeted in the upstairs of a decent house with no officers to answer to, he found these days to be the happiest of his army career. He was no fan of his officers and frequently wrote remarks about his captain, who was living too well, with too much female companionship, isolating himself from the men. Without officers, the garrison at Gabach performed its duties daily and relaxed. It became so relaxed, however, that the eight men began to slack off on their guard duties. They reasoned that the Reds could capture them with ease if they wished to, so standing guard in the bitter cold was pointless. Gradually, they developed a pattern of standing guard only when Allied personnel came through the town.[26] Gabach would be the scene of one of the most bizarre episodes of the expedition.

Sgt. Edward Young had been wounded at Karpogora in December, and his wounds had not healed properly. In mid-March, Young and Sgt. Michael Macalla were detailed to go to Archangel. The two arrived in Gabach on March 16, 1919, and were billeted in the same house as Toornman. Sometime during the night, Young used his service revolver to end his life. Toornman's memoirs indicate the cause of death was ruled accidental, but the official records showed the death was suicide. It was decided that Macalla would continue on to Archangel, still many miles away, taking Young's body with him. He left on his sleigh, alone, in subzero Russian weather. Young's body was frozen stiff in no time; to screen the body from view, it was wrapped in two of Toornman's blankets and rode silently next to Macalla as they departed for Archangel.

Macalla's first night was spent with villagers, who sensed his cargo and offered little in the way of hospitality. His second night was worse, with the villagers refusing to give the pony and sled any shelter; it stood outside for all to see with its blanket-shrouded corpse. The villagers were greatly relieved when he left the next day. The third night he was allowed shelter, but only in the village dead house, where a deceased villager's body awaited burial; Macalla slept between the two cadavers. His last night was the worst. He became lost in a snowstorm and found a little shelter under a large tree. But he was befuddled by fatigue, cold, and the continual presence of his dead friend. Finally, he unwrapped Young's body and used the blankets for his own protection, mumbling apologies to the late Sergeant Young as he did so. "I guess I was a little out of my head at this point," he remarked. He finished his journey with great relief and delivered the body to the medical personnel in Archangel.[27]

Eventually, Toornman's section returned to Pinega where he continued to man his machine gun in the defensive perimeter around Pinega. Although records are sketchy about exact dates, the two platoons of Company G were ordered back to Archangel, leaving the Pinega front to the Russians. A report of U.S. troop disposition for April 17, 1919, indicated the two platoons were then in Archangel.[28] The march back was much harder than the boat trip up to Pinega and lacked the rum supplied on the original passage. It was spring, probably April. Much of the march was on the frozen Pinega River, which unfortunately had begun to thaw, leaving a layer of slush and water covering almost all of the river. Toornman said that the men slept in villages at night, marching all day to the next population center.

> The bad part was that not all the villages were on the same side of the river. The river had several feet of water on top of the thick ice. When we had to cross everyone climbed on the heavily loaded sleighs to keep feet and legs dry. The rivers are very wide and the poor horses would be part way across and stop. It would take only a couple of minutes before the wide wooden runners would be frozen to the ice.[29]

Then it was "everybody off the sleigh" and back to the soggy river ice and wet feet.

Toornman's description of the men of Company G was a pathetic one:

> Some of us looked like tramps—our clothing torn, worn out, or with complete parts missing. Some, like me, wore boots made from reindeer skins. They were up to our knees and warm, bought from Eskimos. Those of us who left Pinega and went upriver where the fighting was never had a good night's sleep, or one good meal. We were always hungry. We had no time off. If one of us got hit, there were no doctors, no nurses, no hospitals, no baths, no shaving, no haircuts, no candles or any light, no matches, no toilet paper, no newspapers, no clean underwear, no new clothes to replace worn out uniforms, no pay (until we reached France), no drinking water unless we hauled it from the river through a hole in the ice, no bandages, and no mail from home to relieve a gloomy winter that was dark from mid-afternoon until late morning the next day. We put up with all of this for $30.00 a month, less the cost of our insurance.[30]

Eventually, the two platoons of Company G arrived in Archangel, set up camp, and did little until it was time for the trip home.

During the company's stay in Pinega, a new shipment of machine guns arrived from Archangel, but they were Russian-style and unfamiliar to the gunners of the American unit. Ivan, a young lad who had recently been discharged from the White Russian army for wounds he had received in South Russia, was able to assemble the new weapons and give simple instructions in how they could best be used. Ivan became attached to Company G, complete with uniform, mess kit, helmet, and all the Yankee equipment. When it came time for the company to leave, Ivan marched alongside, looking to all the world like a Yankee doughboy, and stayed with the unit as they camped in Archangel. He was one of many young Russians who came to the aid of the Americans, learned their methods, and made themselves useful in many ways.

When the Americans of the Pinega Force returned to Archangel after months of duty on the front, they saw an Archangel that was vastly different from the other cities they had visited.

In Archangel

*But those companies, like in the First and Third Battalions that did
get out in the field, they didn't see much of Archangel.*

— Cleo Coburn

BEFORE any Americans arrived, Archangel had already seen
its share of excitement. In January 1918, the Bolshevik Soviet took complete control of Archangel.[1] Although the Murmansk Soviet was friendly toward the Allies, the Archangel Soviet was not.

Because of the hostile Bolshevik government in Archangel, as the
Allied invasion force was leaving Murmansk to occupy Archangel, a
coup arranged by George Chaplin was under way to depose the local
Soviets and replace them with a new government with Chaikovsky at
its head. The coup was highly successful; the Reds fled south on every
conceivable type of watercraft, believing the Allied force to be much
larger than it was. There was only light firing in the south part of the
city on the afternoon of August 2 as the Allied fleet moved toward the
city. "By the evening the town was in the hands of a strong under-
ground force. The old national flag was once again fluttering over the
town hall."[2]

The consuls of Britain, France, and the United States, who were in

113

Archangel, learned of the invasion when they were arrested by Cossack cavalry, who later claimed it was to protect them from the departing Bolsheviks. The arrest was so sudden that the consuls felt compelled to burn codes and records before being carted off to a detention center. The next day, the U.S. consul wired the State Department, "Between hours August 3, 4 A.M. and August 3 11 A.M. counter revolution completed and Allied consuls freed. August 3, 5 P.M. allied forces entered city unopposed and greeted with blowing whistles, cheers and flowers."[3]

One month later, on September 4, the three ships of the American contingent landed at their respective berths near Archangel, causing a new wave of enthusiasm by the natives of Archangel. As the three battalions of infantry, one of engineers, and their supporting medical troops came ashore, a new confidence swept the city. They were convinced the Allies would drive the Reds from their doors.

Archangel itself is only one part of the long waterfront of the port. First, there is Economie at the north fork of the Dvina River; then, upriver past Solombola, the river widens substantially; then, there is the city of Archangel. Bakharitza is several miles to the south and west on the opposite side of the river, and the town of Isaaka Gorka is in the southern part of the metropolitan area. First impressions were varied, but several mentioned the sight of the city's largest cathedral, the Troitski Cathedral, with its impressive five domes. The troops would grow to know the city's good points and its shortcomings during the approaching winter.

In the city, thirteen-year-old Eugenie Fraser, a young Scottish-Russian girl, remembered her first sight of the Allied ships.

> They were all there—Russian, British, French, American. They sailed serenely, majestically, one after the other, in perfect formation, against the pink glow of the setting sun. There was a breathless hush followed by tremendous cheering, growing louder as each ship passed before our eyes. . . . Never before had the banks of our river seen such a glorious armada.[4]

Chaikovsky's new government had only been operating a few weeks, but in those weeks, British commanding general Poole made it clear that the new government existed only because of his support, and the British were in control. Then, just one day after the doughboys arrived, Chaplin staged a new coup to make himself head of the government. On the evening of September 5, he gathered a group of ex-Tsarist sympathizers, surrounded the Chaikovsky governing body as it met in Archangel, took them prisoner and marched them off to a waiting ship.

They were taken to Solovetski Island, where they were held for several days, as Chaplin, with Poole's apparent consent, prepared to assume leadership of the local government.

Ambassador Francis heard about the action the next day in a casual conversation with General Poole, who told him, "There was a revolution here last night." Francis replied with astonishment, "The Hell you say!"[5] He was incensed by the action, and convinced Poole to return the kidnapped government, while Chaplin was led off to exile. To say that the citizens of Archangel were left confused by the bizarre actions would be a considerable understatement.

Later, according to the American newspaper in Archangel, several Cossack officers were tried for the theft of four million rubles taken during the second coup. The Cossacks had been aligned with the Bolshevik Army before the Allies arrived, but decided to take advantage of the confusion during the coup and the arrival of Allied forces. They seized a safe with the rubles from the war department and planned to join the White forces, but were arrested. Captain Bers and Colonel Potapof were accused of the crime and tried. They were found guilty, but granted leniency, based on ancient Russian law justifying war spoils and the unsettled conditions in the city.[6]

As the American 339th Infantry landed and was shipped out to the fighting fronts, a strange aura seemed to cloud all the communications between Washington and Archangel. The president wished to avoid interfering in Russian affairs, yet American infantry were already fighting the Red troops. Much of the confusion was caused by U.S. ambassador David Francis. Francis, an avowed anti-Bolshevik, initially sided with General Poole in his aggressive campaign against the Reds. In one communication with Ambassador Francis on September 30, 1918, Secretary of State Lansing repeated the policy of the United States:

> As it is, in the opinion of the Government of the United States, plain that no gathering of any effective force by the Russians is to be hoped for, we shall insist with the other governments so far as our cooperation is concerned that all military efforts in Northern Russia be given up except the guarding of the ports themselves and as much of the country around them as may develop threatening conditions. . . . You are advised that no more American troops will be sent to the Northern ports.[7]

As clear as that message was, Ambassador Francis, with an agenda of his own, determined military action could be justified by the vague language describing ports, and, ignoring Stewart, allowed General Poole to send American men on his overly ambitious plan to move south. The ambassador, in his eagerness to fight Bolshevism regardless of his government's desires, was the strong American voice in Archangel at the time. It was no secret that the British government considered Bolshevism the enemy in Russia, an enemy to be fought whenever and wherever possible.[8] To his credit, however, it should be stated that Francis kept Washington informed of the units being sent to the various fronts as the AEF landed, and Washington provided him with little criticism.

Col. George Stewart's orders were plain. He was to report and be subject to Allied commander Poole.[9] From the arrival in Archangel, American troops would have little contact with their regimental commander, as all orders passed from British headquarters, through British field commanders, to the units in the field.

Given the circumstances, it was not surprising that friction developed as soon as the doughboys disembarked. The greatest hostility was not against the Russians, but against the British. In addition, General Poole had already alienated many of his Russian subjects. Although the Chaikovsky government was in place, Poole made sure everyone knew it was the British who ruled. The simple subject of flags became an item of contention; Poole refused to let the Russians fly their flags and replaced them with British flags. The Americans would have the same problem with their own flags.

One consistently annoying policy was to promote British officers, often young and inexperienced, to higher ranks in order to make them senior to any other Allied officer. It was claimed that British junior officers carried pips in their pockets, which could be attached at a moment's notice to establish seniority. The British, it is true, had a much more liberal temporary-rank policy than other Allied forces, but it was established without doubt that the promotion of officers at times depended only on their own whims.

In a review of the campaign, American general W. P. Richardson, who later commanded the Americans in North Russia, wrote a scathing summary of British policy in Archangel. Among his criticisms was one directed toward the temporary promotion policy. He noted that British officers commanded almost every unit, even the smallest: "To meet this situation, the practice was instituted and has been followed throughout, of appointing officers to temporary rank without pay, apparently to insure the seniority of British Officers in all cases, but perhaps also as a species of reward."[10] The general then illustrated his criticism with a list of several temporary promotions.

Richardson had further cause for complaint when he visited London on his way to North Russia. A report issued by the British War Office contained a paragraph that said:

On the 4th of September, the American force (1 Regiment of 3 Battalions and 3 companies of engineers) landed, but as it was composed of almost entirely untrained troops, was not of much value, and the bulk of the fighting still fell on the small numbers of French and British troops, who were consequently unable to make any rapid process.[11]

That brought an angry rejection by Richardson, "This comment is a wholly gratituous libel on the American forces and unwarranted by the facts."[12]

Further bitterness developed over rations supplied by the British. Their boring diet consisted of hardtack, meat and vegetables (M&V), and bully beef, or mutton. Stewart, to his credit, complained to both Poole and his seniors in the AEF in Britain, requesting that Americans be allowed their more familiar ration programs. His answers from England were very specific.

1. The British War Office Have Definitely ordered after consultation with French and U.S. Authorities, that only 2 scales of rations be maintained.
   1 for Western European Troops
   1 for Russian Troops
2. It is regretted that no alterations can be made as regards this arrangement.[13]

Virtually every letter or diary of soldiers on the expedition made reference to the poor quality and quantity of food at the front. The Red Cross and YMCA periodically provided additional food variety in the rear areas, but at the front, where the added food was essential, the British prevailed. As mail began to arrive, packages from home would give some relief from the monotony of the M&V, but mail was often delayed, and in one case, the ship *Adventure* was sunk with the loss of three hundred sacks of mail.[14]

In spite of rather strained relations between the Allies, Archangel was a fascinating city. In the first days of the expedition, Companies E, F, G, and H of the Second Battalion were assigned duties within the Archangel metropolitan area, but soon those units departed for various fronts. On September 15, two platoons of Company H left for Onega and were joined by the rest of the company in October. Two platoons of Company G were sent to Pinega on October 20; Company E went to Isaaka Gorka and then to the railroad front; and Company F was split up and sent on various missions along the Dvina River. There were still plenty of Americans in Archangel, mingling with the various troops from France and England, and occasionally with the jaunty Canadian gunners when they were relieved at the front. It was a colorful sight when the British and Russian officers, dressed in their finest uniforms,

strolled down Troitski Prospect to the admiring stares of the young ladies of Archangel.

Soon after the Second Battalion landed, it was called upon to perform some unique services that called into play some civilian occupa-
tions. While Chaplin had the government in custody on Solovetski
Island, the workers in Archangel staged a strike in protest against what
they viewed as an attempt to establish a pro-tsar government. The trolley cars on Troitski were halted, and both the power station and the
water station were shut down. The doughboys were asked to fill in for
the missing workmen, which they did with gusto. "American troops
manned the cars and by their good nature and patience won the respect
and confidence of the populace, excited as it was."[15] It was a lark for
the troops, who had been cooped up in camps and on troopships, but
the strike was soon over and Archangel settled into a wartime routine.

One reason for the Second Battalion's assignment to Archangel
was the presence of a group of Bolshevik sailors who had been manning
the Soviet ships captured by the British. They were not prisoners, but
they were a sullen, unhappy lot as they prowled the streets of Archangel. Many of them had fled south to join the Red forces and proved to
be some of the most vicious of Soviet fighters, but those who stayed on
seemed to be a constant menace to both Allied soldiers and civilians
who accepted Allied rule without complaint.[16] The battalion acted as a
protective force against possible problems.

Before the Allies arrived, food and equipment were in short supply. Almost all of the Allied goods stockpiled there for Russia's war effort had been shipped by the Soviets to Petrograd or Moscow; the little
that the city itself stocked for its citizens had been stripped from local
shelves as well. While the foreign troops and their officers provided
dashing sights and sounds, life was hard for the Russians of the city.
The American and other troops were generous; but the stores were bare
of the familiar Russian products. Bartering became the fashion for both
the occupied and the occupier. Eugenie Fraser remembered that at
Christmastime 1918 there were few presents to buy in local markets,
but they had gained much better food supplies through the friendship
of two American sergeants.[17] These two sergeants she remembered as
Sergeant Grey and Sergeant Boverley. She wrote in her memoir, "Life,
on the whole, was good that winter. British, Americans, and a sprin-
kling of French flocked to our house. In return there were invitations to
receptions, parties and other functions."[18] Sgt. Charles Grace of Headquarters Company wrote in his papers, "Almost every evening I would
go to some Russian home. Now I knew two Russians up there very, very
well." He added that he went frequently to the home of Dr. Papauf, the
head of the Russian hospital. "They had a green house they hadn't used

for several years. I had my family send garden seeds in letters. I took them to Mrs. Papauf. She grew lettuce, etc. and gave me some."[19] Dr. Papauf (Popov) was Eugenie's step-grandfather, Mrs. Papauf was her grandmother, and the garden belonged to the house on the Dvina that was written about with such affection. Sergeant Grace was probably the Sergeant Gray she remembered.

Some of the men told a slightly different version to Dorothea York, author of *The Romance of Company A:*

> With the arrival of the transports, the city took on an unnatural gaiety. Teas, luncheons, dinners, dances, followed each other in quick succession. These were not for the men of the lines but for troops permanently stationed at Archangel. The eight hundred English officers who had nothing to do and all winter to do it in, proceeded to enjoy themselves, as did the two thousand batmen who attended them, and what Russian people could afford it. . . . During the long winter, bottles lay in stacks outside the English Officers' Clubs in Archangel, and within, club members attended to the emptying of such bottles.[20]

The month of September 1918 brought the war home to Archangel, as the funerals for the flu victims filled the city with the sound of dirges. Eugenie Fraser wrote, "Daily throughout the summer, the funeral processions were seen winding along the Troitsky Prospekt on their way to the cemetery. We got to know the sad refrain of the funeral march, the solemn beat of the drum."[21] Many of the men in the Second Battalion remembered those days, too. "September 19—Big funeral we buried twenty-seven men," wrote Fred Krooyers of Company E in his journal.[22] Donald Carey wrote of the physical discomfort of the funeral process. He was recovering from the flu himself when he and other members of Company E were detailed to follow the caskets on a long march to the burial ground. He went on:

> We finally began one hell of a march. I thought it would never end. With the caskets in the lead, followed by the regimental band, we traversed the length of Archangel. Far to the north of the city we entered a cemetery where Private Harold Maybaum and Private John Bigelow of Company E, and seven others were buried with full military honors.[23]

In October the flu epidemic stopped for the Americans as suddenly as it had begun; there were no American flu deaths in Archangel after October. The Russian peasants living in the villages outside Archangel had their own epidemic, which began in November.[24] American doctors organized Russian medical help and assisted the stricken Russian peasants as the epidemic began.

Several American units were permanently based in Archangel, including the regimental supply company, as well as the regimental headquarters. The 310th Engineers had two companies in the area; they were kept busy constructing barracks, mess halls, laundries, recreational buildings, and hospitals. The supply company, however, prospered at the expense of the front-line troops. Shortly after arrival, they set up a thriving business—the sale of American military supplies by some members of the supply unit to anyone who had money. They ransacked barracks bags held in Archangel for delivery to units on the various fronts, selling any items of value. General Richardson's July 23, 1919, supplemental report included a strong condemnation of some members of the supply company, including its officers, who were trafficking in stolen U.S. material and making themselves wealthy men. Several investigations were conducted, but the only concrete evidence of the activity was the large sums of money being sent home by members of the company. Richardson said:

> If Colonel Stewart had had with him a capable and energetic officer as Inspector, this condition could have been dealt with properly long before it reached the proportions to which it evidently grew before the end of the winter; or, in my opinion, Colonel Stewart himself, could have, by proper initiative, prevented its continuance. It is this fact that makes it impossible for me to recommend Colonel Stewart for an award for meritorious service in this Northern Russian Campaign, to which, in my judgment, he would otherwise be entitled.[25]

The only battle casualty suffered by the supply company was Wagoner Carl Berger, who was decapitated by a shell at Visorka Gora while trying to deliver much-needed supplies. Numbers of comments were made by men at the front about the lack of concern for their welfare by officers and supply people in Archangel. One officer, Maj. J. Brooks Nichols, stood out as a protector of his men, who otherwise might have suffered more casualties and hardship. He was heralded as one of the senior officers who would not proceed under orders that seemed to have no logic. After he took over the Third Battalion, he rejected several of the more objectionable orders of the British and found ways to obtain supplies that other front-line forces lacked for his battalion.[26]

The replacement of inept Maj. Charles Young by Major Nichols was a sound tactical move, but Young was then assigned to Archangel, where he continued to trouble the infantrymen of the 339th. As Second Battalion commander, he was given responsibility for courts-martial; this apparently was a responsibility he relished. Of the numerous courts-martial that took place over the nine months of the expedition, two are of particular interest.

Pvt. Julius Stalinski was a twenty-three-year-old Polish immigrant drafted in early 1918 and later assigned to Company I, 339th Infantry. While at Camp Custer, he became Major Young's "dog robber," or personal valet. The major was an ex–first sergeant in the regular army, recently commissioned; a rigid disciplinarian, he was very hard on men in his command. He apparently was dissatisfied by Private Stalinski's work, complaining one time about his unpolished boots. He was so annoyed with Stalinski that he pulled a gun and threatened to shoot the private unless he improved. This scared the poor soldier so much, he reported the episode to his executive officer, Lt. Albert May. May told him it was just Young's way of impressing Stalinski as to the importance of his work and to forget it. Some days later, Stalinski received a letter from his mother pleading with him to come home because she was sick. Camp Custer was not far from his mother's home in Hamtramack, so he applied for and was granted a three-day pass by Lieutenant May. He never returned from his pass.

After the regiment arrived in England, several of Company I's men were detailed to London to escort another soldier to the hospital. While they were in Piccadilly, they spotted Stalinski in a Canadian Army uniform and brought him back to camp to face Lieutenant May. During his questioning, Stalinski told the lieutenant that Major Young had threatened him again, pulling a gun on him, and the soldier was convinced Young was going to kill him. He said he had no idea of deserting when he left Camp Custer, but was afraid to return. So he crossed the Canadian border at Detroit and enlisted in a Canadian infantry regiment. May refused to press charges since Stalinski had been in action with the Canadians against the Germans in France, but Young insisted.

Stalinski was held in custody and brought before a court-martial on December 5, 1918, and charged with desertion.[27] He asked for May to defend him, and May agreed, but the request was denied. May wrote a full explanation of the matter for the court, but it had no effect. Stalinski pled not guilty, but was convicted and sentenced to eighteen months hard labor at Fort Leavenworth and dishonorably discharged. The story later had a happy ending, when Stalinski met May at the gangplank in New York on June 30, 1919, as May debarked on his way home. Stalinski told May that the sentence had been reversed; he was released from Leavenworth, his back pay was reinstated, and an honorable discharge replaced his dishonorable one.[28]

The second unusual court-martial was that of Pvt. Henry Jones, Company E, also held on December 5, 1918. Jones was charged with the murder of Cpl. Martin John Campbell, Company E, 339th Infantry.

Jones pled not guilty, but the court found him guilty. He was sentenced to confinement and hard labor at Fort Leavenworth for the rest of his natural life.[29] The case was not as clear-cut as it seemed. Jones, from Trail City, South Dakota, was depressed by the recent loss of his ranch. He had decided to end it all by shooting himself. He loaded his rifle and put the trigger on a nail; he planned to place himself at the muzzle, yank the rifle, and end his unhappy life. Unfortunately, before he could get himself in position, the rifle fired; the bullet passed through his sleeve, hitting Campbell who was lying on the bunk under him. Campbell, who had recently returned from the hospital at Smolny after recovering from the flu, died shortly after the shooting.[30] Later, a member of Company F painted another picture of Jones. "I happened to draw Pvt Jones of E Company regarded as the most formidable inmate. He had a scar on the right side of his mouth like a knife slash. . . . We got along beautifully, though."[31]

Officers were court-martialed as well, although not many. Capt. Louis Coleman of the 339th was tried and convicted for selling 840 pounds of flour illegally, as well as for "having a Russian woman occupying the same room with him for several days, to the scandal and disgrace of the military service." The sentence, a dishonorable discharge, was reviewed and approved by General Pershing.[32]

There were many other courts-martial as well, in part due to the zealousness of Major Young. There were several trials for self-inflicted wounds, mainly a result of the deteriorating morale and the bleakness of the winter. It became so common that a special board was convened by Colonel Stewart to determine whether wounds that were suspicious were accidental or willfully self-inflicted. The board reported on January 17, 1919, that the wounds of twenty-six men indicated that they might have been self-inflicted. The board determined that nine of the men investigated were wounded by the enemy or by accident; seven confessed to wounding themselves; five were found guilty of the act, based on circumstantial evidence; and five were confirmed to have wounded themselves, but not necessarily willfully.[33]

As late as May two cases remained open, but both soldiers had been returned to their units. The board was not a court-martial, but it did refer those appearing guilty to special courts-martial, where they were judged, and if found guilty, sentenced. Sentences were fairly standard: forfeiture of pay, reduction in rank (if possible), and four to six months' hard labor.[34] One doughboy wrote of his experience:

December 14, 1918
    Food at Selesco was poor and I, Pvt George Paulsen was always hungry. The time came to advance so we marched all day, about thirty versts

with six hard tacks and one can of corned beef each. When we camped that night I was hungry and tired and I guess all the men were. I stood guard on outpost that night and got some rest but couldn't sleep because it rained all night and a dry spot couldn't be found. The next day we marched to the riverbank and opened fire on the Bolshevicki. I lay down in a patch of moss and stayed there for twelve hours, hungry cold and tired and I hadn't had a smoke in two days. During a lull in the battle the thought of home came with all its cheerfulness and the warm bed I used to lay in and while in that mood I wished I could go back for something to eat and a rest and under the impulse of the moment I wounded myself.

I realized I was doing something wrong but the thought of clearing myself seemed so easy that before I thought of the consequences, the deed had been done.[35]

Paulsen turned himself in, but the surgeon reported that his wound "will not interfere with firing of rifle or carrying same." That apparently was enough to keep him off the self-inflicted wound (SIW) list submitted to Colonel Stewart. On the Vaga front, Lt. Henry Katz of the Medical Corps reported on January 29 that he had treated six cases of self-inflicted wounds. "Some seemed intentional."[36]

There were also many other types of courts-martial: summary, special, and even general, for all kinds of misconduct. Being AWOL, drunken- and disorderliness, and failure to obey a superior were typical of the myriad offenses that occur with military forces in overseas locations. There were no recorded executions of Americans, British, or French; although the mutineers of the Yorkshire Regiment were sentenced to be shot, that sentence was commuted by General Ironside. The Russians were a different story. On October 18, one of the engineers noted in his diary that seventeen Bolshevik prisoners were shot that day.[37] Russian executions on both sides were numerous even during the Allied occupation.

Major Young provided other curious programs that proved to the men that he was slightly paranoid about the possibility of danger. In the spring, as the Reds made their aggressive move on Bolshe-Ozerkiye, he became convinced that there were hordes of secret agents and enemy sympathizers in Archangel; he set about issuing a series of orders and required numerous drills to prepare for the anticipated uprising. His complex and detailed instructions in case of riot or civil disobedience were used to drill the doughboys, even those just in from the front. The units coming into the city were almost glad to get back to the more stable fronts, where there was at least some logic to the actions taken.[38]

There were numerous unique characters that appeared and disappeared during the Intervention period. One of the most intriguing was

Mme. Maria Botchkareva, formerly commanding officer of the Women's Battalion of Death, who appeared for a short time, dressed as a Russian army officer. She had recently arrived from the United States, where she had lectured on the Russian Revolution, and was returning to offer her services to the Archangel Government. General Ironside felt sorry for her, but sent her to General Marousheffsky, then the commander of North Russian White forces. Marousheffsky had no empathy for the lady, saying:

> I only consider it my duty to declare, within the limits of the northern region, thank God, the time has already come for quiet creative work, and I consider that the summoning of women for military duties, which are not appropriate for their sex, would be a heavy reproach and a disgraceful stain on the whole population of the northern region.[39]

Botchkareva had already been wounded twice on the eastern front and was penniless, but the general stripped her of all rank and army privileges, and she disappeared from the Archangel scene.

Many of the clashes between the British and the other Allies seemed to stem from the attitude demonstrated by General Poole. He was a typical British colonial military officer, accustomed to the role of the British in their colonies where the military ruled over all; he tended to view anything with which he disagreed as a threat. Finally, the word reached London that Poole was endangering any hope of military or political success by his high-handed actions. His decisions to send his small force in so many directions so many miles from their base was fraught with hazard, and the units were in increasing danger. The farther the two main forces went south, the more they were separated, and communications became almost impossible between fronts. Finally, the Chaplin coup was the last straw.[40] Francis, even though he had fully agreed with Poole's original expeditions, realized that Poole was destroying much of the Intervention's effectiveness and requested that the State Department suggest that American troops be placed under a separate command.

That request stirred London enough to begin a search for Poole's replacement. They soon found one in General Ironside.[41] He arrived on September 30 to be greeted by Poole, who was not at all certain why the War Office would be sending another general officer to Archangel. However, he told Ironside it was fine timing since he was planning to take leave and return to England on October 14.

With the arrival of General Ironside, relations became better among the Allies, but the rift would never be completely healed. Ironside came across as a more tolerant superior, willing to listen to the problems of all his Allied forces. He also recognized the exposure of his various troops, isolated in the midst of a country where the populace might be for or against the Allies. And he was visible; he visited the various fronts personally, talking to the men and their commanders, and listening to their complaints. He was very critical of American forces at first, but soon felt they had warmed to the job at hand and were performing well. His arrival was welcomed by most American officers, who felt that he was a more understanding military officer than his predecessor. Poole never did return from his leave; early in November, Ironside was officially named commander in chief of all Allied forces in North Russia. Poole had been a poor choice for such a force, and Ironside tried to make amends. Ambassador Francis said of Poole that the British had bullied Hindus for so long it was hard for them to put up with Socialists.[42]

One of the new general's first concerns was mutiny in the ranks. It was a problem that would plague the expedition until its final days. Shortly after his appointment as commander in chief, on October 29, he was to review Russian troops in Archangel. When the Russian officers ordered the men to fall in, they flatly refused. They thought that Americans and British had better food and resented having to salute officers, since this was a democratic army. Russian officials and officers scurried around for two days and finally flew in two loyal Russian colonels from the Dvina front, who curtly ordered the men to parade; they sheepishly performed for the British general.

The next incident was much more serious. On December 11 at 11:30 A.M., the Headquarters Company of the 339th was notified of another Russian mutiny. At 1:30 P.M. Colonel Sutherland ordered Headquarters Company to surround the Alexandra Novsky barracks, quarters for the British-led SBAL regiment, and prepare to fire on the Russians, who were shooting indiscriminately from the barracks windows. At 2:00 P.M. the order came to open fire with the company's three trench mortars and two of their Lewis guns. After fifteen minutes, the mutineers raised a white flag and came out of the barracks. They were guarded by the Americans until the British arrived.[43] The doughboys were unhappy that they had to enforce discipline on troops trained and outfitted by the British.

A few minutes later to the immense disgust of the doughboys, a company of English Tommies who by all rules of right and reason should have been the ones to clean up the mutinous mess into which the British officers had gotten the S.B.A.L.'s, now hove into sight . . . singing their insulting version of "Over There the Yanks are Running, Running, Everywhere."[44]

Ironside, however, remembered things differently. He wrote in 1953 that the machine guns and mortars were manned by Russians. He states specifically that no Allied troops were involved in the affair and that only Russians fired on the mutineers.[45] Other reports seem to belie that version. Also disputed was the fate of the ringleaders of the abortive attempt. Colonel Stewart affirmed, in Taylor's "Report of Engagement," that thirteen ringleaders were executed immediately for their part in leading the revolt. Several other versions refer to the executions, carried out by Russian riflemen, but Ironside insists he commuted the sentences and sent the thirteen across to Bolshevik lines.[46] There were numerous other executions that took place in Archangel, according to Naval Intelligence:

> There have been in Archangel, since occupation by the Allies, 56 executions by shooting, of which 17 have been irregular. . . . At the Fighting Fronts there have also been a number, but exact figures are not known. A certain number were inevitable under the conditions, but the total, said to be 270, seems unduly large.[47]

While Ironside as supreme commander was an improvement, the men in the field were still saddled with a large number of incompetent field commanders.[48] When Poole arrived, he brought a large pool of officers, many of whom simply wanted an assignment and had been unsuccessful in finding suitable commands at home.

The day after Ironside was permanently assigned to the North Russian campaign, Ambassador Francis was evacuated on the *Olympia*, suffering from prostate cancer. He and Seaman Perschke, of Force B fame, both left Archangel on the *Olympia* headed for England and further medical treatment.[49] He was replaced at the embassy by Dewitt Poole (no relation to the British general), who had previously been in Moscow. Poole was placed under house arrest in Moscow when the Americans intervened and had only recently made his way from Moscow through Finland to Murmansk and then Archangel.

Then, on a return trip, the *Olympia* brought Rear Adm. Newton McCulley, a new commander for U.S. Naval Forces in North Russia. He had been recommended by the Navy Department and wholeheartedly approved by Francis. He was, according to Francis, "a first class man, having known Russia under Empire and Provisional Government and would comprehend quickly if not acquainted with conditions at present. He is very acceptable."[50] According to naval records, he arrived in Archangel on October 26, after Francis had left. While the navy played only a small role in the North Russian campaign, McCulley's presence was helpful in dealings with Admiral Kemp, the British naval commander of all Allied naval vessels, and with Major General Ironside, McCulley's flag rank was important.[51]

The White Russians, too, were changing their leadership. Under General Poole, Colonel Douroff was the Russian governor-general in charge of military matters, of which Chaikovsky knew, and cared, little. Ironside found him incompetent and eventually replaced him with General Vladimir Marousheffsky. Marousheffsky was a tiny man who had difficulty inspiring his men and was later replaced by Gen. E. Miller, a Russian in whom Ironside had confidence. Miller would stay until the bitter end.

In January 1919, Chaikovsky himself was gone, sent to Paris as a representative to the peace conference; from then on, General Miller would be the nominal head of the Russian forces. Ironside himself was replaced as commander in chief by Lord Rawlinson in August 1919, but the complex plan for evacuation of all Allied troops, civilians, and friendly Russians was left to the capable General Ironside.

An American, Brig. Gen. Wilds P. Richardson, was sent to Archangel to supervise the withdrawal of American troops, arriving from England on April 17. He brought with him a rather complete staff consisting of an acting general staff officer, chief of staff, adjutant, and inspector, his aide, and staff officers assigned to operations, intelligence, personnel, and supply.[52] Had Colonel Stewart enjoyed such a staff, his performance might well have been much different. Stewart had tried, in his own way, to protect his men. Shortly after the Armistice, on November 14, he cabled Washington: "Original object of expedition no longer exists. Allies have not been received with hospitality. My inference is plain. Immediate consideration requested."[53] Stewart was asking that the vast machinery in Washington come to a rapid decision to pull out the doughboys, which did not happen. By the time any serious discussion of removing American troops took place, the frozen White Sea ruled out any winter evacuation plans.

As the armistice was being signed in Versailles, Russia was initiating a new government in Siberia. A coup took place in mid-November, and Adm. Alexander V. Kolchak was installed as Supreme Ruler of all Russia, a rather arrogant and misleading title since his main support came from Siberia. Throughout the Archangel expedition, there were countless references to a linking of the Siberian and Archangel Allied forces, even as the British began their final days in Archangel. There never was any linkage of the two forces reported in the official records, although several sources mentioned that lead forces had joined up.[54]

While the senior officers went about their duties, life for the doughboys in Archangel was improving. There were the usual entertainment opportunities at the Red Cross and YMCA, but they also made up their

own activities. During the winter of 1918–1919, there was a large toboggan slide, which was so popular that the authorities put guards on the
base of the slide to control, not only troops, but youngsters from the city.
Unfortunately, the first guard was a Russian whom the authorities
viewed as too young and too stupid. He was replaced. Eugenie Fraser
and other local youngsters were fascinated by the structure:

> A soldier, standing at the foot of the steps, kept a steady watch. Yet it
> drew us like a magnet and often, succeeding in distracting the guard's
> attention, we dodged past him and, racing down, were followed by a vol-
> ley of strange words which we later learned described us all as being born
> out of wedlock.[55]

Another slide in Solombola drew the attention of the British authorities
as well. They were critical of that one for its construction and were concerned for the welfare of the troops. One soldier went down on skates,
which prompted an official to remark: "The man who used skates for
the descent must have been suffering from a sort of 'tedium vitae', the
thing was suicidal."[56] It was all in good fun, but it was risky for the
youngsters, as well as the soldiers. The *America Sentinel* newspaper in
Archangel reported that five sledders wound up in the hospital after
the slide's first day in operation.[57]

For young Eugenie Fraser, life was good that winter, as the
wealthy Russian families entertained the Allied officers and men. Flir-
tations and romances sprang up between locals and the troops, some
successful, some not. One member of Eugenie's family, Marga, became
engaged to an American officer named Frank; they planned to marry
and live in the United States. Frank left with the 339th in June, and,
sad to say, was heard from only briefly, then disappeared from Marga's
life.[58]

Love sometimes took a more commercial turn; young women of
Archangel, forced to cope with the changing economic times, occasionally turned to other pursuits. Eugenie Fraser's young mind absorbed the
unusual actions involving a house with a green roof. "Although I had
some knowledge of the facts of life, I didn't know the purpose of that
house and imagined it was some kind of club where there was dancing
and perhaps a special entertainment. Enlightenment as to how entertaining it was came some time later."[59]

With the blossoming of commercial romances came a blossoming
rate of venereal disease. Medical reports showed that in March 1919
cases remaining in the Archangel Hospital were for gunshot wounds
(40), influenza (17), gonorrhea (20), syphilis (13).[60] To maintain some
control over the potential problem, the British closed down one of the

most popular spots in Archangel, the Café de Paris, because, the proclamation said, "Women of easy virtue habitually visit the café for purposes of their profession."[61] For health reasons, as well as to protect security, the British declared the café off-limits and suggested the Americans do the same.

Troops also were chided by wives and sweethearts about the possibility of a Russian love interest. John Crissman's wife wrote him in October, " Dearie, don't fall in love with a Russian girl now for that would never do." Then two weeks later wrote again, "I suppose you are 'dating' with a Russian this evening. Sweetie, be careful—Everything is not fair in love and war!"[62] As the Yanks left, there were eight Russian brides accompanying their new husbands.

The local newspaper kept up to date on the various activities; an article published on February 15, 1919, titled, "Who Said That Life Was Dull in Archangel?" mentioned various forms of available entertainment. "Aside from the fascinating past-time of learning the Russian language from a rosy-cheeked Barishna, there are a number of other activities which claim the spare time of the Poilu, the doughboy and the Tommie."[63] They went on to mention the risky toboggan, boxing tournaments, movies, lectures, concerts by the 339th band and other bands, plus some other unspecified "special entertainments."

One puzzling procedure adopted by the military was that of censorship of mail. There may have been some logic for it in the two months while the war still raged in France, but the practice continued for months after the armistice, keeping the true facts of the expedition from even the families of those in Russia. On October 21, a Lt. R. C. Johnson of the 310th Engineers wrote home complaining about his British superiors: "The thing that makes us all so mad, is to have rotten British officers in charge of our troops. No matter how inexperienced our own officers may be, they couldn't be worse than these English. It makes us sick." His letter was returned by the censor to Colonel Stewart with an endorsement stating, "Enclosed find original letter from Lt. R.C. Johnson H.Q. 1st Bn 310 Engs. Archangel, who criticizes the British in violation of Censorship regulations." The letter was returned to Lieutenant Johnson with several forwarding endorsements ending with the lieutenant's apology saying, "Conditions at the time of the writing were very regrettable but have improved. . . . Am very sorry I was so indiscreet as to place the conditions on paper. This will not occur again."[64]

Several of the engineers and doughboys tried to give their letters to sailors to take without the censor's review, and probably many were successful, but there was still little notice in the United States of the beleaguered troops up close to the Arctic Circle. As the various troops were sent home, sick or wounded, the returnees usually carried a large batch of letters to mail when they finally arrived in the United States. Censorship of mail was another thorn in the side of the AEFNR, especially after the armistice, when the only reason for the process seemed to be to prevent home folks from hearing the sordid facts.

The enforcement of the code was purely arbitrary; Pvt. Golden Bahr's seemingly innocuous letter home on November 18, 1918, was literally cut to pieces, whole sentences being cut out, leaving little content. It may have been that he was reporting his physical condition, which was poor. He was admitted to the hospital that same day, sent to England in December, then to New York, and discharged in Michigan in February 1919. He died March 12, 1919, at his home in Marilla, Michigan.[65]

Cpl. Fred Krooyers also had some trouble with the censors. On October 22, his diary noted that he received extra fatigue duty and was told he could write no more letters for a month for "writing the truth home."[66] Officers, on the other hand, sometimes censored their own mail, allowing for considerably more leeway in their communications.

Movies were plentiful in Archangel and even in the forward bases of Obozerskaya and Bereznik. Mary Pickford was a favorite in "The Little American," along with "Up There" and "The Reward of Love," and many other current favorites whose names are lost in time. Dances at the YMCA, the YWCA, and the Red Cross, as well as local events, made Archangel a welcome haven for front-line troops given a breather in town and a good duty station for those who were based there. On all fronts, there still was the Arctic cold, the lack of daylight, and the puzzle over the reason for their presence, but life in Archangel was vastly better than the primitive conditions at the front.

There was a dark side to Archangel, which haunted those who lived in the city. Executions, individual and wholesale, went on in the city. Ralph Albertson was one of the secretaries sent out to provide YMCA services to the troops. He soon became bewildered at the brutality shown by both the Russians and British.

> The execution of suspects made Bolsheviki right and left. The inquisitorial processes of the Russian puppets of the Military Intervention were necessarily so much like that of the old regime that they went far to dispel all illusions about the Military Intervention that remained in the peasant mind.
>
> When night after night the firing squad took out its batches of victims, it mattered not that no civilians were permitted on the streets. There were thousands of ears to hear the rat-tat-tat of the machine guns.[67]

Despite the imminence of the AEFNR's withdrawal, another development was taking place that would put more Americans into the North Russian fighting.

The Murmansk
Railroad Companies

They stopped at Siding 15 and with their bayonets and a broken shovel, dug a grave in the frozen ground for their comrades fallen in the fight of the day before.

—Chaplain John Wilson, North Russian Transportation Corps
Expeditionary Force

DESPITE the War Department's strong opposition to the Intervention and President Wilson's assurance that no more troops would be sent, late in the expedition another contingent of U.S. troops was deployed to the Russian north. In response to a request from the British, two companies of American railroad troops, the 167th and 168th Railroad Companies, were sent to help maintain and operate the existing portions of the Murmansk-to-Petrograd line.

There had been much discussion in Washington concerning withdrawal of American troops from Russia. Secretary of War Baker wrote:

Of course the correct solution to the matter was to withdraw our forces, and the President, not having the War Department at hand to consult

[Wilson was at the Paris Peace Conference], finally called on General [Tasker] Bliss, who was a member of the Peace Conference, for a memorandum on the proposition to send in the two railroad companies.[1]

General Bliss agreed to the British proposal with the understanding that it would be "to assist in the withdrawal of troops in Northern Russia at the earliest opportunity."[2]

In February 1919 General Pershing was authorized by President Wilson to organize two railroad transportation companies to be transferred from France. They would assist in the running of the troubled railroad, which Bolshevik and Allied forces were fighting over. General Bliss reasoned that improving the railroad would contribute to the ease of evacuating American troops. Bliss revealed some confusion as to the geography involved, since the new railroad troops were headed for Murmansk, almost completely cut off from Archangel. The railroaders never came near Archangel, and no U.S. troops were evacuated through Murmansk, except as a quick stopover on the way to England or Scotland.

Wilson was pressured by the Paris Peace Conference and the Allied War Council, plus the various Allied nations, who had proclaimed the urgent need for railroad troops. One of the railroaders wrote:

> The North Russia Transportation Corps Expedition was the response of the Transportation Corps of France to a most urgent radio request received the latter part of 1918, from Archangel, to send special railway troops to open the railroad south from Murmansk far enough to permit overland evacuation of Allied troops.[3]

Wilson's decision on February 12, 1919, committed 720 more men to North Russia, just four days before his decision to withdraw all forces from the region.[4] Some of the railroaders later declared that they had been tricked into volunteering. Charles Tyner claimed he went to rescue the doughboys of the 339th, not to fight Bolsheviks. He told of a recruiting talk given by Brig. Gen. W. W. Atterbury, who maintained the group would be going to rescue a group of marooned soldiers trapped by the ice in the White Sea. "It was a total fabrication, what he wanted was to get U. S. soldiers involved in the war against Bolsheviks, a group of people he had no love for at all."[5]

The men were selected from a number of transportation companies in France with full knowledge of their destination, unlike the men of the 339th who had been mystified as to their real assignment from the time they got to England. On March 5, 1919, American major Edward E. MacMorland was appointed commander of the North Russia

Transportation Corps Expeditionary Forces, made up of the 167th (Operations) and the 168th (Maintenance) Companies Transportation Corps, consisting of 32 officers and 688 enlisted men.[6] The volunteers were sent to St. Pierre-des-Corps, France; there they were organized and outfitted, then shipped to Park Royal Camp near London, where they were reviewed by Gen. John J. Pershing himself.

Their stay in London was brief, but they received their Arctic equipment at Park Royal, complete with the hated Russian Moisin Nagant rifle. Considered fully outfitted, on March 17, the 168th Company sailed for Murmansk from Hull, England, on the HMT *Stephen*. They arrived at Murmansk on March 25, the first American soldiers to be assigned to that port. One man wrote, "If war was hell for Sherman, marching through a southern State in time of abundant harvest, then it was hell frozen over for this battalion marching through the tundras and snows of Russia."[7]

Geographically, Murmansk sits well above the Arctic Circle. It was an unimpressive boomtown, built only three years before. "We saw an unsightly collection of unpainted warehouses and dwellings, sprawled in the snow on the sides of the hills. We saw wharves, railroad yards crowded with decrepit rolling stock, and piles of supplies."[8]

The 168th was already hard at work in Murmansk before the 167th Company left England. MacMorland noted on his arrival, "The British have received us very well and seem glad to have our aid."[9] Unlike their antagonism against Americans in Archangel, the British seemed to appreciate the American help in Murmansk. Another advantage for these men was that they would receive American, instead of British, rations, and supplementary rations would be issued regularly. The English supply forces kept their word; a constant stream of additional rations, cigarettes, candy, and other articles arrived on almost every boat.

Major MacMorland, the commanding officer in Russia, reported to Maj. Gen. C. M. Maynard, the British officer in charge of the Murmansk Allied operation. In addition, for administrative purposes MacMorland reported to American brigadier general Richardson after his arrival.[10] MacMorland believed he would be in Murmansk only briefly, then would be sent back to France. In a letter home on March 6, he wrote, "Although I shall go with this expedition it is probable that I shall return to France by reason of the non-desire of the British to have any American field officers with the unit."[11] However, he stayed with the units until they were withdrawn. While their primary duties were in maintaining and operating the Murmansk-Petrograd Railroad, their eagerness to join in the fighting led them into skirmishes with the Bolsheviks, sometimes with fatal results.

The first order of the 168th was to begin construction of a light railway within the Murmansk area, connecting all the different areas of the port. Capt. C. G. Jones took a section of men and began digging through several feet of ice and snow, building trestles across the hilly sections of Murmansk. Others worked in the railroad shops, repairing and assembling locomotives shipped from England, which had supplied the rolling stock for the little Murmansk line. The rest of the company was sent south some four hundred miles to Soroka to man the repair shops, taking with them some badly damaged cars. They were led by Capt. A. Montgomery, who set up his headquarters in the town of Soroka. Major MacMorland outfitted a boxcar with all his personal and military needs and traveled extensively up and down the railroad to his scattered units.[12]

The first section of the 167th arrived on April 8, 1919, on two U.S. Navy ships, the USS *Chester* and the *Galveston*, accompanied by the new American commander General Richardson.[13] He stayed only a few days, then left on the *Chester* for Archangel. The 167th sent one of its sections to Soroka; the remainder of the company arrived on April 20 on the HMS *Porto*, heading south immediately.[14] As early as April 13, the American unit was given the responsibility of operating the railroad from Soroka south, at that time some fifty miles behind the front line. The British had cleared the territory that far south, but were waiting for the Americans to put the railroad supply lines into shape.

It was important to win the friendship of the Russian peasants, and the Americans made every effort to do just that. The railroaders extinguished a deadly fire in Soroka, supplied food to the destitute, and even brought down boxcars to shelter the homeless from the bitter Arctic cold. The Russian railroad men who manned most of the trains, however, were a different story, as they were poorly paid and envious of the American arrivals. Many of them had been ardent Bolshevik supporters who elected to stay home and keep their jobs, rather than go off to fight. Pay was often late, adding to their unhappiness.

The British decided to launch an attack on May 1, directed toward the town of Maselskaya, en route to the ultimate destination of Lake Onega and Petrozavodsk. Volunteers from the 168th urged the Allied commanders to let them go along on the attack. There had been several occasions when they were under fire, rebuilding bridges blown by the Soviet guerrillas. Major MacMorland provided thirty-five men for the British assault, relieving them from their bridge-building work to join with the attacking units. Lieutenant Garrett commanded a machine gun squad, and at 2 A.M. on May 2, the American volunteers flanked the Bolsheviks and cut the railroad so the Bolos would have no escape route. The group, including the major, waded through the icy waters of the swamps, and eventually, at approximately 1 P.M., came out on a little hill overlooking a railroad bridge about one half mile south of Verst 15.

Unfortunately, before they could destroy the bridge, they were spotted and came under heavy machine gun fire. Several Bolo railcars began to escape south. Lieutenant Garrett was the first casualty, and Sgt. Frederick Patterson the next, both killed by a Red sniper. Pvt. William Parker moved out and shot the sniper; he was later decorated for his bravery. Pvt. Edward Smith was wounded in the same action. Very soon a Bolo armored train appeared, raking the Americans with machine gun and cannon fire. As Soviet forces attacked the American position, the doughboys withdrew in some confusion. Chaplain John Wilson wrote, "The men were fighting stubbornly from behind fallen trees and any protection they could get."[15] They managed to fight their way back to friendly lines, briefly losing the major and two others who showed up later behind Allied lines. During the night of May 2, the Americans, exhausted and cold, slept within British lines at Siding 15, which had been abandoned by the Soviets.

On May 3, the Allies continued to move south toward Maselskaya, helped along by a British artillery piece on a pushcart. After the town was captured, most of the Americans were sent back to their main jobs, repairing bridges and replacing track. Before they left Siding 15, they paid their last respects to Lieutenant Garrett and Sergeant Patterson. "They stopped at Siding 15 and with their bayonets and a broken shovel, dug a grave in the frozen ground for their comrades fallen in the fight the day before. They lined the grave with pine boughs and having wrapped each in a shelter half, tenderly laid them away." Lt. John Wilson, chaplain of the unit, composed a poem titled "Twilight Requiem," which he read over the graves:

> When the glorious northern twilight
> Shed its beauty over all,
> And from swamp and tangled forest
> Came the night bird's plaintive call;
> When the silent heaven's, stooping
> Watched above our fallen dead
> And the pine trees sang their requiem
> Close beside their funeral bed;
> When the quiet stars above them
> Kept their watch like tapers tall,
> And the hillside, hushed from battle,
> Spread for each his funeral pall;
> Then we took our fallen comrades
> From the places where they fell
> And we gave to them the honor

That they each had won so well.
Just a simple gospel service
Ere we laid them 'neath the sod,
"Dust to dust," o'er bodies spoken,
When the soul returns to God.
Then the rifles rang above them
With a soldier's last farewell,
And we turned to leave them sleeping
On the hilltop where they fell;
With the pole star keeping vigil
From its station overhead
And the pine trees standing sentry
O'er the bivouac of our dead.[16]

The important contribution of the railroaders was keeping the railroads running. MacMorland wrote to his wife:

As the Bolsheviki fall back they destroy the railway as they go. One of my men, Capt. [C. G.] Jones, follows right behind the troops and repairs it so fast that the Bolsheviks have been investigating among their people to discover who the guilty one is who makes his demolitions so imperfect as to make possible so rapid an advance on our part.[17]

During the month of May, the 168th continued to move south with Allied forces, doing their special work in maintaining the railroad, bringing supplies and men. Many of the men in the unit were operating the maintenance and repair shops in Soroka, trying to keep up with the necessary equipment to replace the faulty Russian parts. Meanwhile, the 167th manned the many railroad depots as railway transportation offices and often came under fire at the southern end of the line. The 167th suffered only one casualty during the expedition, Pvt. John J. Sheehan, who was killed when he was crushed under a train on June 2. He was later buried beside Lieutenant Garrett and Sergeant Patterson.[18] The final American casualty was Pfc. Joseph Baker, wounded in the chest while working on a bridge at Verst 9. His recovery was rapid and complete.

A novel assignment came to some of the men in mid-June. After the French left North Russia, the 168th took over an armored train, which the French had manned for months in support of Allied infantry. A twenty-five-man gun crew headed by Lt. C. B. Tuttle, a former coast artillery officer, was organized among the railroaders; they boarded their seven-car train, fitted with two three-pounder naval guns and twenty-two Vickers machine guns. There were a kitchen car, a sleeping car, and two ammunition cars, as well as their armored engine tenders.

Almost the only time they could get close enough to do any damage was on June 27 and again a few days later at the town of Kyapeselga.[19]

The final duty of the expedition was providing another unique service to the Allies. Major General Maynard had a plan to station a flotilla of boats on Lake Onega to create a seaplane base there. Medvye-jya Gora, on the northern shore of Lake Onega, was still in Bolshevik hands and under attack by the Allies. Two U.S. Navy fifty-foot patrol boats manned by U.S. sailors appeared on flatcars at Siding 11. The problem was that the railroad tracks passed one and a half miles from the lake. Not to be defeated, the railroad crews under Captain Jones cut a swath through the two miles of forest, then took up track and laid it in front of the boats. As the boats moved along the tracks, the tracks were taken up behind the flatcars and relaid in front of them. It was laborious work, but finally the two boats were launched onto the lake, the first Allied flotilla to operate there. The Stars and Stripes flying proudly on the little boats was a sight for all to see as they rested from their efforts. As soon as Medvyejya Gora was captured, eleven more British boats appeared to join the Onega navy. Jones again had to im-provise, this time by laying track from the main line, right into the frigid waters of the lake so the boats could literally float off the tracks as the water deepened.[20]

The Allied drive continued south toward Petrozavodsk, but Amer-ica's part was coming to a close. The American infantry had left in April; the Italians, Serbs, and French were gone; and on July 12, at the town of Kyapeselga, 576 miles south of Murmansk, orders came for the American railroaders to move north to be sent home.[21] Still, their role was not complete; Major General Maynard requested that they to go from their assembly point at Soroka to Popov for a final construction project, which was completed on July 24. The 168th then moved on up to Murmansk on July 27.

General Richardson had been authorized to keep the railroaders if they volunteered. MacMorland put it to a vote, then reported:

> The men voted to go home. . . . The vote of the men was no reflection on their morale, which had at all times been all that a commanding officer could desire, but was rather the view of railroad men, whose jobs were still being held open for them at home, but might be given to others if they did too much volunteering to stay in Europe.[22]

On July 28, the two companies boarded the HMT *Menominee* for France, then South Brooklyn and Camp Merritt, New Jersey, where the units were disbanded, ending the American participation in North Russia.

Their service had been extraordinary, and differed substantially from that of their infantry counterparts. First, their relations with the British were amicable; second, the rations and supplementary supplies they received were far superior to those supplied the Archangel troops; third, their housing was usually in freight cars or in huts built by them in Soroka. While they did suffer from cold as they worked on the bridges, they were not there in the coldest months and usually returned to snug quarters. Most importantly, although they took occasional fire from the Bolos, it was not as severe as that experienced by the ground troops on the Dvina, Vaga, Onega, and other fronts. Their summer was plagued by the insects of the swamps, but they had netting helmets that gave them some protection.

They worked feverishly on their projects and accomplished more than anyone had expected. They were outstanding representatives of their craft. Recognition of the railroad companies' work was expressed in many ways. The British command decorated nineteen men in the traditional manner, with Distinguished Service Medals and Military Crosses for officers and Military Medals and Distinguished Conduct Medals for enlisted men. Many others were "cited in General Orders" for their roles in the expedition, but, sad to say, no awards or recognition were given to the three dead railroaders. The American commanding general, General Richardson, gave the railroaders high praise, "I take occasion here to add that so far as my own personal judgment and experience extends, no finer or more commendable service has been performed in a like space of time by any body of troops in the American Expeditionary Forces than by these transportation companies in North Russia."[23]

The Withdrawal

Well, we evacuated because they wanted to get us out of the country. It wasn't that we were licked or anything like that—No we didn't lick them, It was a draw, it was just a draw.

—Russell Hershberger, Machine Gun Company

POLITICAL pressures had been mounting all through the winter for evacuation of all forces, especially the American and British. In the United States, opposition to the Intervention in North Russia and Siberia was led by Senator Hiram Johnson of California. He introduced a bill calling for withdrawal of all troops, which, although stymied in committee, still drew the attention of the American public to the inexplicable presence of combat troops in Russia.

On February 16, Wilson decided to call off the North Russian campaign and he cabled that information to Secretary of War Newton Baker, who began preparations for withdrawal. That same month, Baker announced that the 339th would be withdrawn as soon as possible. By April, with no evidence of withdrawal, parents and loved ones of men still in Russia put increasing pressure on their representatives in Congress. Requests to the Army for details about the 339th were unanswered, and anger mounted. In April, a group of concerned

Michiganders wired Army chief of staff Gen. Peyton March, pleading for information about withdrawal. The cable ended, "For God's sake, say something and do something!"[1]

The resentment and pressure came because of President Wilson and Secretary of War Baker's inconsistency, lack of candor, and failure to explain any purpose to the loss of life in Russia. Newspapers, particularly in the Midwest, took up the hue and cry. A *Chicago Tribune* article sounded incredulous when it wrote, "Our men are dying for a cause, the purpose of which they are no more certain than we in America. America has not declared war on Russia, but Americans are killing Russians and are being killed by them."[2]

The British, too, were feeling the pressure from the home front; on April 5, 1919, General Ironside received a telegram from the War Office in London telling him that, regardless of any international decision, his troops would be out as soon as possible.[3] Winston Churchill was the voice of opposition to withdrawal, believing that Communism could be stamped out with increased military action. He had little support from his colleagues or from the public. Then, the issue became how to protect the various Allied troops, as well as their loyal Russian supporters, when the Allies abandoned Russia. It was hoped that knowledge of the decisions to evacuate both American and British forces could be kept from the loyal Russians, but, of course, that was impossible. Even before the Allies boarded their last ships, the apprehensions of the North Russians became obvious.

One of the most enthusiastic Allied supporters was aviator Capt. Alexander Kozakov. He was Russia's earliest and foremost ace, having shot down twenty German and Austro-Hungarian planes. The abandonment of his country by the Allies angered Kozakov. In August, he ordered his little Sopwith Snipe up for a last flight. "At the top of the climb the little fighter stalled and spun, plunging into the centre of the airfield. Other pilots and ground crew raced over to the crumpled wreck, but it was too late. Alexander Kozakov had made his final gesture of defiance."[4]

According to the withdrawal plans, the British were to hold the positions with loyal Russians while U.S. troops gradually withdrew from their various fronts and were transported to Economie, where ships would arrive for the exit from North Russia. In order for British units to hold their ground and protect the withdrawal, British reinforcements were sent to Archangel. On May 27, 1919, a four-thousand-man relief brigade, commanded by Brigadier General Grogan, an experienced western front commander, arrived in Archangel.[5] They were followed days later by a second four-thousand-man brigade, led by another western front veteran, Gen. L. W. Sadleir-Jackson. These relieving brigades even brought a small number of British tanks, which proved utterly worthless in the swamps surrounding the roads.[6]

As the English generals planned the departure, the Americans began to withdraw from the fighting fronts and gather at the port of Economie. The companies came in on various dates: "Early in April B and C companies were relieved at Toulgas and Kurgomen, K company left Kholmogori late in May, G, L, M, I and E companies—in the order named—were withdrawn from the Railroad Front also in May."[7] Company D arrived in Economie on June 8; Company F was the last out, also on June 8.

While the various companies whiled away the hours, the men were reintroduced to the military life: saluting, policing the area, venereal inspections, drills, and kitchen duty. Reviews, too, were required; in one, the company that performed the best in the camp review was picked to march in the Memorial Day parade and ceremony at the Archangel cemetery. That honor went to Company M; Donald Carey was happy it was not his company, E. "When I considered the long, tiresome march as a member of a funeral detail in September, I did not envy their winning first place."[8]

In Economie, the regiment was assembled as a full unit for the first time since it left England. To celebrate that fact, the senior officers required a regimental review in full field pack, although without rifles. It was hot and dusty and no pleasure for the troops. Ironside made an inspection of the ranks, passing through each line. He impressed Private Carey:

> Though I had seen him before I took a good look at this remarkable officer as he passed an arm's length in front of me. Fully six feet four inches in height, he was a man of powerful physique, keen intellect, and unusual personality. His courageous countenance and excellent features combined with blue eyes and clear, ruddy complexion were fairly handsome.[9]

After the inspection, the perspiring doughboys were treated to a series of speeches by their officers. General Richardson made a long and, to Carey, incoherent speech, telling the men how he wished he had been with them during the campaign. General Ironside noted, "Some of the men going home raised a shout of laughter at this."[10] It may be an insignificant omission, but in no recounting of those last days is there a mention of Colonel Stewart. The regiment was ready to depart after the review. The lucky ones left June 2 on the first ship, the transport *Tsar,* headed for Brest, France. The last group left Economie on June 15. Both contingents stopped at Murmansk for logistical purposes and there had their final clash with the British.

As they docked in Murmansk, some fresh British troops were on board a transport docked nearby. Private Henkelman on the *Menominee* wrote:

> On the Kola River near Murmansk we tied up with our bow near an English ship just arriving in North Russia. I was below deck when I heard noises and I sauntered up on deck and saw a pitched battle taking place between our gang and the English throng, each side hurling chunks of coal at each other and cursing loudly. Our men wanted to get off and attack the Limeys, but our officers doubled the guard at the gangplank.[11]

Edwin Arkins wrote in his journal, "English and American troops on opposite transports get into row. One of our men is hit by bottle thrown from opposite ship."[12]

The troops had mixed emotions watching Russia fade from view as they entered the White Sea. Most were delighted to be going home, but puzzled by their experiences. Again and again, the question was asked: why were we there? No reasonable answer ever came. Some of the thoughts of the departing Americans were expressed by Capt. Joel Moore:

> That night scene with the lowering sun near midnight gleaming gold upon the forest shaded stretches of the Dvina River and casting its mellow melancholy light upon the wrecked churches of a village, is an ineffaceable picture of North Russia. For this is our Russia—a church, a little cluster of log houses, encompassed by unending forests of moaning spruce and pine; low, brooding, sorrowful skies; and over all oppressive stillness, sad, profound, mysterious, yet strangely lovable to our memory.
>
> Near the shell-gashed and mutilated church are two rows of unadorned wooden crosses, simple memorial of a soldier burial ground. Come vividly back into the scene the winter funerals of our buddies, brave men, who, loving life, having been laid away there, having died soldier-like for a cause they dimly understood. And the crosses now rise up, mute, eloquent testimony to the cost of this strange, inexplicable war of North Russia.[13]

The Americans and French had departed, and the British evacuation plan was left to Ironside; however, he was plagued by a series of mutinies and desertions that sapped both his enthusiasm and his energy. The Russian garrison at Onega abruptly handed the installation over to the Soviets, then a company of Russians deserted at Seletskoye. But the bitterest blow was the mutiny of the Salvo Batallion Allied Legion (SBAL), Dyer's Battalion, trained and led by British officers and noncoms. On July 7, these Russians turned on their officers, murdered them as they slept, and bolted for the Soviet lines. Four Russian and five British officers died in the mutiny; the event shook Ironside to the core.[14] Until that time, Ironside hoped that the Russian White Army could survive after the Allies had gone, but he began to see the impossibility of that expectation. Even his relief officers questioned the reliability of the Russian troops they commanded. Mutinies on a large scale were not frequent, but individual desertions were a daily occurrence. The situation was disheartening for the British general.

Ironside's plan was to mount a substantial offensive with his new, fresh replacements to push back the Bolos, then to evacuate his men before a Soviet counterattack could be launched. Ironside even had vague thoughts of taking Kotlas, the elusive target of the 1918 fall campaign, and somehow linking up with the Siberian troops. Any chance that this goal might be realized was dashed when word came from Omsk on July 24 that Kolchak's Siberian forces were collapsing and there would be no westward movement of his army. Ironside issued orders for his own offensive to begin August 10 on the Dvina, adding that all units would be withdrawn from Russia by month's end. Right on schedule, the British jumped off on August 10 with a smashing victory, pushing the Bolsheviks back, capturing and sinking their gunboats, and assuring the British that their evacuation would be unhampered by the enemy. Loyal Russian troops were left in the defensive works around Berezenik in case any Soviets showed up, but Ironside breathed a sigh of relief as he returned to Archangel. Casualties in the campaign were 145 killed and wounded.[15]

Capping off the disappointments of the past months, Ironside heard indirectly that a new commanding officer was coming to Archangel to be his superior. This news was confirmed by cable on August 1; Lord Rawlinson would arrive soon to take command. Ironside accepted the news stoically:

> For a moment I had a feeling of disappointment that I was not to be allowed to see the business out by myself, but a little thought soon showed me how necessary such an appointment was. Both General Maynard and I were very much taken up in the affairs of our commands, which were not only widely separated but had indifferent communications between them. And the evacuation of all Allied troops undoubtedly required careful co-ordination.[16]

Fortunately, Ironside and Rawlinson took an instant liking to each other; Rawlinson accepted Ironside's plan, and it was only a matter of withdrawing the troops, arranging transport, and returning to England.

As plans for embarkation progressed, Rawlinson moved on to

Murmansk, leaving Ironside in Archangel to answer the many Russian petitions, pleas, and protests concerning the imminent British departure, which was now well known. One visitor to Ironside's office was a prominent Russian colonel who had been honored with the British Distinguished Service Order.

> He entered my office and saluted me. He then threw his DSO on the table between us. For two minutes he told me what he thought of the Allies and their behaviour. He then saluted again and marched out of the room. I sat in silence looking at the discarded Order which he had so gallantly won.[17]

To complete the British withdrawal plan, Russian general Miller would attack down the railroad on August 29, aided by two Australian companies and a flight of aging RAF planes. Although the attack was a huge success, Ironside had to tell Miller that the British departure date was September 10 and could not be changed. Miller had hoped that his successful offensive would reenergize the Allies, but it was not to be. The actual withdrawal from the front lines began smoothly on August 20; by August 23, all British forces were within a defensive perimeter outside Archangel. In a complex movement of boats, transports, and tugs, the AEF slowly made its way downriver as Ironside watched from the British admiral's yacht.

As General Ironside took his last leave of Archangel and of General Miller and his aide, he was moved:

> The guard turned out again and he was piped over the side. We stood watching them as they walked slowly away. I was half hoping he might turn and wave his hand to us in farewell, but he never once looked back, keeping steadily on till they disappeared behind the buildings once more. He was a very proud and gallant gentleman.[18]

From the White Russian standpoint, the Intervention had been a monumental disaster. Disregarding the suffering of thousands caught in the fighting during the Allied effort, some Russians maintained that the Intervention aided the cause of the Bolsheviks by focusing their propaganda on these foreign "invaders." A Russian professor in Archangel wrote recently, "From our point of view, without the Allied Intervention the anti-Bolshevik struggle in the north could hardly have taken the form of civil war."[19]

Perhaps a more fitting epitaph came from Eugenie Fraser's household.

One morning, a chain of ships, half hidden by the early mists, slowly stole past our shores and vanished behind the island on its way to the White Sea. Only a year earlier these ships had been met with rejoicing and now they were slinking away in silence. We watched them from our windows. Only Seryozha passed a bitter comment. "Why did they come at all? We shall pay a bitter price for this."[20]

And they did.

For a few months the White Army under General Miller managed to hold their ground, but in the bitter winter of 1920, his command began to unravel. In October 1919 the Reds began a slow movement down the Dvina toward Archangel. On February 20, 1920, forces coming up the Vologda Railroad and the Dvina attacked and occupied Archangel. The Red Army also moved up the Murmansk Railroad, taking key cities; Murmansk finally fell on March 20, 1920.[21]

There are few records of the terror that swept North Russia as the Bolsheviks took their vengeance on White Russians and Allied supporters. The continual fighting on the six fronts had burned, shelled, or wiped out most of the towns and cities; when the plundering Reds arrived, those who were fortunate enough to elude the execution squads made survival their only goal. Mass executions took place daily.

Eugenie Fraser, while on an outing picking berries, heard tramping feet behind her and looked back to see a group of guarded prisoners with spades. They passed through a gate into a nearby field, then disappeared into a thicket. Eugenie recognized the school uniform of one of the young prisoners:

> Suddenly the sound of distant shots broke the silence. A flock of frightened birds flew overhead and vanished. Puzzled, Vera and I looked up.
>
> Sometime later, with our full baskets, we were winding our way back past the rough fencing, the strange gate, and onto the road to the town. We were again overtaken by the same soldiers, marching briskly back toward the prison. There were no prisoners in their midst, but flung over their shoulders were bundles of clothing, including the gray uniform of the young boy. Everything fell into place. The prisoners, the gate, the shots, the birds flying overhead, the gray uniform.[22]

Estimates are that as many as thirty thousand North Russians perished at the hands of the Bolsheviks during the next year.[23]

Most of the doughboys had fought bravely and well. There had been unrest, and in a few cases, they had carried out their orders reluctantly, but in spite of many inner feelings, they did their duty. The Canadians and Americans often expressed sympathy for, and even a certain closeness to, the Bolsheviks. "This was not unusual among the

Americans and Canadians of the winter army and was so common among the new army that I felt at one time they were more likely to make trouble for the Military Intervention than the Russians were," wrote Ralph Albertson of the YMCA.[24] But Americans and Canadians, unlike the British, French, or Russians, left mutiny to others.

After Murmansk, the Yanks went to Brest, France, then to Camp Pontanezen near Brest. On June 22, the first units to be sent home boarded the USS *Von Steuben,* headed west for New York. Aboard, in shackles, was Pvt. Harry Jones of Company E, who had been convicted of the murder of Martin Campbell in October 1918. The ship crossed without event; the various companies were moved to Detroit, where the Army routine broke down as families found each other. Carey wrote, "And how glorious it was for Detroit. Her regiment—Detroit's Own— was back from a long campaign on foreign soil; back to receive the hospitable welcome of a gracious city, a happy state and a grateful nation."[25] The final move for most men was to Camp Custer, where they were quietly discharged from service. Other units came from Brest a few days later on the *President Grant,* going first to Boston, then arriving in Detroit on July 15. They were feted and paraded, as the first units had been, and discharged on July 18, 1919, exactly one year after they had left the United States for their unanticipated Arctic experience.

With this episode concluded, the 339th was deactivated as a unit. It would, however, see war again on the Italian front during World War II.

The 310th Engineers, one of the last full units remaining in Russia, left on June 26 and proceeded to Brest, then boarded the USS *Northern Pacific* for the Atlantic crossing to Hoboken, New Jersey. The men were processed at Camp Merritt, New Jersey, and discharged there, so they simply drifted back to their homes without fanfare.

Finally, the 167th and 168th Transportation Companies left Murmansk on July 30 and were demobilized at Brest. General Richardson's return completed the official closing of the American North Russian Expeditionary Force on August 5, 1919.[26]

The AEFNR veterans had a special bond; they formed their own organization, the Polar Bear Association, which met regularly until 1983, when death and illness thinned its ranks to an aged few. Two Polar Bear chapters of the Veterans of Foreign Wars (VFW) still exist, one in Detroit and the other in Muskegon, Michigan.

Although 235 Americans had died in Russia, when the 339th units came home in 1919, they brought only 108 bodies, including those of 5 sailors. More than one hundred bodies lay in marked and unmarked graves throughout the frozen, swampy lands of Russia. But records then, as they often are today, were confused and inaccurate.

Pvt. John Westerhof of Grand Rapids, Michigan, is a case in point. Westerhof died on board a barge on the Dvina River on September 11. His
body was kept on board until the barge docked at Bereznik, where he
was buried in a little churchyard.[27] As the Americans were leaving
Archangel, more than one hundred bodies were exhumed and put on
board the transports. After arrival in the United States, each was sent
to his hometown for burial. Before Westerhof was lowered into the
ground, his parents opened the casket and found that it was not their
son.[28] Who it was, no one knows. There is no record that Westerhof's
body was ever recovered, and, on a plaque in the Meuse Argonne National Cemetery in France dedicated to the missing in action, is the
name of John T. Westerhof, along with others from the 339th.[29]

In one sense, however, the last Polar Bears to return were brought
home many years later in what is one of the most unusual ventures ever
taken by Americans. In 1929 a group sponsored by the VFW with some
State of Michigan funds and some federal funds was able to obtain permission to enter Soviet territory to search for and recover those bodies
left behind. In an odyssey that could fill a book, the group managed to
discover and identify eighty-six remains, even after ten years in that
hostile climate. They were helped by government officials and graves
registration personnel in their frustrating and difficult search. Surprisingly, in 1934 the Soviet government shipped to the United States the
remains of twelve more Polar Bears. They were the last to come home.
But twenty-nine Americans, forever young, still lie somewhere in that
strange hostile land just below the Arctic Circle.

After careful analysis and processing, seventy-five of the eighty-
six bodies recovered in the search were returned to the United States
on board the SS *President Roosevelt* in zinc-lined coffins. The ship
docked at Hoboken, New Jersey, on November 28, 1929, greeted not by
the cheering crowds of ten years ago, but by a seventeen-gun salute and
funeral dirges played by the Army Sixteenth Infantry Band. With dignity and respect, the seventy-five flag-draped caskets were boarded on
a black-creped funeral train that would take them to their final resting
place. Three families requested burial in Arlington, eleven families
asked that their loved ones be buried in Europe, and sixteen Polar Bears
were delivered to their hometowns as the train wound slowly west.

The train stopped in every town or city of any size in New York, New
Jersey, Pennsylvania, Ohio and Michigan. Taps was played at each station
even in the dead of night, the plaintive notes registering on silent crowds
of citizens and VFW honor guards. Nothing like it had been seen since
the train bearing the body of assassinated President Abraham Lincoln
made its sad journey to Illinois in 1865.[30]

On December 1, the train made its last stop at Detroit's Union Station, where thousands gathered in the falling snow to witness the somber procession of fifty-six hearses wind its way to White Chapel Cemetery in Troy. There the bodies would remain in state until Memorial Day 1930, when a proper ceremony could dedicate the new Polar Bear monument and consign the dead to their place of honor. More Polar Bears would join their comrades in 1934, when the Soviets chose to return the remains of twelve soldiers, who would lie in the company of their friends at White Chapel.[31]

There would be no closure for the twenty-nine families left without further knowledge of their missing sons, husbands, or brothers.

While it was a bitter and frustrating winter for the 339th Infantry Regiment, there was a fierce pride in most of them as they came home to live with their memories and wounds and to resume their civilian lives. Lt. John Commons of Company K summed it up not just for the men of Company K returning from the horrors of Kodish, but for all men of the regiment:

> So they stuck and fought, suffering through the bitter months of winter just below the Arctic Circle, where the winter day is in minutes and the night seems a week. And there is not one who is not proud that he was once a "sidekicker" and a "buddy" to some of those fine fellows of the various units who unselfishly and gladly gave the last a man has to give for any cause at all.[32]

Aftermath

ABOUT many of the principal players little is known.

President Chaikovsky was a delegate to the Paris Peace Conference and stayed on to live in the French capital.

Cpl. Earl Collins died in a Bolshevik hospital. In a surprising move, the Soviet government released his body with eleven others in 1934. His family elected to have him interred in Europe, and he remains the only member of the 339th Infantry Regiment buried in England.

Ambassador David Francis recovered from his prostate surgery and plagued President Wilson for years, pleading for massive troop reinforcements.

Eugenie Fraser left Russia in 1920 and moved to her Scottish mother's house in Scotland. She married and lived most her life in Australia, but, widowed, she now lives in Edinburgh.

Gen. Edmund Ironside prospered in his military career, becoming Chief of the Imperial General Staff at the outbreak of World War II, but retired in 1942 and died in 1959 at the age of seventy-nine.

Gen. E. Miller, who stuck with his troops until the disintegration of the northern White Army, sailed out of Archangel with the mysterious George Chaplin just before the Reds took over the city. Reportedly, he lived in Paris, but was abducted and murdered by Red agents years later.

George Stewart passed from sight into an undistinguished Army career. He did make colonel, but never received any recognition for Archangel. He retired on disability in 1931 and died March 2, 1946.

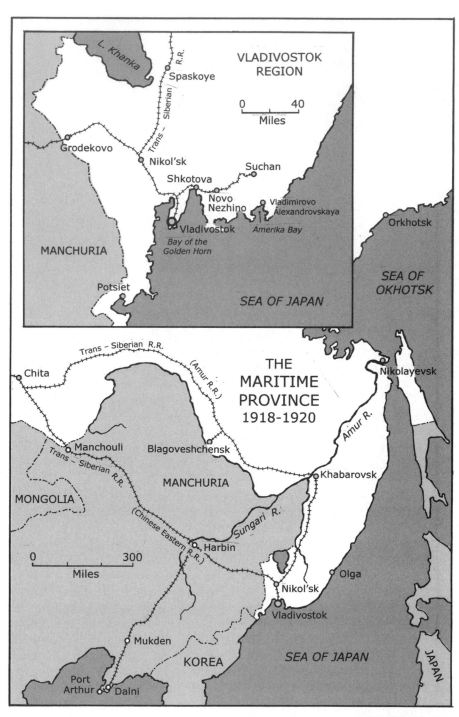

credit: Richard Barber

PART II

Siberia

The American Expeditionary Force Siberia,
1918–1920

The Russian Railroad Story

Anyway, will risk saying that things are looking brighter for the old R.R.S. Corps and we are coming to life, and every man Jack will soon have something to do.

—Lt. Fayette Keeler, RRSC

AT the same time the AEFNR was engaged in North Russia, another American force found itself on the opposite end of Russia, four thousand miles from the 339th Infantry. However, the Siberian expedition was remarkably different from the North Russian expedition. In August 1918, Maj. Gen. William S. Graves, still in Camp Fremont, California, took command of the American Expeditionary Forces Siberia (AEFS), consisting of two infantry regiments sent from the Philippines and bolstered by five thousand replacements from the Eighth Division at Camp Fremont. However, as in North Russia, there were other American forces already involved in Siberia: the Russian Railroad Service Corps (RRSC), and the Navy.

As the American forces began their placement of troops in the Siberian intervention, and the rugged Czech legionnaires struggled toward their eastern goal of Vladivostok, they were completely dependent on the Trans-Siberian Railroad, as was another group of volunteers. This group was unique in its expertise; its members were experienced railroad men, recruited from the northern states to try to salvage the Russian rail system that to all intents and purposes had collapsed. Theirs was a frustrating and disappointing chore that kept them ever in confrontation with the elements, the government, the workers, and even the Allies. They were the members of the Russian Railway Service Corps (RRSC).

When Tsar Nicholas II abdicated in March 1917, President Wilson felt relieved that the only monarchy in the Allied camp had become a democratic government, easing Wilson's concerns about supporting the autocratic tsar and his repressive regime. It was only one month later that the United States entered the war on the side of the Allies. It was still hoped that Russia would remain in the war; however, the condition of the railroads, particularly the Trans-Siberian, was so bad that virtually no supplies could be shipped from Vladivostok to the eastern front. The conditions that existed during those spring months were chaotic; Wilson failed to realize that the provisional government of Luvov and Kerensky, although given the authority to rule, lacked the power to do so.

Hoping that improvements in the railroad systems would be of some encouragement to the Russians, Wilson approved sending a team of U.S. railroad executives to determine the conditions of the railways. They were to meet with Russian railroad officials, review the roadways and make their recommendations to the new Russian provisional government. The Commission, known as the Advisory Railroad Commission to Russia, was selected by a number of railroad experts, and appointed by Secretary of State Robert Lansing, who gave them diplomatic status, important for the Commission members in their travels. The five members were John F. Stevens, Chairman; W. L. Darling, maintenance expert; John Greiner, bridges and structures; Henry Miller, transportation coordinator; and George Gibbs, equipment.

The hastily assembled group met in Chicago and on May 8, 1917, boarded a special train for Vancouver, then went by ship to Yokohama, arriving in Vladivostok on May 31, where they were immediately put to work.

On July 23, 1917, the Commission presented their recommendations to the Russian Railway Ministry, suggesting that the railroads be broken down into smaller operating units, with the United States providing some instructors. The Commission also pledged aid in the form of rolling stock, fifteen hundred railroad engines, and thirty thousand cars of differing types.[1] A more important request made by the Kerensky Government, and agreed to by the American Commission, was to provide a group of experienced American railway operators to assist the inept Russian railroaders.

The Commission visited Prime Minister Kerensky on August 10. George Gibbs was not impressed:

> He appears to be a very active, neurotic, but tired man of about thirty-six; is tall and has a high and fine forehead surmounted by a growth of coarse black hair, a la pompadour. His eyes are fine, but shifty and his nose well proportioned, but his mouth and chin are weak.[2]

Gibbs felt that the regime had little future, and subsequent events proved him right. Kerensky did promise that their recommendations would be carried out and had his full approval. With that assurance the Commission members packed their bags, and on August 14, they left for Vladivostok; they returned to the United States, leaving John Stevens to work with the Russian government.

The Commission arrived in San Francisco on October 5, 1917; within the month the Bolsheviks had gained control of the government, and swept Kerensky from power. Because of the change of government the Commission's recommendations were forgotten, except for the promised cadre of railway workers.

John Stevens remained in Russia to help carry out the recommendations of the American Commission, and was caught in the revolution. Meanwhile, his organization was being formed in the states as a quasi-military organization. This group, called the Russian Railway Service Corps, or RRSC, was actually the first echelon of the American Intervention.

The railroads were one of the critical elements of the Russian civil war that swept the troubled nation in the latter days of 1917. The Trans-Siberian Railroad, as the primary railroad of the country, was a fragile link between European Russia and the virtually undeveloped, but resource-rich, eastern Russia. The route between Murmansk and Petrograd, recently completed across the spongy tundra of North Russia, had just begun to move Allied supplies to the eastern front when the October-November 1917 revolution closed it.[3] The Archangel-Vologda Railroad joined the Trans-Siberian Road at Vologda, but in October 1917 that, too, was shut down.

Whether the Allies or President Wilson realized the importance of the chaotic railways of Russia to the future of the Allied Intervention is subject to debate; however, the creation of the Railway Corps was evidence that there was an awareness. Future use of Russian railroads would not be limited to transportation. Both sides would use the armored trains as weapons; they would be used as housing and hospitals for Allied and Russian troops, as well as refugees; and they would be a battleground for the Czech Legion.

The Russians realized the importance of the railroads when Prime Minister Kerensky sought American help with the Advisory Railroad Commission in mid-1917. Russia agreed to pay expenses for the RRSC technicians, and in the United States the call went out for volunteers. Most of the recruiting was done in the northern states, as the volunteers would be subject to severe Siberian winters. Even the commander, Col. George Emerson, came from the north; he most recently had been general manager of the Great Northern Railroad. In October the recruiting efforts peaked, and before long, the ranks were filled. The literature read, in part, "He [Emerson] will take with him twelve complete division organizations of train dispatchers, trainmasters, traveling engineers, line repairmen, foundry, boiler, machine, engineer erecting, round-house foremen, mechanical Supts. And master mechanics. 206 in all are to go Oct. 25 from Pacific Port."[4] Actually, about three hundred men eventually went as RRSC volunteers.[5] They were promised commissions as Army officers and were furnished uniforms similar to those of the Regular Army troops. They were, however, slightly different in their status. An ID carried by one of the men, Fred E. Brunner, stated, "I certify that Fred Emanuel Brunner is a Civil Agent of the United States detailed for service as 2d Lieut. in the Russian Railway Service Corps and is entitled under the laws of war, if captured, to the privileges of a civil official of the United States."[6] At the time, that designation seemed unimportant; however, later interpretations denied them war veteran status.

Most of the volunteers reported to RRSC headquarters in St. Paul, Minnesota; they were interviewed by Colonel Emerson personally, examined for any physical defects, and told to put their affairs in order for an immediate departure. On November 11, 1917, at 7:45 P.M., witnessed by their apprehensive families and friends, their train pulled out of St. Paul, bound for San Francisco. En route, the men received Russian-language instruction and even drilled in a few of the train stations when time permitted.

In San Francisco, they were joined by eighty men from America's Baldwin Locomotive Company, who would assemble some two thousand locomotives that had been shipped to Russia from the United States and were sitting in crates. They all received the usual overseas shots and uniforms, sent their last letters, and boarded the transport *Thomas*. One last letter from Peter Copeland closed with the enthusiasm most felt: "Do not worry for me as I am all right and would not be out of the fight for anything."[7] As the ship sailed out of San Francisco on November 19, many were pensive as they all wondered what the future might bring. Many of the railroaders were older men with wives and children, unlike the youth of the armed services. After the first week passed, the ship docked in Honolulu on November 26. Three days along the beach of Waikiki raised the men's spirits; there was other entertainment at the YMCA and Elks Clubs, and various parties on the island. On November 29, at 1:55 P.M., the *Thomas* took to the sea again.

The voyage proved to be a quiet one, with only one scare, when a German raider was reported nearby. But there was real concern about the war news that came in over the ship's wireless. Porter Turner wrote home from Honolulu on November 27, 1917, "If the Russians sign up for peace it will change our plans considerable. We are all in hopes we go as planned. In case we do not go to Russia sure hope we can go to France."[8] No one knew then, but events were already unfolding in Russia that would alter their future.

In Petrograd, the Russian capital, the second revolution of 1917 had swept the provisional government from office and the Bolsheviks now ruled. In Vladivostok, nine time zones from Petrograd, there seemed to be no government at all. As the *Thomas* docked at 11:00 A.M. on December 11, 1917, shoving through the ice in the Golden Horn harbor of Vladivostok, the city was in shambles. All *Thomas* shore leaves were cancelled as Emerson and the ship's captain hurried down the gangplank to find Colonel Stevens. The officers finally relented and issued shore passes to the few who showed interest in leaving the safety of the ship. The appearance of three hundred American men in uniform made the city officials nervous; the locals were suspicious and quietly hostile to the few railroaders who left the ship. Stevens and Emerson made the decision to return to Japan, informing Washington by wire: "Impossibility of proceeding with work at the present moment. Danger of harbor freezing makes prompt action imperative. Icebreakers in hands of insurgents. Please arrange quickly for Emerson to have ample credit. . . . I cannot supply him and shore quarters and food in Japan require cash."[9] With an icebreaker leading the way on December 17, the *Thomas* moved out of Vladivostok and headed for the more friendly port of Nagasaki, Japan.

The volunteers could not leave the ship until adequate quarters were found in Japan, which took until January 13. After fifty-three days on board, they disembarked in Nagasaki and watched with mixed feelings as the *Thomas* steamed out of sight on her way back home.[10] Here the corps would sit, many for months, waiting for the call to come from Vladivostok to go to work. As January came and went, the Americans switched from learning Russian to learning Japanese, complaining all the while. "Oh, dear, I wish we were on the move somewhere, Russia, Mesopotamia, Berlin, or home, I don't care which, just as long as we move," wrote Lt. Fayette Keeler. As the time passed new diversions were found: train trips to nearby towns, YMCA meetings, Japanese bathhouses, and endless days of local sightseeing. For half the corps, their Nagasaki stay would last until June.

But Colonel Stevens was not idle; he was in Harbin, China, negotiating with Gen. Dmitri Horvat, the Russian governor and general manager of the Chinese-Eastern Railway. Stevens offered the Russian his skilled men to use on the China railroad. Horvat, an anti-Bolshevik, had been able to chase the Bolsheviks out of his Chinese territory with support from Chinese troops. He was being plagued by the actions of Ataman Gregorii Semenov, a fiercely independent anti-Bolshevik Cossack who operated on both sides of the Russian-Manchurian border in the Lake Baikal area. Semenov had offered his protection to Horvat's railway, but his terms were too steep for Horvat.

In February 1918, Stevens and Horvat came to terms, and the RRSC was allowed to assume responsibility for the Chinese-Eastern Railway. The Chinese-Eastern route was the original route of the Trans-Siberian, but a second route, north from Vladivostok to Khabarovsk and then west, kept the line entirely in Russian territory. On March 30, Lieutenant Keeler wrote home:

> Washington's birthday we received the joyful news we were going to go to Harbin Manchuria within a week, and we were to go in bunches of fifty per day. Two bunches went and then they got orders to hold the balance here, much to our bitter disappointment. And here we have been ever since doing nothing.[11]

Keeler stayed in Japan, but the situation in the Far East was in such confusion that the RRSC in China was confined to menial duties in and around Harbin. Eventually, Keeler went as one of the next five men sent to Harbin in February. Much later, on August 22, he wrote about the Czechs, who had arrived in Harbin, but repeated his hope for more activity: "Anyway, will risk saying that things are looking brighter for the old R.R.S. Corps and we are coming to life, and every man Jack will soon have something to do. This is a relief to think of it, after being inactive for nine months."[12] Unfortunately, more months would pass with little to do.

During those spring and summer months of 1918, one expedition did provide excitement for the corps. A telegram from Secretary of State Robert Lansing ordered Stevens to send Colonel Emerson to Vologda, thousands of miles to the west, to confer with American ambassador David Francis. He was to take several engineers and technicians with him and leave at once. A group of seven with one interpreter left

Harbin for Vladivostok on May 4. Emerson soon learned his would not be an easy mission. First, the Chinese-Eastern refused him any cars with which to make the trip. In Vladivostok, Adm. Austin Knight, American fleet commander, and American consul John Caldwell told him that the United States had no relations with the Soviet government in Vladivostok, so he would have to deal with them himself. Finally, on May 19, enough cars were made available for Emerson to begin his trip. He had more delays in Khabarovsk, but Emerson's crew finally arrived in Chita on May 25, one month after Lansing's order had been received.

In the next town, Krasnoyarsk, he was met by the stationmaster, who said that an armed confrontation between Czechs and Bolsheviks was imminent at Marinsk, just ahead. Emerson volunteered to mediate between the two parties, which was highly agreeable to the officials in Krasnoyarsk. In their new role as mediators, the RRSC train moved slowly toward Marinsk, with the train engine flying the Stars and Stripes, plus a white flag.[13] The Russians wanted the Czechs disarmed; the Czechs wanted to pass through the territory peaceably, keeping their weapons. After some debate it was decided the Czechs were to give up most of their arms, keeping twenty rifles per car for defense. In return, the Russians promised safe passage to Vladivostok. There was much conversation back and forth, but peace, temporary as it was, was established.

After that diplomatic mission, Emerson "hurried" on toward Vologda, still some two thousand miles away. But before he could move on, Emerson wanted to learn about conditions between his location in Marinsk and Vologda. He decided to go back to Omsk until assurance could be received that it was clear ahead, so the RRSC contingent retreated to Omsk on June 26. To his surprise he found that Maj. Alphonse Guinet, French liaison officer with Czech forces, had issued a statement to Czech and Russian papers that Americans and Allies would intervene at the end of June. That would have been a surprise to President Wilson, who was still wrestling with the question of intervention.

By late June, Emerson, in conversations with Harris, decided that the confrontations between the White Russians, Czechs, and Bolsheviks had become a full-fledged civil war, not just a series of local uprisings. With the specific instructions from Washington to stay out of internal affairs, it was decided to refrain from any further efforts to mediate between the various factions. He received a message from Harris in Irkutsk telling him that he had verified the French commitment to intervene at the end of June and that the United States would join the French. Based on that information, erroneous as it was, Emerson made up his mind to help the Czechs. Now, he felt free to assist the Czechs on their movement east, in anticipation of the actual intervention.[14] Emerson never did reach Vologda, nor did he confer with Ambassador Francis; he remained with Czech forces in the Gaida command, waiting for a chance to take his party back to Harbin.

In July Gaida's objective was the capture of Irkutsk, an area that kept him from linking up with the eastern Czech forces in Vladivostok, either across Manchuria or through the northern route to Khabarovsk. The Bolsheviks had fortified Irkutsk, and desperately needed to stop Gaida. Gaida's forces had blown up one of the Red trains loaded with explosives, but the Reds managed to blow the last tunnel of the thirty-nine that ran through the hills and cliffs east of the city, totally blocking the tunnel. With the help of Emerson's group, the way was cleared for the Czechs by August 17.

The Bolsheviks were now in full retreat, blowing bridges, tearing up track, and using other delaying tactics, but Emerson and his team led the repair efforts as they moved through Verkhne-Udinsk, Chita and into Karenskaya. The *Siberian Sojourn* stated, "So it went, mile after mile, with one interruption after another. Wrecked cars were found. Tracks were badly torn up. The tracks, of course, had to be repaired."[15] Near Karenskaya, the Czechs finally met Semenov's Cossacks, many riding on the Czech trains into the city, where the new troops were met with cheers and with delegations welcoming them. Emerson's trip was nearing an end. Czechs from the Third Regiment had been working westward from Vladivostok; the eastern and western Czechs finally met just east of Adrianovka. The report from them was that the Trans-Siberian Railroad was clear from Vladivostok to the Urals.[16]

The Czech Legion had accomplished a minor miracle in their eastward journey: fighting, governing, repairing, and surviving in the unfriendly confines of Siberia. It was probably the high point of the Czech Legion's career. Their future from then on would be full of trouble and conflict, from within and without.

Emerson earned high praise from General Graves:

> He [Emerson] is a man whose language, whose appearance, and whose general attitude towards the duty in hand inspires one with confidence in his integrity of purpose, and the longer one knows him and his work, the greater this confidence becomes.
>
> Colonel Emerson was as disinterested in the political squabbles of the Russian factions as any man I saw in Siberia. He was in Russia for the sole purpose of helping the Russians operate the railroad and took no interest in any other activity.[17]

Graves also blamed Consul General Harris, who had prematurely verified the French statement that Allied help was on the way in early July and had so informed Emerson.

When Emerson arrived in Vladivostok on September 6, he learned that the rest of the Nagasaki members of the RRSC had finally made it to Russia and that most of them were in Vladivostok. He also learned that the Intervention had begun and two American infantry regiments were already in Vladivostok with contingents from other Allies in the city as well.

The RRSC group in Harbin, including Lieutenant Keeler, was still complaining about lack of action and purpose. Keeler was both a wireless operator and a telegrapher, but had almost nothing to do. On August 31, 1918, he wrote, "Things are moving rapidly around Harbin but not as far as we are concerned, although we all hope that something turns up for the R.R.S. to do. It is understood by everyone that our original mission has gone up the spout and we are waiting to see what will be done with us."[18]

Another letter, dated February 15, 1919, shows he was still frustrated: "Harbin told us today that they were hiring all the interpreters they could get and that it is 'rumored' we will be at work very soon. D—— these rumors."[19]

The corps would finally be put to work by an agreement among the Allies assigning various segments of the Trans-Siberian and Chinese-Eastern Railroads to individual nations. As with any agreement between nations whose goals may differ, the signing of the final agreement and its implementation, leading to the real usefulness of the RRSC, would not happen overnight. It would actually not happen until April 1919, nearly a year and a half after the corps left San Francisco. However, the future was dismal as the corps work was continually interrupted by marauding Cossacks and stymied by government bureaucracy. Eventually, the Czechs, the RRSC, and the AEFS would be bound to the vital railroad tracks that crossed Siberia and part of China.[20]

Vladivostok and the Navy

*We had a Filipino Band who never saw snow before. They came out
to play nary a toot of their instrument froze on their lips and the
marines had to carry them inside the ship.*

—Seaman A. Lange, Edith Faulstich Collection, Hoover Institution

THE USS *Brooklyn* arrived on March 1, 1918, establishing the
American military presence in Vladivostok to keep an eye
on Allied, primarily Japanese, actions. The *Brooklyn* joined the other
Allied ships, the British HMS *Suffolk* and the Japanese *Asahi*.[1] While
in port, the *Brooklyn* performed the usual ship's routines, but occasionally had a moment of excitement. On April 1, four sampans came too
close to the ship and were cautioned with warning shots. Then, three
days later, four Japanese merchants were murdered in Vladivostok. A
Japanese reaction was expected, so it was no surprise when on April 5,
lookouts reported that a force of about 160 Japanese sailors landed near
the railway station and marched toward their consulate. Soon after,
fifty British sailors left the *Suffolk* under arms to protect British citizens
and diplomats. Two days later the American commander in chief, Rear
Adm. Austin Knight, and the chief of staff left the ship to attend the
funeral services of the murdered Japanese.[2] Although all forces remained on high alert, there were no major clashes in the city.

162

The Americans were not involved in any fighting; however, during the period March 2 to May 30, the *Brooklyn* lost six of its crew-members, four sailors and two Marines, all of whom died of disease.[3] The memorial services for C. E. Greene, W. B. Frost, H. E. Nelson (USMC), A. A. Helgeson (USMC), W. A. Nicholson, and A. L. Osuna were held on the windswept hill of Vladivostok's Lutheran Cemetery on May 30 as a party went ashore to decorate their graves.

Hostilities began on the morning of June 29, 1918, when the Czechs assaulted the sitting Soviet government in Vladivostok.[4] While the revolt was in progress, all Allied ships sent armed shore parties into the city to protect their consulates and citizens. For those who stayed on board ship, virtually the only excitement was the arrival of two Czechs, who had been run off their posts. They stayed just over an hour, leaving at 3:40 P.M. At 5:25 P.M., a fully armed contingent of U.S. Marines under Lieutenant Grove went ashore to the consulate. "At 6:00 P.M. the firing ceased, the Bolsheviks were defeated, and the city became quiet. At 7:35 the armed guard at the American Consulate was reduced to eight marines."[5] The sailors could hear firing and see movement, but did not see any of the action.

According to the ship's log, trouble in the city began because the local government had ordered the Czechs in Vladivostok to disarm; this made the Czechs most unhappy. So with a minimum of discussion, the Czechs decided to take over the city.[6] They installed a minor political figure, Russian Peter Derber, as the titular head of the new provisional government; but the Czechs, under Maj. Gen. Milo K. Dietrichs, formerly a Russian general, ran the town. The only U.S. naval contribution to the coup, beside guarding the consulate, was tending the Czech wounded. On July 4, Admiral Knight cabled the Secretary of the Navy, "10 Czechs killed in taking city—wounded being taken care of by our surgeons."[7]

However, the *Brooklyn* medical staff soon had an additional workload. On July 4, the Czechs suffered heavy casualties fighting the Reds near Nikolsk, the junction point of the Chinese-Eastern and Trans-Siberian Railroads. Their wounded were brought back to the city for treatment. There were seventy-seven in all; the *Brooklyn* had insufficient space for so many, so they converted a waterfront warehouse into a makeshift hospital for seventy-two Czechs. The five most severely wounded were put on board the *Brooklyn* for surgery. For most of July, wounded continued to come aboard the American vessel.[8] All of the wounded who received treatment survived. Admiral Knight cabled the Secretary of the Navy on July 15:

> The assistance given the Czech's wounded has been appreciated highly by them. The report of the kind service of the men of the USS *Brooklyn*

and of comfort afforded have spread throughout the whole force, producing gratifying sentiment in return. Our men have given up mattresses, blankets, furnished cigarettes and other things cheerfully, and also acted as nurses and waiters. I have ordered additional surgeons and nurses from The Yokohama and Canacao Hospitals.[9]

On July 6, the Allies took control of the city, stating:

In view of the dangers which threaten Vladivostok and the Allied forces here assembled from the open and secret activities of Austro-German war prisoners, spies and emissaries, the city and its vicinity are hereby taken under the temporary protection of the Allied Powers and all necessary measures will be taken for its defense against dangers both external and internal.[10]

While the *Brooklyn* would depart Russia in October 1918, the Navy presence would continue with return visits of the *Brooklyn* and replacement ships, the USS *Albany, New Orleans*, and *South Dakota.*

It was more than a month later that the first units of the AEFS entered the scene.

The AEFS Assembles

Watch your step; you will be walking on eggs loaded with dynamite.
God bless you and good bye.

—Secretary of War Newton Baker

AS the 339th Infantry was en route to England, unaware of their new and frigid assignment in North Russia, another curious development was taking place at Camp Fremont in Palo Alto, California. The Eighth Infantry Division was in training at Fremont, getting ready for the battlefields of France. Ready to lead them was fifty-three-year-old, recently promoted Maj. Gen. William S. Graves. An 1889 graduate of West Point, he was a major when the war began. He was sent on a secret mission to Europe in 1916 to help devise an organizational plan for an American expeditionary force to join the Allies, should such a force be required. He remained on the general staff in Washington, being promoted as his responsibilities increased. After his promotion to major general in June 1918, Army chief of staff Gen. Peyton March offered him command of the Eighth Division. This was the job he really wanted, leading a division in combat. One description of the new major general was that "he was self reliant, well trained, intelligent, and that he had common sense and a self-effacing loyalty."[1]

Graves's happiness with his new command was clouded by an ominous telegram from Washington, which he received on August 2. Graves was to take the first train from San Francisco to Kansas City, go to the Baltimore Hotel, and meet Secretary of War Newton Baker.[2] There were no further instructions, so he had no idea what to take, not knowing when, or even if, he would be returning to Camp Fremont.

Secretary Baker was at the station waiting for Graves when the general arrived, weary after sitting up on the lengthy trip. Baker could spare him but little time, as he was headed back to Washington immediately, so they met in the train depot. Baker told Graves that he was to lead the American Expeditionary Force Siberia. He apologized for the general's change of orders, but offered no explanation. The meeting was brief; Baker handed Graves a sealed envelope with the orders for his new assignment. As Baker left, he cautioned the new commander, "This contains the policy of the United States in Russia which you are to follow. Watch your step; you will be walking on eggs loaded with dynamite. God bless you and good bye."[3]

Graves went to the hotel, opened the envelope, and found the *Aide Memoire,* written by the president just two weeks before. He read it again and again, feeling he had to know every nuance of the document. Early the next day, he boarded the Santa Fe and headed back to San Francisco.

As expressed in Wilson's *Aide Memoire,* his orders, or possibly "directions," appeared to be as much diplomatic as military. He was to assist the Czechs, protect the supplies in the Russian Far East, and "steady any efforts at self-government or self defense in which the Russians themselves may be willing to accept assistance."[4] There were few effective governments in the Russian Far East; the Soviet government in Moscow was four thousand miles away and had little influence over the competing factions in the east.

The War Department lost no time in assembling the various elements of the AEFS, on August 3 telegraphing the Headquarters Philippine Department to release two regiments. The Twenty-seventh Infantry under Lt. Col. Charles H. Morrow departed August 7, 1918, on three ships, the *Merritt,* the *Crook,* and the *Warren.* After one stop at Nagasaki, Japan, they arrived in Vladivostok on August 15 and 16. On August 12, Col. Frederick H. Sargent followed with his Thirty-first Infantry on the *Sherman,* arriving on August 21.[5] Since General Graves would not arrive until later, Col. Henry Styer, stationed in the Philippines, joined the expedition as the interim commander of the AEF.[6] Between the two regiments, there were just over three thousand men. In Vladivostok, they began their participation in the bewildering adventure of the American Intervention.

General Graves, back in Palo Alto, had begun selecting his staff. Knowing that the first elements of his expedition would soon be landing in Russia, he picked carefully from the officers and ranks of the Eighth Division. Fortunately, he had the support and the sympathy of General March, who wired him on August 8 that he could have anything he needed for his mission. It seemed apparent that both Baker and March were aware of problems that would face Graves in the command they had just given him.

On August 14, 1918, General Graves, Chief of Staff Lt. Col. O. P. Robinson, Assistant Chief of Staff Maj. Robert L. Eichelberger, together with 45 other officers and 1,889 men, boarded two troop trains at Camp Fremont. Later that day, at 8:30 P.M., they sailed on the army transport *Thomas*, passing under the Golden Gate Bridge en route to Siberia.[7]

As the *Thomas* sailed out on its still "secret" mission, there was little fanfare, except for an unexpected and unwelcome searchlight that outlined the transport until long after she had passed under the bridge.[8] The battleship *Oregon* and the gunship *Vicksburg* were to convoy the troopship as protection against German U-boats, but Graves impatiently requested their release so the faster *Thomas* could speed its passage.[9]

As the troops on the *Thomas* relaxed, did calisthenics, listened to rudimentary lectures on military subjects, had occasional target practice, and generally whiled away the hours, Camp Fremont was still working frantically to fill the next contingent. These were primarily volunteers from the Thirteenth and Sixty-second Infantry Regiments, with a few left over from the Twelfth Regiment. Several noncommissioned officers actually took demotions to join the expedition, since there was a limit to the number of noncoms authorized. One newly commissioned captain of intelligence, Kenneth Roberts, inveigled his spot on the roster of officers headed for Siberia.[10] He argued that he should replace a certain Captain Ruth; when the orders were published, he told Ruth what he had done, thinking Ruth would be upset. Ruth was delighted. "'Siberia,' he said. 'Sore? Siberia? Gee, thanks!'"[11] Most of the troops craved excitement, and Siberia seemed mysterious, dark, and adventuresome, a change from the monotony of camp life.

Soon, another shipment was ready; two transports sailed away on September 2, 1918, with 1,886 men on the *Sheridan* and 1,811 on the *Logan*.[12] Adventure for these troops would not wait for their arrival in Siberia—they would create their own excitement en route.

The *Logan* was the slower of the two ships, so the *Sheridan* had to slow down to keep her in sight. This meant burning more coal, and after two weeks at sea, it was determined that a refueling stop would be prudent. The port selected, for unknown reasons, was Hakodate, Japan.

It was a poor choice: first, it had no coal, and second, it had a powerful Japanese whiskey.

On the voyage, Captain Roberts met an extraordinary member of the AEFS, Maj. Samuel I. Johnson of Honolulu, who was in charge of the troops on the *Sheridan*. His name wasn't really Sam Johnson—it was Boris Ignuatiev. Born in Russia, he joined a Cossack regiment as a boy and, later, was assigned to a naval training ship. He chafed under brutal treatment, wound up in irons, and when the ship arrived in the United States, jumped ship in Philadelphia. Eventually, he found himself in Honolulu and became a brigadier general in the Hawaiian National Army; he resigned to take a commission in the U.S. Army as a major. He wanted to fight Germans who had killed three of his brothers, but with his Russian background, he was picked for Siberia.[13] It was Sam Johnson who would call on Captain Roberts for help in Hakodate.

As the two ships anchored outside Hakodate on the northern island of Hokkaido, it was decided to let the doughboys get off the ship, visit the city, and stretch their legs. It was not a wise decision. The ships arrived unannounced, and very soon, unwelcomed. As the thirty-seven hundred doughboys, unsteady from weeks at sea, descended on the city, they immediately looked for bars and ladies of the evening. The sign in one bar said:

> Notice!! Having lately been Refitted and preparations have been made to supply those who give us a look-up, with Worst of Liquors and Food at a reasonable price, and served by the Ugliest Female Savants that can be Procured. This establishment cannot boast of a proprietor, but is carried on by a Japanese lady whose ugliness would stand out even in a crowd. The Cook, when his face is washed, is considered the best looking of the company.[14]

That sign was enough to pack the place to the rafters; other even seedier spots prospered as the soldiers sought liquor and companionship. It soon became apparent that Japanese whiskey had a power that affected the men far more than they anticipated. Johnson described the problem to Roberts:

> "All the cheap bars have Scotch whiskey made in Japan," he told us, "If you come across any, don't touch it. It's called Queen George, and it's more bitched up than its name. It must be eighty-six percent corrosive sublimate proof, because thirty-five hundred enlisted men were stinko fifteen minutes after they got ashore. I never saw so many get so drunk so fast."[15]

Johnson enlisted Roberts and a few others to round up the men and get them back aboard the two transports. Roberts described the challenge:

Intoxicated soldiers seemed to have the flowing qualities of water, able to seep through doorways, down chimneys, up through floors. When we slowly edged a score of khaki-clad tosspots from a dive and started them toward the ships, then turned to see whether we had overlooked anyone, the room would unbelievably be filled with unsteady doughboys, sprung from God knows where, drunkenly negotiating for the change of American money or the purchase of juss one more boll of Queen George.[16]

It was not just the enlisted men; officers joined in the orgy and later paid the price.[17] Eventually, order was restored, and the two ships lumbered out of port, still without coal.

They sailed some 150 miles north of Hakodate to another port, Otaru, hoping to find coal enough to get the ships to Vladivostok. As they anchored in Otaru, only a few men were allowed ashore, with cautions that their behavior would be studied carefully.

This time, the problems were of a different nature. Several enterprising doughboys had gilded Philippine one-centavo coins and passed them off as real gold coins, exchanging them for all kinds of merchandise. The merchants in Otaru became suspicious, discovered the fraud, and reported it to police. Meanwhile, as a strong typhoon approached the coast, the men ashore waited for the weather to ease in order to get sampans back to the ships. One of the doughboys, frustrated and drunk, smashed a liquor bottle over the head of a Japanese policeman. This created a true international incident; even after the typhoon subsided, the ships were held in port by local officials until the fraud and assault were satisfactorily resolved. Finally, after four days, Lt. Rodney Sprigg found the guilty parties, made them ante up enough money to satisfy all victims, and they were allowed to leave.[18] More courts-martial followed; Graves telegraphed the U.S. ambassador to Japan, Roland Morris on October 30, "It was undoubtedly a disgraceful occurrence, and the conduct of these men while on foreign soil has been a cause of mortification to us all."[19] Not only was American prestige damaged, but the typhoon winds had blown the *Logan* up on the breakwater causing some damage. However, she was still considered seaworthy for the short voyage to Russia.

After an overnight trip from Otaru to Vladivostok, the remainder of the Camp Fremont contingent docked in that city at 8:30 P.M. on September 29.[20]

Capt. Laurance Packard noted the speedy mobilization in his report:

This within twelve days after orders were issued, and with practically no interference with the colossal effort which the United States was making to decide the issue of the War on the Western Front, an organized and well-equipped force of 145 officers and 4805 men was actually on its way, to a remote and entirely new theatre of action.[21]

There is an explanation for the speedy deployment: on July 6, eleven days before Wilson announced his decision to intervene, a memo written by Col. E. D. Anderson of the General Staff outlined in some detail a plan to send the Twenty-seventh and the Thirty-first Infantries, plus five thousand replacements from Camp Fremont, to Vladivostok, if required.[22]

The Early Days in Siberia

I am entrusted unanimously, by the Allied Powers, with command
of their Armies in the Russian Territory of the Far East.

—Japanese General Otani

WHILE General Graves was assembling, outfitting, and transporting the replacements for the expeditionary force, the two regiments from Manila were already participating in the Vladivostok expedition, an experience often characterized by confrontation and confusion. Colonel Styer commanded the expedition until Graves's arrival, and almost as soon as Styer landed in Vladivostok on August 15, he received this message from Japanese General Otani: "I have the honor to inform you that I have been appointed Commander of the Japanese Army at Vladivostok, by His Majesty the Emperor of Japan, and that I am entrusted unanimously, by the Allied Powers, with command of their Armies in the Russian Territory of the Far East."[1] That was a shock to the American colonel, who immediately cabled Washington. The reply simply said Graves would be there soon to handle matters.

Between August 3 and August 11, the Allies landed five thousand British, French, and Japanese troops.[2] Their purpose was to help the Czechs on the railroad as they struggled northward from Vladivostok

171

in an attempt to clear that portion of the route still harassed by the Reds. The Czechs seemed in complete control of the Trans-Siberian Railroad, but that was not quite true. On the line east of Chita and south of Khabarovsk, Bolsheviks and partisans still harassed the railroad. The Czechs were having difficulty, but were bolstered by the newly arrived Allied troops. Even with that help, the outcome was in doubt. The day was saved for the Czechs at the Nikolsk railroad junction by artillery that British colonel John Ward, commander of the Middlesex Battalion, had begged from the *Suffolk* and brought up by train in time to stop Bolshevik advances. Although Ward later became an open critic of the American policy in Siberia, he was a hero to the Allies in August.[3]

As that Nikolsk battle continued, Otani decided to commit his Twelfth Division and withdrew the Czechs, British, and French. Otani requested American troops to move north against the Reds and also requested two companies of the Twenty-seventh Infantry to relieve Czech troops guarding the railroad between Vladivostok and Nikolsk. On August 18, Companies F and G of the Twenty-seventh moved up to spell the weary Czechs along the railroad. The following day Company F underwent the expedition's first baptism by fire. It was a minor affair, not with the Bolsheviks, but with Chinese bandits, who were menacing a small village north of Razdolnoye. Lt. George Herrick led a team from Company F to the rescue; Pvt. Stephen Duhart became the first American casualty in Siberia when he was slightly wounded by a Chinese bullet.[4]

The rest of the Twenty-seventh stayed on the ships until August 20, when they all disembarked and put on a grand parade for the Allies and U.S. Navy already there. On August 19, Colonel Styer cabled Washington with the Japanese plan, of which he was to become a part. It was also a Japanese plea for help. Styer's cable describing Otani's plan read:

> First take Khabarovsk, 15,000-armed enemy this sector; then advance west by Amur and Manchuria.—General Otani stated that in his judgment present forces, assigned to expedition, are insufficient to accomplish mission which was and remains solely the extrication of the Czechs west of Irkutsk, between whom and us are 40,000 enemy forces and a double line of communications to make secure; the Czechs, west of Irkutsk, have little ammunition left and otherwise are in a pitiable plight, so much so that their relief before winter is imperative, if they are to survive. He asked all Allied Commanders to so represent to their Governments, and that they themselves, send all forces immediately available, and request Japan to send troops at once in sufficient numbers to meet the situation. Japan has ready many troops.[5]

The message displayed the Japanese lack of knowledge of the true situation, or lack of candor. There were no more than a few thousand troops in Khabarovsk, and nowhere near forty thousand Reds between Vladivostok and Irkutsk. And the "pitiable" Czech troops actually were closing in on Verkhne Udinsk, capturing it in mid-August.[6] That made the Czechs the masters of the route of the Trans-Siberian Railroad, which crossed Manchuria.

Although the Czechs were successful in the Baikal area, the railroad between Khabarovsk and Vladivostok was stubbornly defended by a Bolshevik force. The Twenty-seventh Infantry was assigned to the Japanese, who launched the Ussuri offensive to clear the railroad between Khabarovsk and Vladivostok on August 24. General Otani committed his Twelfth Division, with the U.S. Twenty-seventh Infantry as rear guard. Colonel Styer was still confused about his position, uncertain whether he should join an offensive under a Japanese commander, but receiving no clear answers from Washington and with Graves at sea, he made the decision to participate. General Otani ordered the Twenty-seventh Infantry to Sviyagino, as he positioned his troops for an attack on the Bolo stronghold at Kraefski.

As the American units traveled on the railroad north toward Sviyagino, repairing burned out bridges and disrupted communications, they came upon some of the carnage left from the previous battles. One source said it was the Chinese bandits who performed the wanton pillage, murder, and burnings that the Americans saw with horror. One of the men wrote of seeing several boxcars full of horribly cut and mangled women and children on their way to medical help.

> The dying mass of humanity was so mutilated it made us feel dreadful. The poor souls were being taken by train to Nikolsk so that those in one piece could have some treatment but that was a distance of some 25 miles or more and we were pretty sure that not many would survive.[7]

The Japanese attack on Kraefski crushed the Red defense, and the Bolos fled northward. The British and French forces were pulled out of the line at that point and sent farther west; little would be heard from them, except for the critical comments of the British, during the next eighteen months. The Twenty-seventh Infantry, being held in reserve, was not in the fight, but marched along with the Allied troops as they followed the fleeing Reds. After the battle one of the American intelligence officers, viewing the battleground, drew the conclusion that the Bolshevik strength estimated by Otani was vastly exaggerated.[8] Thereafter, Japanese details of enemy strength, position, and condition were viewed with some skepticism.

As the U.S. Twenty-seventh Infantry took part in the Ussuri campaign, the understrength Thirty-first Infantry landed in Vladivostok on

August 21 with 1,424 members.[9] The landing of both regiments was far from smooth; no one seemed ready for the American troops. The city was not prepared to house the three thousand Americans who had just landed. Many units of the Twenty-seventh Infantry had stayed only briefly in the city before being sent north, but most of the Thirty-first Infantry remained in the city. They managed to erect a tent city west of the city in a valley, but with Russian generosity and the hard work of the doughboys, they were soon in barracks scattered around the city. The Thirty-first Infantry did send part of its Third Battalion to relieve Companies F and G of the Twenty-seventh Infantry, leaving three hundred men between Vladivostok and Baronovski.[10]

After the battle of Kraefski, the Japanese cavalry cleared the roads north to Ussuri, and the Japanese infantry headed north on the railroad, delayed by bridges destroyed by the Bolos, damaged tracks, and obstacles placed on the tracks. Meanwhile, the Americans were ordered by General Otani to march on the right flank from Sviyagino to Ussuri, about ninety miles, so they did not have the luxury of train travel. The roads were hardly deserving of the name, being no more than tracks in many places. Some of the days were fine, but when the rains came, filling the roads with muck and mud, the regiment covered only eighteen miles in two days. The men took all their equipment and rations with them in carts pulled by mules; they soon found that the U.S. carts were no match for the Russian roads.

As they moved north, they came on another area where a battle had been fought, with dead men and animals left on the scene. The complete lack of respect for, or even interest in, the dead stunned the Americans.

> When men regained some semblance of composure, their voices came in whispers. In that mangled pile of bloated corpses, lying in a mush of bone and flesh, men felt that what they had come to regard as civilization must have died there. There had been dead men on top of dead horses, dead horses on top of men, and flies thick and black everywhere.[11]

This was the aftermath of the Battle of Kraefski.

As the march wore on and discomfort became agony, the doughboys thought of the Japanese at Sviyagino waiting to be moved up to Ussuri by train; they began to question the Japanese commander's selection of the Twenty-seventh Infantry for the miserable march. "Allies," remarked Pvt. George Billick, "I'll bet they will give us more trouble than the Russians before we are through."[12] Passing through villages, their interpreters heard tales of Japanese troops pillaging, raping, and stealing, giving the Americans more to think about on their lonely advance. Every time they stopped as they passed through swampy areas, huge mosquitoes would attack them. Russian mosquitoes have a quality all their own; one British officer claimed they could suck blood through a blanket. Their bites were painful, itchy, and long-lasting, making nights unbearable for many. Each day brought a new grisly discovery of the rotting bodies of Russians killed by the Japanese.

In a moving finale to the miserable march, as the advance party neared Ussuri, they could hear martial music coming faintly through the trees. As the battalions came into sight of the village, they saw the Thirty-first Infantry band, recently arrived by train, playing "The Stars and Stripes Forever," and, as weary as they were, they picked up their step and with tears in their eyes, finished their misery-plagued trek.[13]

The ninety-mile march was said by many to be the worst experience of their Siberian stay. The doughboys did themselves proud, though, and Japanese General Oi, General Otani's second in command and commander of the Japanese Twelfth Division, gave them high praise.[14] The Japanese cavalry swept through Khabarovsk, with the main body of Japanese troops following on September 6. Colonel Styer was requested to send one company to join the Japanese in the formal occupation of the city; he selected Company E. On schedule, the parade and formal occupation took place on September 10. On September 13, the commander of the Japanese Seventh Division, part of the occupying force, issued a declaration disclaiming any desire of the Japanese to interfere in any way with the Russians in their internal affairs, or to take any lands, but only to bring peace and harmony to the people, "its only purpose being to perform the will of our most humane and merciful emperor." He added:

> It may be said that the Japanese Army is the real savior of the Russian people. If, however, anyone should oppose our Army or endeavor to prevent the carrying out of our avowed purposes, it will be necessary to invoke a severity of action and such obstructionist will be pursued and dealt with regardless of his nationality, as nothing must stand in the way of the execution of the work of our Army.[15]

Ultimately, many would oppose the will of the "humane and merciful Japanese emperor" with tragic consequences.

The Twenty-seventh Infantry Regiment set up its headquarters in Khabarovsk, with Japanese and Russian units also assigned to that sector. Shortly after arriving in Khabarovsk, Companies E and C went after the scattering Soviet troops, going as far west as Ushumun, almost five hundred miles from Khabarovsk. Much of the trip was on the newly completed Trans-Siberian Railroad Amur section, but part of the route was by foot, in rugged weather, with the doughboys, recently arrived from Manila, still in summer uniforms. Again, the Japanese were impressed. The history of the regiment said that it snowed during the march to Ushumun, and the lack of winter wear made life miserable. Still, they arrived well in advance of the Japanese, prompting General Oi to once again send his compliments.[16]

By September 7, the Reds were passing through Khabarovsk, pursued by Japanese cavalry and fleeing along the northern Amur River, losing any semblance of organization. The Reds still put up resistance in spots, but being pressed from the west by advancing Czech units and from the east by the Japanese, they had little hope of success. By September 18, the Czechs and Cossacks, pushing westward from Verkhne-Udinsk were only one hundred miles from a linkup with the Japanese and Americans at Ushumun. Many of the Reds fled to the north or crossed the border into China, but the Japanese pursued them and captured most of them. The Japanese navy played its part, bringing gunboats up the Amur to search for Reds and placing a few boats on the Zeya River. How they managed to get boats into that remote area, near Ushumun, is a puzzle, but reports indicate they were there.[17] The remaining Reds still did what the Bolsheviks did best: fought a guerrilla warfare along the railroad.

The Ussuri campaign ended with Companies C and E returning to Khabarovsk on October 11, 1918, and other elements of the Twenty-seventh Infantry scattered. The regiment suffered no casualties, but the Japanese lost 306 men in the bitter fighting.[18] After the campaign, Second Battalion, without Company E, was sent to guard the railroad west of Khabarovsk, at Bira and Prokrofka, about 150 miles west of regimental headquarters. Later, in November, Company C was sent to Spasskoye to join the First Battalion, and Company E was sent to guard the prisoners at Krasnaya Retchka.[19] The rest of the regiment remained in winter quarters in Khabarovsk to suffer through the long, bitterly cold, boring winter.

Some of the Allies noted with concern that after the campaign, Japanese troops occupied most of the territory north of Khabarovsk to the sea and west virtually to Chita. The Japanese had a goal of acquiring Siberian territory, and that strategy seemed to be working. And their troop strength continued to increase, eventually reaching seventy-two thousand.

In the midst of the confusion and distrust between the Americans and Japanese, Gen. William S. Graves arrived, determined to follow the principal guideline of his president: to stay out of Russian affairs.

General Graves
Arrives in Russia

*International relations are quite unlike relations subsisting between
individuals. Morality and sincerity do not govern a country's diplomacy which is guided by selfishness, pure and simple. It is considered the secret of diplomacy to forestall rivals by every crafty means
available.*

—Kokumin, Japanese newspaper

AFTER Graves's arrival, the assembled AEFS with the two infantry regiments, AEF Headquarters, Company D Fifty-third
Telegraph Battalion, 146th Ordnance Depot Company, Seventeenth
Evacuation Hospital, and other signal, medical and ambulance units
numbered 8,117.[1] Their stated purpose was to aid the Czechs, securing
the lines between Czechs in Vladivostok and those fighting in the west.
Some Czechs were heading west to help their comrades in the Baikal
area, some were trying to break through the Bolshevik line that was entrenched across the Ussuri line of the Trans-Siberian, and some remained in Vladivostok.

Confusion reigned in Vladivostok. Nine Allied nations were rep-
resented in Siberia—the United States, Great Britain, France, Japan,

China, Canada, Italy, Serbia, and Czechs. The Russians had twenty-four separate governments stretching from the Urals to Vladivostok with no common bond except a hatred of Bolshevism and a distrust of Tsarists.[2] The Japanese in Siberia, seeking territorial expansion, were willing to join the Siberian expedition, so long as the Americans joined in as well to pay part of the cost. In an accord reached before the Intervention, Japan and the United States agreed to limit the number of their own troops to roughly seven thousand; that was the understanding as Graves landed in Siberia.[3] The notion of not interfering in internal affairs in the middle of a revolution, with nine Allies sending in armed units, seemed incredible. Newton Baker's caution in Kansas City was a considerable understatement of the risks involved for Graves. His eggs were loaded with dynamite, and he soon found the fuses had been lit.

Until Graves arrived with his troops, it had begun to look as though the Siberian expedition would resemble the ill-fated North Russian experience: American troops serving under a foreign commander who immediately sent the doughboys off to fight Bolsheviks with widely separated units spread over large tracts of land.

General Graves took steps to change the status in Siberia. As soon as he landed on September 2, 1918, he met with Colonel Styer and Adm. Austin M. Knight, commander of the Asiatic Fleet, who showed him the orders from General Otani, appointing himself commander of all Allied troops. One of Graves's first visits was to the Japanese general on September 2; he made it clear to Otani that American units were to be controlled by American officers and could be used only with Graves's consent. Otani said that he had been requested to assume control of all troops by the American State Department.[4] After some discussion, Otani accepted Graves's limitation on the use of U.S. troops. "The question was never again mentioned, except once in February, 1920 by General Oi, who had succeeded Otani in command of Japanese troops."[5]

One of the few pieces of information Graves had received from the War Department concerned the Japanese Siberian strategy, which was simply to keep Russian forces as fragmented as possible and to oppose any strong Russian central authority. The Japanese were to support weaker fragmented Russian units as much as possible. Graves wrote in September 1919:

> It is not known from what sources the War Department received the reports upon which the foregoing telegram to me was based, but events of the past year have borne testimony to the accurateness of that estimate as evidenced by the Japanese support of the notorious Kalmykoff, Seminoff and Ivanoff-Rivanoff.[6]

He also mentioned the problems the Japanese were giving Mr. Stevens and the RRSC. The Japanese plan was working; any prospect of a central government in Siberia, let alone Russia, was improbable while the Japanese supported separate factions.

Even with that uneasy situation, as late as September 1919 Graves still maintained good relationships with Japanese General Otani, describing him as "a man of kindly character, of temperate habits, and as the Senior Allied Commander he has been manifestly fair in dealing with all of us."[7] He also recognized other Japanese traits:

> [T]he Japanese have simply been following a different policy. They have resorted to bribery and trickery in every way. . . . They spend money in a way and follow methods that Americans can not and must not follow. . . . I doubt very much whether it is possible for us in the face of such obstacles to realize American ideals of honesty, liberty, and justice in Siberia for years and years to come.[8]

A Japanese paper, the *Kokumin,* gave an interesting explanation of Japanese diplomacy: "International relations are quite unlike relations subsisting between individuals. Morality and sincerity do not govern a country's diplomacy which is guided by selfishness, pure and simple. It is considered the secret of diplomacy to forestall rivals by every crafty means available."[9]

General Graves found himself in a vast turbulent arena that contained numerous factions with conflicting strategies and goals and several dominant figures with whom he would soon clash. One of the members of the expedition, Lt. Sylvian Kindall, wrote about Graves's arrival:

> Contrary to expectations, the arrival of General Graves did not remove any of the mystery which hitherto had surrounded the American Expeditionary Force in Siberia. The fact turned out to be that the general himself, although he had been sent direct from the United States to assume command, had not been entrusted with any information which could be construed to define what had been the real purpose in sending American troops to Siberia.[10]

Graves, however, had found one point in Wilson's *Memoire* to which he adhered: he was in no way to interfere with the internal affairs of Russia. That specific order of the president brought him into conflict with virtually every faction of Siberia. There was no communication between Vladivostok and Archangel, so Graves may well have had no knowledge that the British had thrown American doughboys into open battle with the Bolsheviks, and the Allies probably expected the same thing would happen in Siberia. But Graves, throughout the twenty months of his expedition, never wavered from his position, offering battle only when necessary to protect his troops. He clashed principally with the British, whose commander Gen. Alfred Knox, an avowed foe of Bolshevism, looked with disdain on America's late entry into the Great War as well as their reluctance to join the Allies in Russia.

An early evidence of difficulties among the Allies was in the guarding of the vast mountains of material stored in and around Vladivostok. When Graves arrived he suggested to his Allied partners that an inventory be made of all Allied stocks in the area. That seemed to him a reasonable request, but the British and French requested time to think the suggestion over. The French and British thought there should be some exceptions to any control of these vast amounts of material, specifically arms and ammunition. Eventually, agreement was reached on a complicated series of procedures requiring the permission of the commission, then proceeding with a series of forms, requisitions, and receipts.[11] There appeared to be little discussion of the preservation of the stockpiles of materials that remained and that, in many cases, were subjected to the hazards of Siberian weather and poorly guarded.[12]

The American general was faced with the question of troop placement. He had authorized Colonel Styer, now commanding the Twenty-seventh Infantry after his brief role as AEF commander, to participate in the Ussuri campaign. Graves reasoned that the battle was primarily against the elusive Austro-Hungarian-German war prisoners who Otani had claimed were the cause of the stubborn resistance on the Khabarovsk line. Graves wrote:

> I learned that the Twenty-seventh Infantry was taking part in a combined action against the enemy. The enemy being represented to me as Bolsheviks and German prisoners. I was satisfied that the American troops were not departing from the announced policy of the United States Government to refrain from taking part any part in Russian affairs.[13]

Shortly afterward, Graves released the Twenty-seventh Infantry to Otani and Oi to use at their discretion.[14]

Earlier, in March 1918, a thorough report had been made concerning POWs in Russia by Mr. Webster of the American Red Cross and Captain Hicks, British Army. Their opinions were that any expectation of armed German or Austro-Hungarian prisoners playing a role in the Russian revolution was utter nonsense.[15] In spite of the lack of evidence of any armed prisoners being involved anywhere, and that the Bolsheviks obviously were a part of the Russian internal scene, Graves ordered the

Twenty-seventh Infantry to support the Japanese drive against the Bolsheviks. It should be noted that this was his first day in Siberia; while he spent weeks at sea, Colonel Styer had already made the troop commitment.

The following days brought more decisions to make, not the least of which was where he should locate his headquarters. On September 8, he requested guidance from Washington. He pointed out that everyone was moving west except the Japanese; Czechs, British, and French were all making preparations to move, possibly as far as the Volga, with visionary dreams of a renewed eastern front. Graves recommended, under certain conditions, that he move west with them, citing the fact that few troops were needed in Vladivostok. He said he would need several additional units if he headed west: a regiment of mountain artillery, a provisional artillery battery, and one company of engineers.[16]

On September 27, the War Department cabled that any move to Omsk or beyond was disapproved. They thought Harbin might be a good central location, but left the decision to Graves. He was cautioned to be sure his supply lines stayed intact, that he in no case should send troops west of Lake Baikal, and that guarding Czech lines was still a priority.

Deciding that his headquarters would remain in Vladivostok, Graves told Otani that he would not to move to Harbin, where quarters were at a premium, but was thinking of sending a battalion to some place between Chita and Lake Baikal. The Japanese garrisoned all the areas east of Chita, but they had no troops west of Chita. Graves eventually decided not to spread his troops out as far as the Baikal area; thus, as winter set in October 1918, Americans were located almost exclusively on the Khabarovsk-Vladivostok Railroad, with only one unit, Company B of the Thirty-first Infantry, in Harbin, China. The Thirty-first Infantry headquarters was in Vladivostok with companies A, C, E, H, I, and K in areas near the city. Companies F and G were at Spasskoye, L was at Razdolnoye, B at Harbin, and M at the Suchan Mines. Most of the Twenty-seventh Infantry was at Khabarovsk, with its First Battalion at Spasskoye and one platoon at Ussuri.

General Graves visited Khabarovsk in September, going as far west as Bira on the railroad. He found the troops in Bira quartered in Russian boxcars, made reasonably livable by the doughboys' ingenuity, but still boxcars. At two other outposts Graves found similar situations and wrote, "I could see no reason for keeping these troops at any of these stations, so ordered that all be brought to Khabarovsk."[17] There they were housed in almost luxurious barracks where they spent the winter.

In Khabarovsk the Twenty-seventh Infantry was given responsibility for the Austrian-German prison camp a few miles from the city in a place called Krasnaya Retchka (Red River). When Company E was sent to the camp, the men found a mess: filthy, refuse-strewn, unsanitary, inefficient, and generally dark and gloomy, it was a challenge for the Americans. Of the 2,000 prisoners, 460 were sick and feverish, and there were no medical facilities. "The Russians had no individual records of these prisoners, nor did they know how many prisoners they held in confinement." The Americans discovered that about fifteen hundred of the prisoners were officers. With their tattered clothes, minimum rations, and without medical care, they faced the Siberian winter with little hope.[18]

That all changed with the arrival of the Americans under the command of Capt. Edward Larkin. Within thirty days, a transformation had been made in the way the prisoners were treated. Soon the camp was entertained by the strains of two inmate orchestras, a thirty-seven-piece Austrian symphony, and another made up of Hungarian musicians. The cost of caring for these victims of the war was considerable, but it was agreed that the expenses would be shared equally by the United States, Japan, England, France, Italy, and China.[19] The POWs held in this camp and others run by Americans were lucky; in thirty other prison camps in Siberia run by Russians and Czechs, life was far from pleasant.[20]

One of the most poignant scenes at the prison was the cemetery, where there were about fifteen hundred graves. They lay neglected and deserted in tangles of overgrown vines and weeds with only rough wooden markers to identify those who lay beneath. In the center stood a magnificent limestone monument made by the prisoners.

> The hands of the war prisoners that erected it had apparently been guided by no thought of reviving any soreness of heart from the graves of the dead comrades around it, who from shattered battlefields had been marched and carted across two continents into this distant corner of the world, here to rot away the remaining days of their lives, in pestilential prison barracks. In contrast to the bitter things that might have been said, the shaft bore a single, simple inscription, which Sperati translated to read, "Here all are friends"[21]

The prison became part of a struggle between Cossacks and Americans. For several months, Ataman Ivan Kalmykof, part of the Kolchak White Army, had roamed the Amur territory, robbing, burning, raping, and executing hundreds of Russian peasants. In October he arrested a Swedish Red Cross representative, Sven Hedblum, and a Red Cross assistant, tried them for espionage, and hanged them both in a boxcar in Khabarovsk, while stealing 1.6 million rubles from Red Cross dispatches. A Red Cross typist was then raped and shot by Cossacks.[22] At the same time, a group of Hungarian musicians, POWs, was executed by Kalmykof's men. One of his lieutenants, a man named Julienk, carried out the killings with obvious relish:

> Some Cossacks and I caught them all—16 men—like dogs; at 12 o'clock noon I led them into a garden by the Amur near the Muaviev Memorial where there is a chasm extending down to the river. . . . I lined them up, the Cossacks stood ready, I commanded "fire" and they rolled into the Amur to the Devil's Mother.[23]

Word of these executions and arrests reached Graves on an almost daily basis; by December 1, he had had enough. Under his orders, American soldiers could do nothing, even when they were witnesses to Kalmykof's crimes; that created serious morale problems for the troops. General Graves finally wrote to Otani, suggesting that they both notify Kalmykof that the next time he murdered, he would be turned over to the civil courts. The Japanese responded, "Kalmykoff had promised them, on November 28, that he would not kill any more people, and that he had kept that promise, but, if I desired, they would join me in notifying him as I had suggested."[24] That was no solution, but Kalmykof did become more careful, hiding his actions from the Americans while apparently continuing his purges.[25]

The atrocities became so flagrant that even the Kalmykof Cossacks could take no more. On the night of January 27, 1919, a large body of his Cossacks came to the American headquarters in Khabarovsk while Kalmykof was away. Their grievances were presented to the Americans, listing, "enforced enlistment; prisoners of war being forced to serve under penalty of death; whippings and executions for slight offenses; fear of being shot; insufficient food and clothing; arrears and reduction in pay; drunkenness and cruelty of officers; great numbers of execution and mutilation of civilians."[26] Even Cossack tribunals had been disgusted by the Cossack leader. On February 12, 1919, a decision of the Volna Special Cossack (Ussuri) Assembly declared, among other things:

> Ataman Kalmykoff has filled the cup of endurance by his shooting down of Cossacks. . . . The numerous cases of shooting the civil inhabitants of the town of Khabarovsk—guilty or not guilty of having taken part in Bolshevism—have excited the population of the province to such an extent and have instilled such disgust towards the Cossacks that only threats of the Kalmykoffites holds back the civil population of the province from taking the law into their own hands and applying it to the Cossacks.[27]

That slowed, but did not stop, his brutality.

After complaining to the Americans, the rebelling Cossacks, some 700 strong, went in different directions: 300 disappeared into neighboring villages, 30 turned themselves in to the Chinese detachment, and 398 marched in a body, with animals, rifles, and machine guns, to the headquarters of the Twenty-seventh Infantry. Colonel Styer refused to turn over the mutineers to Kalmykof or any representative of Horvat, but decreed that they should be released to return home.

During this time, Kalmykof remained near Khabarovsk making threats against Americans, blaming them for the defections, and accusing American soldiers of various offenses. The Japanese responded to Styer's decision concerning the mutinous Cossacks, saying, "The desertion involved, and your reception the soldiers, is an event within Kalmykoff's detachment, and is simply a matter of its military discipline. This case is believed as interference with the interior administration of Kalmykoff's detachment." The rest of the message was equally troubling.[28] Colonel Styer fired back to the Japanese on March 25, with Graves's blessing:

> The situation grows grave and most serious. On several occasions I have reported the conduct of this detachment towards the Americans and each time you have informed me that you had no authority over Kalmikoff. The mere fact that he is controlled by the Japanese and supported by them makes you responsible for his acts.[29]

There was much discussion, but Colonel Styer still refused to turn the mutineers back to their Cossack fate; he had already sent them down to Krasnaya Retchka on February 1.

The Japanese, whose attitudes toward Americans had been cooling as the winter progressed, sided with Kalmykof's Cossacks; Japanese papers slandered the United States repeatedly over the event, and Japanese officers made dangerously biased reports about the American role in the mutiny. Daily contact became even more difficult between the lower ranks of the two forces. General Otani maintained his diplomatic approach, writing in response to Styer:

> In view, however, of the facts that the Japanese Government has hitherto assisted them in their equipment and supplies, and that Japanese troops have been operating in co-operation with them, we feel it is our duty to see that Kalmikof be duly advised and that a satisfactory and smooth solution be reached in connection with the matter lately informed by Colonel Styer.[30]

A special Cossack trial of the mutineers, with local communities having input, convened on February 21, but arrived at no conclusion;

most of the mutineers apparently drifted back to their homes. The arms and equipment were turned over to the Japanese, who claimed they had paid for them.[31] It was acknowledged that the Japanese were now openly supporting both Cossack Atamans Kalmykof and Semenov. Relations were rapidly deteriorating as the various forces in the Russian Far East realized that U.S. troops would not be participating in the struggle on either side.

However, as the men relaxed and bided their time in various ways, the armistice on the western front took effect and the guns in France were silent. The effect on the Siberian troops was minimal. Graves, feeling very much as did Colonel Stewart in Archangel, wrote:

> I expected Allied troops, as well as United States troops, to be withdrawn from Siberia soon after the signing of the Armistice, and I seemed to be the only military representative who was not aware that we had a war of our own in Russia, and that our War was independent and separate from the war in France. The Armistice had absolutely no effect in Siberia. It seemed to me, as all the reasons the United States took part in military action in Siberia had entirely disappeared before the Armistice, or at the time of the Armistice, we would withdraw our troops from Russian territory and naturally the question repeatedly came to my mind, why are American troops kept in Siberia?[32]

The questions became more frequent and more specific regarding their mission, but there were no visible signs of a departure. Unknown to the troops, Secretary of War Newton Baker wrote the president immediately after the armistice:

> My own judgment is that we ought simply to order our forces home by the first boat and notify the Japanese that in our judgment our mission is fully accomplished and that nothing more can be done there which will be acceptable to or beneficial to the Russian people by force of arms, and that we propose to limit our assistance to Russia hereafter to an economic aid in view of the fact that our armies by the armistice have been required to withdraw their armed forces from Russian territory.[33]

But, that, of course, was not to be.

Another event of critical importance was a coup on November 18, 1918, in Omsk, which installed Adm. Alexander Kolchak as the new head of the Siberian government. The coup was similar to that in North Russia, organized and carried out with British blessing, placing the ex-Tsarist naval officer at the head of a new government. He called himself the Supreme Ruler of all Russia, yet Vladivostok was governed by Czechs, Khabarovsk by Japanese, and other cities by local governments, many with differing agendas. His selection did nothing to solidify the vast regions of Siberia, let alone European Russia, still struggling with the new Soviet government in Moscow.

Dmitri Horvat, formerly head of the Chinese-Eastern Railway, was the virtually powerless governor-general of the Far East. In March 1919, he was replaced by Gen. S. N. Rozanov, a Cossack who turned out to be as much a barbarian as Kalmykof and Semenov. Rozanov's first order when he replaced Horvat was, if his men could not find partisan leaders, "then shoot one out of every ten of the people." If his troops entered a town and failed to find enemy leaders, "a monetary contribution should be demanded of all, unsparingly. The villages where the population meet our troops with arms, should be burned down and all the full grown male population should be shot; property, homes, carts, etc. should be taken for use of the Army."[34] These were Russians committing these outrages on fellow Russians.

Other tyrants gained power at that time in the Far East. In October 1918, General Ivanoff-Rinoff, formerly a Tsarist official, appeared in eastern Siberia and was put in command of all White Russian troops in the area. One of his first mandates was to declare martial law in Amur, Primorskaya, Sakhalin, and Kamchatka, an area that reached virtually from Korea north to Alaska, including the islands off the coast.[35]

As the winter wore on, tension increased among Allies. The Japanese had greatly expanded both their area of occupation and their troop strength. In an October memorandum to the adjutant general in Washington, Graves stated that there were then sixty thousand Japanese troops in eastern Russia and China, far exceeding the seven thousand limit agreed on prior to the Intervention.[36] Actually, at one point the Japanese had seventy-two thousand men in the area.[37] American intelligence reported that Japanese troops had garrisoned the mouth of the Golden Horn Bay in the villages of Posyet and Slavyansk on the Korean border. They had also sent troops as far north as Nikolaevsk na Amur at the mouth of the Amur River on the Sea of Okhotsk.[38] This was in violation of the original outline of territories.

By mid-winter 1918–1919, the Kolchak government was relying heavily on the two Cossack bands of Ivan Kalmykof in the Ussuri region and Gregorii Semenov in the Baikal area. According to Graves, Kalmykof "was the worst scoundrel I ever saw or heard of and I seriously doubt, if one should go entirely through the Standard Dictionary, looking for words descriptive of crime, if a crime could be found that Kalmikoff had not committed." About Semenov Graves said, "Kalmikoff murdered with his own hands, where Semenov ordered others to kill, and therein lies the difference between Kalmikoff and Semenov."[39] The actions of these two evil forces caused the people of Russia to turn against Kolchak and his armies as they raped, plundered, and murdered their way across Siberia.

As early as October 1918, the U.S. troops in Spasskoye reported various minor disagreements with the Japanese over use of water, latrines, loitering, and general misbehavior of Japanese troops in the Spasskoye compound. The Americans took over various buildings and supplies from the British as the British moved west, but the Japanese also claimed them. The U.S. Spasskoye commander sent a detailed report of his grievances both to the Japanese officer at Spasskoye and Colonel Sargent, which brought a rather tart response from the American colonel: "I am not at all surprised that the answer to the attached letter was more or less insolent in tone, as your letter to the Japanese Commanding Officer was anything but diplomatic." He went on to caution that Japanese were Allies with different customs and habits, so be nice to them.[40]

Other incidents were disconcerting. On November 3, 1918, Pfc. Frank Werkstein and Sgt. Frank Baelski were traveling from Khabarovsk to Vladivostok by rail. The train stopped in the village of Viasimskaya and Werkstein got off, only to be surrounded by Japanese soldiers, one officer, and a civilian. There was much shouting, gesturing, and prodding with the Japanese bayonets. Minutes later, Sergeant Baelski got off the train, and the Japanese turned their attention to him. The civilian had told the soldiers that he had been struck by an American soldier and pointed out Baelski. The Japanese officer ordered Baelski held and told the civilian to hit Baelski in the face, after which he was released and reboarded the train. He reported the incident; when word of the episode reached Graves, he immediately advised General Otani of the seriousness of the occurrence. Otani performed his own investigation and wrote Graves, "it was confirmed that what really happened was, to my hearty regret, evidently the same as was stated in your note, and I earnestly desire that the most cordial friendship which has long been existing between the two countries will not be affected by this occurrence." He told Graves the officer responsible had been relieved of his command and sent back to his regiment.[41]

However, by January the tone of Japanese replies had changed. Sgt. Ignacio Borda was harassed by Japanese soldiers on an American car on the same railroad. The Japanese took Borda's pistol while pointing their rifles at him and took over the car. When he arrived at Khabarovsk and the Japanese had left, Borda learned that several U.S. Army items were missing. He reported the loss, but no action was taken by the Japanese, "as it was considered unworthy to be discussed about specially, being a trifling matter." Further, they stated that they knew nothing of the missing items, which were the responsibility of Sergeant Borda.[42]

There were other incidents involving the two Allies, and the doughboys were increasingly appalled at the Japanese soldiers' treatment of the area peasants. Lieutenant Kindall wrote of one of the most extreme examples of Japanese outrages. Late on a Saturday night, Russian men were celebrating the week's end with the usual vodka and song. A Japanese patrol raided the vodka house and seized three men and two boys. Bound with rice straw ropes, they were taken to the Japanese camp at Sviyagino and pushed into boxcars. The next day they were marched down the railroad tracks to five shallow graves and forced to kneel by the graves. The executioner, a Japanese officer, proceeded to measure the saber he carried and its distance from the condemned man's neck. All things being in order:

> [T]he Japanese officer hopped into the air with both feet, gave an odious grunt, and brought down the keen blade through the neck. As the body tumbled forward into the dirt and squirmed about the shallow grave, the Japanese standing alongside jeered at it and prodded it with their bayonets.[43]

The stunned Russians and two American officers who were there could never again believe that the Allies were there to help Russians. The Russian countryside was being ravaged by their own countrymen, the Cossacks, and the uncontrollable Japanese. Americans often witnessed bestial behavior toward Russians, but under their strict orders they were not to interfere. In the minds of many, it was a determined effort to force the Americans into confrontations and eventually drive them from Siberia, leaving the Far East solely in Japanese hands.

As the winter wore on, the bitter cold kept activity to a minimum, yet more atrocities were reported as the Cossacks and Japanese continued their incursions. Even Graves could not believe the degree of brutality that was being reported to him. In March 1919, he sent one of his officers to verify the story of a young woman who had come to American headquarters to ask for protection. The American officer who went to Gordievka reported:

> The first woman interviewed said her husband was on his way to the school house with his rifle to turn it in to the Russian Troops as ordered. He was seized on the street, beaten on the head and body with his rifle, and then taken to a house a short distance from the school where he was stretched by the neck to a pin in the rafter, his hands tied, and terribly beaten about the body and head until the blood was splashed even on the

walls of the room, and the marks on the body showed me that he had been hung by his feet also.

He was later stood in a row, with eight other men, and shot to death at 2 P.M. There were ten men in line and all were killed but one, he being left for dead by Ivanoff-Rinoff's troops.[44]

Other details in the officer's report shocked Graves so much he asked the young officer to report to him. Graves said:

I always remember the remark this officer made to me after I had questioned him. His remark was: "General, for God's sake, never send me on an expedition like this. I came within an ace of pulling off my uniform, joining these poor people, and helping them as best I could."[45]

Not only the Russian peasants felt the pressure of White Russian troops, but American senior officers as well. Newly promoted Lt. Col. Robert Eichelberger, head of intelligence for the AEFS, was sent on an assignment into the Suchan Mine area in the spring of 1919, hoping to meet with partisan leaders and dissuade them from attacking American guards in the area. Frequent reports from the American Mine Guard commander, Col. Gideon Williams, and Maj. Emile Cutrer in Shkotova indicated that the partisans were getting more aggressive, firing into trains and raiding the smaller villages. There also was the unpleasant news that the White Army was recruiting in the area, using its brutal tactics.

Eichelberger took the train and cable car, passed through the mine area, and entered the town of Pyratino near the Suchan River. As he walked in with Lt. O. P. Winningstad and a sergeant, he discovered that the Whites had started burning the town and killing the villagers as part of their recruiting methods. The partisans were holding out against the Whites as Eichelberger, "being young and enthusiastic," decided to try to mediate a peace. Under terms of the Allies, White Russians were not allowed in that area, which made the young colonel's job difficult. Colonel Rubetz, commanding the Russian White unit, arrested Eichelberger and his aides. Rubetz was convinced that the American was leading the Bolshevik resistance. Eichelberger and Winningstad were put in the schoolhouse under guard.

As local peasants ran to the American mine headquarters and reported Eichelberger's danger, Colonel Williams, the Mine Guard commander, was in a quandary whether to try to rescue him or not. Eichelberger wrote his wife, "Then the Bolsh general went to [American Lieutenant] Rumans and reported that we were confined in the schoolhouse and were to be shot. He [the Bolshevik general] volunteered to go to Pyratin to rescue me."[46]

The next morning the Whites disappeared and the two Americans walked back to more friendly territory, meeting a rescue party that had finally been sent by Colonel Williams.[47]

Back in Vladivostok, the Americans were finding that life at times could be very pleasant, but there were many times when bitterly cold weather, unfriendly Allies, uncertain living conditions, and increasingly hostile locals could make life anything but home-like.

Eight soldiers at Camp Custer, Michigan, in August 1918 just before the regiment left for England. Top row, left to right, William J. Walsh, Joseph P. Curry, Matthew G. Grahek, Norman H. Zapfe; bottom row, left to right, Walter H. Rosenau, Jonathan Davis, Howard Durrant, Charles O. Dial. Dial was killed in action in March 1919. *(Bentley Historical Library, University of Michigan)*

Col. George E. Stewart, commanding officer, 339th Infantry Regiment, 85th Division, in 1928. *(U.S. Military Academy Museum)*

Members of the landing party from the USS *Olympia* just before joining the Allied Force B in August 1918. *(U.S. Naval Historical Center)*

Capt. Otto Odjard, commanding officer, Company A, 339th Infantry Regiment, in 1919. *(Bentley Historical Library, University of Michigan)*

Capt. Joel Moore, commanding officer, Company M, 339th Infantry Regiment, in 1919. *(Bentley Historical Library, University of Michigan)*

The USS *Olympia* in Philadelphia Harbor, now a museum. *(Author's collection)*

Alexander Kozakov, Russian air ace and member of the Slavo-British Squadron of the Royal Air Force in 1919. He was killed near Archangel in August 1919. *(Courtesy of the Imperial Russian Air Service by Allan Durkota, Thomas Darcey, and Victor Kulikov, and assisted by Jack Herris)*

Pvt. Floyd A. Sickles, Company M, in 1918. Private Sickles was killed by friendly fire on December 6, 1918, on the railroad front. *(Bentley Historical Library, University of Michigan)*

Sgt. William Bowman, awarded the DSC for heroism at Toulgas, died of wounds received on patrol along the Dvina River in March 1919. *(Davis Collection)*

Troops of Company M moving up to the railroad front in September 1918.
(Bentley Historical Library, University of Michigan)

Toboggan slide in Archangel erected by the 310th Engineers in January 1919.
(Archangelsk City Museum)

Left to right: Lt. Edmund Collins, Company H, died of wounds on March 24, 1919; Russian Captain Maknuff; Lt. Howard Pellegrom, Company H. Photo taken on the Onega front in 1919. *(Bentley Historical Library, University of Michigan)*

Camouflaged Allied blockhouse on the Kodish front in 1919. *(Bentley Historical Library, University of Michigan)*

Campfire on the railroad front in 1918. *(National Archives, College Park, Maryland)*

Patrol on the railroad front in February 1919: (left to right) Charles Metcalf, Company I; Harold Holliday, Company M; Sgt. Maj. Ernest Reed, Third Battalion. *(National Archives, College Park, Maryland)*

Forward blockhouse at Toulgas on the Dvina front in January 1919. *(National Archives, College Park, Maryland)*

Maj. Gen. William S. Graves, commanding officer, American Expeditionary Force, Siberia, in 1918. *(National Archives, College Park, Maryland)*

Lt. Col. Robert L. Eichelberger, intelligence officer, AEFS—later promoted to lieutenant general—in 1918. *(National Archives, College Park, Maryland)*

Lt. Alfred E. Ward, USMA Class of 1919, in 1918. Ward was killed in action at Novitskaya on June 22, 1919. *(USMAM Library Special Collection and Archives)*

Czech Gen. Radola Gaida (Czech Legion) in 1918. *(The History Institute of the Army of the Czech Republic, Prague, Czech Republic)*

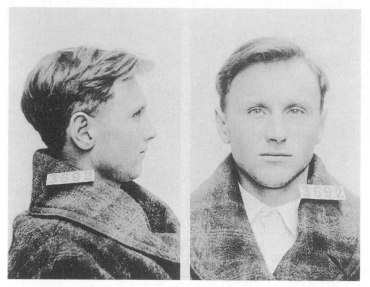

Pvt. Anton Karachun, Machine Gun Company, 31st Infantry Regiment, was tried and convicted of desertion and fighting against Americans and was the only American sentenced to death during the two Russian campaigns. *(National Archives, Pacific-Alaska Region, Spokane, Washington)*

Machine Gun Company, 31st Infantry Regiment, in Vladivostok in 1918. *(National Archives, College Park, Maryland)*

Czech Armored Train in 1918. *(National Archives, College Park, Maryland)*

Czech soldiers en route to Vladivostok in boxcars in 1919. *(The History Institute of the Army of the Czech Republic, Prague, Czech Republic)*

Trans-Siberian Railroad station in Vladivostok. Scene of the fighting during Gaida's unsuccessful revolt in November 1919. *(National Archives, College Park, Maryland)*

Allies parading in Vladivostok on November 15, 1918, in honor of the Armistice. *(National Archives, College Park, Maryland)*

Soldiers of Company M, 31st Infantry Regiment at Suchan Mines near Vladivostok on Thanksgiving Day 1918. *(National Archives, College Park, Maryland)*

Bolshevik prisoners en route to prison camps in 1918. *(National Archives, College Park, Maryland)*

Members of the Bolshevik Council at Ekaterinburg captured by the Czechs in the fall of 1918. All were executed. *(National Archives, College Park, Maryland)*

Cable car used as part of the Suchan Mines rail spur in 1918. *(National Archives, College Park, Maryland)*

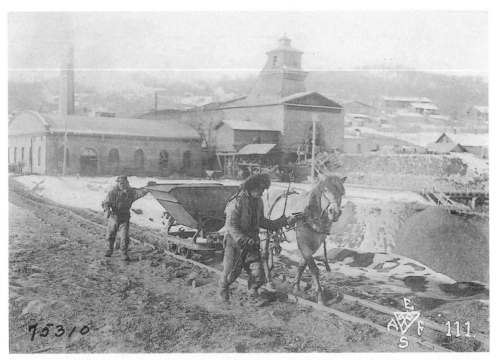

Hauling coal from Mine #1 in 1918, Suchan Mines, one of the trouble spots during the Allied Intervention. *(National Archives, College Park, Maryland)*

Nurses at the Evacuation Hospital #17, Vladivostok. *(National Archives, College Park, Maryland)*

Coffins of Americans killed at Romanovka on June 25, 1919, being taken to ships for transport home in 1919. *(National Archives, College Park, Maryland)*

1919 poster promoting war bonds to support the boys in Siberia. *(Hoover Institution of War, Revolution and Peace, Poster Collection, Stanford University)*

Life in Siberia

I don't think I had better go into any of the details of the various crimes for with the true artistic spirit of the orient, the criminals try to frighten the citizens with their atrocious conduct.

—Capt. Rodney Sprigg

VLADIVOSTOK, the largest city in Siberia, was a haven for refugees from the western part of revolution-torn Russia. Refugees came flooding into Vladivostok daily, swelling the population significantly. The prewar population was estimated at 100,000, but an estimated 250,000 more had slipped in by railroad, cart, boat, foot, or litter.[1] It was an excellent port; although frozen in during some winter months, a channel was kept clear from the port entrance to the docks by great, hulking icebreakers.[2]

In the city, local trams were suffocatingly crowded; little horse-drawn carts called *droskies* trotted along the waterfront, and marching troops often filled the streets. The city resembled San Francisco in topography, rising virtually from the banks of Golden Horn Bay to hills dotted with houses, shacks, and buildings of all sorts. The main street, Svetlanskaya Street, was lined with impressive homes and buildings belonging to wealthy merchants and businessmen. It could have been

191

a beautiful city, but it held little beauty for arriving Americans. In December, one young soldier wrote a friend that he was enjoying new sights and was impressed by Vladivostok's downtown area, but once he left the center, he did not find much to like. "The houses are mean, one-story, stucco structures, the pavements are rotten boards, full of gaps and holes, dangerous to walk upon. The streets are either roughly cobbled or unpaved and full of mud, and cows and pigs and dogs and goats run around in happy confusion."[3] He added in his letter a description of his brief stopover in Japan: "The Japanese on his own soil is a much more attractive person than he is abroad."

Most of the comments about the city mentioned the stench: rotting garbage, human and animal filth, fish, and sewage seemed to blend into an unforgettable stink. Refugees slept where they could, finding shelter in improvised lean-tos, filling every covered space; and still, many slept on doorsteps, hallways, or any other spot available. Fortunately, the doughboys were offered good quarters in barracks by their Russian hosts. In September, the weather in Vladivostok was still warm, and the troops from the Philippines were still in summer uniforms.

Soon after their arrival, Maj. Sam Johnson and his adjutant 1st Lt. Rodney Sprigg located a likely barracks at Fort Churkin at the mouth of the harbor. But before they took over the fort, General Graves summoned them both. He was anxious to have a combat-ready force available in the city for defense should it become necessary. Col. O. P. Robinson had suggested forming a replacement battalion that would always be trained and ready should he need it. Major Johnson was given command of the battalion with Sprigg as his adjutant. So the term replacement battalion actually was not used for replacement troops, but for men trained in the use of automatic weapons and tactics to be ready when needed in the midst of a city in turmoil. Sprigg wrote home, "In the past week we have had two changes of government in the city of Vladivostok, we have had one large fire, and any number of holdups, murders and other miscellaneous goings."[4]

Some two months after the replacement battalion was formed, Sam Johnson was selected for an even tougher job: commanding officer of the International Military Police (IMP), formed to combat the civil disturbances and the unrest in the city. This new organization included individually selected men of all nationalities: American, British, French, Italian, Polish, Czechoslovak, Chinese, Lettish, Romanian, and Serbian. "Almost every man in each army wanted to become a member of the IMP but size was important. You had to be big."[5]

The international patrols were highly effective in a city known for its lawlessness and crime. Lieutenant Sprigg wrote to his wife, "Twenty four hours never pass without the report of at least two or three violent deaths. . . . So far they have been Czecho-Slovaks or Japs, Thank goodness, but there's no telling when some good natured assassin decides to bump off one or two of our men." Sprigg added a thoughtful note, "I don't think I had better go into any of the details of the various crimes for with the true artistic spirit of the orient, the criminals try to frighten the citizens with their atrocious conduct."[6]

The men of the IMP had beautiful uniforms but dirty jobs, yet they maintained a sterling record during the expedition's stay in the Far East. Johnson became the expedition's most highly decorated member by the end of the campaign for his work with the IMP and for his part in a rescue during a later Vladivostok uprising. The IMP's role was not without cost; it sustained fifty-one casualties in its brief existence. In 1919, the IMP reports that it assisted the Russians in 851 cases and handled 3,532 Allied cases, almost 10 per day.[7]

The AEF troops found they had little to do in the fall and winter months. A few units were sent out on various missions, but the majority of American soldiers were housed in reasonably comfortable barracks in either Khabarovsk or Vladivostok. Company M of the Thirty-first Infantry had joined a Japanese company and a Russian company assigned to guard the Suchan Mine area, under command of Lt. Col. Sylvester Loring. Companies F and G were housed in Spasskoye on the railroad. In November 1918 the Twenty-seventh Infantry, First Battalion moved down from Khabarovsk to Spasskoye to join the Thirty-first Infantry units and a small Russian and Japanese garrison. Lonely units from Company B were housed in far-off Harbin, China, on the Chinese-Eastern Railroad.

Snow came in October, and while it was welcome at first, the novelty wore off as it grew deeper and heavier. By November 1, Golden Horn Bay had a thick coating of ice. Sprigg's fort was across the bay from the city; he could walk across the ice when the wind wasn't blowing, but when the winds blew, and the gusts dealt body blows to walkers, it was impossible to cross the bay. "The cold here is of a peculiar dry, penetrating sort. Any exposed part suffers. For instance I can sit with my feet in the stove and they will get quite warm while my hands a few feet away are stiff with cold, and yet not once have I suffered with my body being cold."[8] January 1, 1919, recorded one of the worst snowstorms of recent years. It became so severe that the commander of the guard of Company C in Vladivostok pulled in all his guards, afraid they might become disoriented. Instead, he sent out patrols every half hour to keep watch.[9] In various sections of the American military territory, temperatures were reported as being consistently 30 degrees below zero.

The men from Camp Fremont were supplied with adequate cold

weather gear before they left California; the others received their winter
clothing before the bitter cold set in. The staple garment for the outdoors was a sheepskin-lined greatcoat that kept out the frigid weather.
They wore woolen uniforms topped off with fur hats, with lumber-
men's socks in place of leggings. Some had regular field boots, while
others preferred moccasins. But there was no sign of the Shackleton
boot. They were also issued parkas, shoe packs, heavy olive-drab un-
derwear, and fur mittens, all of which were in sufficient supply
throughout the campaign.[10] Private Reynolds of the 146th Ordnance
Depot Company wrote that with the winter clothing they were issued
and the reasonably comfortable barracks they lived in, "On the score of
creature comforts . . . we don't deserve much sympathy."[11]

As the cold set in, tempers began to fray, even among the senior
officers. Colonel Robinson, Graves's chief of staff, assigned Capt. Kenneth Roberts to go to Khabarovsk on an intelligence mission. Colonel
Barrows, head of intelligence, objected. Roberts described their shouting match: "The resulting scene between Barrows and Robinson was
both embarrassing and ludicrous; for those two full-grown, dignified officers screamed at each other like Italian ditch diggers."[12] Captain Roberts noted that between Thanksgiving and January (1919), "most of the
participants in the Siberian Expeditionary Force seemed semi insane
with cold, idleness and the depression that accompanies these two cur-
ses."[13] Roberts solved his depression by writing as much as he could;
others slept, wrote letters, sang the old songs, badgered each other, and
tried to cope. Sometimes, though, the boredom got to them:

> A couple of guys were stationed deep in the Trans-Baikal, waiting, wait-
> ing for something to happen. They rarely talked for they'd each spoken
> their piece.
>   Finally one day the major arrived and called one of them up.
>   "What under the sun made you beat up your buddy the way you did?"
> he asked.
>   "Oh, he gets on my nerves," was the answer.
>   "Well, what has he done now?"
>   "The Soldat: 'He tore the leaf off the calendar and it was my turn.'"[14]

One of the ways to cope was with vodka. A doughboy wrote of its
many uses:

> Vodka is a liquor discovered about A.D. 1918 by the American soldiers. Its
> qualities are varied; its virtues many. It has the appearance of oily water
> and the effects of a young volcano. One little can will cause more men to
> come to parade rest in less time than two Major Generals. One can is ca-
> pable of producing any number of Carusos, several pugilists and lots of

> dancers and many jail-birds. It is great to moderate the weather, makes
> bees hum and causes little birdies to flit among the trees. . . . As a cleanser
> it has no equal, for it is the finest thing ever known to remove the stripes
> from a non-com's sleeve.[15]

Wartime prohibition restrictions at home made liquor hard to get, so
the wild abundance of the local vodka made the drink even more attractive to bored and lonely young men.

The sanitary systems in Russia were strange and sometimes embarrassing to the new arrivals, but they found that necessity overcame
modesty at times. One of the men was in town and suddenly needed to
find a toilet facility. He found one nearby, went in and seated himself.
Shortly afterward a young lady came in and seated herself beside him.
In spite of the awkward situation, they struck up a minimal conversation, neither knowing much of the other's language. Then a young Russian man came in and sat next to the young lady and they began to talk.
The American was put out and told his buddies later, "We were getting
along okeh until he showed up!"[16]

There were duties that kept them busy some of the time—machine
gun school, Officer Candidate School (until the armistice, when OCS
was discontinued), guard duty, drills, and parades—but there really
was little to do to fulfill the expedition's elusive mission.

Dull and boring as it was, the troops were able to find amusements
in several ways. The YMCA had several fine canteens, which were usually crowded. One of the women at the Y wrote in her diary:

> Several afternoons I have helped at the International Hut canteen, and
> now recognize tea, coffee, cocoa with or without milk or sugar, in Rus-
> sian, German, French, Czech, and Italian, to say nothing of the welcome
> sound of our own boys' voices which range from the Southern boy's "Cof-
> fee with cream an' sugah, please M'am," to Tony from Chicago's South
> side who always cuts a pigeon wing and then says, "Good evening, Miss
> Boig. Got a hand-out fer me?"[17]

There were books, games, movies, and sometimes concerts by the
POW orchestras. The prisoners were primarily housed in the prison
compound on Russian Island, a short ferry ride from the Vladivostok
docks, but they had a variety of assignments throughout the area. One
of the men from Company E of the Thirty-first Infantry, Russell Swihart,
was assigned the duty of guarding prisoners and found them a conge-
nial group, well-mannered, polite and helpful in many of ways. Once
there was a concert at a nearby orphanage on Russian Island, which had
young women as counselors. One of the American guards, against all
orders, took several POWs to the concert. They had a wonderful time;

after the evening was over, one German prisoner told the doughboy with a great deal of emotion, "I will never forget this night!"[18]

Music was plentiful for everyone, with the orchestras, the military bands from the Thirty-first Infantry, the USS *Brooklyn*, and the HMS *Kent*, plus some improvised jazz groups. Some of the members of the Thirty-first put together a performing group that successfully toured the various bases.

And there were always the boy-girl friendships that sometimes blossomed into romance. One story went this way:

> She leaned tantalizing across the table toward him; gloriously youthful, vivacious and trim. Wagging a worn spoon around in her tea, she bewildered him with a sun-shiney smile:
> "Pochimo vi niet gavareet po Russkie?" she challenged.
> He moved to his feet uneasily, adjusted his neck, and answered:
> "I niet habla Ruskie ochen much. Ya cachew to though"
> They both laughed, relapsed into silence and drank chai.
> And the people about thought:
> "How quickly these Russians learn English."
> "How quickly these Americans learn Russian."[19]

Love frequently blossomed in the months the doughboys spent in Siberia. At the end of the expedition, the chaplain had rush orders from the general to sanctify seventy-eight marriages of doughboys with local ladies.[20] The officers did not encourage the couples, but did not forbid the marriages. Not all of the dalliances ended in marriage. One soldier wrote, "Was interested in a Russian girl but never asked permission to marry. Didn't think it would be granted so I forgot about it. People there were broadminded. I made love to a girl with her parents right there in the house."[21]

There was a show called "Roadhouse Minstrels," including several Royal Canadian Mounted Police, starring Raymond Massey, who later became a Hollywood star.[22] There were lectures, plus sing-alongs that featured still-popular classics like "There's a Long, Long Trail," "I Want to Go Home," "Over There," and "I Didn't Raise My Boy to Be a Soldier."

As winter approached, the summer recreations were no longer available: swimming in the bay, walking along the waterfront, and outdoor games. With the lack of alternatives, boys began to frequent the ladies of Kopeck Hill. There the ladies of the evening provided their own form of entertainment, but along with it, diseases that plagued the expedition. Kopeck Hill did more damage to American youth than any Bolshevik, Cossack, Japanese, or Chinese bandit. Venereal disease was more common than the flu or even gunshot wounds.[23]

The Navy provided some entertainment for both officers and men. For officers there were frequent dances and dinners on board the various naval vessels. Each morning certain ceremonies began the day. On the *Brooklyn,* Marines raised the American flag, while the sailors stood at rigid attention. The flag raising was accompanied by the playing of the American national anthem; when that was finished, the British played their anthem, followed by the Japanese and any other ships that might be in the harbor. One sailor, Ernest Hoskins, wrote with some candor, "It would take some time before we could carry on."[24] Added to that symphony of sound were the Japanese bugles, the British bagpipes, and the U.S. whistles that continued throughout the day. On still days, the sound carried throughout the district. Winter made these ceremonies difficult, however, as a Filipino band discovered.

> When the icebreaker made our passageway through to the dock at Vladivostok and we tied up it was time for the band to play the Star Spangled Banner and the lowering of the flag. We had a Filipino Band who never saw snow before. They came out to play nary a toot of their instrument froze on their lips and the marines had to carry them inside the ship.[25]

On May 14, 1919, the British cruiser HMS *Kent* with the Russian steamer *Georgie* went on a mission that was as confusing as it was successful. The mission was to remove Russians who wanted to evacuate from two areas, Olga Bay and Tethue, on the coast several hundred miles north of Vladivostok. The plan was to have a committee of Allied representatives interview the refugees and meet with a partisan committee to assess the state of affairs. The Allied committee was made up of an Englishman, a Czech, and U.S. Maj. Sidney Graves, son of the commanding general. Graves pointed out in his May 17 report that both the British officer and the Czech seemed determined to spread propaganda for Kolchak.[26] The ships visited the two areas and discussions were held with local Red committees. While the delegations in both areas expressed some friendship toward American troops, they detested Japanese policy and behavior. They were unanimous in hoping for the withdrawal of all Allies.[27] Those Russians from both Olga Bay and Tethue who wished to leave their homes stayed on the ships as they all returned to Vladivostok.

General Graves had difficulty charting a course, as pressures continued to mount. He clung rigidly to the one clear message of Wilson's *Memoire*: stay out of Russian affairs. The problems might have eased after the German surrender, but just a week later, Admiral Kolchak came to power, producing a government that went from bad to barbaric. The U.S. State and War Departments seemed to have no communication with each other as messages sped across the Pacific. Secretary of War Newton Baker, in the forward to Graves's book many years after the war, said:

> I cannot even guess at the explanation of the apparent conflict between the War Department and the State Department of the United States with regard to the Siberian venture, nor can I understand why the State Department undertook to convey its ideas on Siberian policy, as it seems to have occasionally done, directly to General Graves.[28]

Graves himself attributes the rift to a State Department message sent to the War Department and then forwarded to Siberia. In essence, it said that local consular officials were free to give advice and counsel to any local governments along the railroad. Since the railroad and its supporting communities were basically controlled by the Whites, it became obvious that the United States was, in fact, interfering in Russian internal affairs. Graves said, "The instructions above referred to, in my judgment, were the entering wedge to, what proved to be, a distinct cleavage between the representatives of the State and the War Departments in Siberia."[29]

It was not only his own government that tried to move Graves off his neutral course. In the last message he received from Britain's General Knox, Knox sounded peeved, but resigned to the American position on the Intervention:

> I wish we could see more eye to eye in matters here. The objects we wish are undoubtedly very similar but we are falling into different ruts. The policy of our Government is to support Kolchak, and I believe in that policy, for if he goes there will be chaos. I don't pretend for a moment that Kolchak is the Angel Gabriel, but he has energy, patriotism and honesty, and my eight years in Russia has taught me that when you get these qualities combined in one man he is a man to keep.
>
> There is a widespread propaganda to the effect that your Countrymen are Pro-Bolshevik. I think in the interest of Allied solidarity, and of the safety of Allied detachments, you should try to contradict this.[30]

According to Graves, this was Knox's last attempt to convince him of the error of his ways; Knox, in Omsk, turned his efforts toward the American diplomats there.[31] It would probably be safe to place the blame for the utter confusion on the original *Aide Memoire* with its vagueness and subsequent lack of clarification. That vagueness turned Graves into a Bolshevik in the eyes of the Whites and a White in the eyes of the Bolsheviks. Graves cabled Washington on November 21 that conditions were growing steadily worse. General Horvat had just been appointed as the Omsk government's east Russian representative; Graves considered him to be another monarchist. Graves felt the only thing allowing the Kolchak government to continue was the presence of the Allies. "I think some blood will be shed when the troops move out but the longer we stay the greater will be the blood shed when the allied troops do go."[32]

Soon after his arrival in Russia, Graves had made it a point to visit all of the units along the railroad to evaluate conditions and get a feeling for the land. On several of his stops, the general asked the troops what they were doing in their mission. Most replied they were ordered to fight the Bolsheviks. Graves, each time, explained:

> Whoever gave you those orders must have made them up himself. The United States is not at war with the Bolsheviki or any other faction of Russia. You have no orders to arrest Bolsheviks or anybody else unless they disturb the peace of the community, attack the people or the Allied soldiers. The United States army is not here to fight Russia or any group or faction in Russia. Because a man is Bolshevik is no reason for his arrest.[33]

As in North Russia, one of the aggravations of the troops was censorship. The chief of the censorship section was Kenneth Roberts, who had no liking for the duty. But he was to enforce the requirements of the censorship restrictions as outlined in AEFS Memorandum #4 (Censorship Regulations). Roberts was told emphatically by Colonel Robinson that censorship was to concern itself not only with military information, but with political information as well. Roberts pointed out the dangers of such a policy to the colonel:

> Colonel Robinson couldn't see it. Correspondents, he held, had no call to come uninvited into the sphere of influence of an expeditionary force and criticize things they didn't understand; and he, as chief of staff, wouldn't tolerate such criticism. And my orders were to see that no such criticism was sent.[34]

Pvt. William Johnson wrote his sister in February 1919, "I don't have the least idea of what was in that letter of Dec. 12 that wouldn't pass the censor. I must have told the truth about something."[35]

The end of censorship happened as a result of a single soldier's letter. Pvt. Willard Simonton wrote to his father about some of the conditions in Siberia. He told of being punched out by his sergeant and how, after he reported the assault to his commanding officer, no disciplinary action was taken against the sergeant. In general, he said that the recruits in Siberia were worse off than slaves before the Civil War.

Then he said they were told by the American consul that they were in Siberia because Wall Street had money invested there "and they don't give a dam about you." The letter, after his father read it, was sent on to U.S. Senator Hiram Johnson of California, an avowed advocate of bringing the boys home. He lost no time in sending a copy of the letter to Graves in Vladivostok. That began an investigation that lasted for several weeks, with the results announced on July 27 that the following action would be taken:

1. Simonton was to be reprimanded for violating Memorandum #4.
2. Sgt. John Powers was to be reprimanded for laying hands on a private.
3. Capt. Laird Richards was to be ordered before an efficiency board to determine his fitness to remain in the service.
4. Memorandum #4 was to be rescinded.

Thus ended censorship, but not until nine months after the Armistice, and one month after the AEF in North Russia had abandoned its campaign.

There was a censorship of local media as well, although not in the early days of the expedition. As time passed, local papers became more critical of the Allies and Kolchak; on two occasions local newspapers were closed by Allied orders. The *Echo,* a paper owned primarily by the British, was shut down in July 1919 by the Kolchak government after it published articles critical of the government. The Kolchak officials carried it one step further by ordering the arrest of the editor, Mr. Lopatin, who fled the area. In a confusing series of events, the British deputy high commissioner in Vladivostok heard of the editor's difficulty and arranged to have him stowed away on a British vessel. Lieutenant Gruner, the British military control officer, reported that plan to the British police, who then arrested Lopatin and turned him over to the Russians.[36]

A second closing took place in late August of the same year when the Russian newspaper *Golos Primoria* was closed by order of the commander of the Vladivostok fortress, Colonel Butenko, one of the few officials consistently friendly toward the Americans. He gave the order, apparently, because of an article entitled "Yankee," which was critical of the Americans. On August 29, Major Johnson of the IMP called on the newspaper office with Maj. Sidney Graves and ordered the paper closed. The editor was not arrested, but a guard was placed around the premises, supposedly to make sure the paper remained closed.[37]

While there was little actual fighting for the Americans in Vladivostok, occasionally snipers fired at the sentinels manning outposts around the city, and there were sometimes clashes between Allied, Russian, and Chinese forces within the city. For the most part, the duty there was reasonably peaceful, comfortable, and boring. Mail was the main morale booster, and in Vladivostok, mail came very promptly and very efficiently. However, the farther from Vladivostok the soldier was stationed, the smaller his chances for frequent contact with home. In spite of the efforts of the RRSC, trains were constantly disrupted by the partisans and the Bolsheviks. The trains provided the delivery system for all of the basic goods and the personal mail of those up the line, and for passenger movement as well. When train service was disrupted for any length of time, as it frequently was, deliveries and passenger services were halted.

Units were stationed in various locations outside Vladivostok in the early days of the Intervention. The Americans came into frequent contact with the Japanese, particularly on the railroad; on these occasions, doughboys were alarmed by the Japanese troops' actions and conduct. By January 1919, the Japanese had firmly established themselves all along the railroads and in key Siberian locations.

The closest post outside the big city was Razdolnoye, about thirty miles north of Vladivostok on the Trans-Siberian Railroad. Duty there had its benefits, with a YMCA canteen, some free time, and a chance to see Russians in a more natural setting than that of the big city. After their brief baptism by fire early in the expedition, life remained quiet in this little village. However, one particular day provided considerable excitement. It was reported that partisans were planning to stop a train and seize a Kolchak officer. According to Pvt. Joseph Ahearn, one platoon of Company F, Thirty-first Infantry was called out to man the station to stop the partisans from taking the officer. As the train approached, tensions mounted; the doughboys crouched behind a hastily put together barricade. The train thundered into the station without a pause, and the men breathed a sigh of relief. Captain Bishop ordered the platoon commander to unload the rifles. The lieutenant's sheepish reply was, "Golly, captain, I forgot to have them load!"[38] Ahearn wrote that it was a dull, boring existence, but he was convinced he was there to avoid a Japanese takeover of Siberia.

Spasskoye was the main base for troops along the Ussuri line of the Trans-Siberian. Actually the troops were about two miles from Spasskoye in Yerfgenyefka, which was not on the railroad, but the camp became known officially and unofficially as Spasskoye, a much easier name to deal with. The first to arrive were Companies F and G of the Thirty-first Infantry; in November the First Battalion of the Twenty-seventh Infantry was dispatched from Khabarovsk to provide men to staff the various areas between Ussuri and Nikolsk.[39] They were housed in old Russian barracks built originally for Russian Army Siberian troops. After much cleaning, the barracks became very livable. Other similar buildings were quarters for Russian and Japanese troops sharing the Allied responsibilities with the Americans. The Russians were aviators from a nearby Russian airbase and a few engineers. The regimental history of the Thirty-first Infantry recorded that the Russians and Americans got along well in the early days. "However, in the late spring and in the summer of 1919 this relationship changed."[40]

Throughout the expedition, troops were frequently moved from one station to another. Sviyagino, not far from a railroad tunnel, was typical of the towns that housed American units. A normal small village, reached virtually only by train, it was described by one doughboy: "35 miles from nowhere, or introducing Sviyagino, an unknown spot in Siberia located on the railroad about 35 versts north of the end of the earth (called Spasskoye by the Ruskies)."[41]

Shmakovka, much farther up the line, was home for a short time to Lt. Sylvian Kindall, who became a rather outspoken critic of the Japanese allies. One of his complaints was that the Japanese sanitary conditions were disgusting:

> The Japanese across the railroad from our camp were even more careless than the Russians about the requirements of nature, using the open ground in plain view of everybody with no more shame about themselves than a herd of swine. Whenever a breeze blew from the direction of their camp, sheets of crumpled toilet paper, like a flock of white butterflies, would come flying over into our area.[42]

He also noted the bathroom facilities at the train stations on the main line left much to be desired. Most stations had two-seater accommodations in the stationhouses, described by Kindall as "limited to two bellyaches at one time." Whenever a train stopped, there was a race to those two-seaters; the losers were forced to ease their discomfort in the open ground behind the station. "Privacy here, the same as privacy at the bathing places along the Ussuri River, depended largely on how well the other person kept his head turned."[43] The village was peaceful enough, with some entertainment locally provided. One Chinese magician baffled the doughboys by pulling a live snake out of his nose!

It was here that Kindall visited a true Cossack village, one that provided warriors loyal to the Whites. He was impressed by their dignity and pride, unlike the Semenov/Kalmykof variety of Cossack. While Kindall was in Shmakovka, the Kalmykof Cossacks rode into town on an armored train. They jumped down from their cars, went to the station market, and grabbed food and bread from the old ladies tending their stalls. Without any pretense of paying, they then marched off to a Chinese moneylender, who was changing American dollars for rubles. Since they forbade exchanging money of any kind, the Cossack officer grabbed the Chinese man, took out his saber, and cut off part of the man's nose, slashed the rest of his face and lip, and took his money. Then, they threw him in their boxcar and prepared to leave. Kindall drew his pistol, jumped on the car, and rescued the old man, then found the Cossack officer and dragged him across the station so he could return the stolen money.[44] It was a vivid demonstration of Kalmykof's callous treatment of his fellow Russians, with a little taste of American justice.

All through Siberia, roads were merely paths unable to support the expedition's vehicles, so the train was vital for bringing supplies from the south to the troops along the railroad. In the beginning, the villagers were friendly and life was bearable. Some men were quartered in tents, others in local houses, but many lived in boxcars that had been taken off the rails, stripped of their wheels, and insulated by ingenious methods to prepare for winter's subzero temperatures. These quarters were much like the boxcars used in North Russia, lacking only mobility.

In Khabarovsk, the Japanese Twelfth Division was housed in barracks similar to those of the doughboys, although they remained aloof from the Americans. Khabarovsk in the past had been part of a garrison along the Chinese border, which was only a short distance from the city, and had housed various Tsarist units in bygone days. As the Allied troops wintered there, the drill fields rang with the various units honing their skills: machine gun practice, close-order drill, bayonet practice, and even mounted Cossacks with their saber charges across the drill fields. North of the city, Japanese gunboats plied the Amur River between the river's mouth at Nikolaevsk and Khabarovsk, providing cover for Japanese troops north of Khabarovsk, who were driving out the few Bolshevik units still causing problems.[45]

Desertion was a periodic problem. Desertion would seem an unattractive alternative given the language barrier, climate, ongoing revolution, and the different lifestyle of the Russians, but official records indicate that fifty U.S. soldiers deserted during the expedition.[46] Many of the expedition members were native-born Russians, chosen for the Intervention force for that very reason. None of the defections was more devastating to American units than the desertion of Anton Karachun. Karachun, a coal miner from Minsk, Russia, emigrated to the United States in 1914 and enlisted in the army in 1917. At Camp Fremont he was selected for the Siberian expedition because of his fluency in Russian. His first assignment was as a censor in the post office in Vladivostok, where he became friendly with a number of Russians, mostly of the Bolshevik persuasion. After he began to distribute their Red literature against Army policy, he was transferred to the Suchan Mine area as a gunner with Machine Gun Company K of the Thirty-first Infantry. It was from his post at the Suchan that Karachun deserted to play a significant role in the tragic days ahead.

The winter was a cold but quiet one for most of the men stationed in the various cities along the Trans-Siberian Railroad. Spring was just around the corner, however, and spring would change everything.

Spring Comes to Siberia

The Siberian railroads belong to the Russian working people, not to the Kolchak Gvoernment, [sic] which usurped the people's power and will on the territory of Siberia and which is not recognized by anyone.

—Partizan Detachment of Olga County

WITH spring came the first open acts of aggression against the Allies. Initially, they consisted of sniping at the railroad trains, a result of the strong feelings that the Russian people were expressing against almost everything. It was not necessarily a pro-Bolshevik emotion that galvanized them, but an anti–everything else sentiment. They hated the tsar, they hated Kolchak, they hated the Cossacks Semenov and Kalmykof, they hated the Japanese, and now they hated the Americans. Those emotions peaked in the late spring, bringing confrontations and hostility to the troops of the AEFS. This feeling was encouraged by the anti-American sentiments that prevailed in Japanese newspapers.

A significant event in the spring of 1919 was the signing of the Railroad Agreement by representatives of the various Allied forces. This agreement was signed in March and implemented in April.[1] The document made "Russians" the chairman of the Inter-Allied Committee, and all railway heads were to be "Russian." According to Graves, these various officials were rapidly appointed by Kolchak; thus, most of the railway employees were strong supporters of the Omsk government.[2]

The agreement also required that various sections of the railroad be guarded by military forces, separate and distinct from the railroad operators. The assignments split the two routes, the Chinese-Eastern and the Trans-Siberian, into several areas of responsibility. Both the British and French announced that they would not have any troops available for such guard duty.[3]

The United States was assigned to guard the following:

1. Vladivostok to Nikolsk including the Suchan Mine line—a total of 144 miles
2. Spasskoye exclusive to Ussuri inclusive—70 miles
3. Verkhne-Udinsk to Baikal City (later changed to Mysovaya)— 316 miles

Japan would be responsible for:

1. Nikolsk to Spasskoye, both inclusive—81 miles
2. Guberovo exclusive to Verkhne-Udinsk exclusive and from Manchuria Station to Karymaskaya—2,220 miles

China would be responsible for:

1. Ussuri, exclusive, to Manchuria Station inclusive, including the line to Chanchun—1,225 miles

The Russians were given the road between Mysovaya and Baikal City, and the Czechs the roads west of Baikal. It was hoped that the agreement would end the frustrations and inactivity of the members of the RRSC, as they would be empowered to play a more important role in railroad affairs. This turned out to be an empty hope; the Kolchak government and the White military continued to stymie the efforts of this dedicated group of experts.

The railroads, even when maintained by well-trained American railroaders, remained in a state of chaos and disrepair. In part it was pure politics, with Japanese, Russians, and Americans disagreeing on almost everything. In addition, partisan raids were stepped up during the springtime, wreaking havoc on the already mangled railroad.

The Americans assigned to the Baikal area arrived to find Russian troops already there, and intending to stay. Graves protested to the Omsk government; that body, after considerable procrastination, admitted that a mistake had been made, apologized, and allowed the Americans to take their proper places. On the Manchurian line, the Chinese had responsibility for the largest section, but shortly after they arrived, the Japanese dropped off troops in almost every Chinese installation, citing their need to build and maintain a telegraph line.[4] The records are full of protests, explanations, and apologies, all diplomatically worded, but having few positive results for those trying to maintain the railroads.

The railroads had been increasingly monopolized by the two Cossack brigands, Semenov and Kalmykof. They acquired a number of armored trains, which bristled with weapons and were protected by sandbags, or in some cases, actual armor plating. These trains roamed the countryside virtually uncontrolled in the spring and summer months. In these trains, they housed their troops, entertained them with captured prisoners, held court, and in some cases actually carried out their sentences. Since both Cossack groups were supported by the Japanese, many of the complaints filed by Russians and Americans were directed toward the Japanese, who maintained they had little control over the horsemen and could do nothing. In some cases, the Cossacks expressed their contempt for Americans by driving their armored trains through American sections and throwing dead horses into the doughboy's camps near the railroad.[5]

The Railroad Agreement had one positive effect: the Americans now had a specific assignment, rather than the vague goals that had never really been fully understood or accepted. Unfortunately, the Americans were now guarding a railroad that was used exclusively by the White forces. The armored trains of the Cossacks and the movement of military goods were all destined to help Kolchak; there was never any pretense that the railroads could be used by the Bolsheviks. So even the appearance of noninterference was eroding. General Graves, although unhappy with the agreement, tried to explain the new U.S. role in a proclamation issued on April 21, 1919, just days after the agreement was put into effect.

> TO THE RUSSIAN PEOPLE
> Whereas, under existing disturbed and distressed conditions in Russia, it appears of general benefit and to the equal advantage of the Russian people, irrespective of political connections or belief, to insure the safe, prompt and regular movement of freight and passengers over the railroads in Siberia, and,
> Whereas, for such desired accomplishment, agreement has been made

between the Allied Powers having military forces in Siberia, including Russia, for the safe-guarding of the operation of the railroads by means of troops within the territory in which Allied military forces are now at work, and,

Whereas, pursuant to such agreement, the railway from Vladivostok, exclusive, to Nikolsk, exclusive, and including the branch line from Ugolnia to and including Souchan mines; from Spasskoye, exclusive, to Ussuri, inclusive, and from Verkhne-Udinsk to Baikal City, both inclusive, has been placed under the protection of troops of the United States of America.

Now, therefore, the Russian people are notified and advised, that in the performance of such duty, the sole object and purpose of the armed forces of the United States of America, on guard between the points above stated, is to protect the railroad and railway property and insure the operation of passenger and freight trains through such sector without obstruction or interruption. Our aim is to be of real assistance to all Russia protecting necessary traffic movements with the sectors on the railroad assigned to us to safeguard. All will be equally benefited, and all shall be treated alike by our forces irrespective of persons, nationality, religion or politics. Cooperation is requested and warning given to all persons whomsoever, that interference with traffic will not be tolerated.[6]

The Russians saw through the pretense of equal treatment. In a memo to Graves in May, the Olga County partisans praised the United States for its concerns for the Russian people, but they made their real feelings plain:

The Siberian railroads belong to the Russian working people, not to the Kolchak Gvoernment, [sic] which usurped the people's power and will on the territory of Siberia and which is not recognized by anyone. This certainly is known to the American Government.

In spite of this the latter reckons with the Government of Kolchak as if it were the Russian authority, makes different agreements with him, among them the guarding of the Siberian railways. It is necessary to call attention to the fact that the working population of Siberia, including the population of Olga County in whose name we are speaking, does not recognize any of the above-mentioned agreements, and will act as the interests and demands of the revolution move them.[7]

The proclamation ended with a pledge of full noninterference with railway traffic as long as the railroads were truly accessible to all Russians. The partisans made it plain that they would like to believe in the sincerity of Graves's words, but the actions of the Allies in their obvious support of Kolchak "makes us, to our regret, disbelieve." The message from Olga County in the Suchan area seemed to speak for all

Siberia. It was a remarkable document that rationally put forth the very dilemma that the United States had tried to avoid.

Fulfilling the requirements of the Railroad Agreement meant shifting troops farther west than any American troops had been previously. The first deployment sent parts of the Twenty-seventh Infantry to cover the section between Verkhne-Udinsk and Mysovaya on Lake Baikal. Orders came from Vladivostok for the Third Battalion to take up station on the Baikal route; they joined Companies A and B, which had been sent there in March, before the agreement was signed. Regimental headquarters and the medical staff went with the Third Battalion to Verkhne-Udinsk, where Colonel Morrow established his new center of operation.[8] Shortly afterward, the Second Battalion was ordered to Spasskoye's railroad territory, joining Companies C and D, leaving Khabarovsk to the Russians and the Japanese. As the companies moved to their headquarters area, they were soon split into smaller units and sent out to safeguard the railroads against any intruders. One of the little villages became home to a platoon of Company M. Pvt. Pat O'Dea found it a place of peace and beauty:

> Many of the men did not know it when they were there but later when they were home again they missed that beautiful north country. Its beauty and difference crept into their being without them even being aware of it at the time. You would see it and feel it all around you and you would still not know what it was. It was something that just took hold of you. I remember the moonlight too. It was so bright at midnight we could read a newspaper outside our barracks. . . .
>
> I used to get up sometimes at night and watch out the window of the barracks just to see that clear beautiful moonlight night and ponder at the mystery of all the peace. Perhaps I would hear a few distant wolves howl but that would be all—not another sound.[9]

But not all was so peaceful in the sector. The armored trains of Ataman Gregorii Semenov, known as Broneviks, had rolled virtually unchecked through that territory until the Twenty-seventh Infantry arrived. Americans had witnessed with disgust the atrocities of Kalmykof in the Ussuri area, but his brutality was equaled by the wholesale slaughter accomplished by Semenov. Semenov was not a favorite of Admiral Kolchak when he took over in November of 1918, but Semenov's control of a number of anti-Bolshevik troops became increasingly important. As recently as January, Kolchak had declared Semenov a traitor and ordered his arrest, but in May he revoked that order and made him a corps commander in the White Army.[10] Reports indicated that Semenov's promotion was entirely the result of Japanese pressure, the Japanese being the force behind both Cossack leaders.[11]

On May 22, Private Karas of Company K, serving with the Military Police, shot and killed Corporal Kyakoff of Semenov's command while attempting to stop a drunken rampage by the Cossack, an act that increased friction between Cossacks and Americans. "Full and complete investigation fully exonerated Private Karas," according to Colonel Morrow.[12]

In May, Semenov created more tension by demanding a railroad car from Captain Gilliland of the RRSC. Semenov's demand was denied, and a guard was assigned to the car. The next day, however, Gilliland released the car. On June 1, a detachment of Russian engineers (6 officers and 105 soldiers) was en route to the front at Perm under orders from Kolchak himself, when its train was stopped by Semenov. "All members of the Engineer Company except those who escaped, were arrested. About 34 of them were forced to serve on the armored train, the whereabouts of the others is not known."[13]

The situation continued to worsen in the Baikal area until Colonel Morrow, known for his somewhat gruff manner and short temper, finally decided to take matters into his own hands. He had repeatedly requested that Semenov's trains be kept out of American sectors. He also had received a series of telegrams concerning Semenov's trains, including one from John Stevens, head of the RRSC, telling Graves that there was no need for any armored trains in Verkhne-Udinsk. The Cossacks had arrested citizens and taken them aboard their trains to be whipped, tortured, and sometimes shot.[14] The charge was always "suspected Bolshevik," and no proof was necessary for a guilty verdict. In early June 1919, some railroad personnel were arrested by the Cossacks; when the next Semenov train pulled into the Verkhne-Udinsk station and tried to arrest the stationmaster, Morrow issued an ultimatum regarding the removal of armored trains. Morrow then wired Graves:

> Owing to Semenov's armored cars continual interference with the railroad, seizure of cars, threatening employees, interference with working parties, continued menace to my guard, and firing upon and arresting Russian troops proceeding to the front, I yesterday at 5 P.M., June 8, at a conference between Major General Yoshe, Japanese Army, General Mejak, Military Governor and General Pechinko, Commander of Russian troops in Beresova, requested them on grounds stated above to cause the removal of the armored cars out of the American sector and at the same time, informed them that if my request is not complied with within twenty-four hours I would destroy these cars.[15]

The threat was enough to bring a medical unit to the train station. "On the afternoon of June 10th Three aid stations were established for the care of wounded that might be sustained in the attack on the Armored car.''[16]

There was no need for the armored train to be there. There were ample Allied and White troops available to handle any attack by the few Reds reported to be in the area.[17] But the Japanese, supporting the Cossacks, put themselves between the Semenov train and the firepower of the Americans, proclaiming that they would fight with the Cossacks if the Americans opened fire. Morrow brought up his little 37mm cannon with all the machine guns he could find and placed them in position to fire on the Japanese. Again, it appeared that a significant incident was about to happen. Finally, the Japanese conferred with their headquarters and with the Cossacks and decided to withdraw, backing the armored train into more friendly territory.[18] "The Japs came to regard Morrow as a fellow with a short fuse already lit."[19]

In July 1919 the Inter-Allied Commission sent a telegram to the Kolchak government describing the misuse of the rail system by Semenov and requesting that other Russian railway officials conform to the various conditions set up to restore the railroads. Their first requirement was for Semenov to cease his disruption of traffic and his wanton acts of violence.[20] To this request they received no response.

In Spasskoye, the American headquarters for the area, the winter ended with a bitter Russian-American clash. An American interpreter was on duty at the train station when a drunken White Russian captain came in and made some insulting remarks. The American, Private Rubanovitch, took exception to the remarks and hit the Russian. The Russian left and Rubanovitch went to sleep in his bunk at the station. The officer found a pistol, came back, and awakened the sleepy private. The Russian fired one shot, which grazed the American, but the pistol jammed, giving Rubanovitch time to get his own Colt and pump five bullets into the captain.[21] "The officer sagged to the floor with a load of bullets in his body. 'Please don't shoot me any more' he begged, 'I'm dead.' And these were the last words he said," according to Lieutenant Kindall.[22] Lt. Fairfax Channing, the officer of the day, arrested the private; however, he was found innocent of any wrongdoing after the facts became clear.[23]

Shortly afterwards, Rubanovitch was involved in another drama. One evening in Sviyagino, Lieutenant Kindall was on duty at the train depot. As the evening train slid to a halt, Kindall received two garbled messages with instructions to hold the train. One car of the train was a Kalmykof armored car carrying several long-haired Cossacks; they, along with the conductor, demanded to know why the train needed to be held. The irate conductor shouted, "By what authority do you stop my train? You are not in America now you are in Russia!" Kindall called on Rubanovitch to translate; the interpreter pulled his revolver from his holster and shoved it in the belly of the conductor. "By this authority if you must know."

After thirty minutes, another indistinct message came through, allowing the train to leave. When the train was only five miles out of Sviyagino, it was riddled with Bolshevik bullets; when the train reached Spasskoye, the dead and wounded were removed. To the spectators in Spasskoye, it seemed as if the train was deliberately held long enough for darkness to fall and the Bolsheviks to creep to the edge of the tracks and pour their deadly fire onto it. Kindall later believed the messages he received were not from Vladivostok, but from an American-born partisan named Baranof, a local Bolshevik leader.[24]

In other American sectors, bullets were replacing bulletins in conveying messages. In May, several reports came into Vladivostok of shots fired into trains in the Spasskoye sector. An intelligence report showed three villages near Sviyagino appeared to be the centers of unrest. Belaya Zerkov, Kronstadka, and Vasilkovka lay only about ten versts east of Sviyagino in the center of heavily forested, mountainous area perfect for defense.[25]

Attempts were made to meet with Bolsheviks to reduce tensions. On one occasion, Capt. Lindsay P. Johns met with Bolshevik leader Baranof near Sviyagino. Baranof asked perplexing questions regarding the American position of allying itself with Semenov, Kalmykof, and other White Russian groups that had committed so many barbarous acts against the peasants of Russia. Johns could only read the proclamation of General Graves regarding the railroad. While Johns was in his meeting with Baranof, Lt. Montgomery Rice observed Baranof's soldiers:

> Rice could perceive a spirit of purpose that distinguished them from most other soldiers. No matter if their rifles were foul with rust, their clothing worn to rags, their bodies sour with filth, their cheeks sunken from malnutrition, or otherwise how far below the standard of professional soldiers they were in appearance, it could not be denied that they were inspired men.[26]

This meeting and others accomplished nothing. In his conversation, however, Baranof denied any connection with American deserter Karachun and said they would make every effort to capture him.

On May 21, Maj. Fitzhugh Allderdice, commanding the Spasskoye units, received a frantic wire from Sviyagino: "Thirty five hundred Bolsheviks surround us send help for God's sake." Actually, about five hundred Bolshevik horsemen had come into the town simply to use the telegraph. They sent four wires, harmed no one, and left.[27] On

May 21, two bridges near Razdolnoye were blown up; a detachment was sent out to find the guilty parties, but found nothing.

June would be the bloodiest month of the campaign.

On June 2, a train was fired on between Sviyagino and Ussuri. On June 7, the bridge near Shmakovka was blown, but quickly repaired, and there were repeated attempts by the Bolos to sabotage train tracks during this period. On June 9, a patrol of White Russians was attacked five miles southeast of Spasskoye, and two were killed. That same day, a raiding party of four hundred Reds entered a village near Sviyagino; ignoring the presence of American guards, they stole telephones and raided the post office and a flour mill.

As a result of those events, an expedition was sent on June 11 to the suspected headquarters of the Bolsheviks at Uspenka, several miles off the railroad. A detail from Company F was sent from Shmakovka; they had to cross a swampy section just in front of the town, so they spent the night of June 11 at a monastery. Pvt. Sam Liberberg wrote years later:

> Early the next morning, there were several sightings of the Reds on top of a ridge; as soon as the firing began, a patrol went forward to find their positions. The patrol, under Lt. Fairfax Channing, fired on the Reds and sparked immediate return fire. The lieutenant dashed forward and jumped in the Bolo trenches, which were filled with dummies to fool the doughboys. He found himself alone, with several of his patrol wounded and seeking cover. Channing's situation was serious. He was drawing fire from both the Reds and the Americans, who had no idea he had made it to the enemy trenches. Eventually, he was rescued and the Bolsheviks driven back. The next morning, before dawn, Channing led six squads into the village and drove out the Reds who had stayed behind.[28]

The cost to the Americans was four wounded, two seriously, all of whom were sent to the hospital at Spasskoye.[29] They claimed two enemy killed, several wounded, and several captured. Both Channing and Lt. Christian Cross won the DSC in that action.[30]

A few miles down the railroad was the village of Kraefski, home to a platoon of Company F of the Twenty-seventh Infantry. Shortly before the Uspenka fight, a squad of Company C had garrisoned the town, but they were surrounded by Bolsheviks early one morning and gave up some telephone equipment to the raiders without a fight. The leader of this raiding party was identified as the deserter Karachun.[31] Soon after, the platoon was replaced by Lt. Wilson Rich and his men. Major Wallace came through on June 11, taking two squads of Rich's platoon on an expedition to Uspenka, leaving Rich with only two squads. That night, about midnight, a Russian woman came into the American compound and tried to tell them something, but the language barrier was too great. However, Rich felt she was trying to warn them, so he took his men from their warehouse quarters and had them sleep in a trench near a railroad embankment. They were awakened early the next morning by 150 Bolshevik infantry, plus about thirty-five Chinese "bandits" about to attack their warehouse. At 5:20 A.M. the attackers opened fire, riddling the empty warehouse, but the Americans held their fire. The Reds came charging up to the compound and were met by the first volley of American fire, which stopped them in their tracks.

Two Chinese found refuge behind a pile of aspen logs and had a clear shot at the doughboys. Fortunately, two lucky shots killed the two Chinese; that broke the attack, and the Reds took to the woods. The cook, John Evans, placed himself on the thatched roof of a cook shed and shot nine more Bolsheviks, ending the half-hour battle.[32]

Shortly after the firing stopped, Pvt. Walter Kellerman, while searching for wounded, came across a badly wounded Red soldier. As Kellerman knelt to tend to him, the wounded soldier, expecting to be killed, raised his rifle and shot Kellerman through the heart. His stunned buddies emptied their rifles at the Red; as he died, he muttered "Natcheevo, natcheevo," which meant, "It really didn't matter."[33]

Evans won a DSC for his bravery. The Americans lost one dead, and Pfc. Steve Trask was slightly wounded. Two members of Company F, not involved in the fighting, were captured while returning from a patrol. Pvt. Chester Burt was held only a few days, returning June 15, but Sgt. Chester Batchelor stayed with the Red units for fourteen days before he was released.[34]

Both men identified one of the leaders of the attack as the deserter Karachun. The man in charge was called Gorko, an American-educated Russian who spoke perfect English. Batchelor reported that Karachun was the leader of forces in the Kraefski section and had a wife living in Uspenka.[35] Karachun was now not only a deserter, but an active part of the group responsible for at least one American death. He was quoted as saying, after the Kraefski battle, "It was a great scrap, we shot them all to pieces. . . . I killed Lt. Rich myself I shot him and I saw him fall."[36] His enthusiasm for the raid and his part in it was somewhat premature given the few American casualties and the fact that Lieutenant Rich was neither killed nor wounded, but it was puzzling that someone could turn on his friends so viciously.

There were additional clashes along the Trans-Siberian in those middle days of June. The Bolsheviks tore up rails a few miles north of Sviyagino and wrecked a train, although no one was injured. Japanese on the train claimed they killed one Red. On June 13, another train was wrecked, followed by a Bolshevik attack that killed three Russians and wounded eighteen civilians, plus one Japanese. While the wounded were being taken off the cars in Spasskoye, two Bolsheviks broke into a roundhouse nearby, started a locomotive, and rolled it downhill into the train, causing more injuries. "Japanese soldiers later picked up the Russians marched them up the tracks and bayoneted them from the rear allowing their bodies to fall in a ditch along the right of way."[37] The next day, few trains moved because of more track damage, and on June 15, Reds fired on Japanese patrols in the village of Dobovskaya, just outside Spasskoye, killing two, so the village was burned to the ground by the Japanese. To say the least, there was little peace in the area.

A confrontation in Sviyagino on June 25 involved only Allied forces. Just after the Kraefski fight, a Japanese troop train pulled into town, unloading a detachment of its soldiers and their equipment. Captain Johns protested to headquarters in Vladivostok, since the village was well within the boundaries of the American sector. The Japanese set up camp across town and, for some reason, were allowed to stay. They began night patrols, while the Americans did the same. There were attempts to designate patrol areas, passwords, and responsibilities, but the inevitable happened on a dark night on June 25.

Lieutenant Kindall was leading a patrol when, without any warning, he was fired on from out of the darkness. Kindall thought he heard Japanese voices and ordered a cease-fire; a call for recognition brought only silence. After a few minutes, firing broke out again. "We fought back at them once more, and during this second round of the fighting were able to do better shooting on our side." One American bullet struck home, and the shriek of the wounded Japanese brought the firing to a halt. As the two sides slowly approached each other, the Japanese found one of their men dead and two wounded. The Americans counted only one wounded, Lieutenant Kindall. Kindall later wrote in his book that his "only distinction is that he happened to be the first American to qualify for the award of the Purple Heart for a wound received in a fight with the Japanese."[38]

After the fight, Johns met with the surly Japanese commander; their brief conversation ended with the Japanese threat that war between his country and the United States would come of the matter. Johns's brief reply was, "you'll find us good and ready!" As a result of the late-night encounter, Captain Johns requested assistance in removing the Japanese unit, but found to his dismay that his Company C was the one ordered to move out.

Another fight at about the same time was not between Reds and Americans, nor between Japanese or Cossacks and Americans, but between Americans themselves. Late in June, Lieutenant Kindall found himself in command of two squads ordered to patrol a hotly contested section of the railroad between Sviyagino and Drosdov Siding, some three miles away. There was a wooded area close to the section of the track that concealed Red troops, who would wait for passing trains, open fire, and then disappear. As Kindall and his men moved up the tracks, the sky darkened and the rains came, making it almost impossible for them to see each other.

The lieutenant put nine men on one side of the tracks and ten on the other, then scurried between the two columns to keep control. As the rain began, they heard a train approaching slowly behind them. They decided to make themselves conspicuous as the train approached and waved, shouting "Amerikanski!" as loud as they could, but the darkened train passed slowly into the darkness ahead with no sign of recognition. A few minutes later they heard firing from the direction of the vanished train. Kindall was not sure what the firing meant, but realized that his men appearing out of the darkness might well be mistaken for unfriendly forces and draw fire. He cautiously approached the sound of the firing, which died out as they neared. They still could not see the train, but a match lit briefly in the distance showed the location of some force.

Kindall's two columns were still on both sides of the track; he crossed and recrossed the track to give the columns directions. As he crossed, a rifle fired, and he, without the least bit of ceremony, threw himself down the bank and ordered his unit to open fire. He was amazed to hear the sound of machine guns and dozens of rifles and see their twinkling flashes ahead of him and on his left. He was sure he was done for, outnumbered and outgunned. Suddenly, one of the old-timers, Corporal Durham, recognized the distinctive sounds of a Browning automatic rifle and realized the men they were fighting were Americans. He sent a shout down both columns to cease fire, and suddenly all was quiet. When the din of battle receded, Kindall found he had been facing Company E and another infantry company with a machine gun section.

The men had been on the train, transferring from Khabarovsk to Spasskoye.[39] The Bolsheviks had fired into the train and the men dismounted just as Kindall approached. Kindall guessed that the match was from a Bolshevik, that the firing from his left was from the Reds, and that the Bolos, recognizing superior firepower, beat a hasty retreat. The engagement was costly; Sgt. Andrew Buchanan of Kindall's patrol was killed and Pvt. William A. Roberts was wounded in the scalp.[40] Company E's only loss was Pvt. William Miller; severely wounded in the thigh, he was taken to the Spasskoye hospital where he died on June 23.[41]

After this disheartening event, the Twenty-seventh Infantry Regiment began a quiet period that would last until the waning days of the campaign. There were still serious problems keeping the trains on some semblance of a schedule. With interference from the Cossack's armored trains, White government officials, and Bolshevik trickery, there was little hope that an efficient railroad would ever emerge. The Americans were exposed to the excesses of the Cossacks on all their sectors, but were powerless to interfere.

During the summer, a verification of the enormity of Semenov's cruelties was made in a report by Lt. J. S. Davidson of the expedition's Intelligence Section. On September 3, 1919, he reported to his headquarters that on August 19 a trainload of Bolshevik prisoners and suspected Bolsheviks were taken out of the cars at Adrianovka, led some three versts outside town, and executed. Davidson visited the scene three days later:

> There were four graves, three of which were about fifteen feet long and ten wide each, the other, a smaller one, was completely covered with dirt, the other three only a thin layer of dirt covered the bodies. In one there were three or four bodies exposed and from the position of the bodies it seemed as though they were dumped in. One particular thing I noticed was that all of the feet were gone of the bodies exposed, with the exception of one, and only one foot remained on that body, the privates of another man gone. In my opinion the prisoners were tortured before they were killed, which is the custom of Semenov's guards.[42]

The people of the Baikal district were terrified of Semenov, "[I]t means death if you are found expressing your opinion, regarding Semenov or his officers."[43] It was painful for the men of the Twenty-seventh Infantry to accept that these were the men they were sent five thousand miles to support, but sadly they realized that they were now being identified as among Kolchak's defenders, atrocious as those defenders were.

These railroad guards remained in their locations with relatively little action until the chaos and confusion of the expedition's final days. However, the smoldering embers of the Suchan Mine unrest were already bursting into a consuming flame.

The Battles Begin

I reached the passenger train first and told the train guard that Company "A" was getting massacred.

—Cpl. William Heinzman

FROM the very beginning, the Suchan Mine area, located north and east of Vladivostok, had been troublesome to the Americans.

In September 1918, General Graves sent Company M of the Thirty-first Infantry with a Japanese company, a Chinese unit, and a few White Russians to the mine area under the command of Lt. Col. Sylvester Loring.[1] Colonel Robinson accompanied the units to judge the reception they might get. He also distributed Graves's notice, which said:

> *To the Citizens of the Suchan Mine District*
> The Allied nations have come to Russia to help the Russian citizens and help win the war against Germany. In the prosecution of this mission they have found it necessary to operate the mines temporarily in order to increase the production of coal, thus making possible the distribution of supplies from one section to another, to keep the Russian people from starving and Russian women and children warm this winter.[2]

Graves offered a few more details in his notice:

1. He reinstated Mr. Egroff, former mine superintendent (who was highly unpopular when he was relieved earlier), because he was most familiar with the mines.
2. The citizens did not need arms, since they were now being protected by the Allies. Mr. Egroff would issue permits for any weapons deemed necessary for hunting.
3. Machine guns must be turned in.
4. The local government was still in charge.[3]

Robinson left confident that the situation was well in hand.

During the winter months, life remained relatively quiet; the Americans even thought they had established friendships with the locals, although there were undercurrents of unrest. Springtime, however, brought significant changes; signs of trouble appeared as the trees began to bloom. Many of the miners were definitely anti-Kolchak, even if not pro-Bolshevik. The mine managers were Whites, and there had been tensions for some time between managers and workers.

The scene in Suchan was confusing. There were villagers who tended to their businesses; there were partisans who could at times be moved by impassioned leaders to take action against enemies; there were Bolsheviks who were determined to keep some pressure against the Whites recruiting in the area; and now there were Allies. The Suchan Russians were primarily Bolshevik sympathizers. They were very disorganized, but constituted a significant force when aroused. The Bolshevik leaders made it their job to keep anti-Kolchak feelings at fever pitch; the White Army's current recruiting tactics played perfectly into the Bolshevik leaders' plans.

After the Railroad Agreement, Allies guarded the spur railroad, which left the Trans-Siberian at Ugolnaya and turned east to the rugged hills of Suchan. From Ugolnaya, the line passed through a number of towns and villages, including Shkotova, Romanovka, Novo Nezhino, and Kangaus, as it wound toward the Suchan Mines. From Kangaus the rails turned to a cable car, which went through Tigrovia, then a narrow gauge which ran from Fanza through Sitsa, ending at the mines. The cable cars were used to climb the steep mountain grades and to transport the coal to the railroad cars. Since coal was critical to the operation of the locomotives of the all-important Trans-Siberian system, operating the coal mines was considered a logical addition to the Allied assignments along the main line. One observer described the passengers' experience getting to the mines: "We went into this area by a very unique method. First by regular train then by coal train on a narrow gage rail then by bucket line, two men to a bucket."[4]

At the time of the Railroad Agreement, Graves increased the troops in the Suchan area by sending Company E under American major Emile Cutrer to establish a base at Shkotova on the Suchan main rail line. In mid-March, he sent Company H to relieve Company M at the mines, but once they arrived, it was decided to keep both companies there. As more Americans came to guard the railroads and their presence increased, the friendship of the locals soon vanished. Animosity was increased by a number of White Army troops recruiting in the mine area, killing and torturing anyone trying to evade conscription. On his exploratory trip in April, Colonel Eichelberger had witnessed firsthand the belligerence of the Kolchak men when he was captured and later released.

Colonel Eichelberger returned to Suchan again in April to try to determine what could be done to keep conflicts in check. Earlier, Graves had reported to Washington that Cossacks under Ivanoff-Rinoff conscripting White Army recruits had executed ten men in Gordievka. His comment was, "The actions of these punitive Cossack expeditions is a disgrace to present day civilization and in my judgment the history of atrocities committed by the Bolsheviks will not be much worse than the history of those being committed by these Cossacks."[5] The White Army presence had left strong resentment against anything connected to the Kolchak regime. Eichelberger saw for himself the results of some of their methods when he asked for some evidence. "I had some bodies dug up, took photographs of the men who had been tortured— fingernails off and hundreds of burns with red hot irons."[6] Repeatedly, the locals pleaded with the Americans for help, but, in spite of their sympathy, the Americans obeyed their orders to stay neutral. Graves told Ivanoff-Rinoff to curtail his troops or the Americans would withdraw, so Ivanoff-Rinoff agreed to keep his men out of Suchan.[7]

There were several changes in command in the Mine Guard during the winter and early spring. On February 12, Colonel Loring was replaced by Lt. Col. L. L. Pendleton, who in turn was replaced by Maj. F. B. Allderdice on May 30.

On April 23, two Japanese soldiers were murdered and mutilated near Mine #10. "Their men were very nervous and would only leave their barracks in armed parties."[8] As the tensions mounted, on May 17 Graves ordered a full battalion from Vladivostok to Shkotova in an effort to stabilize the situation. The First Provisional Battalion, under Maj. William H. Joiner, consisted of four companies, plus one platoon of machine gunners and its 37mm cannon. This brought the number of companies in Shkotova to five: A, C, D, E, and I. Graves himself went to Shkotova and was there on May 21.[9] That same spring, a new Bolshevik figure appeared in the area, A. N. Iaremenko, who provided partisan leadership, as well as close contact with Bolshevik circles in other areas. A proven Bolshevik and partisan leader, he was joined by a more fanatical Bolshevik, Yakov Triapitsyn; together, they were able to pull the various factions together and begin a series of organized raids on the Suchan rail line.[10] They arrived in Suchan in time to witness the virtually complete blockade of the area by the Kolchak government. Believing that the White army's recruiting and terror methods had failed, the government stopped shipment of goods to Suchan. But far from forcing people to abandon the partisan movement, it only strengthened their numbers and their resolve.[11] By spring, no coal was being produced and even as the Allies deployed, the partisans began their campaign.

The campaign opened with a series of attacks on the Suchan trains carrying various Allied troops, supplies, and Russian troops and civilians. On May 18, a train was fired on between Ugolnaya and Shkotova, wounding five civilians and killing a Russian major. The same day a train was ambushed near Romanovka. Four days later a general strike of the miners was declared. The next day the revolutionary headquarters of the Olga district demanded the withdrawal of Allied troops, threatening to use force if necessary to make them leave.[12] Headquarters had become uneasy, and Major Cutrer had issued a blunt order to Lt. H. Krieger at Romanovka on May 23: "[Y]ou will disarm or kill every Red Guard in Romanovka. Don't parlay with them one minute longer."[13]

Because of the threats and demands of the partisans, on May 21, Company E under Capt. Laird Richards was sent from Shkotova to attack the village of Maihe. General Graves said:

> [T]here was nothing left for us to do but to take the field and break up these small bands which were getting together and rapidly forming into larger groups under the leadership of men who were reported as being extremely radical and who would not hesitate to resort to hostile measures.[14]

The orders to Company E stated that these overt acts justified the use of troops.

When Company E attacked the partisan stronghold at Maihe, it was not a major battle as battles go, but it was the first action the Thirty-first Infantry had seen since the old days of the insurrection in the Philippines. On May 21, the rains were heavy as the company moved along the road to Maihe. To reach the village, the men had to cross an icy river. Pvt. Wilber Goreham slipped and fell as he crossed. Two of his squad pulled him out of the river, but he found later that the three hundred dollars he had in his wallet had became stuck together.[15] Pvt. William Kislingburg was walking point, leading the advance; as they neared the village, he was sent on a flanking mission. The Americans drew some partisan fire, but had no casualties. He watched as the main body approached the bridge over the river, but had to deploy as the Reds opened fire. As the Browning automatic rifles fired back, the partisan fire slackened, then stopped.[16]

Back at regimental headquarters in Vladivostok, Colonel Sargent reported that Company E met "vigorous resistance" in the attack, and withdrew to encamp on the river across from town. A machine gun section was supposed to support Company E in its assault, but communications were confused, so Captain Richards and Company E left without the machine guns. Reinforcements arrived the next day, parts of companies C, D, and I, with the missing machine gun section.

The next day, May 22, the Americans launched a new assault, which successfully cleared the town of the partisans. Most of the attackers had to wade the frigid Maihe River, although some managed to cross on the bridge. They stayed in Maihe until 1:00 P.M., when they were ordered back to Shkotova. One of the machine gun company's reports said it was a miserable march in the rain. The men of the weapons section, ordered to take a shortcut back to camp, found themselves in a sucking swamp; they had to turn around to find the main road. It took them seven hours to cover the five miles; they arrived mud-caked and soaked.[17] American casualties were three wounded; Red casualties were unknown.[18]

The third day, Major Joiner sent a column with units from companies C, D, and I farther north and west, where they encountered sporadic firing, but chased out the snipers. On May 25, Joiner sent Companies C and D with a machine gun section from Shkotova west on the railroad, riding the cars a few miles, then detraining to clear two tiny villages, Knevichi and Krolovets, where they ran into heavy fire. These companies attacked from the south; Company E, sent from Shkotova, attacked from the east. The Americans, returning fire with their automatic weapons, swept the entire area, suffering no casualties. Colonel Sargent reported, "These operations effectively cleared the country north of the Ugalnaya-Shkotova sector."[19]

Although the area may have been cleared, it was far from secure. Graves, recognizing this, sent detachments from both the Shkotova base and the Mine Guard base, stretched to cover important rail stations. Allderdice wired Graves on June 7 saying he had been informed of an attack to be staged on the mines and Mine Guard within the next ten days. He asked permission to launch an attack on the two Bolshevik centers, Frolovka and Kazanka, which he felt was "the only solution to the problem in my opinion."[20] In spite of recent fighting, the answer was no. Allderdice's request might have had a bearing on the decision to relieve him on June 10, 1919; he was replaced by Col. Gideon H. Williams. On June 21, Major Joiner took Companies C and D from Shkotova to the Mine Guard base with a machine gun platoon and a section of heavy weapons, including a small one-pounder cannon.[21] This left Major Cutrer in command at Shkotova, and Colonel Williams commanding the Mine Guard.

Significant hostilities began on June 21 in an unexpected way. The fishing had been good along the Suchan River; three men from Company H walked the three miles to the river, took off their shoes, and began casting. Without warning, a group of partisan Red Guards surrounded and captured them. These three, Cpl. Harlan Daly, Pvt. Harold Bullard, and Pvt. Forrest Moore, were bound and taken across the river to Novitskaya, a partisan center. Early the next morning, two more American fishermen, Lt. Custer Fribley of the Quartermaster Corps and Cpl. Eastland Reed of Company H, were caught at almost the same spot, along with Lieutenant Fribley's mule.[22]

At 11:00 A.M. on June 22, the first three men were reported absent, and a patrol set out to find them. They learned that the three had been taken prisoner by the Red Guard and were now at Novitskaya. At about 2:00 P.M., Fribley and Reed were reported absent as well. The patrol returned to Suchan; Lt. Gilpin S. Rumans took out a larger expedition, following the mule tracks until they came to the Suchan River. Rumans' orders were not to cross the river, so he called to partisans on the other bank, asking about the prisoners, but there was no response.

Certain that the men were in Novitskaya, and knowing of the partisans' usual treatment of prisoners, Colonel Williams moved rapidly. He formed two platoons with 3 officers and 110 men and left on his mission at 5:40 P.M., leading the column personally. It was still raining and the roads were thick with mud, but the column moved rapidly, fording the river, arriving in Novitskaya at 8:00 P.M. They moved in quietly, even passing some Reds with rifles in their hands, but neither side made any move to open fire. Lieutenant Rumans led the advance party toward the center of the town. Colonel Williams demanded the release of the men, but as he did so, bells began to ring from the church steeple, and with that signal, the partisans opened fire.[23] The doughboys spread out immediately and returned fire, moving slowly toward the town center to stop the snipers. Williams was in the midst of the fighting, "[H]e rode up and down the skirmish line to see if everything was all right and did not show the slightest fear," one infantryman reported.[24]

It was all over by 9:00 P.M., but the Americans had lost four killed.

One was 2d Lt. Albert F. Ward from Chicago, a June 1918 graduate of West Point, the only Military Academy graduate killed in either Russian expedition. A report on the events of Ward's death was written by Sgt. Herbert Reeves, who was with him when he died:

> The organization was marching to the town where the American soldiers were imprisoned and as we were not really at war with the Bolsheviki, it had been decided to first request the release of the Americans before we took them by force. Lieutenant Ward and his orderly rode into the town with a flag of truce, suddenly two shots rang out and Lieutenant Ward and his orderly both fell from their horses. The shots came thick and fast then but I managed to get to Lieutenant Ward and got him back to cover. He was shot through the head and I knew he was done for. I think he knew it too. As I picked him up, he said, "Don't mind me, Sergeant, look after Jim he is hurt worse than I am." He said no more and he died a couple of hours later, before we could get him to the hospital. But think of what a man he was, sir; his first thought was of the poor kid who was serving him and who was dead when we picked him up.[25]

Killed with him were his orderly Pfc. Dee Craig, Pvt. Jesse Reed, and Pvt. Charles Flake, who died of his wounds the next day. Lieutenant Ward and Pfc. Craig were from Company F, Reed and Flake from Company M. In addition to those killed, two men were wounded and two were missing, Pfc. Charles Alison and Pvt. Anthony Calcao. They were apparently left behind as Company M made its retreat back to Suchan Mine #1 at 1:00 A.M. in a pouring rain, soaked and depressed over their tragic introduction to Siberian combat.[26]

It was ironic that the prisoners they had tried to rescue were held in Novitskaya only a few hours, then were moved some twenty miles to Frolovka, according to one of the prisoners. It is doubtful if they were even in town when the attack occurred. It was at Frolovka that the two groups of prisoners met.[27] Five Americans were in enemy hands; however, the two missing men from Company M, Alison and Calcao, straggled in the morning of June 23.

On June 23, Colonel Williams was handed a letter from the chairman of the temporary revolutionary headquarters of the Olga district, blaming the Mine Guard for interfering in internal affairs by arresting comrades Setti, Ivan Samuschenko, Iakovleff, and others. In retaliation, they had captured and were holding the five Americans. The message said that an exchange could be made if the Russians were released. They also asked that Vasily Shedko, who lived in the mines, be turned over to them for prosecution of a civil offense.[28] Williams fired back a response saying that he was about to give Samuschenko back to him anyway, that he knew nothing of Iakovleff, and that he had explained somewhere else about Setti. He also said he could not turn Shedko over to the partisans.

Just to make sure that Colonel Williams knew the situation, Lieutenant Fribley sent a message through the lines, stating that he and Corporal Reed were indeed prisoners of the partisans. He also said the other three men, Daly, Bullard, and Moore, were being held with them. He repeated the demands of the partisan committee that Samuschenko, Iakovleff, and Setti be released. It was assumed those were the same men requested in the partisan's formal demand. He closed with a terse, "Request that you make every possible effort for our release." Then, he asked for some cigarettes.[29] Williams reply was brief. "You may be assured that everything within my power will be done to secure the release of all captured. Am sending cigarettes."[30]

While these negotiations were being pursued, the Suchan area had exploded into a minor war. Two cable houses on the cable section of the railroad had been dynamited and put out of action, and bridges between Kangaus and Fanza were burned on June 23. A train carrying U.S. and Japanese soldiers was fired on near Sitsa, wounding one American. Lt. F. C. Shepard, based at Tahe, heard firing in the direction of Fanza and took four squads to investigate. He got as far as Kishmich, where he found that two Chinese soldiers stationed there had been killed, while five other Chinese had beaten off a Red Guard attack.[31]

In addition, partisans fired into the camp at Suchan; no one was hit, but all telephone lines into the mine area were cut.[32] Companies C and D were still struggling to reach the mines, but it was a rugged march, even though Colonel Williams had cautioned them about the route. In some spots, with the cable cars out of commission, they literally used the cog tracks of the cable cars as ladders to reach the tops of the grades.[33] Not only were these troops headed for Suchan, but Maj. Sidney Graves, the general's son, and Lieutenant Colonel Eichelberger had been ordered to Suchan as well. Eichelberger brought a message from Graves suggesting that any punitive expedition wait until the captives were released to avoid any possible harsh treatment toward them.[34]

With the obvious change in the partisan attitude toward the Americans and their obvious attempt to drive out the railroad guards, General Graves ordered that his outlying detachments should be reinforced so that none would number fewer than one hundred. A reinforcing platoon of twenty-one men under Lt. Lawrence Butler was sent off to Romanovka. While Colonel Eichelberger and Major Graves were traveling from Vladivostok to Suchan, they passed through Romanovka on June 24 and became concerned about the camp.

The American garrison was camped on the bank of a stream in this village and the Russians were walking through the camp.[35] The whole garrison looked in poor condition for defense and I made a note to communicate as soon as I reached Suchan with Major Graves and recommend that this garrison be told to prepare trenches around their camp which was made of tents with one or two log houses.[36]

The two senior officers continued on their way to Suchan virtually as Lieutenant Butler was arriving in Romanovka. Earlier in the day a platoon of Company C had been stationed there along with Company A, but for unknown reasons, they moved out as Butler moved in. The Romanovka camp had as a permanent detail fifty-one men from the third platoon of Company A, with Lt. Krieger in charge. Their duty was to guard a nearby bridge and the section of rail assigned to them. By nightfall on June 24, with Butler's arrival, the Yanks in Romanovka numbered seventy-two men.

Relations had seemed cordial between the townspeople and the doughboys, who exchanged money and goods when possible, and passed out small presents from time to time. The camp was located between the village and the tracks, with three log houses next to the camp. The village was adjacent to the railroad tracks, but was overshadowed by a large bluff covered with shrubs on the other side of the tracks. Lieutenant Krieger had established several outguards to be manned, including one on top of the bluff, where they had dug a small trench. Other guards were set on either side of the camp along the railroad.

The area had been quiet for some time, so the guards had become very relaxed about their duties. It was normal for guards to come in about daylight, but daylight there arrived early. Dawn came about 4:00 A.M. on the morning of June 25, ushering in one of the bloodiest days of the two Russian interventions.

By 4:30 A.M., all of the outguards were back in their tents, most of them asleep. One of the guards was Pvt. Abel Anderson, posted about two hundred yards north of camp on the railroad. The previous night there had been two men on that post, but on that night, Anderson was alone. "I walked from midnight to 4:00 A.M., no one inspected my post between midnight and daylight. I just came in at 4 A.M. when my time was up and I went to bed. I was asleep when the firing started."[37] At the same time, the guard on the bluff scrambled down the hillside, headed for his bunk. By 4:30 A.M. the platoon was virtually unguarded; apparently, the only ones up were the cook, Claude Hollis, and two interior guards, Pvt. Pete Uteralt and Pvt. William Roberts, walking their posts inside the camp.

As the Americans went about their routines, the partisans, Bolshevik leaders, and Red Guards had been studying the increasing laxness of the American camp. With knowledge of the unit's procedures, a decision was made to strike the Americans at Romanovka. As a part of the plan, the Reds burned one of the bridges on the northwest side of Romanovka, hoping to prevent any reinforcements from that direction. During the night of June 24, one of the fiery Bolsheviks, Sergei Lazo, and his men, estimated to be about two hundred, crept up the back side of the bluff. As dawn came and the sentry left his post, they slipped over the top of the rise and filtered silently into the tall brush.

At about 4:45 A.M., they opened fire from the brush only a short distance away directly into the tents. Many of the men were killed as they slept. One man was reportedly hit seventeen times.[38] The first volleys were deadly for the sleeping Americans, toppling cots, smashing furniture, and shredding the tents. As the doughboys stumbled from their tents, half naked, many wounded, but all in shock, the partisans called, "Throw up your hands and we won't fire!" Those who did so were promptly shot.[39]

But after the first volleys, the stunned Americans began firing back. Lieutenant Butler, whose jaw and mouth had been shattered in the first minutes, swept the brush with an automatic weapon, and the others who could, joined in his fire. His wounds were horrifying, but he kept his men inspired with his leadership. He wrote orders, pointing or muttering through his shattered face, directing fire, withdrawing the men to the log houses, and sending for help. For four hours, Butler directed his men despite severe bleeding and immense pain. He, among others, was awarded the DSC for his heroism on that day. The survivors directed a withering fire into the hillside brush. Two automatic riflemen, Emmet Lunsford and Roy Jones, inserted fresh twenty-round magazines and broke up a Red charge that was just beginning; George Strakey was exposed outside the log house, but with his single shot '03 rifle kept many of the attackers pinned down.[40] There were others, too, who never made the record books, but kept the remaining men of Company A alive.

Wounded or not, the doughboys rallied, moving first to a makeshift cover, then to the three log houses. Some of them died getting there, but once in the houses, they had reasonable protection; with their automatic weapons, they held the Reds at bay. Running low on ammunition, Lieutenant Krieger, Pfc. Oscar Tucker, Pvt. Densie Carr, and Pvt. Gustav Schlicter sprinted to the tents to get more.[41] When they got back to the log house in which Butler had established headquarters, they found a bloody shambles. Many of the wounded, who had been dragged from the tents to the houses, had died there. Many others were waiting for medical attention, which was provided by two Russian girls. One was the girlfriend of Sgt. Almus Beck of Company C, who had remained in the village when Beck departed with his company.[42] As the wounded lay quietly in the log huts, Beck's girl bound up their wounds, washed them and even, at her own peril, went outside to get water for the injured Americans.[43] Another tale of heroism was that of a crippled young girl nicknamed Peggy who lived in one of the three log houses where many of the wounded and dying were taken.[44] Fifty years later Pvt. Alan Ferguson remembered the aid she provided the wounded.

While the firing was at its peak, two volunteers, Cpl. Leo Heinzman and Cpl. Valeryan Brodnicki, were sent to find a way to get to Novo Nezhino, some seven miles away, to find help. They each chose different routes, but Heinzman was the luckiest; unwounded, he heard the train coming from Novo Nezhino, which had stopped after being fired on. It was actually backing up to gain cover from a nearby hill when the American sergeant-in-charge, Sylvester Moore, spotted Heinzman signaling frantically. Here the stories conflict. Moore's report said he had seventeen men on board and that Heinzman told him that would do no good against the estimated two hundred Reds attacking them. With that information, Moore took his train back to Novo Nezhino and passed the word of the disaster to nearby stations.[45] However, Corporal Heinzman remembered the train episode differently:

> I reached the passenger train first and told the train guard that Company "A" was getting massacred. Instead of detraining the train guard the sgt in charge of his own accord went back to Novo Nezhino where the train remained for at least two hours before it started back to Romanovka. The train first reached Romanovka during the heaviest firing. It did no good whatever when it reached Romanovka the second time. The fighting was all over then. I was the first man to board the train and it was then about 3 miles from Romanovka *backing* toward Novo Nezhino. No one that I know of sent it back to Novo Nezhino for reinforcements.[46]

Brodnicki arrived somewhat later and was tended by the medics, reinforcing Heinzman's version. Sergeant Moore returned to Romanovka, bringing half of the Novo Nezhino Company E detachment under Lt. Lewis Lorimer. Lorimer took these men, with the few unwounded Company A survivors, and swept the area, finding only a few dead Bolsheviks. Other reinforcements began to arrive long after the fighting had stopped. Company K arrived about 9:00 P.M., slowed by the burned out bridge northwest of Romanovka, and had its first look at the devastation. Private Rohrer from K Company wrote:

It will always be imminent in the minds of us who witnessed the surroundings. It was unbelievable that anyone could have been fortunate enough to have survived the tents were literally riddled, there wasn't an object in the camp that didn't have several bullet holes through it the field cots were still damp with blood from the men killed as they slept.[47]

Lieutenant Butler was badly wounded and would be hospitalized for years; Pvt. William Roberts was among the dead, killed as he quietly walked his sentry post.

The dead and wounded were tended to, but the casualty count was numbing. Nineteen had been killed outright and twenty-six wounded,[48] five of whom later died of their wounds. The camp cleanup began; Company E returned to Novo Nezhino, and the wounded and dead were sent to Vladivostok on a hospital train. Hospital Train #1 had been at Kangaus; as soon as he received word of the disaster, Capt. Oscar Frundt of the Medical Corps ordered the train to the site. Under sporadic sniper fire, the dead and wounded were loaded onto the train. Since the bridge between Shkotova and Romanovka had been burned, it was necessary to unload the Kangaus train and ferry the doughboys across the river to the waiting Vladivostok train. So, the wounded had one more painful ordeal, being ferried on litters across the river, jarred and jolted in a difficult crossing. The dead were put on one open boxcar and the wounded on two other cars. They even managed to transfer the mattresses and blankets to the Vladivostok train.

More help boarded at Shkotova; while on the trains, the wounded were cared for by three Russian nurses and two American doctors with all the equipment and comfort that could be provided.[49] As they arrived in Vladivostok, the personnel at Evacuation Hospital #17 took responsibility. Pvt. Sam Richardson, who was on duty, wrote, "The entire personnel of the Hospital worked through out the night, operating, administering medicine and embalming the bodies. I worked during the night preparing the casualty list to be sent by wireless to the United States."[50]

As the remaining men of Company A viewed the few partisan dead, they realized with anger that some of these were the very villagers with whom they had traded, shared meals, and become friends.[51] It gave them a new perspective on the war that now raged and raised questions regarding who might become the enemy.

In Romanovka, Major Cutrer and Company K's commander, Capt. William Crom, had no desire to see a repeat of the deadly attack, so late that afternoon, Cutrer had a train waiting at Romanovka to take two platoons to Novo Nezhino in case of a partisan attack. They planned to arrive just at daybreak to flank the Reds if they attacked there. In the meantime, Sgt. James Gardner, in charge of the remnant of Company E still at Novo Nezhino, had the same concern; his men slept outside beneath a hastily built barricade of railroad ties, awaiting dawn on June 26.

The partisans had achieved such success the previous day that they used the same tactic, this time creeping along the railroad tracks, still protected by heavy brush. They began by firing into the tents, but Gardner fired a volley from behind his ties, and the Reds took cover. Gardner's men kept firing away at the Reds, not sure of their effect, but kept the enemy from charging. Eventually, Gardner heard firing from the railroad tracks on the west side of town, heralding the arrival of Lieutenant Lorimer and parts of Company K.[52] Cutrer had hoped they would arrive earlier to cut off the Reds, but train personnel, lacking urgency, were two hours late.[53] Still, little damage was done to the Americans: only one Company E man was wounded. Lorimer led the men toward the village, chasing the remaining Bolsheviks; there was sporadic firing on both sides, but by evening, all was quiet.

Later, in August, when the Thirty-first Infantry band was sent to the area to play, Bandsman Pvt. William Johnson noted that the Romanovka tragedy was still very much in evidence. There were trenches and dugouts, but most noticeable were the bullet holes still very visible in the tent sides. The next day, they played at Novo Nezhino and remarked that those tents were punctured by bullet holes as well.[54]

As Lieutenant Colonel Eichelberger passed through Romanovka on June 24, he spotted Karl Phillips boarding the train there. Phillips was one of three Russian spies identified by Major Cutrer as constantly feeding alarming information to Lieutenant Otto at Kangaus, keeping his unit on constant alert, which exhausted them. Eichelberger believed that Phillips was responsible for the attack on Romanovka.[55] Phillips was arrested, but not disarmed, and subsequently taken to headquarters in Shkotova, where he hoped to see Major Cutrer. When he was refused, he grew angry and demanded to see the major. He drew his pistol, putting it to his head and claiming he was ready to die. His guard, Sgt. Arthur Chedister, reached for his own pistol and put in a clip, then ordered Phillips to drop his gun. Instead, Phillips fired; a shootout followed with one other guard, Corporal Hunsaker, shot in the leg. Phillips died on the headquarters floor, shot six times.[56]

On the day of the Romanovka attack, a train near Sitsa was fired on, and one Company H private was wounded. A few miles away from Novo Nezhino, other units were attacked the next day. After their grueling mountain crossing, Companies C and D and other elements on their way from Kangaus to Suchan got as far as Sitsa, where they were able to board the narrow gauge headed for Suchan. They cautiously sent out an advance unit, squads from C and D Companies. The advance guard was fired on from the hills; one man was slightly wounded. Soon the main body moved up, but the advance party took more fire, and a member of Company D was severely wounded. The report estimated Red casualties were thirty killed, "actual dead Bolsheviks actually counted—nineteen."[57]

On June 30, Company K, with parts of Company E, left Novo Nezhino to move against a partisan stronghold south and east of the town, in the village of Petrovka. They came in from the north, while a landing party of 140 sailors and Marines under Lt. Comdr. F. D. Manock, plus a company of White Russians, landed at 7:50 A.M. on July 1 at Andrieva Bay, preparing to attack Petrovka from the south.[58] By 10:35 P.M. the naval landing parties had returned to the ship and were back aboard. The two forces found only light resistance from the Reds in Petrovka so the doughboys returned to Novo Nezhino at 3:00 P.M. on July 2, suffering no casualties.

The next action would be down the Suchan Valley to meet ships at Amerika Bay, ships bringing badly needed supplies from Vladivostok to the beleaguered Suchan garrison.

The Suchan Valley

[Y]ou are now authorized to move against gangs which are now formed or that may be in the process of formation in your vicinity.

—AEFS Headquarters

BY July 1, Colonel Eichelberger and Major Graves were in Suchan with Companies C, D, H, and M, one platoon of Machine Gun Company, and a one-pounder gun section. They were essentially cut off from the Shkotova units, both in communications and in supplies, because the hill country between Kangaus and Fanza was in Red hands. The Suchan Valley, including the mines, became a separate campaign with Colonel Williams in charge, having virtually no communication with his superiors in Vladivostok. On June 26, an official communiqué from General Graves came through Colonel Robinson to all AEF commanders:

> [Y]ou are now authorized to move against gangs which are now formed or that may be in the process of formation in your vicinity. Use your own judgment as to the distance from the railroad that you go. In view of acts of these people it is considered that only by destruction of these gangs can railroad be operated successfully. Acknowledge.[1]

The funerals of Lieutenant Ward and the three men killed at Novitskaya were held in Suchan on June 24 and attended by men of the Mine Guard, as well as a platoon of Japanese troops. It was a brief service that brought somber thoughts to those attending. On June 27, Eichelberger wrote his wife a poignant comment on Ward's death. "On a little hill near here are four fresh graves—Lt Ward and 3 soldiers killed at Novitskaya last Sunday. He was just graduated from West Point last fall and now lies way off on the other side of the world with faded flowers on his grave."[2]

On June 27, Eichelberger set out to accomplish the exchange of the men captured earlier while fishing. He took to the meeting an interpreter and the partisan leader Samuschenko, who was to be exchanged; he was followed by two platoons of Company D, which quietly stayed about a mile back. His proceedings with the partisan leader Ilyakov took much longer than he expected; the men of Company D began to push toward the village, concerned about the colonel and the prisoners. Eventually the exchange was made, and the five much-relieved prisoners were escorted back to the mines, along with Fribley's mule.[3] Colonel Eichelberger was the official head of G-2 (Military Intelligence) in Vladivostok, but in Suchan, he became at one time simply a rifleman and at another time a squad, then a platoon, leader. In each of those roles, he was a great addition to the units involved.

It was fortunate that all Americans captured by the Reds during the expedition, the fishing party and Burt and Bachelor from the Twenty-seventh Infantry, were released unharmed. Eichelberger wrote of his first negotiations with the partisans, "In my talks with Colonel Williams, I realized I did not see any means of getting Fribley and his men back alive."[4] The Czechs, Japanese, Bolsheviks, and partisans never took prisoners, preferring to kill them rather than bother with them; yet, all captured Americans were, if not well treated, at least not harmed. One of the released prisoners, Harold Bullard, wrote in his memoirs, "This bunch of Russians were commanded by one big Russian and an American Sgt. who had deserted. He was still wearing his U.S. uniform and had a Springfield rifle and Colt automatic pistol."[5] Although Karachun was reported to be over on the Trans-Siberian Railroad, Bullard's description seemed disturbingly familiar.

With the release of the prisoners and the aggressive new orders, it took little time for Williams to begin pursuit of the partisan Reds who plagued his mission. The mines themselves were shut down, both by strike and by threats against the workers, so he turned toward the villages that were home to the partisans. He also was worried about supplies; since he needed to receive some support from Vladivostok, and the railroad was unusable, he determined that supplies would have to come by sea.

Williams planned his first attack on Novitskaya as a prelude to hitting Kazanka, a partisan headquarters. He began his assault at 1:30 A.M. on July 2, sending Major Graves with Company C, less one platoon, plus two machine guns. This column attacked Novitskaya from the north at 2:00 A.M., while Colonel Williams led Company M, two machine guns, and a Japanese infantry company into town from the south. The combined force met some heavy sniper fire, which wounded two men, but Novitskaya was in their hands by 5:00 A.M. At 11:00 A.M., Company C with its two machine guns went back to Suchan, while the others camped north of the town; snipers interrupted their rest, but did no damage.

The next day they launched an attack on Kazanka, again using two columns. The first column under Major Joiner was made up of Company C, less one platoon, Company D, two machine guns, and two one-pounders. They left Suchan at 3:30 A.M., found the Reds one mile from town and had a short but fierce fire fight, in which Pvt. Peter Bernal was killed and two wounded. The town was taken by 9:45 A.M. Meanwhile, Colonel Williams took a column of Company M, plus heavy weapons and the Japanese infantry company, by a different route, but ran into trouble. The heavy weapons proved difficult to move over the hills, and twice the column became lost. He finally arrived at 11:00 A.M. with his men exhausted, after Joiner had successfully taken the town.[6] At Kazanka, it wasn't the Reds that committed crimes, it was the Americans. A lieutenant in Company C emptied his automatic pistol into a doorway filled with women. One of his platoon, Cpl. Oscar Woutilla, put a gun to the officer's stomach to make him stop shooting. Eichelberger witnessed the shooting and wrote, "How many were hit I do not know nor care to know."[7] Next, the lieutenant ordered a squad to shoot a blind man being led by his daughter. For some reason, the lieutenant felt the blind man and those with him were a threat. Someone in the squad fired on the man, wounding him badly, then the officer finished him off with a borrowed bayonet. It was then discovered the man's daughter had been given a pass by Major Graves, but was too terrified to show it to anyone.[8]

With the victory complete, they all marched back to Suchan, taking their dead and wounded. Williams felt satisfied. "It is believed that by defeating the enemy at Kazanka he lost practically all of his prestige in Suchan Valley, and that it will take several months, if unmolested, for him to again gain the support of farmers of this locality."[9]

On July 4, the Suchan units attended the funeral of Private Bernal, killed at Kazanka. He was the fifth American buried at the mines.[10] Ber-

nal, Lieutenant Ward, and the others would rest in the Suchan grave-
yard until August, since that area was cut off from rail transport to
Vladivostok. Those killed in areas west of Kangaus were sent immediately to Vladivostok, properly treated, and transported to the United
States. A naval relief force finally made it possible to send to Vladivostok the bodies of those killed in the beleaguered Suchan area. On August 17, 1919, a work party opened the graves, placed the bodies in
hermetically sealed caskets, and "as the coffins were loaded on *droskies* . . . rode down to the ocean sitting on the coffins." The remains
were taken to Vladivostok by ship for transport home.[11]

Colonel Williams's next challenge was to open a supply route. Between Suchan and Amerika Bay, the nearest open water allowing passage to Vladivostok, there were still nests of Reds who opposed the
Americans. Word of the need for supplies was received by AEF headquarters; Company G in Vladivostok was ordered to join White Russian
troops and board the USS *Albany* to take supplies to Amerika Bay. The
plan called for Williams to clear the hostile partisans between the bay
and Suchan to establish a line of supply. It was an awkward route, but
the only alternative, since the cable cars and bridges were out between
Kangaus and Fanza.

On July 5 at 4:00 A.M., a sizeable column left Suchan headed for
the bay. Included were Companies D and M, machine gun sections,
one-pounders from Headquarters Company, and one Japanese infantry
company. Williams led the column himself, but was accompanied by
Lieutenant Colonel Eichelberger and Major Graves, both of whom
hoped to board a ship and get back to their duties in Vladivostok. As
they left Suchan, they had no assurance any ships would be meeting
them, but they assumed the Navy would come to their rescue.[12]

The march to their destination, the town of Vladimir-Alexan-
drofsk, six miles inland on the Suchan River, was hazardous. As they
neared the town of Piryatino on the Suchan River, they were met by
heavy fire from the hills, which wounded six men from Company D.
Williams sent the Japanese infantry to root the gunmen out with two
machine guns, which they did very efficiently, and the column was
then protected by the high ground. They had one more encounter as
they neared their destination: a group of partisans opened fire near Un-
ashi, but was quickly subdued. When they reached Vladimir-Alexan-
drofsk, the Reds were entrenched on the hills overlooking the town, but
a healthy barrage of Allied machine gun and artillery fire chased them
off the hills, which were then occupied by Company M. They then set
up their camp in the village.

July 6 was a day filled with activity. The Suchan soldiers sent a
patrol down to the bay; they reappeared with the happy news that the

fleet was, indeed, there. The *Albany* had arrived and anchored at 6:44
A.M., accompanied by a fleet of Chinese junks loaded with supplies and
Russian naval ships, as well. The Russian ships landed three hundred
White Russian troops, while the *Albany* unloaded Company G and
whaleboats to move officers who were needed to direct the supply-
laden junks to the Vladimir camp.[13]

The men who did not journey to the bay remained in the Vladimir
Camp or on outposts in the hills. From those hills, some of the men
claimed they could see the *Albany* in the bay. Eichelberger thought it
was a different ship, not the American cruiser, but he and Major
Graves, anxious to get back to headquarters, scavenged a launch and
had some minor repairs made to fix it for the trip downriver. Eichelberger and Graves, with Lieutenants Winningstad and Greenway, made
the trip in the patched-up launch. Eichelberger wrote his wife, "The
soldiers worked on the Bolshevik steam launch and we got away at 5:00
A.M. A heavy Browning machine gun with several sand bags forward
and aft. I expected to get shot at all the way down but we never heard
a shot though we passed a town on the right for a mile."[14] The launch
reached the *Albany,* and its passengers were taken on board at 7:45 A.M.,
their Suchan adventure over. The *Albany* also took on four of the
wounded from the valley campaign, one of whom, Pvt. Alphia Schur-
ter, wounded at Piryatino, died in Vladivostok on July 8. Its duty finished, the ship left for Vladivostok at 9:30 P.M. on July 7.[15]

The following days in Vladimir were spent organizing and stock-
piling the welcome supplies. On July 9, with Colonel Williams still
leading, the column left with all the supplies it could convoy, arriving
back in Suchan with only minor disturbances. One platoon of Company D remained behind with Company G to guard the rest of the supplies. On July 10, Major Joiner took Company H and a Japanese
company with an empty wagon train back to Vladimir to bring the remaining supplies; they were back in Suchan by 3:30 P.M. on July 11.
The following day Company G returned to Vladivostok from Vladimir,
although it is not clear how they made the trip.

In his report, Colonel Williams ended by saying, "From all reports
and indications it is believed that Suchan Valley is practically free of
Bolsheviki, and that it can be kept so with the present force at Souchan
without assistance from outsiders."[16] Eichelberger wired Graves from
the *Albany*, bringing him up to date on the Suchan Valley: "No reinforcements of any nationality believed necessary. Present force actively
handled should be able to roam at will through country."[17]

During the next month there were regular patrols, with occasional
sightings of Reds, but little real threat to the mines. The cable cars were
still not operating, and so many bridges had been blown or burned that

time estimates of repairs ran into months. As the need for troops slackened, Company D was released from Major Joiner's command and sent back over the rugged hills to join the Shkotova contingent at Kangaus.

General Graves had no intention of keeping his units in Suchan. He had no plan to garrison the isolated Vladimir on Amerika Bay, which was virtually the only way to supply Suchan. As early as July 5, he telegraphed Colonel Williams to keep a minimum supply of all things needed to maintain the base. "No surplus should be taken in because it will be necessary to move it again."[18] As Eichelberger and Graves described the Suchan situation upon their arrival in Vladivostok, it became obvious to the general that Suchan had lost any value it once had. There was no coal being produced; the rugged country might be safe for the moment, but new partisans could return at any time to break the fragile line of supply.

On August 13, Colonel Williams received a telegram from General Graves requesting a plan of evacuation. Williams knew this would have to be accomplished by wagon to Amerika Bay and by ship back to Vladivostok. The major problem was rounding up enough wagons; however, by August 16, he had acquired three hundred. Word was received that a ship would be in Amerika Bay on August 19 to take off all Allied troops and equipment. In a soaking rain, the chilled and weary men of the Suchan Mine Guard found themselves on the beaches of Amerika Bay. They were loaded onto the *Merritt*, their transport out of the mine country. A lieutenant wrote in the regimental newspaper:

> [B]y the light of a wonderful moon, and to the accompaniment of the melodious Filipino string orchestra, [we] steamed out of Amerika Bay, steamed away from the country where we had hiked so many weary versts, and where we had fought so many nasty engagements, steamed back to the city called Queen of the East on the Golden Horn Bay.[19]

In the hold were the bodies of Lieutenant Ward and the others who had died during the brief mine occupation.

The Suchan expedition ended, but those in Shkotova were still tending to their guard duties as they had been since Major Joiner's force left to join Williams in Suchan. They patrolled and reconnoitered from their duty stations along the still functioning portions of the railroad leading into the cable station at Kangaus. Several times they went back to Petrovka; one man was wounded in one expedition, but they never encountered any significant force.

Their one major venture was up the New Russian Valley, through the town of Bronchi, where a force of Russians, Company K, and a machine gun platoon were to meet a command from Novo Nezhino. Together they were to find the Reds at Bronchi and at Gordievka; however, before they joined forces at Bronchi, they had "a stiff engagement"—so stiff that one intelligence officer was wounded, Pvt. Albert Rooney was killed, and three other men were wounded. They finally met the Novo Nezhino column on July 9, but shortly afterward returned to their base.[20]

Throughout the summer, reports showed the concern of commanders for the loss of their veteran troops; many of their replacements were untrained and certainly inexperienced in the skills needed in Siberia. Major Cutrer was replaced by Maj. Thomas Arms, who ended his August report, "During this month the command lost some of its best men, due to transfer to the United States for discharge and many recruits were received in their place." In September he wrote:

> The fighting capacity of the command has been seriously impaired, due to the transfer to the United States of the best men and the securing of recruits in replacement, mostly under 21 years of age and not of sufficiently mature age or growth to properly withstand the hardships of campaigning.[21]

But the men still patrolled and occasionally skirmished; the last recorded wound received was by Private Cathermon on September 11.[22] The major reported no operations in October and November, and few in December as winter descended.

The Kolchak government was in flight by December, and the White Russians everywhere were in total disarray. At Shkotova on December 27, 1919, the Russian garrison mutinied, killing two of its officers; between four and five hundred men deserted to the Reds. Companies D and E remained there with two hundred loyal Russians.[23]

Elsewhere in Siberia—1919

Semenof has given until 11:00 A.M. this date when he will take rifles by force.

—Ryan wire to Morrow, October 25, 1919

AFTER the Suchan mine area was abandoned in August 1919, the Thirty-first Infantry remained primarily in the Vladivostok area, except for Company B, which was still in Harbin, China, and other contingents along the Trans-Siberian and Suchan Railroads. The Twenty-seventh Infantry was scattered all the way from the Lake Baikal area to Vladivostok, still sparring with partisans, Cossacks, and Japanese. By then the Thirty-first Infantry had its nickname: like the 339th in North Russia, they became the Polar Bears. The Japanese called the Twenty-seventh Infantry the Wolfhounds after the Russian wolfhound, whose characteristics were speed and tenacity; the Japanese thought both characteristics were evidenced by the Twenty-seventh's marches in the early Ussuri campaign.

The Thirty-first Infantry returned from Suchan, proud of its combat record and ready to assume its duties in Vladivostok, but still uncertain of its mission. Nearly a year after the Armistice had been signed and with the AEFNR on its way home, it appeared that the Siberian

239

expedition was readying for yet another winter in Russia. Congressmen questioned by their constituents had few answers. Pressure was building on the president to make some firm statements about the purpose of the expedition and the time frame for departure. Some of the drafted men were trickling home, and, as the local commanders acknowledged, their replacements were not always prepared for Siberian conditions. One of those who went home was Col. Frederick Sargent. He had commanded the Thirty-first Infantry from its early days at Fort McKinley in the Philippines, until he was replaced by Col. Fred Bugbee on October 8, 1919.[1]

Colonel Bugbee arrived September 7 and took a few weeks to acquaint himself with the Siberian situation. The Thirty-first Infantry regimental headquarters was the base and line of communications center in Vladivostok, and Bugbee was not totally happy with his assignment. On September 23, he wrote his wife, "I am slated to take command of the 31st. . . . I don't fancy it very much." His immediate concern was finding quarters for the units that had been withdrawn from the mines with another Siberian winter approaching. "I will be caught holding the bag, as I will be in command of the regiment when the shoe pinches."[2]

Other changes in the expeditionary forces command personnel were taking place. Colonel Robinson, Graves's chief of staff, had caused so much friction among other officers that he was sent home in September and replaced by Col. Joseph D. Leitch.[3] The Twenty-seventh Infantry had been commanded by Lieutenant Colonel Morrow in the early days while Colonel Styer was AEFS commander; Styer became regimental commander from September 8, 1918, until April 8, 1919, when Morrow, then a full colonel, took command.[4]

Through it all, General Graves remained in command of the AEFS and was continually pressured and harassed by virtually everyone. With the United States ostensibly allied with Japan, it was understandable that the average Russian felt no liking toward any of those representing the Kolchak government, be they Cossacks or Allies.

One major break in United States–Japanese harmony came in February 1919. The Japanese had been fighting Bolsheviks on the Amur near Blagovestchentsk, where they took large losses. Graves cabled Washington, recounting Japanese losses: between February 11 and 16, eighty-one men were killed. He then reported, "On the same day two peace-strength companies of Infantry, total of about two hundred and fifty men, one company of Artillery and one section of Infantry met the same Bolshevik force at different times and only three escaped." When General Oi asked Styer for a company of the Twenty-seventh Infantry, Styer cabled Graves requesting instructions. Graves sent Robinson to meet with the Japanese chief of staff in Vladivostok, who requested that Styer do nothing until further notice. No instructions came, and the Japanese were left to their fate.[5] Actually, the U.S. troops were hundreds of miles from the fighting and could have done nothing to help, but the Japanese press had a field day, depicting the United States as failing to aid an ally and allowing the slaughter of Oi's troops.

Friction between Graves and the State Department continued, with Graves particularly disturbed when he found that the president was relying on information from State Department representatives in Russia, rather than the War Department.[6] When Graves questioned Army chief of staff General March, asking if his reports were faulty or inadequate, March reassured him that he was sending exactly the kind of information the War Department needed.[7] Graves repeatedly telegraphed the War Department about the deterioration of relations with other Allies and with the Russians themselves. As early as March 1919, he requested new instructions from Washington, saying:

> Japan and the United States are in Siberia with the same announced purpose and are following opposite courses relative to taking part in internal troubles. This has made it seem advisable to me to ask if my policy, in considering the Bolshevik trouble in Siberia, entirely an internal trouble, in which I should take no part, is the policy the Department desires me to follow.[8]

The message was forwarded to the president, who did not reply. Therefore, General March told Graves to follow the only policy set forth, that of the *Aide Memoire*, until further direction came from Wilson. March ended by saying, "Keep a stiff upper lip, I am going to stand by you until _____ freezes over."[9]

On June 27, Major Johnson reported that there was information about bomb making and bomb threats against Horvat and spectators along a parade route during a celebration of the Czech takeover the previous year. It was reported that the bomb parts were coming from Tethue, north of Vladivostok on the coast, and some were being stored at Olga. Graves requested the navy to move troops to those areas to stop the partisan activity. On July 31, the USS *New Orleans* picked up 175 men from Company B, Thirty-first Infantry, under Capt. H. W. Lee and sailed to the coastal towns, three hundred miles up the coast. The infantrymen, joined by Russians, landed one hundred yards offshore and waded into the town of Tethue.[10] The soaking wet doughboys were somewhat disgruntled when the ship managed to off-load fifty Marines on the dock; but since it was pouring rain, everyone was soaked before long. Ashore, they spent the night outdoors in the rain, then moved inland, with the Marines leading the way, following narrow-gauge tracks that supposedly led to a mine. At noon they stopped for lunch while the Russians went on ahead. Snipers began firing and five Russians were killed.

The Marines went back to the ship, but the Russians and dough-boys went on toward the mines. That night as they camped, a Bolshevik turned himself in. Pvt. E. V. Hockett wrote, "He claimed to be a Lt. Col. in the Bolshevik army. We turned him over to the Russians and they made him dig 6 graves the 6th grave was for him."[11] Another member of Company B on that expedition, Clifford Catlin, wrote, "We did capture a Bolshevik major, who had been in the American army. Our first sergeant knew him—they had gone to the Philippine Islands together."[12]

The next day they reboarded the ship and sailed back to Vladivostok. Eichelberger wrote that he was highly disappointed not to be on that raid. "I have had a lovely grouch on since I learned that I couldn't go on this expedition up country on the New Orleans. It is the most ridiculous proposition I have ever heard of to send an expedition out under a boy of two years service. The navy men are sore about it."[13] Not much was written of the Olga expedition, except that one hundred men of Company K joined a Russian force to land in Olga. Graves reported no resistance and the landings were completed as scheduled.[14]

In July Graves was ordered to join Ambassador Rowland Morris for a fact-finding trip to Omsk to assess the situation there. The U.S. government had no diplomatic relations with Soviet Russia, and Morris, ambassador to Japan, was the senior diplomat in the Far East. The Allies in Omsk felt that the general's exposure to just the Far East prejudiced his thinking about the government in the interior. Morris and Graves had worked reasonably well together before the trip to Omsk; on that trip, their relationship deteriorated. Graves was reluctant to go, as noted by Eichelberger in a letter to his wife July 10, 1919: "The Ambassador came today enroute to Omsk. Gen. Graves has been ordered to accompany him much against his will. They probably will not find any government when they get there."[15] The diplomats still pushed for recognition of the Kolchak government and a commitment that American units would enter the fight against the Reds. Morris and Graves spent two months in western Siberia, witnessing numerous defeats of White forces, the firing of Gaida, and the mass movement of west Russian refugees. By the time Graves returned in September, Wilson had made it clear that the United States would not recognize Kolchak, and Britain was withdrawing support as well.[16]

The trip gave General Graves assurance that his estimates had been right. In a visit to the front west of Omsk, he found few Kolchak troops and scant enthusiasm for the fight. On his return trip, he heard from U.S. RRSC men more reports of Semenov's killing sprees. Yet, despite all of the evidence, Ambassador Morris was convinced that recognition of Kolchak was the only solution. From then on, Graves and the ambassador found little common ground.[17] Graves would be proved right, as the Kolchak government, under pressure from advancing Bolshevik forces, was forced to flee Omsk in mid-November.[18] Western Siberia became a scene of total confusion and turmoil with the government, the Czechs, and refugees all seeking a way east. The already troubled Trans-Siberian Railroad became chaotic.

Numerous incidents kept the Americans off balance in all areas in the fall of 1919. In Spasskoye, the Kolchak government appointed a new chief of garrison, Colonel Staripalov, who was openly anti-American. He found numerous ways to show his disdain for the Americans based in the area. An episode on September 2 added to American humiliation. Capt. Lindsay Johns of the Twenty-seventh Infantry was ordered to search for the deserter Karachun, now a wanted man for his role in various Red raids. The captain took with him Cpl. Benjamin Sperling of Company F, Thirty-first Infantry, who reportedly knew Karachun before he deserted. Their target was reported to be near Iman, well north of Spasskoye. Iman was the headquarters for a Kalmykof detachment, plus a Japanese and Chinese contingent.

As the two Americans explained their mission to the Cossacks, they were asked to produce passports. Captain Johns produced his military papers, but that was not sufficient, according to the Cossacks, and the Americans were confined to the railroad station in Iman as prisoners. Two days later, Captain Johns escaped and hopped a train back to the American zone headquarters in Spasskoye, where he told of Corporal Sperling's predicament.

Major Shamotulski was in command of the Twenty-seventh Infantry units at Spasskoye; he started a train from the southernmost end of his sector, picking up every trooper he could find in full combat gear. As the train jolted to a stop in Iman, the doughboys jumped off; yelling and brandishing their automatic weapons, they scattered over the entire town. The Japanese told Shamotulski they would fight on the side of the Cossacks if the Americans wanted a fight; it appeared as if another incident was imminent. Shamotulski said he intended to rescue Sperling, and if that included a fight, he was ready.[19] The Japanese then explained that Sperling had been taken to Khabarovsk, and a clash in Iman would accomplish nothing. Shamotulski decided to retreat, but not without assurance of Sperling's release. That assurance took the form of three hostages, Cossack horsemen who were taken with the retreating Americans, despite threats and protests from both Cossacks and Japanese.[20]

Graves was outraged; he protested to Horvat, demanding Sperling's immediate release. He was released several days later, after having been badly beaten by Cossack officers while on the train and again at the Khabarovsk station.[21] Although Graves believed the Japanese to have engineered the affair, he demanded an apology from General Rozanov, then head of White Army forces in Siberia, but received no reply. Warnings then went out to the Americans along the railroad to be doubly alert. This had been a humiliating series of events: sneak train raids, an attack led by a deserter, and an American soldier whipped and beaten with no apology, reprimand, or explanation. Unfortunately, the situation would only worsen.

As Graves and Morris left Omsk on August 20 to return to Vladivostok, conditions in the Lake Baikal area were unsettled, not because of Bolsheviks, but because of Cossacks. The Twenty-seventh Infantry had its headquarters and units of the Third Battalion in the Baikal area at the time. Graves visited some of these units on his return from Omsk. Lt. Benjamin A. Dickson, regimental transportation officer, wrote from Verkhne-Udinsk on August 31, "This day is memorable for the presence of the Commanding General, William S. Graves and Ambassador to Japan Morris in our camp."[22] Dickson found a fellow West Pointer, William Chapman, Class of 1917, who was an aide to General Graves. Chapman made little comment beyond that it was not an especially interesting trip. Dickson mentioned that he was expecting the winter quarters for the Twenty-seventh Infantry to be at Beresovka, a location he visited and found not wholly to his liking.[23]

Those units based in the Baikal area were uneasy about the Kolchak government and its army. More and more evidence indicated that the White Army west of Baikal was in disarray and retreating, leaving the Bolsheviks to take over abandoned areas. When Graves visited the Ural front in August, he found the Kolchak reports of proposed offensives were highly inaccurate. The White Army west of Omsk had meager support from Semenov or Kalmykof, who, with their Japanese support, continued to harass and intimidate the people in their areas of Baikal and Ussuri. While the American dignitaries were in Omsk, the White Army was retreating in turmoil. Gaida, who had enjoyed a measure of respect from the Americans, had been dismissed, and Kolchak was relying increasingly on his lawless Cossacks. Graves and Morris arrived back in Vladivostok in September, and the ambassador returned to his duties in Japan.

In October there was another incident involving an arms shipment. Lt. Albert Ryan was in charge of a shipment of fifteen thousand rifles to be taken across Manchuria and delivered to Kolchak in Irkutsk. On October 24, when Ryan was in Chita with his loaded train, he was confronted by a Cossack lieutenant who demanded that the rifles be turned over to Semenov. Ryan's response was that he had orders to deliver the rifles to Irkutsk and that was where they would go.

The American consul in Chita, Henry Fowler, became involved in the negotiations, which included Colonel Morrow, General Graves, Japanese General Oi, and Semenov. On October 25, Graves telegraphed Ryan, "Do not give arms to Semenof." Ryan wired Morrow, "Semenof has given until 11:00 A.M. this date when he will take rifles by force."[24] Morrow repeated Graves's instructions that the rifles were not to be released, then telegraphed Semenov, "Urgently request you take no action against small American echelon now at Chita." He emphasized that Kolchak should decide who should receive the rifles.

As Morrow was wiring Semenov, he was also ordering his troops to be ready to move. Ryan telegraphed that a Semenov armored train was opposite his train, but he had barricaded his train and was ready to fight. Apparently, the Japanese put pressure on Semenov; the 11:00 A.M. deadline passed with no action. Finally, Ryan reported at 2:45 P.M. that the Russian armored train was moving out; he was told to be ready to leave at 3:00 P.M. A final note came to Morrow from Semenov himself: "Dear Colonel We understand each other I see Don't worry I shake your hand." Morrow replied, "Thank you for your courteous message its spirit and its understanding."[25] Once again the threat of a fight had forced Semenov to back down.

Ryan did not leave until 10:15 P.M.; with stops at Verkhne-Udinsk and the Twenty-seventh Infantry's winter quarters at Beresovka, he made it to Irkutsk on October 27 and turned the rifles over to the Kolchak authorities. It was a hollow victory; the Japanese later told Graves that the rifles had gone straight to Semenov. A puzzling end to the rifle story came in Vladivostok in early 1920. Graves discovered that those same rifles were sitting in four rail cars in the Vladivostok rail yards. Eventually, he persuaded the Japanese to turn the cars over to him; he counted fifty-nine hundred rifles still in their boxes.[26]

In November 1919 Lieutenant Dickson in Missovaya wrote about the approaching Red Army. "The Reds are going on a rampage now that Omsk has fallen," he said, "and we of the 27th are in for a dance and a song. The last British pulled out Friday."[27] He reported that Semenov's armored trains were at the front, as was a battalion of Japanese troops. He seemed happy to be in the midst of such turmoil, "I am glad I came to Missovaya, whether I ever leave it or not." Dickson became increasingly disenchanted with the mission, his assignment, and his regiment, as the winter progressed.

Problems in other American sectors of Siberia continued to mount. Not only had the quality of the troops suffered by the rotation of veteran soldiers, but numbers had decreased as well. Graves's report indicated that on July 1, 1919, the AEFS had a total of 8,367 officers and men. By December 31, that number was down to 7,293.[28] General Rozanov, who had replaced General Ivanoff-Rinoff in Vladivostok, was a constant source of irritation to Graves. While Ivanoff-Rinoff had been ruthless to the Russians in his territory, his tactics were benevolent compared to Rozanov's. Graves said of him, "Rozanov proved to be the third worst character known to me in Siberia, although he could never quite reach the plane of Kalmikoff and Semeonoff [sic]."[29]

Graves was warned in October that Semenov and Kalmykof were planning to attack American outposts. On October 7, he consolidated the small units stationed along the railroad at Spasskoye, and no attacks were made. On November 2, he spread his men out again to their old locations.[30] But with a hostile chief of garrison, Colonel Staripalov, in Spasskoye, the uncontrollable Rozanov in Vladivostok, the Suchan mines shut down, and the two Cossack Atamans roaming the rails with their armored trains, the prospect for winter was bleak for the general and his expedition. Two men were shot by Russians in September in Vladivostok; one was an American private, James Long, the other a Czech. As a result the Allies demanded that Rozanov remove his troops from the area. Graves reported to Washington, "This demand was not complied with, due to the attitude adopted by Kolchak and the Allied representative in Omsk."[31] More clouds were forming over Vladivostok as the cold weather set in.

General Gaida had been fired from his job with the Kolchak army and had no status in the Czech ranks, but he had a burning ambition. He believed that Rozanov should be deposed, and he considered himself the likely replacement. He began discussions with the many factions in Vladivostok, planting the seeds for a revolt. General Ivanoff-Rinoff, when appointed commander of all Russian armed forces in the Russian Far East in 1918, declared the whole territory to be under martial law.[32] This gave him and his successor, Rozanov, life-and-death powers over the people in his territory. By November 1919, Gaida was ready to organize the many factions of anti-Bolshevik, anti-Kolchak, and anti-Japanese to begin a revolution within a revolution. Gaida was asked to join a group called the Siberian National Directorate, which included Pavel Yakushev as president with Colonels Morovsky and Krakovetsky as vice presidents. It was an invitation the ambitious Czech welcomed; he became the pivotal member and the military commander.[33]

Convinced that the Kolchak reverses and evacuation of Omsk in mid-November were the precursors of the Kolchak decline, Gaida made his move on Monday, November 17, 1919. He opened a recruiting station in the Vladivostok railroad yards within sight of Rozanov's office and proceeded to enlist all of the dissatisfied citizens and Rozanov soldiers he could find. At first the results were encouraging, but later, about 2:00 P.M., a few shots broke the calm. It is uncertain who fired them, but they started an open fire fight between the Rozanov forces and the Gaida recruits. As the day passed with more and more firing in the yards, the Allied Council met to decide what role it should play. Most members were sympathetic to the overthrow of Rozanov, but they hesitated to take sides openly. Eventually, they decided to stay neutral. They assigned Maj. Sam Johnson additional troops for his police force from the Allied units, but his role was simply to maintain order and confine the fighting to the railroad yards.

The yards, surrounded by hills, were under artillery fire from the high ground. The harbor came virtually up to the station itself; government naval ships lobbed shells from gunboats, so Gaida's troops in the station or the yards were at a considerable disadvantage. With the Allied decision not to take part, but to keep the fighting in the yards, Gaida's small contingent was in peril from the start. Shells began coming from artillery on the hills, Russian gunboats began firing point-blank at the yards, and as evening wore on, the Rozanov forces located in the station pinned the rebels down under the railroad cars. At midnight, Gaida rushed the station and drove out the Russians. So far, his losses had been small, with only six killed, but the Rozanov troops now could concentrate all their fire on the station.[34] The firing from the Russian ships began again at midnight, aided by the searchlights of the *New Orleans, Brooklyn,* and a Japanese cruiser. The fighting ended by 9:00 A.M., and the revolt was over. Gaida was captured, slightly wounded, and Rozanov lost no time in executing the men who had fought against him.

Although the Americans took no part in the revolt, scores of soldiers, sailors, Red Cross workers, and others, were witnesses. George Miller, a sailor on the USS *Brooklyn* anchored out in the bay, was a member of a team sent on board the *New Orleans,* which was tied up at the dock, close to the fighting. Miller reported Russian destroyers and torpedo boats firing at the station, but the *Brooklyn* threatened to fire on them unless they moved away from the dock area.[35] The *Brooklyn*'s log recorded that Marines were sent ashore to protect the consulate, while a tug brought two wounded Russians aboard the ship for medical help. The log also noted that a number of shots from shore hit the ship. One of the stray shots struck Sailmaker's mate, Theodore Williams Rowland, on the *New Orleans;* he died the next day, the only American casualty.[36]

Russell Miller of the Twenty-seventh Infantry was on a train en route to the ship that would take him home; he arrived in Vladivostok the night of November 17. He was roused from his sleep in a boxcar and taken up the hill to waiting trucks as the revolt began, relieved to have no part in the battle. Colonel Eichelberger wrote his wife that he was convinced the Russian cadets from Russian Island, who were trained by the British and brought into the fight on Rozanov's side, were the deciding factor in the fight. The Red Cross stepped in to help the wounded; by Tuesday night fifty-six wounded had been treated.[37] The only Americans involved were a handful of men under Major Johnson, who were asked to go into the heavy fire in the railroad yard to rescue Kolchak's lieutenant general Romanovsky and his family, caught by the rebels and trapped in their railroad car under guard. Majors Graves and Johnson took a number of men and crawled across bodies, track, and rubble to find the general and his family. They were eventually rescued with a great deal of risk to the Americans and a bayonet wound to Major Johnson.[38] All members of the rescue party were awarded the DSC for their valor.[39]

The aftermath was a bloody one. As soon as the outcome became obvious, Colonel Krakovetsky and several others escaped and rushed past the American sentry at AEF headquarters to beg for asylum. Graves knew that a consulate was American territory and could grant asylum, but a military headquarters was not the same thing. As the colonel and his men waited for a decision, Rozanov was already beginning the methodical execution of the men captured at the station. Graves knew the fate of his guests should he refuse their plea; he could not in good conscience turn them over to Rozanov for certain execution. He wired the War Department in Washington for instructions and Washington replied that he was not authorized to grant sanctuary. He wired again, but no answer came.

A simple solution to the problem was devised by Colonel Bugbee. While waiting for an answer to the second telegram, Colonel Bugbee came to Grave office's, saluted, and reported, "General, the prisoners have escaped." Graves wrote later:

> I could not say to him that I was glad, as a matter of fact, I could not say anything, but I know of nothing in my whole life that removed such a load from my conscience as did that report of Colonel Bugbee, and I decided I would not report this to Washington, as nothing could be done about it.[40]

After his capture, Gaida was released to the Czechs with the provision he leave Siberia immediately. Wounded and shaken by the events, Gaida left as soon as he could be taken to a ship.

Most of the Americans in Vladivostok viewed the carnage in the railway station, where many of the first executions had taken place, adding to the bodies of those killed in the uprising. "When I reached the railway station the last batch of prisoners was lined up against the wall to be shot, however, they marched them into the station and shot them while they were going downstairs. . . . About noon it started to snow and the bodies were soon covered," wrote Eichelberger.[41] Another witness was more disturbed:

> The aftermath was dreadful and unbelievable and more than one man belched up good army rations as he looked down at dead bodies in parts everywhere. Headless trunks and thighs and pools of dried blood in the cold streets and station. . . . The only things in quantity that seemed to have escaped the massacre were the lice and rats who ran like little armies over the corpses piled in places like cordwood.[42]

Eventually, the bodies were removed, the debris cleaned up, and life in Vladivostok resumed. Of the four leaders of the revolt, Gaida was gone; Col. Pavel Yakushev was dead, his body found in the bay; Morovsky was dead, killed in the station; and Krakovetsky had disappeared.

The abrupt ending of the revolt, which had hoped to establish at least some form of democratic rule, was to put the brutal Rozanov in almost total control, with Kalmykof and Semenov unchecked. Eichelberger wrote, "It was a sad blow to democracy as these murderous cut throats backed by the Japanese are in full control."[43]

There is some irony in the fact that in late summer 1919, after the U.S. forces had left North Russia, the White Army was really at the height of its success. The Kolchak Army, even without Czechs, had driven the Reds west of Kazan, only five hundred miles from Moscow. Gen. Anton Denikin's southern army was in the outskirts of Moscow, Gen. Nikolai Yudenich and his ragged army pressed on to Petrograd and were virtually in the suburbs by fall. Also, Ironside's final offensive in July had come close to Kotlas on the Dvina River and seemed able to continue.

But it was all an illusion. Ironside's push was only for the purpose of protecting his already planned evacuation; Kolchak by July was in retreat; and by late fall Denikin and Yudenich had begun their retreats. Christopher Dobson and John Miller, in their book *The Day They Almost Bombed Moscow,* write, "By the end of the year nothing remained of the White Russian Army."[44]

In Vladivostok, one positive event took place when the deserter Anton Karachun was captured while trying to bribe a supply company guard in February. He was trying to obtain clothing for himself and his colleagues when he was recognized and seized.[45]

Christmas came and went with few celebrations for the Americans or their Russian hosts; however, on December 29, 1919, Graves received orders to prepare the troops for withdrawal. The information was not passed to the Japanese diplomats in Washington until January 9, 1920, a fact that caused the Japanese much resentment since information leaked before their official notice was received.[46] As one historian summed it up, "In fact, the Americans abandoned intervention without any grace at all."[47]

The American Red Cross

From the beginning the purpose of the Red Cross was to help the people of Russia without regard to political situations, and with utter indifference to the policies of the political party that happened to be in power.

—Henry Davison, *The American Red Cross in the Great War*

MANY months before the decision to intervene was made, Col. Raymond Robins of the Red Cross Mission in Moscow played an important, though unsuccessful, role in the complicated formation of U.S. Russian policy.

Robins became convinced that recognition of the Soviet government by the United States was the proper protection of U.S. interests in the region. To reinforce his views, he developed a relationship with Trotsky; it was through Robins that Trotsky's overtures to the United States were directed. In the opposite camp was U.S. consul general Maddin Summers, who was equally adamant that the new Russian government posed a real threat to U.S. interests.

One explanation of the two opposing views was their interpretation of Germany's threat to Russia. In March 1918, Summers believed that the Bolsheviks were agents of the German government, while Robins was convinced that the Soviets were as strongly anti-German as the remaining Allies. In fact, both men were deeply troubled about German domination of Russia, but disagreed about how to prevent that domination.[1] This disagreement shaped the widely varying information sent to Washington in the spring of 1918. The friction between Summers and Robins ended abruptly in May with the death of the consul general and the recall of Colonel Robins. But the Red Cross was established as a part of the turbulent Russian scene even before the Allies landed.

President Wilson hoped that humanitarian efforts could be included in his Russian Intervention and voiced that hope in his *Aide Memoire*. The Red Cross had a very visible presence in Russia throughout the Intervention and sometimes found itself at cross-purposes with General Graves and his mission. Interestingly, the Red Cross in Siberia was managed by Mrs. Wilson's first cousin, Dr. Rudolf Teusler.

American Red Cross workers landed in Vladivostok in July 1917, met by the Russian Red Cross, an organization in some disarray.[2] A history of the Red Cross set forth the role of the organization in Russia: "From the beginning the purpose of the Red Cross was to help the people of Russia without regard to political situations, and with utter indifference to the policies of the political party that happened to be in power."[3] They would find that lofty goal difficult to achieve.

First, the Czechs required medical care not only in the Far East, but in their new participation on the Ural front. Also, the refugees, a constant stream of displaced humanity, needed not only medical care, but the basics of housing and food. As the Intervention neared, the navy assisted in medical help in Vladivostok, and the Red Cross began to set up a network of hospitals across Siberia. Vladivostok became the relief base, distributing food and supplies, procuring housing, and eventually entertaining the masses of refugees and military. Russian Island in Golden Horn Bay became a hospital and a refugee camp and, later, an orphanage, which involved new and unusual requirements of the Red Cross volunteers.

In North Russia, the Red Cross was important for its humanitarian efforts. A Red Cross shipment arrived in Murmansk in 1917 before winter set in, and the cargo was distributed to the various needy population segments. In 1918 a chain of Red Cross hospitality centers sprang up as American troops fanned out across the vast and frigid lands of the north. However, in Siberia they found it difficult to stay out of internal Russian affairs.

One of the volunteers was Grace Bungey of Palo Alto, California. She explained their role: "The Red Cross went in with the army and we ran trains of supplies up into the interior for the Army camps guarded by American servicemen. The Red Cross established hospitals, and American railway engineers helped the Russians get the railroads running."[4] The Trans-Siberian Railroad provided the transportation that linked all these organizations across eastern Siberia: Czechs, Red Cross, Allied armies, Railway workers, and Cossacks. It was obvious that most of these factions supported the Kolchak government, in spite of the disclaimers of the organizations involved. It would have been almost impossible for Bolsheviks to obtain Red Cross supplies, let alone use the railroad for its own purposes.

The Red Cross not only sent supplies and medical equipment by train, but even equipped many of the cars as hospital cars to be used primarily for Czech, Kolchak, or Allied sick or wounded. Adding more weight to the identification of the trains with the White cause were the U.S. Army troops sent to guard them. There were refugee trains, and later typhus trains that attempted to halt the spread of the deadly disease. What they found often were appalling conditions.

Rudolph Beckley, a Red Cross captain, reported his arrival in Omsk in May 1919 to distribute medicine to a Kolchak prison camp housing Bolshevik prisoners. He found 1,935 prisoners, 1,040 of them with typhus.

> Think of it and try and imagine the horror of the scene and the fearful, indescribable stench that greets you as you open the door. . . . These men are prisoners of the Kolchak Govt, a Govt recognized by the Allied powers, and these things are happening in this, the 20th century under the very eyes of the representatives of these Allied powers, who do not interfere, I presume from matters of "policy."[5]

Beckley's was one of the few attempts made to aid Bolshevik forces, and he faced an overwhelming task.

One of the train guards on Red Cross Train #15 was Cpl. Jesse A. Anderson of the 146th Ordnance Depot Company. He was ordered to take ten men to guard a train headed for the Ural front. The train left Vladivostok on June 3, 1919, rolled across Manchuria, and arrived in Chita, Russia, on June 11. From there they began to see the effects of the civil strife. They were escorted by a Czech armored train after Lake Baikal, passing a refugee train headed east. Anderson wrote, "It is an awful sight to see, the refugee passengers getting on their trains (boxcars). We saw one car of gypsies. They had two naked children, about four years old." After they passed Irkutsk, he wrote, "We are in Bolshevik territory now. Had lots of fun and hard work fixing our bunks and putting in sandbags, blankets, fish plates and rails. Let the B's come."[6]

Anderson was disturbed by the chaos of the railroad. Even though the American railroaders had identified problems in management and efficiency, they could do little to correct the problems. The Red Cross cars were continually being hooked onto various train segments; they were never really sure where they would be the next day. On June 19, in Kansk, Anderson wrote in his journal, "We have seen a lot of the dirty work of the Bolsheviks today. Buildings burned, railroad track blown up and 12 wrecks from 3–30 cars each."[7] Train #15 reached its destination, Ekaterinburg, on July 12, unloaded its medical supplies and headed back east, finally reaching Vladivostok on September 4. The round trip took just over three months.[8]

The largest hospital in Siberia was the Red Cross Hospital in Omsk, which was organized in November 1918 with twelve nurses and six doctors who arrived with Colonel Teusler on Train #2. Their first tasks were to find a building suitable for a hospital, staff it, and obtain supplies and equipment. The Red Cross personnel had a frustrating beginning; they spent eight weeks in the Omsk train yards waiting for the bureaucratic approvals required for them to occupy, convert, and staff the warehouse they had selected. However, by the end of 1918, they had a building, beds, supplies, and staff, but no patients. Gradually, the word spread that they were in operation, and their first Russian patients arrived on a sanitary train coming from the front near Perm. Nurse Gertrude Pardee Carter described the sight:

> [A] more neglected crowd of individuals I have never set eyes upon, from a medical and human standpoint. We had them scrubbed, bathed, shaved and put into clean pyjamas and bathrobes then sent them to bed between clean sheets, apparently the first articles of this kind many had seen for months and I doubt whether many of them had ever known some of these things before.[9]

By mid-1919 the Red Cross had established three divisions: eastern, from Vladivostok to Manchuria Station; central, from Manchuria Station to Krasnoyarsk; and western, everything west of Krasnoyarsk. There were Red Cross hospitals in Omsk, Irkutsk, and Manchuria, as well as Vladivostok and Russian Island. There were also supplemental facilities for typhus, hospital trains equipped for surgery, and dressing stations in various rail yards.[10] Soon, however, many of those installations would have to be abandoned as the Kolchak government collapsed and the safety of Red Cross staff became paramount.

The evacuation of Red Cross personnel in Omsk began September 4, 1919, when Train #52 pulled out at 6:45 P.M., headed for Irkutsk. It was a difficult trip with seemingly needless delays and confusion. The Red Cross personnel left depressed by feelings of helplessness and frustration. An Army officer, E. Alfred Davies, wrote in his diary on September 4:

The American Red Cross has surely spent millions, while the Russian Railway Service is trying hard to help. . . . Officialdom—the same petty type of official which betrayed Russia's great army before, and which is betraying Russia today. Department jealous of department, each working against each other, conscious of only one thing—their own interests.[11]

The evacuation of Red Cross personnel from Siberia would take months. They abandoned medical equipment and supplies as the American support of the hospitals was withdrawn. One of the last trains to leave Irkutsk with Red Cross staff was that of Consul General Harris, which was part of a fleet of trains evacuating Irkutsk, shepherded by Czech armored trains. Even with that protection, Semenov's and Japanese trains interrupted their journey repeatedly.[12] The last train reached Vladivostok on February 6, 1920. The first group to return to the United States left on the *Great Northern* on February 5. The ship would return on March 30, leaving Vladivostok on April 1 to take most of the remaining personnel to Manila and then to San Francisco. As the ship sailed, it left eight women to liquidate Red Cross affairs.[13] On the same ship were General Graves, quartered in the finest accommodations, and Anton Karachun, locked up in the ship's brig.

The Red Cross found itself at cross-purposes with the AEFS. General Graves was hostile to the mission of Colonel Teusler's group, because of their virtually total connection to Kolchak's government. They established a medical branch of his army, delivering supplies to his troops, including Semenov.[14] A crowning blow was the January meeting, only days after Americans were killed by Semenov at Posolskaya, when Harris reported his and Teusler's relations with Semenov were most cordial, even though he knew of the killings.

There was, however, one Red Cross success story that rivals fiction. It involves Mrs. Hannah Campbell, "Mother" to many in Siberia. She began her Red Cross duties as a housemother for personnel in Vladivostok, a challenging enough position, but she became famous for her work with the children at Russian Island. During the turbulent days of 1917, a group of Russian children living in and around Petrograd was sent to Siberia, away from the violence. It was anticipated that they would be sent back home in a few months, but with war raging across the whole country, the children were put under the care of the Red Cross, first in Omsk and later on Russian Island.

After the Americans left Vladivostok in 1920, the Red Cross chartered a ship to return the eight hundred children to Petrograd. The *Yomei Maru* would be the home for the 350 girls and 450 boys, twelve to fifteen years old, for months as they crossed the Pacific to San Francisco, then through the Panama Canal to New York, and on to Brest,

France, finally ending in Finland. In those months, Mother Campbell was helped by numerous volunteers, but the incredible responsibility of that exodus rested squarely on her shoulders. Eventually, the children were repatriated across the Finnish border to Petrograd, where they were reunited with their families after years of separation. The success of her personal dedication showed when in July 1973, one hundred of the children were located and attended a reunion in Petrograd, meeting with some of the Red Cross workers who had been on the ship. It was an emotional gathering.[15]

It is fitting that this episode should close the chapter on the role of the Red Cross in Siberia. They had become embroiled in the politics of the times, as had so many other organizations, trying to do what they did best, distribute humanitarian aid and medical help. Sadly, some of their efforts were channeled in directions that were contrary to the Siberian mission. The organization paid a price for its service: seven of its personnel died of disease during their Siberian stay.[16]

There were other organizations that helped the Army in Siberia: the Salvation Army, YMCA, and the Knights of Columbus. Graves wrote, "As far as I could see, all American welfare organizations, excepting the Red Cross, were not only in favor of, but followed the policy of non-interference in the internal affairs of the Russian people."[17]

The Exodus—1920

On the afternoon of 9 January 1920 I received word from a ser-
geant's Russian girl friend that the villagers were leaving because
the Destroyer [Semenov's armored train] was coming.

—Lt. Paul Kendall

TECHNICALLY, the withdrawal of Allied troops started in
November 1918 when Kolchak assumed power. From that
moment, the Czechs, not approving of the new dictatorship, began to
withdraw from the Ural front and prepare their departure. More than a
year later, in December 1919, they made their first actual exit from Siberia.[1] The Japanese were the only ally reluctant to see the Czechs leave;
they believed that as long as there were Czechs in Siberia, there was a
reason for the Japanese to stay. The other Allies, the Reds, and even the
Cossacks, were happy to see them go.

In December 1919 the major project facing Major General Graves
was the evacuation of his seven thousand men from locations scattered
across thousands of miles of hostile Russia. In addition, he was to protect those Czech elements still drifting toward Vladivostok, while defending his own units from possible attacks from Bolsheviks, partisans,
Cossacks, or Chinese bandits—all of this while facing a bitter Siberian

winter. Fortunately, he had two able regimental commanders. Colonel Morrow had been thoroughly tested in his remote Baikal location, and Colonel Bugbee, although new to Siberia, had endeared himself to Graves by his performance during the Gaida revolt.

The decision was made to consolidate troops in Vladivostok while awaiting ships, which would follow the icebreakers into the docks. With Morrow still in the Baikal, Bugbee had much of the responsibility for loading the expedition's horses, equipment, and supplies. He wrote home on January 22, "I have never worked harder in my life than I have done lately. Have shipped six companies of the 27th Inf. and a lot of property on the Great Northern."[2] He also had to arrange temporary quarters for these units coming into Vladivostok from other regions. First to arrive were the Spasskoye units of the Twenty-seventh Infantry Regiment on about January 13; they were loaded on the *Great Northern* and left on January 17. The next arrivals were several Shkotova units, which boarded the *Crook* on February 15 and left for Manila that same day.

The forces withdrawing from Shkotova to Vladivostok had only one recorded run-in with the partisans. On January 5, Captain Scroggs moved a section of Company H from Kangaus to Shkotova; about three miles out of Kangaus a bridge was blocked and the train stopped. An estimated three hundred Reds surrounded his twenty men and demanded that the Americans give up their arms. After some discussion, Scroggs led his men off the train and started walking to Novo Nezhino. Bugbee's report said, "I believe it would have been far better to have stayed and fought it out."[3]

Most of the troop movements were uneventful, but after their arrival in the city, the weather turned bad. On January 13, the temperature dropped to below zero and winds whipped across the bay at more than one hundred miles per hour. The remaining Shkotova units were to be evacuated on the *Sheridan,* but it was so loaded with equipment and supplies that there was no room for men. The *Crook* was the next ship due, but she was late due to heavy ice in the bay. The icebreakers finally led her to the dock and the Thirty-first Infantry Shkotova contingent left its freezing barracks to board the ship, bound for the warmer climate of Manila. After the Shkotova units and local Twenty-seventh Infantry units were taken out, it then became possible to move the Twenty-seventh Infantry units from the Baikal area, followed by the Thirty-first Infantry units protecting the movement of the Baikal companies. It was far from a simple operation. The Kolchak government was also evacuating to the east under Czech protection with a hoard of gold that had belonged to the now-dead tsar. Numerous Czech units were trying to move east as well, on a railroad that was in chaos.

In the Baikal area, it was reported that Bolsheviks were gathering in Mukheene, some twelve versts southwest of Verkhne-Udinsk, to attack the city and the railroad. Since the town was in the American sector, an expedition was sent to investigate. On January 3, Lt. Col. A. C. Gillem led parts of Companies I and L and Machine Gun Company with a mounted section toward Mukheene. Gillem was to have support from a White Russian company, but it refused to go.[4] After some preliminary firing, the Reds told Gillem they were about to attack, but their purpose was to wipe out Semenov's train, not attack the Americans. While Gillem confiscated a few arms from the Reds, he gained their pledge that they would not attack the railroad. His report also mentioned that the march was made in snow during a windstorm at 20 degrees below zero and that the new recruits performed admirably.[5] He reported no casualties.

After the Reds had promised Colonel Gillem they would not attack the railroad, Lieutenant Dickson wrote on January 4 that the Reds had blown up two bridges west of Verkhne-Udinsk. He reported he was a little short of supplies since the train couldn't get through, but was not worried. To relieve his boredom, "I had some fun patrolling after snipers this last week in the woods by moonlight. I went alone to show the men there was no danger. It was really quite thrilling—harmless sport. But those people never turn up when expected."[6]

The evacuation orders for the Baikal troops came on January 7, orders that they had all looked forward to for a long time; but there were still some duties to perform before they left. Third platoon of Company M, stationed in Posolskaya, east of the regimental Beresovka winter headquarters, was guarding a bridge near the town. Their winter quarters were boxcars on the rail siding. The platoon of thirty-three men was commanded by Lt. Paul Kendall and one other officer. Kendall remembered:

> On the afternoon of 9 January 1920 I received word from a sergeant's Russian girl friend that the villagers were leaving because the Destroyer [Semenov's armored train] was coming. I'd heard such rumors before, but nevertheless took the precaution of ordering the men to sleep on the floor of their cars, to remain dressed with rifles loaded and locked, and put double guards at the railroad station and at the bridge. Sure enough by dusk the hundred or so villagers had departed.[7]

His precaution saved a number of lives. It was a bitterly cold night, 20 degrees below zero with six inches of snow on the ground. While Lieutenant Kendall stood outside, at 1:00 A.M. an armored train came alongside the American boxcars. The port holes on the armored car opened and the Cossacks opened fire on the boxcars. The Americans jumped out into the bitter cold to attack the Cossack train. In the first fire, Pvt. John Montgomery was killed as he stood guard outside the boxcars, and in the next action, Sgt. Carl Robbins was killed as he climbed into the engine of the attacking train and tossed in a grenade. Under the heavy American fire, the Destroyer slowly began to back away from the station. As it was backing out, Pfc. Homer Tommie tried to climb on the train, but fell under the wheels and lost his leg. Kendall's men followed the train on foot; when reinforcements from Company I arrived, the two groups closed on the train and captured it with all of its personnel. American losses were two killed and two wounded; Semenov lost General Bogomoletz captured, five killed, several wounded, and forty-eight taken prisoner.[8]

Colonel Morrow held the train and the prisoners until he left the Baikal area for Vladivostok; he learned from the prisoners that they had "robbed and brutally murdered over forty men and three women were raped and brutally killed."[9] When Graves learned of the attack and the capture of the Cossack general and crew he said:

> I was sorry that Lieutenant Kendall, who first got hold of Bogomoletz, did not hang him to a telegraph pole, but he acted within the law and really exhibited better soldierly qualities in doing as he did. This young officer is entitled to great credit for his leadership in resisting this unwarranted attack, and in capturing a force with vastly superior armament.[10]

It was another American humiliation when Morrow was forced to give the train and its crew back to Semenov as the Americans left the area of Baikal. By then Kolchak was no longer a factor; he had deputized Semenov and Kalmykof, but the supreme ruler himself was making every effort to escape to the east. There was virtual anarchy in the Baikal area: Jews were being slaughtered in Ekaterinburg, hostages taken by Semenov were executed and thrown into the freezing Lake Baikal, and the press of eastbound trains was creating a travel nightmare.

A high degree of animosity had developed between General Graves and the State Department's general consul Ernest Harris. Lt. Col. B. B. McCroskey, a military observer in Kolchak's White Army, was relieved of that duty and assigned to Consul Harris in Irkutsk. In December, Graves wired Washington that McCroskey was giving out an official communication stating, "The American troops are in Siberia primarily to support Kolchak against Bolsheviks by keeping his line of communications open along the Trans-Siberian." Graves requested that McCroskey not show that communication to anyone in Siberia.[11] On

January 14, five days after the Posolskaya attack, Harris telegraphed the American consul in Peking: "I called on Ataman Semenof today with Colonels Teusler [Red Cross] and McCroskey. Arranged with Semenof distribution of certain Red Cross material to needy population. My relations with Semenof cordial and I have no fear for safety of Red Cross nurses here." In this same wire, he stated that three American soldiers were dead in a clash with Semenov.[12]

McCroskey was headed west on a Semenov train near Chita when he encountered Morrow, who was traveling east to Vladivostok. Morrow was told that McCroskey had taken part in a railroad meeting in Chita; Morrow considered that interfering in area affairs. He arrested McCroskey and held him in Manchuria. That action instigated a series of messages—McCroskey to Graves, McCroskey to Harris, Harris to Graves, Harris to Morrow—each of which increased in intensity. Harris telegraphed Washington, "Colonel Morrow's arbitrary action in this and other matters, together with his personal conduct on many occasions has not placed him above the severe criticism of those who are familiar with his doings."[13]

Graves wrote that Morrow had found that McCroskey was with Semenov on some of his raids. Morrow asked McCroskey, "Do you know what a murderer he is? Do you know he has killed some of my men?" His reply was, "Semenof is the only thing standing between civilization and Bolshevism, and I do not intend to listen to anything against Semenof."[14] Morrow reported that he thought McCroskey was mentally unbalanced and stated that he would bring him to Vladivostok, which he did. Graves had McCroskey examined; he was found mentally stable, but of a "very nervous temperament and they thought it unwise and unsafe to leave him in Siberia." Graves eventually sent him to the United States.[15]

As Morrow's forces were leaving the Baikal area, Joseph Loughran, a chaplain with the Thirty-first Infantry, brought with him German-Austrian prisoners for repatriation. With the Posolskaya incident fresh in his memory, Morrow was so uneasy about the Cossacks he told Loughran to arm the prisoners in case of trouble. "Had the Cossacks attacked us the German and Austrian prisoners would have been our staunch allies."[16]

Only a few days later, Admiral Kolchak was taken from his train at Irkutsk and handed over to the local Communist Party, a group of political and fringe parties making up the Irkutsk government. They were inflamed by Kolchak's recent execution of hostages—members of the Political Center who had been murdered and thrown in Lake Baikal. Kolchak was under the Czech protection, but the Czechs had no love for the old dictator; on January 15, following orders, they turned him over to the locals. His court-martial took place a few days later and lasted nine days, but there was little doubt of its outcome. His only defense was ignorance of the atrocities performed by others, saying he only had vague knowledge of the sordid events. On the last day of the trial, he was found guilty of the outrages attributed to his regime; the next day, he and his prime minister Victor Pepeliaev were taken from their prison cells into the subzero day and shot.[17]

Vladivostok was hardly a tranquil city as U.S. troops gathered, waiting for their ships. Another coup took place on January 31: the Russian Thirty-fifth Infantry Regiment surrounded key buildings in the city and arrested Rozanov and his henchmen. The new government resembled the old Zemstvo form of government that existed in pre-Intervention days and, according to Graves, provided welcome relief to the excesses of Rozanov.[18] Events of more concern to Americans took place as well. One of those events was a tragic fire that burned one of the barracks of the replacement battalion as the men waited to board ships. An investigation determined that a fire of unknown origin swept through the barracks on the night of March 6, 1920, killing four privates, Alex La Beaux, Quartermaster Corps; Julius Morris, Company M, Thirty-first; Merrill Mastin, Company M, Thirty-first; and James Brantley, Company I, Twenty-seventh.[19]

After the death of Kolchak, with the Cossacks' armored trains on the loose, it became imperative to get the U.S. forces out of Russia as quickly as possible. The first echelons left the Baikal area on January 16, and the final one left on January 29. They all had reached Vladivostok by February 25, and most of them left on the *Thomas*, bound once again for Manila.[20]

The Thirty-first Infantry Regiment contingent in Razdolnoye was pulled back to Vladivostok with the other units: Company D, Fifty-third Telegraph Battalion, Field Hospital #4, Ambulance Company #4, 146th Ordnance Depot Company, and other small units. All were shipped to the Philippines on the *South Bend* on March 30; Evacuation Hospital #17 and its personnel followed the next day on the *Crook*.

The last ship, the *Great Northern*, left on April 1 carrying General Graves, the remaining elements of the Thirty-first Infantry Regiment with AEF headquarters staff and Red Cross personnel. The Japanese waited on the dock to see the Americans off; as the ship backed slowly away from the dock, the Japanese band played a Stephen Foster melody, "Hard Times Come Again No More."[21]

While most of the Americans were gone, there were still a few left in Vladivostok. Colonel Eichelberger and his recently arrived wife awaited transport to Tokyo; four officers and fifty-three men were to assure the exit of the Czechs still in Siberia; and two officers and two enlisted men stayed to assist the surviving German Austro-Hungarian war prisoners who were waiting for the *Mount Vernon*.[22]

Eichelberger and his wife were witnesses to the next Japanese move, the retaking of the Far Eastern governments. On April 4 and 5, 1920, the Japanese attacked throughout the Far East, ousting the new Vladivostok government and inflicting large losses on the unsuspecting Russians. General Graves and Eichelberger had watched the Japanese prepare their installations in Vladivostok in late March, setting up automatic weapons in key city locations. By then, there was little they could do about it. The last ship was hardly out of the harbor when the Japanese launched their attack. In the coming months, the Far Eastern Republic emerged to become the central government, under the watchful eye of the Japanese. Semenov established a short-lived government in Chita, but by October, he had been driven back to Manchuria.[23]

In later days, Eichelberger, then a lieutenant general, mellowed slightly in light of later events, although he had no liking for the White Army. While his hatred of the Japanese did not diminish, he remarked in his memoirs, "Looking back, now, and realizing the world dominance given the Reds by FDR and Churchill in World War II, I regret that we did not put troops into Siberia for the purpose of defeating the Reds and eliminating that group from the picture." He added:

> Having witnessed the seizure by the Japs of Eastern Siberia on April 4, 1920, and this seizure without the authority of even their own central government impressed me with our future dangers. From that time I never had any doubt that we faced danger of future war with the Japanese.[24]

That opinion was mirrored by a number of other Siberian veterans.

The evacuation of 34,933 Czechs on thirteen American ships was finally accomplished by September 1920, leaving thousands of their comrades in unmarked graves along the Trans-Siberian tracks.[25] Those who survived found in their old homeland a new democracy formed on October 28, 1918, the Republic of Czechoslovakia.

The Americans were gone, the Czechs were about to depart, and the British and French were also withdrawing; only the Japanese were left in Siberia. In North Russia the Bolsheviks had taken Murmansk and Archangel in February 1920 and were purging those who had given service to the Allies. The purposes of intervention had been thwarted in virtually every case. Although the Japanese remained in Siberia after the other Allies left, they, too, would depart by the end of 1922. It remained only to evaluate the Intervention and its lasting effects.

General March, who had never favored either expedition, wrote after the war, "The sending of this expedition was the last occasion in which the president reversed the recommendation of the War Department during my service as Chief of Staff of the Army." He added, "Almost immediately after the Siberian and North Russian forces had reached their theaters of operations, events moved rapidly and uniformly in the direction of the complete failure of these expeditions to accomplish anything that their sponsors had claimed for them"[26]

Conclusions

THE Intervention did not exist in a vacuum; it was shaped by other events as it progressed. The first and foremost factor affecting its course was the end of World War I. Historian George Kennan wrote, "The American forces had scarcely arrived in Russia when history invalidated at a single stroke almost every reason Washington had conceived for their being there."[1] A second factor was the severe stroke suffered by President Wilson on October 2, 1919. A third factor was the Senate's failure to ratify the Versailles Treaty and the resultant defeat of Wilson's dream of the League of Nations in November 1919.

The effects of these events on the Intervention, or how these events were shaped by the Intervention, are subject to much debate. It is obvious that Soviet-Western relations were off to a very rocky start. It has been argued that the Cold War may have started as the Allies openly challenged the fledgling Soviet government, and it is safe to say that, even though we recognized the Soviet government in 1934 and stood beside her as an ally in World War II, there was great distrust between the West and the Communist Russian government.

How much support Wilson lost in the Senate by not removing the troops from Russia after November 1918 is difficult to measure. But when he badly needed the Senate ratification vote as he campaigned for the League of Nations, he faced public and Senate demands to bring home the troops from Russia.

The original pressure to intervene came from America's chief allies, France and Britain. The reluctance of the United States to join the
Allies in Russia, and President Wilson's instructions to stay out of internal affairs, gave them little satisfaction. In Siberia, where Graves followed the president's directions faithfully, there was even more
disappointment. The Japanese in Siberia violated their original promise that they had no territorial interest in Siberia, and their goal of territorial expansion became obvious to all the world as the Americans
sailed out of Vladivostok.

Japanese-U.S. relations were strained as Japan began an anti-
American press campaign that continued throughout the expedition.
While Graves and General Otani maintained a certain cordiality, the
deep distrust of Japanese troops was obvious, as evidenced especially
by Eichelberger's writings and the vast majority of soldiers' letters, diaries, and journals.

Continued feelings of hostility would be evident when the
Twenty-seventh and Thirty-first Infantry Regiments faced the Japanese
Imperial Armed Forces after December 1941. The Twenty-seventh was
in Hawaii on December 7, and participated in a number of battles in the
steamy South Pacific jungles. The Thirty-first was captured on Bataan
and faced more than three years of torture and imprisonment.

Bruce Lockhart, the British consul in Moscow at the time of the
Intervention, recorded his thoughts when he first heard of the small
force being sent into North Russia:

> It was a blunder comparable to the worst mistakes of the Crimean war.
> . . . It raised hopes which could not be fulfilled. It intensified the civil war
> and sent thousands of Russians to their deaths. Indirectly, it was respon-
> sible for the Terror. Its direct affect was to provide the Bolsheviks with a
> cheap victory, to give them new confidence and to galvanize them into a
> strong and ruthless organization.[2]

Adm. N. A. McCully, commander of naval forces in North Russia,
recognized the consequences as the Allies abandoned their mission.
"This will leave compromised and hopeless a portion of the Population
of Northern Russia, a population which has been encouraged if not in-
cited by Allied Power to war with the Soviet Government, and now exposed to the vengeance of the Bolshevik troops, the character of which
is well known." The admiral determined that in North Russia there
would be left unprotected 96,320 Russian military, civilians, and rural
peasants.[3] Only about six thousand White Russians accompanied the
withdrawing British as they left Archangel, and there is no record of
any Russians leaving Vladivostok with the Allies.

While there can be various interpretations of the effects of the Intervention on relations between the Soviets and the Allies, there is one undisputed fact: 446 American lives were lost—424 soldiers and 22 sailors, including those killed in action, by accident, or by disease and those missing, who were later classified "killed in action, body not recovered." North Russia was the deadlier of the two expeditions, with 235 dead out of approximately 5,000 men involved, while the larger Siberian expedition counted 189 dead from all causes. At least twenty-two sailors died supporting the two expeditions. In Siberia no men were listed as missing, but there were large numbers of wounded in both campaigns, some of whom would be disabled for the rest of their lives.

The military action formally known as the Allied Intervention into Russia has been described by historians and its veterans by many titles—the Forgotten War, the Midnight War, the Secret War, the Unknown War, the Winter War, and the Frozen War—but to the 427 Americans who died there, it was the Last War.

While the casualties were not significant in comparison to other conflicts, they were particularly painful when evaluated with the purpose for which they suffered. The Intervention should have taught future politicians and militarists valuable lessons—lessons that, in light of current events, may not have been learned at all.

As the doughboys stood on the decks watching Vladivostok disappear across the ice-filled harbor, Lieutenant Kindall wrote in his journal:

> We were out of Siberia—at last. We stood upon the deck and across floes of ice watched fade from our sight the same glittering church domes that had first come into our view many weary months before. Among us there was no cheering and little to be said. In the long months past, perhaps something of the dark, brooding Asiatic spirit had crept into our own lives.[4]

Epilogue

General Bogomoletz—Captured by Lieutenant Kendall at Posol-skaya in January 1920, he later fled to Manchuria, then Japan, and came to the United States in the 1930s. Paul Kendall saw him in Hollywood running a shoe-repair shop in 1941. He was then sixty-six.

Maria Botchkareva—Last seen in Archangel in 1919, she was arrested by Soviets in Omsk and was executed there on May 15, 1920. She was posthumously "rehabilitated."

Lawrence Butler—He was evacuated to the United States and treated at Letterman General Hospital for more than a year. He was married to his nurse, Sylvia, in October 1920; one of his fellow Wolf-hounds, who visited him in the hospital, remarked that he looked wonderful after his many surgeries. He was awarded the DSC (U.S.), Military Cross (British), and the Croix de Guerro (Italian). His youngest son, Reed Butler, was killed in World War II.

Robert Eichelberger—He remained in the Army and in World War II became a lieutenant general in General MacArthur's Pacific campaign. He was a significant factor in the Japanese occupation. He was awarded the DSC for Suchan. He retired in 1948, but came back as an advisor during the Korean War and died in 1961.

Rudolf Gaida—He left Siberia after the November revolt and returned to Czechoslovakia to become Army chief of staff, but was demoted in 1926. He led an unsuccessful revolt by Czech fascists in 1933. He formed the Czech Fascist Party, but broke with Hitler and supported the republic against the Nazis. Still seen as a Nazi, he was imprisoned briefly after World War II. He died in 1948, in Czechoslovakia, at age fifty-six.

General William S. Graves—He was haunted by his Siberian assignment and was labeled a Bolshevik sympathizer when he came home. He retired as a major general in 1928, but complained that he was hounded by the FBI as a security risk after that time. He died in New Jersey in 1940.

Sam Johnson—He was decorated by eleven nations, including the United States. He received the DSC for his role as head of International Police in Vladivostok and was wounded during Gaida's revolt. He became a Prohibition officer after the war and retired in 1926.

Ataman Kalmykof—He fled Russia when the Japanese left, going to China where he was captured and shot while trying to escape.

Anton Karachun—He was captured in February 1920 while trying to steal supplies from a Vladivostok warehouse. He was taken to the Philippines, court-martialed, and sentenced to be hanged. His death sentence was commuted, and with ACLU assistance, he was paroled on condition he return to Russia. From Russia he continued to hound the ACLU to help him return to the United States. In Russia he was penniless, unemployed, and miserable. He was last heard from in 1927, living in Vladivostok, trying to emigrate to Canada.

Paul Kendall—He remained in the Army and in World War II became a major general commanding the Eighty-eighth Division.

Kenneth Roberts—He became the editor of the *Saturday Evening Post* and a prolific novelist. His most famous historical novels were *Northwest Passage, Lydia Bailey,* and *Arundel.* Several of his novels were made into movies. His stay in Siberia was brief; he returned home in January 1919.

Ataman Semenov—He survived the revolution and moved to Japan, becoming a Japanese officer in World War II. He was caught by the Russians in 1945 and hanged in 1946.

NOTES

Preface

1. Carol Wilcox Melton, *Between War and Peace: Woodrow Wilson and the American Expeditionary Force in Siberia, 1918–1921* (Macon, Ga.: Mercer University Press, 2001), 94.

Introduction

1. Carol Wilcox Melton, *Between War and Peace: Woodrow Wilson and the American Expeditionary Force in Siberia, 1918–1921* (Macon, Ga.: Mercer University Press, 2001), 211; and David S. Fogelsong, *America's Secret War against Bolshevism* (Chapel Hill, N.C.: The University of North Carolina Press, 1995), 12.

2. *Encyclopedia Britannica, 15th ed., Vol. 19, "World Wars," 957.*

3. *Norman E. Saul, War and Revolution: The United States and Russia, 1914–1921* (Lawrence, Kans.: University of Kansas Press, 2001), 95.

4. Saul, *War,* 98–99.

5. Saul, *War,* 99.

6. B. O. Johnson, "American Railway Engineers in Siberia," *The Military Engineer,* Vol. 15, No. 81 (May–June 1923): 187–192.

7. George F. Kennan, *The Decision to Intervene.* Vol. 2, *Soviet-American Relations, 1917–1920* (Princeton, N.J.: Princeton University Press, 1958), 166–189.

8. Richard Abraham, *Alexander Kerensky: The First Love of the Revolution* (New York: Columbia University Press, 1987), 216.

9. There is a thirteen-day difference between the Western (Gregorian) calendar and the Russian (Julian) calendar in use in Russia until February 1918. Some calendars mark the revolution in October, some thirteen days later in November.

10. Richard Luckett, *The White Generals* (New York: The Viking Press, 1971), 93; and Brian Moynahan, *Claws of the Bear* (Boston: Houghton Mifflin Co., 1989), 32.

11. Saul, *War,* 234–244.

12. Saul, *War,* 237–240.

271

13. Saul, *War,* 302.

14. Rudolf Medek, *The Czechoslovak Anabasis across Russia and Siberia!* (London: The Czech Society, 1929), 9.

15. John Albert White, *The Siberian Intervention* (Princeton, N.J.: Princeton University Press, 1950), 252.

16. Kennan, *Decision,* 152.

17. Kennan, *Decision,* 150.

18. Richard Goldhurst, *The Midnight War: The American Intervention in Russia, 1918–1920* (New York: McGraw-Hill, 1978), 75

19. William S. Graves, *America's Siberian Adventure* (New York: Peter Smith, 1941), 72.

20. John Bradley, *Allied Intervention into Russia, 1917–1920* (London: Weidenfeld and Nicolson, 1968), 104.

21. Gustav Becvar, *The Lost Legion* (London: Stanley Paul & Co., 1939), 195.

22. Becvar, *Legion,* 196.

23. Becvar, *Legion,* 199.

24. National Archives, Washington, D.C., Log of the USS *Brooklyn*, April 4–5, 1918, Naval Records, RG 24.

25. Kennan, *Decision,* 364.

26. Congressional Research Service, Library of Congress, October 7, 1993.

27. Murray Oliver Roe, *American Military Intervention in Russia, 1918–1920* (San Diego: University of San Diego, 1969), 31.

28. Betty Miller Unterberger, *America's Siberian Expedition, 1918–1920: A Study of National Policy* (Durham, N.C.: Duke University Press, 1956), 30.

29. Graves, *America's Siberian Adventure,* 5–10.

Chapter 1

1. George F. Kennan, *The Decision to Intervene.* Vol. 2, *Soviet-American Relations, 1917–1920* (Princeton, N.J.: Princeton University Press, 1958), 22.

2. Today, Murmansk has a population of 450,000 and is the largest city above the Arctic Circle.

3. Kennan, *Decision,* 43.

4. Kennan, *Decision,* 56.

5. Rear Adm. Kemp Tolley, "Our Russian War of 1918–1919," *U.S. Naval Institute Proceedings* (February 1969): 62; and NADC, Telegram, R. A. Murmansk to U.S. Force Commander, May 10, 1918, Naval Records, RG 45.

6. Kennan, *Decision,* 45.

7. Kennan, *Decision,* 46.

8. Christopher Dobson and John Miller, *The Day They Almost Bombed Moscow* (New York: Atheneum, 1986), 39.

9. Maj. Gen. Sir C. Maynard, *The Murmansk Venture* (London: Hodder and Stoughton, 1928), 14.

10. Kennan, *Decision,* 372.

11. Maynard, *Murmansk,* 19.

12. E. M. Halliday, *The Ignorant Armies* (New York: Harper, 1960), 22.

13. Halliday, *Armies,* 22.

14. Leonid I. Strakhovsky, *The Origins of American Intervention in North Russia, 1918* (New York: Howard Fertig, 1972), 67.

15. Kennan, *Decision,* 376; and Dennis Gordon, *Quartered in Hell* (Missoula, Mont.: Doughboy Historical Society, 1982), 7.

16. UMBHL, J. A Ruggles, Chief of American Military Mission to Russia, No. 1366, "Reports Concerning American Morale," February 27, 1919, AEFNR, RG 120.

17. Maynard, *Murmansk,* 117, 120.

18. Maynard, *Murmansk,* 110–111.

Chapter 2

1. Richard Goldhurst, *The Midnight War: The American Intervention in Russia, 1918–1920* (New York: McGraw-Hill, 1978), 86.

2. National Archives, Washington, D.C. (NADC), Cable, Washington from Sims, August 13, 1918, Naval Records, RG 45.

3. NADC, War Diary, USS *Olympia,* Capt. B. B. Bierer, August 1, 1918, Naval Records, RG 45.

4. Goldhurst, *War,* 93.

5. NADC, War Diary, USS *Olympia,* August 1, 1918.

6. National Archives, College Park, Maryland (NACP), War Diary, British HQ Archangel, AEFNR, RG 120.

7. Olga Melikoff Collection, Montreal, Leslie Lawes to Mr. W. A. H. Hulton, July 27, 1918.

8. Olga Melikoff Collection, Montreal, Leslie Lawes to his mother, August 8, 1918.

9. Rear Adm. Kemp Tolley, "Our Russian War of 1918–1919," *U.S. Naval Institute Proceedings* (February 1969): 64.

10. NADC, War Diary, USS *Olympia,* August 10, 1918. Several histories report that Ensign Hicks, immediately upon landing, commandeered a Russian locomotive and led his men on a railroad chase, trailing the retreating Bolsheviks anywhere from thirty to seventy-five miles down the railroad. These histories indicated that they were finally repulsed by the Bolos, returning August 9 with fifty-four prisoners; Goldhurst, *War,* 94; E. M. Halliday, *The Ignorant Armies* (New York: Harper, 1960), 35; George F. Kennan, *The Decision to Intervene.* Vol. 2, *Soviet-American Relations, 1917–1920* (Princeton, N.J.: Princeton University Press, 1958), 425; Joel R. Moore, Harry H. Meade, and Lewis Jahns, *The History of the American Expedition Fighting the Bolsheviki: Campaigning in North Russia* (Detroit: Polar Bear Publishing Co., 1920), 53; and others. These all indicate that Hicks was wounded, which is not correct. Neither Hicks's own report, nor a diary of one of his sailors, nor the log of the *Olympia* makes any mention of this raid; however, it may have taken place.

11. NACP, War Diary, British HQ Archangel.

12. Andrew Soutar, *With Ironside in North Russia* (London: Hutchinson and Co., 1940), 155.

13. The Russian verst equals roughly two thirds of a mile.

14. NADC, Lt. Henry F. Floyd, Weekly Report (quoting Hicks's report), September 7, 1918, Naval Records, RG 45.

15. Christopher Dobson and John Miller, *The Day They Almost Bombed Moscow* (New York: Atheneum, 1986), 66.

16. NADC, Lt. Henry F. Floyd, Weekly Report, September 7, 1918.

17. NADC, Lt. Henry F. Floyd, Weekly Report, September 7, 1918.

18. Dennis Gordon, *Quartered in Hell* (Missoula, Mont.: Doughboy Historical Society, 1982), 55.

19. NADC, Lt. Henry F. Floyd, Weekly Report, September 7, 1918.

20. Gordon, *Quartered,* 55.

21. Gordon, *Quartered,* 56.

22. Except for the quotes by Seaman Gunness, the narrative of the Force B expedition is taken from the official record of Hicks as quoted in Lieutenant Floyd's weekly report. Gunness's version, as set forth in Gordon's *Quartered,* differs slightly on the dates involved.

23. NACP, War Diary, British HQ Archangel.

24. NADC, Lt. Henry F. Floyd, Weekly Report, September 7, 1918.

25. The numerous citations referring to American Marines as participants in various activities of the *Olympia* would seem to be in error, as the roster of the cruiser shows no complement of Marines aboard during the AEFNR campaign.

Chapter 3

1. *Trench and Camp Newspaper,* Battle Creek Enquirer. Willard Library, Battle Creek, Michigan, July 4, 1918.

2. The last draft would include men up to forty-five, but the war ended before any of them were actually inducted.

3. *Trench and Camp Newspaper,* July 4, 1918. The beautiful cemetery across from the present Fort Custer was not opened until World War II; all World War I bodies were shipped to the hometown of the soldier.

4. University of Michigan, Bentley Historical Library (UMBHL), Gordon Smith, Diary.

5. Donald E. Carey, *Fighting the Bolsheviks* (Novato, Calif.: Presidio Press, 1997), 26.

6. UMBHL, Charles Simpson, Diary.

7. Joint Archives, Hope College, Holland, Michigan, James Siplon, Diary.

8. Carey, *Fighting,* 31.

9. UMBHL, Roy Rasmussen, Diary.

10. UMBHL, Douma Collection, Frank Douma, Journal.

11. E. M. Halliday, *The Ignorant Armies* (New York: Harper, 1960), 37.

12. U.S. Military Academy Museum (USMAM), Stewart Papers.

13. Richard Goldhurst, *The Midnight War: The American Intervention in Russia, 1918–1920* (New York: McGraw-Hill, 1978), 96.

14. Carey, *Fighting,* 34.

15. Joint Archives, Hope College, Holland, Michigan, Russell Hershberger, Memoirs.

16. Stanley Bozich and John Bozich, *Detroit's Own Polar Bears* (Frankenmuth, Mich.: Polar Bear Publishing Co., 1985), 21.

17. Bozich and Bozich, *Polar Bears,* 21.

18. Peyton C. March, *The Nation at War* (Garden City, N.J.: Doubleday, Doran and Co., 1932), 139.

19. Dennis Gordon, *Quartered in Hell* (Missoula, Mont.: Doughboy Historical Society, 1982), 47.

20. Gordon, *Quartered,* 48.

Chapter 4

1. Donald E. Carey, *Fighting the Bolsheviks* (Novato, Calif.: Presidio Press, 1997), 38.

2. *Encyclopaedia Brittanica*, 15th ed., s. v. 15, "Diseases of the Respiratory System," 745. *Encyclopedia Britannica* puts the number of deaths at 20 million worldwide and 850,000 in the United States. It names the epidemic as one of the world's worst catastrophes.

3. Dorothea York, *The Romance of Company A* (Detroit: McIntyre Printing Co., 1923), 20.

4. University of Michigan, Bentley Historical Library (UMBHL), Charles Simpson, Diary.

5. Joel R. Moore, Harry H. Meade, and Lewis Jahns, *The History of the American Expedition Fighting the Bolsheviki: Campaigning in North Russia* (Detroit: Polar Bear Publishing Co., 1920), 43.

6. UMBHL, James R. Longley, "Report on the Work of the Medical Department," April 1, 1919, RG 120.

7. The same report shows that in September 1918 a total of 378 cases of flu were admitted to hospitals in the Archangel area; 60 of them died in that month. Also listed were three deaths from pneumonia, which were probably flu-related. The October report showed another 43 cases of flu admitted to the hospital in October, but no deaths.

8. UMBHL, Charles Lewis Papers.

9. A Chronicler (John Cudahy), *Archangel: The American War with Russia* (Chicago: A. C. McClurg and Co., 1924), 78.

10. Dennis Gordon, *Quartered in Hell* (Missoula, Mont.: Doughboy Historical Society, 1982), 64.

11. Moore, Meade, and Jahns, *History,* 299–302.

12. Joint Archives, Hope College, Holland, Michigan, John Oudemuller, Diary.

13. Author's collection, Golden Bahr Papers, Surgeon General's Report on Patient Evacuation, November 26, 1918.

14. U.S. Military Academy Museum (USMAM), George Stewart Papers, Cable, Biddle to Stewart, September 17, 1918.

15. Harry J. Costello, *Why Did We Go to Russia?* (Detroit: Harry J. Costello, 1920), 60.

16. E. M. Halliday, *The Ignorant Armies* (New York: Harper, 1960), 56.

17. Edmund Ironside, *Archangel: 1918–1919* (London: Constable and Co., 1953), 14.

Chapter 5

1. Joel R. Moore, *'M' Company: 339th Infantry in North Russia* (Jackson, Mich.: Central City Book Bindery, 1920), n.p.

2. Joel R. Moore, Harry H. Meade, and Lewis Jahns, *The History of the American Expedition Fighting the Bolsheviki: Campaigning in North Russia* (Detroit: Polar Bear Publishing Co., 1920), 21.

3. Moore, Meade, and Jahns, *History,* 21.

4. U.S. Military Academy Museum (USMAM), George Stewart Papers, "Report of Expedition to the Murman Coast," 2.

5. A verst is a Russian measurement equaling roughly two thirds of a mile.

6. USMAM, Stewart Papers, "Report," 2.

7. Dennis Gordon, *Quartered in Hell* (Missoula, Mont.: Doughboy Historical Society, 1982), 170.

8. E. M. Halliday, *The Ignorant Armies* (New York: Harper, 1960), 62.

9. USMAM, Stewart Papers, "Report," 3.

10. Moore, Meade, and Jahns, *History,* 246.

11. Halliday, *Armies,* 64; and Harry J. Costello, *Why Did We Go to Russia?* (Detroit: Harry J. Costello, 1920), 84.

12. In Major Young's report dated October 12, 1918, after he had been relieved of command, he mentioned, "The half of 'I' Company attacking at Verst 458 was to be accompanied by a trench mortar section, three guns and 19 enlisted men, the trench mortar section had been given a special mission by the O.C. 'A' Force, with which I was not made acquainted."

13. Moore, *'M' Company,* n.p.

14. Gordon, *Quartered,* 176.

15. National Archives, College Park, Maryland (NACP), Lt. Laurence P. Keith, "Report of Engagement," October 1, 1918, AEFNR RG 120.

16. Gordon, *Quartered,* 176.

17. In *'M' Company,* Moore remarks, "But where is the cutting? Have we missed it? Then we are done for! Where is 'I' Company again? Lost? Here, Corp. Grahek, Sgt. Getzloff, you old woodsmen, scout around for that rear party of ours and see if you can spot the cutting."

18. Moore, *'M' Company,* n.p.

19. Moore, Meade, and Jahns, *History,* 26.

20. University of Michigan, Bentley Historical Library (UMBHL), Cleo Coburn, Diary.

21. Michigan's Own Museum, Frankenmuth, Michigan, Godfrey Anderson Manuscript.

22. UMBHL, Godfrey Collection, *Detroit News* clipping, n.d.

23. Moore, *'M' Company,* n.p.

24. Moore, *'M' Company,* n.p.

25. UMBHL, Cleo Coburn, Diary.

26. USMAM, Stewart Papers, "Report," 9.

27. Moore, Meade, and Jahns, *History,* 28.

28. NACP, Capt. Horatio G. Winslow, "Report of Engagement," AEFNR, RG 120.

29. Moore, *'M' Company,* n.p.

30. USMAM, Stewart Papers, "Report," 30.

31. NACP, "Notes from War Diary of British HQ Archangel," November 3, 1918, AEFNR, RG 120.

32. Edmund Ironside, *Archangel: 1918–1919* (London: Constable and Co., 1953), 33–34.

33. NACP, "Notes from War Diary of British HQ Archangel," November 3, 1918, AEFNR, RG 120.

34. Ironside, *Archangel,* 31–32.

35. NACP, "Operation Order" HQ, Vologda Force, December 18, 1918 (translated from French), AEFNR, RG 120.

36. NACP, Capt. E. Prince, "Allied Offensive on Vologda Force Front," January 2, 1919, AEFNR, RG 120.

37. Ironside, *Archangel,* 90.

38. Ironside, *Archangel,* 90.

39. Ironside, *Archangel,* 90.

40. NACP, Capt. E. Prince, "Allied Offensive on Vologda Force Front," January 2, 1919, AEFNR, RG 120.

41. NACP, Capt. E. Prince, "Report on Trip to Vologda Force Front," February 20, 1919, AEFNR, RG 120.

42. NACP, Capt. H. S. Martin, "Report on Mutinies," July 1, 1919, AEFNR, 5, RG 120.

43. NACP, Capt. E. Prince, "Report."

44. Gordon, *Quartered,* 174.

45. Hoover Institution on War, Revolution and Peace (HIWRP), Lt. Forest J. Funk Papers.

46. In *At War with the Bolsheviks* (London: Tom Stacey, Ltd, 1972), Robert Jackson refers to the units as the Green Howards.

47. Ironside, *Archangel,* 112–113. The sergeants were court-martialed, found guilty, and sentenced to be shot. Ironside commuted the sentences to life imprisonment under orders from King George that no British subject be executed after the Armistice, although other records indicate the execution was carried out.

48. Ironside, *Archangel,* 114

49. Gordon, *Quartered,* 177–178; USMAM, George Stewart Papers, "Conduct Company 'I'," June 14, 1919.

50. The "mutiny" made headlines in U.S. newspapers, particularly in Detroit, and led to a congressional investigation.

51. UMBHL, Cleo Coburn, Diary.

52. One of the three was twenty-four-year-old Semeon Timoshenko, who would later be a field marshall and hero of World War II.

53. Gordon, *Quartered,* 296.

54. Gordon, *Quartered,* 296. In *History,* Moore et al. reported that only one American, Private Fulcher, was released, but a French soldier was the other lucky prisoner, and that the Allies gave up only four Bolshevik officers.

55. NACP, Secretary of War to Acting Secretary of State Frank Polk, May 12, 1919, AEFNR, RG 120.

Chapter 6

1. Richard Goldhurst, *The Midnight War: The American Intervention in Russia, 1918–1920* (New York: McGraw-Hill, 1978), 92.

2. National Archives, College Park, Maryland (NACP), Capt. A. G. Martin, "Summary of Principal Military Events in the Archangel District," March 26, 1919, AEFNR, RG 120.

3. Christopher Dobson and John Miller, *The Day They Almost Bombed Moscow* (New York: Atheneum, 1986), 66.

4. University of Michigan, Bentley Historical Library (UMBHL), Edward Flaherty Collection, Richard W. Ballensinger, Company H Field Diary, 2.

5. UMBHL, Roy Rasmussen, Diary.

6. UMBHL, Edward Flaherty Collection, Ballensinger, Field Diary, 1.

7. UMBHL, Edward Flaherty Collection, Ballensinger, Field Diary, 2.

8. U.S. Military Academy Museum (USMAM), George Stewart Papers, "Report of Expedition to the Murman Coast," Stewart Papers, 8.

9. UMBHL, Roy Rasmussen, Diary.

10. UMBHL, Edward Flaherty Collection, Ballensinger, Field Diary, 3.

11. UMBHL, Roy Rasmussen, Diary.

12. UMBHL, Roy Rasmussen, Diary.

13. In his "Report," Col. George Stewart reports one American killed January 1, 1919, but neither Ballensinger's Field Diary, nor the compiled list of American dead shows that death.

14. UMBHL, Edward Flaherty Collection, Ballensinger, Field Diary, 4.

15. UMBHL, Edward Flaherty Collection, Ballensinger, Field Diary, 4; Dennis Gordon, *Quartered in Hell* (Missoula, Mont.: Doughboy Historical Society, 1982), 201.

16. Goldhurst, *War*, 180.

17. NACP, Colonel Thornhill, "G.H.Q. Intelligence Report," February 27, 1919, AEFNR, RG 120.

18. Edmund Ironside, *Archangel: 1918–1919* (London: Constable and Co., 1953), 114.

19. Goldhurst, *War,* 183.

20. Joel R. Moore, "The North Russian Expedition," *Infantry Journal* Vol. 29, No. 1 (July 1926).

21. The unlucky six men, Cpl. Earl Collins, Pvt. Augustus Peterson, Pvt. Earl Fulcher, Pvt. William Scheulke, Pvt. John Frucce, and Pvt. Josef Ramatowski, met a variety of fates. Collins was apparently killed and is buried in Brookwood, England; Peterson died in a Bolshevik hospital, Fulcher and Scheulke were exchanged with a few others through Stockholm on April 25, 1919; Frucce was reported to have died in a Bolshevik hospital, but his body was never found; Ramatowski was killed before the others were captured and his body never recovered. In *History of the American Expedition Fighting the Bolsheviki: Campaigning in North Russia* (Detroit: Polar Bear Publishing Co., 1920), Moore et al. state that Frucce was exchanged through Finland, but gives no reference; however, the *Muskegon (Michigan) Chronicle* on November 11, 1934 reported the twenty-four-year-old Italian killed in action March 22, 1919.

22. NACP, Statement of Earl Fulcher, May 7, 1919, AEFNR, RG 120.

23. UMBHL, Edward Flaherty Collection, Ballensinger, Field Diary, 5.

24. Ironside, *Archangel,* 121. There is some confusion about what happened to Colonel Lucas. Ballensinger's report indicated Lucas suffered a frostbitten

hand, but returned eventually to Chekuevo. Stewart's report indicated Collins retired to Chenova, assuming Lucas was still with them. However, both E. M. Halliday's *The Ignorant Armies* (New York: Harper, 1960) and Goldhurst's *War* indicate that Lucas was separated from the patrol and wandered all night, finally being picked up with badly frostbitten hands by a later patrol.

25. UMBHL, Edward Flaherty Collection, Lt. Col. W. Morrison, "Operation Order #1," April 1, 1919, Company H Field Diary. A report from Captain Ballensinger, commanding Company H, however, said Lieutenant Collins was in command of the Americans in that attack.

26. USMAM, Stewart Papers, "Report," 52.

27. UMBHL, Edward Flaherty Collection, Ballensinger, Field Diary, 5.

28. UMBHL, Edward Flaherty Collection, Ballensinger, Field Diary, 5.

29. UMBHL, Edward Flaherty Collection, Ballensinger, Field Diary, 6; USMAM, Stewart Papers, "Report," 50.

30. USMAM, Stewart Papers, "Report," 49.

31. Donald E. Carey, *Fighting the Bolsheviks* (Novato, Calif.: Presidio Press, 1997), 148,

32. Carey, *Fighting,* 150.

33. Carey, *Fighting,* 152.

34. NACP, Report of 2d Lt. Howard Pellegrom, March 26, 1919, AEFNR, RG 120; and UMBHL, Roy Rasmussen, Diary.

35. Joel R. Moore, *'M' Company: 339th Infantry in North Russia* (Jackson, Mich.: Central City Book Bindery, 1920), n.p.

36. Sergeant Leitzel, Hogan, and Laursen were released to go to Finland after a trip to Moscow.

37. Moore, *'M' Company,* n.p. Ryal was released at the same time as Leitzel, Hogan, and Laursen.

38. UMBHL, Edward Flaherty Collection, Ballensinger, Field Diary, 8.

39. Moore, Meade, and Jahns, *History,* 299–302.

40. There are a number of references to the use of gas, particularly from airplanes, but it seemed to play no significant role in the North Russian campaign

41. UMBHL, Roy Rasmussen, Diary.

Chapter 7

1. Joel R. Moore, Harry H. Meade, and Lewis Jahns, *The History of the American Expedition Fighting the Bolsheviki: Campaigning in North Russia* (Detroit: Polar Bear Publishing Co., 1920), 55, reports that only half of Company K went to Seletskoye on *droskies,* pony-driven carts.

2. U.S. Military Academy Museum (USMAM), George Stewart Papers, "Report of Expedition to the Murman Coast," 2.

3. National Archives, Washington, D.C. (NADC), Lt. Henry F. Floyd, Weekly Report, September 7, 1918, Naval Records, RG 45.

4. U.S. Army Military History Institute (USAMHI), Harold Weimeister, World War I Survey.

5. USMAM, Stewart Papers, "Report," 3.

6. The battle had exhausted both sides, and one report indicated that the Bolsheviks assassinated their commander in order to break off the fight; Rich-

ard Goldhurst, *The Midnight War: The American Intervention in Russia, 1918–1920* (New York: McGraw-Hill, 1978), 103.

7. USMAM, Stewart Papers, "Report," 3.

8. Goldhurst, *War,* 103.

9. Henderson was reportedly relieved because he refused to send the Americans across the river (Ryan diary). USMAM, Stewart Papers, "Report," 5.

10. University of Michigan, Bentley Historical Library (UMBHL) Charles Brady Ryan, Diary.

11. Michigan's Own Museum, Frankenmuth, Michigan, Roster of K, Percy Walker Papers. Walker was evacuated to the Seletskoye Medical Station, then sent to the Archangel Hospital.

12. Dennis Gordon, *Quartered in Hell* (Missoula, Mont.: Doughboy Historical Society, 1982), 318–319; USMAM, Stewart Papers, "Report," 6.

13. USMAM, Stewart Papers, "Report," 10.

14. USMAM, Stewart Papers, "Report," 10.

15. UMBHL, Charles Brady Ryan, Diary, October 13, 1918.

16. Joint Archives, Hope College, Holland, Michigan, Gerrit Knoll Papers, Journal.

17. UMBHL, Charles Brady Ryan, Diary, October 18, 1918.

18. Moore, Meade, and Jahns, *History,* 59; USMAM, Stewart Papers, "Report," 17.

19. USMAM, Stewart Papers, "Report," 17.

20. USMAM, Stewart Papers, "Report," 17.

21. Moore, Meade, and Jahns, *History,* 61.

22. USMAM, Stewart Papers, "Report," 19.

23. USMAM, Stewart Papers, "Report," 19.

24. Donald E. Carey, *Fighting the Bolsheviks* (Novato, Calif.: Presidio Press, 1997), 80.

25. UMBHL, George Albers Papers, Fred Krooyer, Diary, 6.

26. UMBHL, George Albers Papers, Fred Krooyer, Diary, 6.

27. USMAM, Stewart Papers, "Report," 22, 24, 26, 27.

28. UMBHL, George Albers Papers, Fred Krooyer, Diary.

29. Carey, *Fighting,* 103.

30. Carey, *Fighting,* 84.

31. Leon Trotsky was a former journalist whose real name was Lev Davidovich Bronstein. Trotsky was reported to be commanding Red forces at that time, and it is possible that he was the journalist mentioned.

32. NACP, M. J. Donoghue, "Report of Engagement on December 30–31, 1918," 2, AEFNR, RG 120. On November 3, Pvt. George Albers of Company I was captured while he was on a remote observation post. His saga finally ended when he was released, in good condition, in Stockholm on April 25, 1919.

33. George Stewart's papers list these elements of the Right Wing; however, they fail to mention the presence of Company E.

34. Just when Donoghue became a major is not certain. Stewart refers to him as a captain on December 27 and as major on January 2. Donoghue's engagement report of December 30–31 is signed as a major.

35. NACP, M. J. Donoghue, "Report," 4–5, AEFNR, RG 120.

36. National Archives, College Park, Maryland (NACP), 1st Lt. John Baker, "Report of Engagement," March 5, 1919, AEFNR, RG 120.

37. There is some confusion about casualties; Stewart's papers indicate seven killed in the two days. Three honor rolls listing individuals killed in action show nine killed: Sgt. Floyd Austin, Pvt. Frank Mueller, and Pvt. Harold Wagner of Company E, killed on December 30; Sgt. Bernard Crowe, Sgt. Michael Kenney, and Pfc. Alfred Fuller, all of Company K killed on December 30; Lt. Carl Berger, Pvt. Walter Franklin, and Pvt. James J. Mylon, all of Company E, died of wounds on December 31.

38. Manistee Historical Museum, Manistee, Michigan, *Manistee News Advocate*, June 2, 1919.

39. NACP, M. J. Donoghue, "Report," 5.

40. Gordon, *Quartered*, 194.

41. Harry J. Costello, *Why Did We Go to Russia?* (Detroit: Harry J. Costello, 1920), 108.

42. It is not known if this was told about Haselden or one of the many other British commanders of that front.

43. NACP, M. J. Donoghue, "Report," 7, AEFNR, RG 120.

44. NACP, M. J. Donoghue, "Report," 8, AEFNR, RG 120.

45. Edmund Ironside, *Archangel: 1918–1919* (London: Constable and Co., 1953), 91.

46. UMBHL, George Albers Papers, Fred Krooyer, Diary.

47. NACP, British Headquarters War Diary, 7, AEFNR, RG 120.

48. USMAM, Stewart Papers, "Report," 33.

49. Carey, *Fighting*, 120–121.

50. UMBHL, Charles Brady Ryan, Diary.

51. Moore, Meade, and Jahns, *History*, 132.

52. Moore, Meade, and Jahns, *History*, 132.

53. Moore, Meade, and Jahns, *History*, 133.

54. USMAM, Stewart Papers, "Report," 45.

Chapter 8

1. Edmund Ironside, *Archangel: 1918–1919* (London: Constable and Co., 1953), 203.

2. Benjamin D. Rhodes, *The Anglo-American Winter War with Russia: 1918–1919* (New York: Greenwood Press, 1988), 39–40.

3. University of Michigan, Bentley Historical Library (UMBHL), Sgt. Silver Parrish, Diary.

4. Michigan's Own Museum, Frankenmuth, Michigan, Sgt. Robert Roy, Diary.

5. UMBHL, Edwin Arkins, Journal, 3.

6. UMBHL, Sgt. Silver Parrish, Diary.

7. UMBHL, Pvt. Joseph Noonan, Diary.

8. Joel R. Moore, Harry H. Meade, and Lewis Jahns, *The History of the American Expedition Fighting the Bolsheviki: Campaigning in North Russia* (Detroit: Polar Bear Publishing Co., 1920), 33–34.

9. National Archives, College Park, Maryland (NACP), Chief Surgeon's Correspondence, "Deaths, AEFNR," AEFNR, RG 120.

10. Lieutenant Smith was awarded the Distinguished Service Cross for the Seltso action.

11. Dennis Gordon, *Quartered in Hell* (Missoula, Mont.: Doughboy Historical Society, 1982), 219.

12. UMBHL, Edwin Arkins, Journal.

13. UMBHL, Sgt. Silver Parrish, Diary.

14. In two of the best books on the AEFNR, E. M. Halliday, *The Ignorant Armies* (New York: Harper, 1960) and Richard Goldhurst, *The Midnight War: The American Intervention in Russia, 1918–1920* (New York: McGraw-Hill, 1978), there are references to Company B attacking Puchuga, suffering casualties, and having to withdraw to Seltso. Both also mention Captain Boyd's adventure with his Company B returning to Seltso; however, Stewart's official report makes no mention of any fighting near Puchuga or of any casualties. Diaries of Company B soldiers (Parrish and Davis) also make no reference to a fight, and Boyd, quoted extensively in *History,* Moore et al. describe the march to Puchuga in detail, but makes no comment about fighting.

15. Moore, Meade, and Jahns, *History,* 34–35.

16. U.S. Militay Academy Museum (USMAM), George Stewart Papers, "Report of Expedition to the Murman Coast," 7.

17. USMAM, Stewart Papers, "Report," 9–10.

18. Michigan's Own Museum, Frankenmuth, Michigan, Lt. Ray McCurdy, Diary.

19. Michigan's Own Museum, Frankenmuth, Michigan, Thomas Hancock, Diary.

20. Moore et al.'s *History* sets forth the names, units, dates of death, and other information about AEFNR casualties. He lists Connor as another victim of the drowning incident, apparently in error.

21. Moore, Meade, and Jahns, *History,* 299–301.

22. Robert Jackson, *At War with the Bolsheviks* (London: Tom Stacey, 1972), 76.

23. UMBHL, Sgt. Silver Parrish, Diary.

24. UMBHL, Sgt. Silver Parrish, Diary.

25. According to a captured communist captain, the Bolos had sixteen hundred men on both sides of the river, and six-inch howitzers and six-inch naval guns on rafts in the river. "Does not see any reason why the Americans retreated from Seltzo." (AEFNR, RG 120)

26. Wisconsin State Library (WSL), John Hall, Diary, Wisconsin manuscripts.

27. WSL, John Hall, Diary, Wisconsin manuscripts.

28. USMAM, Stewart Papers, "Report," 9.

29. Lieutenant Cudahy was from a very wealthy meat-packing family in Wisconsin.

30. UMBHL, Sgt. Silver Parrish, Diary.

31. USMAM, Stewart Papers, "Report," 34.

32. A Chronicler (John Cudahy), *Archangel: The American War with Russia* (Chicago: A. C. McClurg and Co., 1924), 145.

33. Moore, Meade, and Jahns, *History,* 106–107.

34. Gordon, *Quartered,* 245.

35. Moore, Meade, and Jahns, *History,* 107.

36. Karan was visiting with his family in Europe when war broke out. He tried to enlist with the Czechs. Too young, he was finally hired by the British in the Balkans, but was sent to his home in New York. He then went to Canada, enlisted in 1917, was sent to England, then to Murmansk, and finally to Archangel, where he joined the 339th Infantry, Company B. He stayed in Russia until the British left in July 1919.

37. Gordon, *Quartered,* 247–248.

38. UMBHL, Gen. R. G. Finlayson, "Toulgas Engagement," November 11–14, 1918, AEFNR, RG 120.

39. Gordon, *Quartered,* 249.

40. Moore, Meade, and Jahns, *History,* 21.

41. Ironside, *Archangel,* 54.

42. Goldhurst, *War,* 137.

43. UMBHL, Sgt. Silver Parrish, Diary.

44. UMBHL, Gen. R. G. Finlayson, "Toulgas Engagement," November 11–14, 1918, AEFNR, RG 120.

45. UMBHL, Finlayson, "Toulgas."

46. Prince was the last prisoner released by the Soviets on August 16, 1920.

47. NACP, Albert M. Smith, "Report of Engagement, B Company," March 12, 1919, AEFNR, RG 120.

48. NACP, Erastus Corning, "Investigation of Complaint," June 9, 1919, AEFNR, RG 120.

49. A more stinging indictment was filed by a naval aid investigating the American fronts. "When he arrived at the America hospital in Bereznik [from the British hospital] he had a bed sore in his back two inches deep and six inches long exposing five inches of the spinal column with the nerves. This sore the British Medical Authorities did not know he had . . . . I myself saw this man and it is impossible to believe that his condition could have come from anything but gross neglect" (NADC, Oliver E. Cobb to Admiral McCully, Naval Records, RG 45).

50. Gordon, *Quartered,* 216.

51. UMBHL, Sgt. Silver Parrish, Diary. Company B was ordered across the river to Turgomin on March 20 and replaced by Company C on April 6.

52. NACP, Capt. E. Prince, "Report on Morale of American Troops on Dvina Front," February 2, 1919, 1, AEFNR, RG 120.

53. Moore, Meade, and Jahns, *History,* 112.

Chapter 9

1. U.S. Military Academy Museum (USMAM), George Stewart Papers, "Report of Expedition to the Murman Coast," 6.

2. Dennis Gordon, *Quartered in Hell* (Missoula, Mont.: Doughboy Historical Society, 1982), 222.

3. University of Michigan, Bentley Historical Library (UMBHL), John Sherman Crissman, Diary, 4; and USMAM, Stewart Papers, "Report," 10.

4. Joel R. Moore, Harry H. Meade, and Lewis Jahns, *The History of the American Expedition Fighting the Bolsheviki: Campaigning in North Russia* (Detroit: Polar Bear Publishing Co., 1920), 64.

5. UMBHL, John Sherman Crissman, Diary.

6. Wisconsin State Library (WSL), Glenn Weeks, Diary.

7. Roy MacLaren, *Canadians in Russia* (Toronto: MacMillan of Canada, 1976), 74.

8. WSL, Glenn Weeks, Diary.

9. Michigan's Own Museum, Frankenmuth, Michigan, Robert Ray, Diary.

10. UMBHL, Edward Brock, Diary.

11. WSL, Glenn Weeks, Diary. Records indicated that six bodies were recovered.

12. In *The Ignorant Armies* (New York: Harper, 1960), E. M. Halliday notes that Cuff's mutilation was the only atrocity documented; however Cpl. G. J. Anderson in Gordon's *Quartered* notes several incidents he witnessed where bodies had had heads "bashed in" and forearms severed.

13. Halliday, *Armies*, 151.

14. WSL, Glenn Weeks, Diary.

15. Gordon, *Quartered*, 105.

16. Halliday, *Armies*, 159.

17. NACP, Chief Surgeon's Correspondence, AEFNR, RG 120.

18. Stier was posthumously presented the Distinguished Service Cross.

19. Dorothea York, *The Romance of Company A* (Detroit: McIntyre Printing Co., 1923), 80.

20. York, *Romance*, 83.

21. UMBHL, Edward Trombley, Diary.

22. MacLaren, *Canadians*, 78.

23. York, *Romance*, 85.

24. UMBHL, John Sherman Crissman, Diary.

25. Moore, Meade, and Jahns, *History*, 138.

26. Gordon, *Quartered*, 112.

27. UMBHL, John Sherman Crissman, Diary. The dates are somewhat confusing, but the GHQ War Diary shows the sequence of "Leave Ust Padenga night of the 22, arrive at Shalosha at 10 P.M. for rest, go to Spasskoye on the 23d, withdraw to Shenkursk on Jan 24, evacuate Shenkursk beginning 1:30 A.M. Jan 25."

28. York, *Romance*, 89.

29. MacLaren, *Canadians*, 78

30. Gordon, *Quartered*, 115.

31. Halliday, *Armies*, 132–133.

32. Grand Rapids Public Library, Grand Rapids, Michigan, Godfrey Johnson Memoir, Godfrey Johnson Collection.

33. Vanis was released in Sweden on April 25, 1919.

34. National Archives, College Park, Maryland (NACP), Lt. Harry Steele, "Attack on Shagovari," War Diary GHQ, May 2, 1919, AEFNR, RG 120.

35. Grand Rapids Public Library, Grand Rapids, Michigan, Godfrey Johnson Collection, Godfrey Johnson Memoir.

36. Gordon, *Quartered,* 143.

37. Grand Rapids Public Library, Godfrey Johnson Collection, Godfrey Johnson Memoir.

38. Grand Rapids Public Library, Godfrey Johnson Collection, Godfrey Johnson Memoir.

39. Gordon, *Quartered,* 144.

40. USMAM, Stewart Papers, "Report," 45.

41. Moore, Meade, and Jahns, *History,* 147–148.

Chapter 10

1. Joel R. Moore, Harry H. Meade, and Lewis Jahns, *The History of the American Expedition Fighting the Bolsheviki: Campaigning in North Russia* (Detroit: Polar Bear Publishing Co., 1920), 85.

2. Dennis Gordon, *Quartered in Hell* (Missoula, Mont.: Doughboy Historical Society, 1982), 264.

3. Gordon, *Quartered,* 264–265.

4. National Archives, College Park, Maryland (NACP), "Report of December 7 on Pinega Situation" to O.C. L. of C. by illegible lieutenant colonel, AEFNR, RG 120.

5. U.S. Military Academy Museum (USMAM), George Stewart Papers, "Report of Expedition to the Murman Coast," 25.

6. Gordon, *Quartered,* 268.

7. Gordon, *Quartered,* 294.

8. USMAM, Stewart Papers, "Report," 25.

9. Gordon, *Quartered,* 270.

10. NACP, "Report of December 7 on Pinega Situation" to O.C. L. of C. by illegible lieutenant colonel, AEFNR, RG 120.

11. Joel R. Moore, *'M' Company: 339th Infantry in North Russia* (Jackson, Mich.: Central City Book Bindery, 1920), n.p.

12. Moore, *'M' Company,* n.p.

13. Moore, *'M' Company,* n.p.

14. Moore, *'M' Company,* n.p.

15. USMAM, Stewart Papers, "Report," 35.

16. USMAM, Stewart Papers, "Report," 40.

17. Gordon, *Quartered,* 271.

18. Gordon, *Quartered,* 272.

19. Gordon, *Quartered,* 272.

20. Gordon, *Quartered,* 266.

21. Gordon, *Quartered,* 271.

22. Moore, Meade, and Jahns, *History,* 154.

23. Moore, Meade, and Jahns, *History,* 117.

24. USMAM, Stewart Papers, "Report," 41.

25. USMAM, Stewart Papers, "Report," 46.

26. Gordon, *Quartered,* 277.

27. E. M. Halliday, *The Ignorant Armies* (New York: Harper, 1960), 216–217;

Detroit Free Press, November 17, 1929. Macalla would return again to Archangel in 1929 to assist in recovering bodies of the Americans left behind in the Allied retreat and departure in 1919.

28. NACP, *Disposition of U.S. Troops in North Russia*, April 17, 1919, AEFNR, RG 120.

29. Gordon, *Quartered,* 280.

30. Gordon, *Quartered,* 280–281.

Chapter 11

1. Eugenie Fraser, *The House by the Dvina* (New York: Walker and Co., 1984), 207.

2. Fraser, *House,* 215.

3. National Archives, Washington, D.C. (NADC), Telegram, Cole [Felix, U.S. Consul] to State Department, August 12, 1918, Naval Records, RG 45.

4. Fraser, *House,* 215. There were, however, no American ships in the fleet, only American naval personnel.

5. E. M. Halliday, *The Ignorant Armies* (New York: Harper, 1960), 50.

6. Willard Library, Battle Creek, Michigan, *American Sentinel Newspaper*, Archangel, April 12, 1919.

7. National Archives, College Park, Maryland (NACP), Telegram, Secretary of State Lansing to Ambassador Morris in Japan, September 26, 1918 (copy to Francis), Naval Records, RG 45.

8. George F. Kennan, *The Decision to Intervene.* Vol. 2, *Soviet-American Relations, 1917–1920* (Princeton, N.J.: Princeton University Press, 1958), 427.

9. NACP, Cablegram, Biddle to Stewart, September 17, 1918, AEFNR, RG 120.

10. U.S. Army Military History Institute (USAMHI), Carl Russell Collection, WWI Survey, Supplemental Report, AEF, to the Adjutant General of the Army, July 23, 1919, 2.

11. USAMHI, Carl Russell Collection, WWI Survey, Supplemental Report, AEF, to the Adjutant General of the Army, July 23, 1919, 2.

12. USAMHI, Carl Russell Collection, WWI Survey, Supplemental Report, July 23, 1919, 2.

13. NACP, undated memo, Brig. Gen. H. Needham to Stewart, AEFNR, RG 120.

14. University of Michigan, Bentley Historical Library (UMBHL), Charles Brady Ryan to his wife, February 15, 1919.

15. Joel R. Moore, Harry H. Meade, and Lewis Jahns, *The History of the American Expedition Fighting the Bolsheviki: Campaigning in North Russia* (Detroit: Polar Bear Publishing Co., 1920), 40.

16. Moore, Meade, and Jahns, *History,* 41.

17. Fraser, *House,* 220.

18. Fraser, *House,* 220.

19. Joint Archives, Hope College, Holland, Michigan, Charles Grace Papers.

20. Dorothea York, *The Romance of Company A* (Detroit: McIntyre Printing Co., 1923), 41.

21. Fraser, *House,* 227.

22. UMBHL, George Albers Papers, Fred Krooyer, Diary.

23. Donald E. Carey, *Fighting the Bolsheviks* (Novato, Calif.: Presidio Press, 1997), 46.

24. NACP, "Report of the Work Accomplished by the Medical Department," 5, AEFNR, RG 120.

25. USAMHI, Carl Russell Collection, WWI Survey, Supplemental Report, AEF, to the Adjutant General of the Army, July 23, 1919, 3.

26. Harry J. Costello, *Why Did We Go to Russia?* (Detroit: Harry J. Costello, 1920), 67.

27. NACP, General Court-martial No. 2, Headquarters U.S. Troops (Murmansk Expedition) AEFNR, RG 120.

28. Dennis Gordon, *Quartered in Hell* (Missoula, Mont.: Doughboy Historical Society, 1982), 169–171.

29. NACP, General Court-martial No. 1, Headquarters U.S. Troops (Murmansk Expedition) AEFNR, RG 120.

30. Carey, *Fighting,* 62.

31. UMBHL, Paul Totten Memoirs.

32. Fred L. Borch, III, "Bolsheviks, Polar Bears and Military Law," *Prologue: Quarterly of the National Archives and Records Administration,* Vol. 30, No. 3 (Fall 1998): 183–184.

33. NACP, Lt. Col. Edmund S. Thurston, "Memorandum As to Cases of Self Inflicted Wounds," Headquarters, American Expeditionary Forces, May 10, 1919, AEFNR, RG 120.

34. NACP, Lt. Col. Edmund S. Thurston, "Memorandum As to Cases of Self Inflicted Wounds," Headquarters, American Expeditionary Forces, May 10, 1919, AEFNR, RG 120; and various court-martial records, same source.

35. NACP, Chief Surgeon's Correspondence, AEFNR, RG 120.

36. UMBHL, Henry Katz Collection, "Short Summary of Activities of Medical Personnel with First Battalion 339th Infantry," 3, RG 120.

37. UMBHL, G. T. James, Diary.

38. Moore, Meade, and Jahns, *History,* 178.

39. Edmund Ironside, *Archangel: 1918–1919* (London: Constable and Co., 1953), 77–78.

40. While there was no direct evidence that Poole was in on the coup, most felt that he was undoubtedly aware of its planning. Ironside wrote, "There was, of course, no truth in such a stupid accusation" (*Archangel,* 21).

41. Due to the strange methods of British promotions, Ironside was a major in the Gunners, a lieutenant colonel by brevet, and a temporary brigadier general. Ironside cites a classic case of rank increase: "Lieutenant (Temporary Brigadier General) E. A. Bradford, V.C. to be brevet major on reaching the rank of captain." Unfortunately, before Bradford became a regular captain, he was killed in action.

42. Richard Goldhurst, *The Midnight War: The American Intervention in Russia, 1918–1920* (New York: McGraw-Hill, 1978) 94.

43. Joseph V. Taylor, "Report of Engagement," AEFNR, RG 120.

44. Moore, Meade, and Jahns, *History,* 178.

45. Ironside, *Archangel,* 69–70.

46. Ironside, *Archangel,* 70.

47. NADC, General Intelligence Report #5, April 13–July 9, 1919, Naval Records, RG 45.

48. Costello, *Why,* 116.

49. Gordon, *Quartered,* 6–7.

50. NADC, Cablegram, Francis to Navy Department, September 13, 1918, Naval Records, RG 45.

51. Interestingly, McCulley's orders from the Navy Department addressed him as captain, not rear admiral.

52. Wilds Richardson, *Notes on the War and on the North Russian Expedition,* AEFNR, RG 120, n.d., 38–39.

53. U.S. Military Academy Museum (USMAM), George Stewart Papers, Cable, Stewart to Adjutant General, November 14, 1918.

54. Michael Kettle, *Churchill and the Archangel Fiasco: November 1918–July 1919* (London: Routledge, 1992), 269.

55. Fraser, *House,* 221.

56. NACP, "Memo to Base Commandant," February 14, 1919, AEFNR, RG 120.

57. UMBHL, *The American Sentinel Newspaper,* February 15, 1919.

58. Fraser, *House,* 263. In a review of all officers in the 339th Infantry, there is no officer with the first name of Frank.

59. Fraser, *House,* 224.

60. NACP, Office of the Chief Surgeon, Report, April 9, 1919, AEFNR, RG 120.

61. NACP, GHQ, "Memo to Stewart," September 25, 1918, AEFNR, RG 120.

62. UMBHL, John Sherman Crissman, Diary.

63. Willard Memorial Library, Battle Creek, Michigan, *American Sentinel Newspaper,* February 15, 1919.

64. NACP, Robert C. Johnson to his father, October 21, 1918, AEFNR, RG 120.

65. Historical Museum, Manistee, Michigan, Red Cross Records, Golden Bahr.

66. UMBHL, George Albers Papers, Fred Krooyer, Diary.

67. Ralph Albertson, *Fighting without a War* (New York: Harcourt Brace and Howe, 1920), 71.

Chapter 12

1. Peyton C. March, *The Nation at War* (Garden City, N.J.: Doubleday, Doran and Co., 1932), 148.

2. March, *Nation,* 149.

3. John E. Wilson, "When Murmansk Went Yank," *American Legion Magazine* (February 1940): 12. While such a request might have been radioed, there is no mention of it in the discussions, nor is such a cable found in the files of the 339th.

4. Richard Goldhurst, *The Midnight War: The American Intervention in Russia, 1918–1920* (New York: McGraw-Hill, 1978), 171.

5. U.S. Army Military History Institute (USAMHI), Albert Galen Papers, Brian Clark, *Russia, 1919,* February 15, 1980.

6. USAMHI, E. E. MacMorland, "American Railroading in North Russia," *The Military Engineer* (September–October, 1929): 417. MacMorland would obtain the rank of major general before he retired in 1953.

7. Wilson, "Yank," 44.

8. MacMorland, "Railroading," 419.

9. USAMHI, Edward MacMorland Papers, undated letter.

10. USAMHI, AEFNR, U.S. Army, Harold Weimeister Collection, "Battles and Engagements," 380–384.

11. USAMHI, Edward MacMorland Papers, Edward MacMorland, letter, March 6, 1919.

12. University of Michigan, Bentley Historical Library (UMBHL), John Wilson, *Arctic Antics* (Salina, Kans.: Padgett's Printing House, 1919), n.p.

13. NADC, Navy Logs of the *Chester* and *Galveston,* RG 24.

14. Goldhurst, *War,* 192; Wilson, *Antics,* n.p.

15. Wilson, *Antics,* n.p.

16. Wilson, *Antics,* n.p.

17. USAMHI, Edward MacMorland Papers, Edward MacMorland, letter to his wife, May 18, 1919.

18. Wilson, *Antics,* n.p. In 1919, the bodies of the three railroad men killed in North Russia were returned to the United States with the bodies of the dead of the 339th.

19. Wilson, *Antics,* n.p.

20. Wilson, "Yank," 46.

21. Dennis Gordon, *Quartered in Hell* (Missoula, Mont.: Doughboy Historical Society, 1982), 287.

22. MacMorland, "Railroading," 426.

23. MacMorland, "Railroading," 426.

Chapter 13

1. University of Michigan, Bentley Historical Library (UMBHL), Roger Crownover, "Stranded in Russia," *Michigan History* (January–February 1999): 40.

2. David S. Fogelsong, *America's Secret War against Bolshevism* (Chapel Hill, N.C.: University of North Carolina Press, 1995), 228.

3. Edmund Ironside, *Archangel: 1918–1919* (London: Constable and Co., 1953), 123–125.

4. Robert Jackson, *At War with the Bolsheviks* (London: Tom Stacey, 1972), 172.

5. Jackson, *At War,* 151–152; National Archives, Washington, D.C. (NADC), "Re-Enforcements and Withdrawals," Naval Records, RG 45.

6. One of the tanks still remains in Archangel, sitting on the sidewalk of a main street outside a group of small shops.

7. Donald E. Carey, *Fighting the Bolsheviks* (Novato, Calif.: Presidio Press, 1997), 194.

8. Carey, *Fighting,* 198.

9. Carey, *Fighting,* 201.

10. Ironside, *Archangel,* 150.

11. Dennis Gordon, *Quartered in Hell* (Missoula, Mont.: Doughboy Historical Society, 1982), 225.

12. UMBHL, Edwin Arkins, Journal.

13. Joel R. Moore, Harry H. Meade, and Lewis Jahns, *The History of the American Expedition: Fighting the Bolsheviki* (Detroit: Doughboy Publishing Co., 1920), 296.

14. E. M. Halliday, *The Ignorant Armies* (New York: Harper, 1960), 244.

15. Ironside, *Archangel,* 168.

16. Ironside, *Archangel,* 169.

17. Ironside, *Archangel,* 176–177.

18. Ironside, *Archangel,* 186–187.

19. Vladislav Goldin, "The Russian Revolution and the North," *International Politics* (December 1996).

20. Eugenie Fraser, *The House by the Dvina* (New York: Walker and Co., 1984), 232.

21. Map of North Russia, Murmansk City Museum, Murmansk, Russia.

22. Fraser, *House,* 272.

23. George Kennan, *Russia and the West under Lenin and Stalin* (Boston: Little, Brown and Co., 1960), 90.

24. Ralph Albertson, *Fighting without a War* (New York: Harcourt Brace and Howe, 1920), 74.

25. Carey, *Fighting,* 223.

26. Stanley Bozich and John Bozich, *Detroit's Own Polar Bears* (Frankenmuth, Mich.: Polar Bear Publishing Co., 1985), 106–145.

27. UMBHL, Henry Katz Collection, "Short Summary of Activities of Medical Personnel with First Battalion 339th Infantry," RG 120.

28. UMBHL, James B. Sibley Collection, *Grand Rapids Press*, undated.

29. American Monuments Battlefield Commission, Washington, D.C.

30. Herbert M. Mason, Jr. "Mission to North Russia," *VFW Magazine* (April 1999): 12–16.

31. UMBHL, Hugo Salchow Collection.

32. Moore, Meade, and Jahns, *History,* 134.

Chapter 15

1. Christopher Dobson and John Miller, *The Day They Almost Bombed Moscow* (New York: Atheneum, 1986), 69.

2. Wisconsin Historical Society (WHS), Joe Michael Feist, ed., "Railways and Politics: The Russian Diary of George Gibbs, 1917," *Wisconsin Magazine of History*, Vol. 62, No. 3 (Spring 1979): 196.

3. Richard Goldhurst, *The Midnight War: The American Intervention in Russia, 1918–1920* (New York, McGraw-Hill, 1978), 88.

4. Edith Faulstich, *Siberian Sojourn* (Yonkers, N.Y.: Edith Faulstich, 1972) 47.

5. John White, *The Siberian Intervention* (Princeton, N.J.: Princeton University Press, 1950), 147.

6. Hoover Institution on War, Revolution and Peace (HIWRP), Brunner Papers.

7. Faulstich, *Sojourn*, 55.

8. Faulstich, *Sojourn*, 61.

9. Faulstich, *Sojourn*, 66.

10. WHS, Joe Michael Feist, ed., "A Wisconsin Man in the Russian Railway Service Corps: Letters of Fayette W. Keeler, 1918–1919," *Wisconsin Magazine of History*, Vol. 62, No. 3 (Spring 1979): 221.

11. WHS, "Wisconsin Man," 221.

12. WHS, "Wisconsin Man," 228.

13. Faulstich, *Sojourn*, 90–92.

14. William S. Graves, *America's Siberian Adventure* (New York: Peter Smith, 1941), 50.

15. Faulstich, *Sojourn*, 109.

16. Faulstich, *Sojourn*, 110.

17. Graves, *Adventure*, 52–53.

18. WHS, "Wisconsin Man," 229.

19. WIIS, "Wisconsin Man," 243.

20. After the war, and as late as 1972, efforts were made to include these men as veterans with the rights afforded other WWI veterans; however, as their numbers dwindled with death, less effort was made. In 1971 there were only 30 of the 300 still living. Finally, in 1973, a U.S. Court of Appeals ruled in favor of the surviving RRSC veterans.

Chapter 16

1. U.S. Army Military History Institute (USAMHI), Joseph B. Longuevan Papers, David R. Opperman, "Army Transports and Navy Warships Participating in the Siberian Intervention," January 5, 1984.

2. National Archives, Washington, D.C. (NADC), Log of the USS *Brooklyn*, April 5, 1918, Naval Records, RG 24.

3. NADC, Log of the USS *Brooklyn*, May 30, 1918, Naval Records, RG 24.

4. NADC, Log of the USS *Brooklyn*, June 29, 1918, Naval Records, RG 24.

5. NADC, Log of the USS *Brooklyn*, June 29, 1918, Naval Records, RG 24.

6. NADC, Log of the USS *Brooklyn*, June 29, 1918, Naval Records, RG 24.

7. NADC, Cablegram, Flag, Vladivostok to Secnav, Washington, July 3, 1919, RG 45.

8. NADC, Log of the USS *Brooklyn*. July 2–26, 1918, Naval Records, RG 24.

9. NADC, Cablegram, Flag, Vladivostok to Secnav, Washington, July 15, 1918, Naval Records, RG 45.

10. NADC, Log of the USS *Brooklyn*, July 6, 1918, Naval Records, RG 24.

Chapter 17

1. Richard Goldhurst, *The Midnight War: The American Intervention in Russia, 1918–1920* (New York: McGraw-Hill, 1978), 77.

2. William S. Graves, *America's Siberian Adventure* (New York: Peter Smith, 1941), 2.

3. Graves, *Adventure,* 4

4. Graves, *Adventure,* 8.

5. National Archives, College Park, Maryland (NACP), Philippine Department Telegrams, August 6 and 12, 1918, RG 135.

6. George A. Hunt, *History of the Twenty-Seventh U.S. Infantry* (Honolulu: Honolulu Star Bulletin, 1931), 49.

7. NACP, Laurance B. Packard, "An Account of the American Expeditionary Forces in Siberia, August 1918 to March 1919," 7, AEFS, RG 395.

8. Graves, *Adventure,* 36.

9. Graves, *Adventure,* 36.

10. Roberts later became famous as a novelist; he wrote *Northwest Passage, Lydia Bailey,* and other famous books.

11. Kenneth Roberts, *I Wanted to Write* (Garden City, N.J.: Doubleday and Co., 1949), 76.

12. Hoover Institution on War, Revolution and Peace (HIWRP), Edith Faulstich Collection, Military folder, "Organizations that Served in American Forces in Siberia with Dates of Arrival in and Departure from Siberia," Box 9.

13. HIWRP, Edith Faulstich Collection, Samuel Johnson file, Florence Johnson, "Some Notes on the Life of Col. Samuel Johnson," Box 8.

14. Roberts, *Write,* 86.

15. Roberts, *Write,* 86.

16. Roberts, *Write,* 88.

17. Records indicate that courts-martial were held in Vladivostok for at least three officers; two were found guilty, but sentences were not revealed.

18. HIWRP, Edith Faulstich Collection, Rodney S. Sprigg file, Rodney S. Sprigg Manuscript, 35, Box 21.

19. HIWRP, Edith Faulstich Collection, Military folder, Box 9.

20. HIWRP, Edith Faulstich Collection, Military folder, "Organizations That Served in American Forces in Siberia," Box 9.

21. Packard, "Account," 8, AEFS, RG 395.

22. NACP, "Memorandum, Expedition to Vladivostok," July 6, 1918, AEFS, RG 395.

Chapter 18

1. William S. Graves, *America's Siberian Adventure* (New York: Peter Smith, 1941), 58.

2. National Archives, College Park, Maryland (NACP), Laurance B. Packard, "An Account of the American Expeditionary Forces in Siberia, August 1918 to March 1919," 13, AEFS, RG 395.

3. Richard Goldhurst, *The Midnight War—The American Intervention in Russia 1918–1920* (New York: McGraw-Hill, 1978), 74.

4. In North Russia, just four days before, Seaman Perschke had received the

first wound in that campaign. U.S. Army Military History Institute (USAMHI), Millard S. Curtis Papers, "History of the 27th Infantry Regiment," unpublished.

5. Goldhurst, *War,* 74.

6. Goldhurst, *War,* 74.

7. Edith Faulstich, *Siberian Sojourn,* Vol. 2 (Yonkers, N.Y.: Edith Faulstich, 1977), 64.

8. Graves, *Adventure,* 62.

9. Packard, "Account," 8, AEFS, RG 395.

10. Packard, "Account," 33, AEFS, RG 395.

11. Faulstich, *Sojourn,* Vol. 2, 101.

12. Hoover Institution on War, Revolution and Peace (HIWRP), Edith Faulstich Collection, George Billick Papers, Box 16.

13. Faulstich, *Sojourn,* Vol. 2, 114–115.

14. George A. Hunt, *History of the Twenty-Seventh U.S. Infantry* (Honolulu: Honolulu Star Bulletin, 1931), 53.

15. Packard, "Account," 56, AEFS, RG 395.

16. Hunt, *History,* 55.

17. Hunt, *History,* 55.

18. Packard, "Account," 22, AEFS, RG 395.

19. Packard, "Account," 59, AEFS, RG 395.

Chapter 19

1. National Archives, College Park, Maryland (NACP), Laurance B. Packard, "An Account of the American Expeditionary Forces in Siberia, August 1918 to March 1919," 66, AEFS, RG 395.

2. Richard O'Conner, "Yanks in Siberia," *American Heritage,* Volume 25, No. 5 (August 1974): 15.

3. William S. Graves, *America's Siberian Adventure* (New York: Peter Smith, 1941), 63.

4. Graves, *Adventure,* 57.

5. Graves, *Adventure,* 59.

6. NACP, William S. Graves, "Report on Operations of the AEFS to June 30, 1919," September 25, 1919, 7, AEFS, RG 395.

7. Graves, "Report," 7.

8. Graves, "Report," 8.

9. Graves, *Adventure,* 289.

10. Sylvian G. Kindall, *American Soldiers in Siberia* (New York: Richard R. Smith, 1945), 19.

11. Packard, "Account," 96.

12. Packard, "Account," 95.

13. Graves, *Adventure,* 57.

14. Packard, "Account," 51.

15. Graves, *Adventure,* 24–25.

16. Graves, "Report," 3.

17. Graves, *Adventure,* 89–90.

18. U.S. Army Military History Institute (USAMHI), Millard S. Curtis Papers, "History of the 31st Infantry Regiment," 14.

19. Graves, "Report," 11.

20. Elsa Brandstrom, *Among Prisoners of War in Russia and Siberia* (London: Hutchinson and Co., 1929), 261.

21. Kindall, *Soldiers,* 28–29.

22. Hoover Institution on War, Revolution and Peace (HIWRP), *Goles Rodini Newspaper,* January 2, 1920; Brandstrom, *Prisoners,* 259.

23. Edith Faulstich, *Siberian Sojourn,* Vol. 2 (Yonkers, N.Y.: Edith Faulstich, 1977), 81.

24. Graves, *Adventure,* 127.

25. Faulstich, *Sojourn,* 81.

26. Packard, "Account," 106.

27. Packard, "Account," 106–107.

28. Packard, "Account," 111.

29. Packard, "Account," 115.

30. Graves, *Adventure,* 136.

31. George A. Hunt, *History of the Twenty-Seventh U.S. Infantry* (Honolulu: Honolulu Star Bulletin, 1931), 59–60.

32. Graves, *Adventure,* 144.

33. Betty Miller Unterberger, *America's Siberian Expedition, 1918–1920: A Study of National Policy* (Durham, N.C.: Duke University Press, 1956), 104.

34. Graves, *Adventure,* 214.

35. Graves, *Adventure,* 143–144.

36. NACP, "Memorandum from Graves to the Adjutant General," October 31, 1918, AEFS, RG 395.

37. Graves, *Adventure,* 64.

38. NACP, "Intelligence Officer David Barrows to Chief of Staff," October 23, 1918, AEFS, RG 395.

39. Graves, *Adventure,* 90–91.

40. NACP, Message from Colonel Sargent to Commanding Officer, 2d Battalion, 31st Infantry, Spasskoye, October 16, 1918, AEFS, RG 395.

41. NACP, K. Otani to Graves, November 21, 1918, AEFS, RG 395.

42. NACP, Chief of Staff of the 18th Division to Commander 27th Infantry, undated, AEFS, RG 395.

43. Kindall, *Soldiers,* 163.

44. Graves, *Adventure,* 154.

45. Graves, *Adventure,* 155–156.

46. HIWRP, Edith Faulstich Collection, Suchan Mines folder, Eichelberger to his wife, April 23, 1919, Box 14.

47. USAMHI, Virginia Cooper Westall Collection, "Recollections of Robert L. Eichelberger."

Chapter 20

1. Richard Goldhurst, *The Midnight War: The American Intervention in Russia, 1918–1920* (New York: McGraw-Hill, 1978), 78.

2. U.S. Army Military History Institute (USAMHI), Joseph B. Longuevan Papers, Director, 2d Year Class, Command and General Staff School, Ft. Leavenworth, Kansas, "A Study of the Supply of the 31st Infantry, AEF."

3. Hoover Institution on War, Revolution and Peace (HIWRP), Elliott Reynolds Collection, Elliott Reynolds to Miss Sutcliff, December 30, 1918.

4. USAMHI, Joseph B. Longuevan Papers, Rodney S. Sprigg folder, Rodney Sprigg to his wife, March 3, 1919.

5. HIWRP, Edith Faulstich Collection, International Military Police folder, Box 7.

6. USAMHI, Joseph B. Longuevan Papers, Rodney S. Sprigg folder, Rodney Sprigg to his wife, March 3, 1919.

7. HIWRP, Edith Faulstich Collection, Samuel Johnson folder, Box 8.

8. HIWRP, Sprigg Collection.

9. USAMHI, Joseph B. Longuevan Papers, Richardson folder, Letter, Sam Richardson to Joseph Longuevan, February 13, 1973.

10. USAMHI, Joseph B. Longuevan Papers, Director, 2d Year Class, Command and General Staff School, Ft. Leavenworth, Kansas, "A Study of the Supply of the 31st Infantry, AEF."

11. HIWRP, Elliott Reynolds Collection, Elliott Reynolds to Miss Sutcliff, December 30, 1918.

12. Kenneth Roberts, *I Wanted to Write* (Garden City, N.J.: Doubleday and Co., 1949), 111.

13. Roberts, *Write,* 115.

14. HIWRP, Edith Faulstich Collection, Military folder, Box 9.

15. HIWRP, Edith Faulstich Collection, "From Here and There with the 31st," February 22, 1919, Box 6.

16. HIWRP, Edith Faulstich Collection, Entertainment folder, Box 6.

17. Author's collection, Gail Berg Reitzel, "Shifting Scenes in Siberia," unpublished journal.

18. USAMHI, Joseph B. Longuevan Papers, Russell Swihart, "German Prisoners of War in Siberia," Box 1.

19. HIWRP, "From Here and There with the 31st," February 22, 1919, Kinslingbury Collection.

20. USAMHI, James Loughran, World War I Survey.

21. HIWRP, Edith Faulstich Collection, Charles Maxwell Papers, Box 21.

22. HIWRP, Edith Faulstich Collection, Entertainment folder, Box 6.

23. National Archives, College Park, Maryland (NACP), James S. Wilson, "Medical History of the Siberian Expedition August 1918–June 1919," AEFS, RG 395.

24. HIWRP, Ernest Hoskins Collection, "In the Service of the U.S. Navy," unpublished memoir.

25. HIWRP, Edith Faulstich Collection, Naval folder, Box 9.

26. NACP, Sidney Graves, "Report on Operations of HMS *Kent* and Inter-Allied Committee," May 17, 1919, AEFS, RG 395.

27. Graves, "Report," AEFS, RG 395.

28. William S. Graves, *America's Siberian Adventure* (New York: Peter Smith, 1941), xiv.

29. Graves, *Adventure,* 98.

30. Graves, *Adventure,* 189.

31. In a telegram, dated January 4, 1920, an intelligence summary from

Eichelberger stated: "Colonel Wickham, the head of the British Mission, informed me that on the day that General Knox left for England he telegraphed his Government that Bolshevism was sure to come to Vladivostok. He stated further that the support given by the British Government to Admiral Kolchak has been the most disgraceful page in British History. . . . Colonel Wickham further stated that the Commanding General of the American Expeditionary Forces had long ago gained the correct view point of the Siberian situation."

32. NACP, Cablegram, Graves to AGWAR, Washington, November 21, 1918, AEFS, RG 395.

33. Carl Ackerman, *Trailing the Bolsheviki* (New York: Charles Scribner's Sons, 1919), 189.

34. Roberts, *Write,* 101.

35. HIWRP, Edith Faulstich Collection, William H. Johnson folder, William Johnson to his sister, February 12, 1919, Edith Box 19.

36. HIWRP, Elena Varneck, Translation of *The Closing of the Echo,* by Hector Boon, Box 1.

37. HIWRP, Elena Varneck, Translation of "The Death of a Newspaper," September 18, 1919, Box 1.

38. USAMHI, Joseph Ahearn Papers.

39. USAMHI, Millard S. Curtis Papers, "History of the 27th Infantry Regiment," unpublished.

40. George A. Hunt, *History of the Twenty-Seventh U.S. Infantry* (Honolulu: Honolulu Star Bulletin, 1931), 58.

41. HIWRP, Edith Faulstich Collection, *Here and There*, 31st Infantry newspaper, June 5, 1919, Spasskoye folder, Box 13.

42. Sylvian G. Kindall, *American Soldiers in Siberia* (New York: Richard R. Smith, 1945), 186.

43. Kindall, *Soldiers,* 185–186.

44. Kindall, *Soldiers,* 193–194.

45. NACP, Laurance B. Packard, "An Account of the American Expeditionary Forces in Siberia, August 1918 to March 1919," 45, AEFS, RG 395.

46. Peyton C. March, *The Nation at War* (Garden City, N.J.: Doubleday, Doran and Co., 1932), 132.

Chapter 21

1. National Archives, College Park, Maryland (NACP), William S. Graves, "Report to the Adjutant General of the Army, Operations to June 30, 1919," May 26, 1920, 15–18, AEFS, RG 395.

2. William S. Graves, *America's Siberian Adventure* (New York: Peter Smith, 1941), 178.

3. Graves, *Adventure*, 182.

4. Hoover Institution on War, Revolution and Peace (HIWRP), Benjamin O. Johnson Collection, B. O. Johnson to H. H. Fisher, May 19, 1931.

5. Sylvian G. Kindall, *American Soldiers in Siberia* (New York: Richard R. Smith, 1945), 199.

6. Graves, "Report," 17–18.

7. NACP, "Proclamation of the Field Staff of the Partizan Detachment of Olga County," May 1919, AEFS, RG 395.

8. U.S. Army Military History Institute (USAMHI), "History of the 27th Infantry Regiment," unpublished, 1922.

9. HIWRP, Edith Faulstich Collection, Pat O'Dea memoir, Entertainment folder, Box 6.

10. NACP, Robert L. Eichelberger, Intelligence Report, May 17, 1919, AEFS, RG 395.

11. NACP, Intelligence Summary No. 199, June 13, 1919, AEFS, RG 395.

12. NACP, Telegram #282, Morrow to Vladivostok, May 25, 1919, AEFS, RG 395.

13. NACP, "Report of Operations of the 27th Infantry, from January 1, 1919 to June 30, 1919," May 26, 1920, AEFS, RG 395.

14. George A. Hunt, *History of the Twenty-Seventh U.S. Infantry* (Honolulu: Honolulu Star Bulletin, 1931), 72.

15. Graves, *Adventure*, 254–255.

16. NACP, Medical Officer's Report, Field Hospital #4, AEFS, RG 395.

17. NACP, Telegram, Morrow to Vladivostok, June 19, 1919, AEFS, RG 395.

18. NACP, Intelligence Summary #196, Vladivostok, June 10, 1919, AEFS, RG 395.

19. Internet, *http://www.geocities.com/Pentagon/6215/siberia.htm*, "Wolfhounds"; Graves, *Adventure*, 183–184.

20. USAMHI, William Donovan Collection, "Memo from Inter Allied Commission to Omsk Government," July 16, 1919.

21. Fairfax Channing, *Siberia's Untouched Treasure* (New York: G. P. Putnam's Sons, 1923), 276–279.

22. Kindall, *Soldiers*, 233.

23. Channing, *Treasure*, 276–279.

24. Kindall, *Soldiers*, 113–120.

25. HIWRP, Edith Faulstich Collection, Spasskoye folder, intelligence map, July 15, 1919, Box 13.

26. Kindall, *Soldiers*, 75.

27. NACP, Telegram #147, Allderdice to Vladivostok, May 21, 1919, AEFS, RG 395.

28. George A. Hunt, *History of the Twenty-Seventh U.S. Infantry* (Honolulu: Honolulu Star Bulletin, 1931), 70–71.

29. NACP, Report, "R. H. Sillman to Vladivostok," June 16, 1918, AEFS, RG 395.

30. Hunt, *History*, 143.

31. Hunt, *History*, 66.

32. Hunt, *History*, 67.

33. Hunt, *History*, 66–68; Edith Faulstich Collection, Casualties folder, Telegram, Graves to Washington June 18, 1919, Box 3; Kindall, *Soldiers*, 81.

34. NACP, Report, "R. H. Sillman to Vladivostok," June 15, 1918, AEFS, RG 395; USAMHI, Leroy W. Yarborough Papers, "Report of Sergeant Bachelor," August 6, 1919.

35. USAMHI, Leroy W. Yarborough Papers, "Report of Sergeant Bachelor," August 6, 1919.

36. HIWRP, Gretchen Haskin Collection, "Cause Celebré," n.d.

37. HIWRP, Edith Faulstich Collection, Spasskoye folder, Lieutenant Morse, Box 13.

38. Kindall, *Soldiers,* dedication.

39. Kindall, *Soldiers,* 139–151.

40. NACP, Telegram, R. H. Sillman to Vladivostok, June 23, 1919, AEFS, RG 395.

41. NACP, Telegram, R. H. Sillman to Vladivostok, June 24–25, 1919.

42. NACP, Report, "Davidson to Chief Intelligence Officer," September 3, 1919, AEFS, RG 395.

43. NACP, Report, "Davidson to Chief Intelligence Officer," September 3, 1919.

Chapter 22

1. National Archives, College Park, Maryland (NACP), Laurance B. Packard, "An Account of the American Expeditionary Forces in Siberia, August 1918 to March 1919," 73, AEFS, RG 395.

2. NACP, Laurance B. Packard, "Account," 75.

3. NACP, Laurance B. Packard, "Account," 75.

4. Hoover Institution on War, Revolution and Peace (HIWRP), Edith Faulstich Collection, Souchan Mines folder, Box 14.

5. NACP, Telegram, Graves to Washington, March 7, 1919, AEFS, RG 395.

6. U.S. Army Military Institute (USAMHI), Robert L. Eichelberger Papers, "Career of Robert Eichelberger," E 78.

7. USAMHI, Robert L. Eichelberger Papers, "Career" E 75.

8. NACP, Report, "Commanding Officer Allied Mine Guard to Vladivostok," July 10, 1918, AEFS, RG 395.

9. The only mention of Graves's visit is a brief note added to Cutrer's telegram on May 21: "The general is here."

10. Eric Smith, "Partisans and Polar Bears," master's thesis, San Jose State University, 1993, 100.

11. Smith, "Partisans," 100.

12. NACP, Report, "Commanding Officer."

13. NACP, Telegram, Cutrer to Krieger, May 23, 1919, AEFS, RG 395.

14. NACP, William S. Graves, "Report to the Adjutant General of the Army, Operations to June 30, 1919," May 26, 1920, AEFS, RG 395.

15. HIWRP, Edith Faulstich Collection, Shkotovo folder, Wilber Goreham, Box 13.

16. HIWRP, Edith Faulstich Collection, Maihe folder, Box 13.

17. NACP, Report, "Month of May Machine Gun Company," June 10, 1919, AEFS, RG 395.

18. NACP, "Report of Operations 31st Infantry, January 1–June 30, 1919," July 20, AEFS, RG 395.

19. NACP, "Report of Operations, January 1–June 30, 1919"; and Telegram, Cutrer to Vladivostok May 25, 1919, AEFS, RG 395.

20. NACP, Telegram, Allderdice to Vladivostok, June 7, 1918, AEFS, RG 395.

21. NACP, Graves, "Report," 20.

22. Smith, "Partisans," 110; and NACP, Report, "Commanding Officer Allied Mine Guard to Vladivostok," July 10, 1918, AEFS, RG 395.

23. NACP, Monthly Report, Company M, June 30, 1919, AEFS, RG 395.

24. HIWRP, Edith Faulstich Collection, Eastland Reed file, POWs folder, Box 10.

25. U.S. Military Academy Museum (USMAM), U.S. Military Academy Annual Report, June 14, 1920, 68.

26. NACP, Telegram, Williams to Vladivostok, June 23, 1919, AEFS, RG 395; and NACP, "Report of Operation in Suchan Valley June 22 to July 6, 1919," Suchan Mine Guard, n.d., AEFS, RG 395.

27. HIWRP, Edith Faulstich Collection, Eastland Reed file, POWs folder, Box 20.

28. NACP, Letter from the Temporary War Revolutionary Headquarters of the Olga District, Frolovka to AEF at Suchan June 22, 1919, AEFS, RG 395.

29. NACP, Fribley to Williams, June 25, 1919, AEFS, RG 395.

30. NACP, Williams to Fribley, June 26, 1919, AEFS, RG 395.

31. NACP, Intelligence Report, June 24, 1919, AEFS, RG 395.

32. NACP, Earle Jennings, "History of the Suchan Campaign," August 12, 1919, AEFS, RG 395.

33. Smith, "Partisans," 119.

34. USAMHI, Robert L. Eichelberger Papers, "Memoirs," E 81.

35. Eichelberger's memoirs were written many years after the event. He probably meant "railroad tracks" instead of "stream." There appeared to be no stream in the village.

36. USAMHI, Robert L. Eichelberger Papers, "Memoirs," E-81.

37. USAMHI, Leroy W. Yarborough Papers, Daily patrol reports and weekly battalion intelligence summary, July 13–19, 1919, Box 5; Reports by survivors, Commanding Officer Shkotovo to Vlad, July 18, 1919.

38. HIWRP, Edith Faulstich Collection, Joseph Longuevan folder, Letter to fellow Siberians and friends, September 1968, Box 21.

39. Smith, "Partisans," 124.

40. Smith, "Partisans," 125.

41. USAMHI, Leroy W. Yarborough Papers, Daily patrol reports and weekly battalion intelligence summary, July 13–19, 1919, Box 5; Reports by survivors, Commanding Officer Shkotovo to Vlad, July 19, 1919.

42. Sergeant Beck and his girl were later married and returned to the United States, where Beck remained in the Army.

43. HIWRP, Edith Faulstich Collection, Joseph Longuevan folder, Letter to fellow Siberians and friends, September 1968, Box 21.

44. USAMHI, Joseph B. Longuevan Papers, Stan Stephenson to Joseph Longuevan, June 25, 1969.

45. HIWRP, Edith Faulstich Collection, Romanovka Massacre folder, Sylvester B. Moore to Sargent June 29, 1919.

46. USAMHI, Leroy W. Yarborough Papers, Daily patrol reports and weekly battalion intelligence summary, July 13–19, 1919, Box 5; Reports by survivors, Commanding Officer Shkotovo to Vlad, July 19, 1919.

47. HIWRP, Edith Faulstich Collection, Harry Rohrer folder, Box 20

48. NACP, C. D. Meloy, "Report of Men Killed and Wounded in Action of Co. 'A' 31st Inf.," June 25, 1919, AEFS, RG 395.

49. NACP, Commanding officer Hospital Train #1 to chief surgeon, "Care and Transportation of Wounded," July 5, 1919, AEFS, RG 395.

50. USAMHI, Joseph B. Longuevan Papers, Sam Richardson folder, "The Romanovka Massacre."

51. USAMHI, Leroy W. Yarborough Papers, Daily patrol reports and weekly battalion intelligence summary, July 13–19, 1919, Box 5; Reports by survivors, Commanding officer Shkotovo to Vlad, July 19, 1919.

52. USAMHI, Joseph B. Longuevan Papers, Romanovka folder, "Report of Operations in Shkotovo Sector."

53. HIWRP, Edith Faulstich Collection, William H. Johnson folder, Box 19.

54. USAMHI, Robert L. Eichelberger Papers, "Memoirs," E 82.

55. USAMHI, Leroy W. Yarborough Papers, "Discipline Cases Siberia," Box 4, 1919–1920.

56. NACP, "Engagement at Sitsa, Siberia," June 29, AEFS, RG 395.

57. National Archives, Washington, D.C. (NADC), Log of the USS *Albany,* July 1, 1919, Naval Records, RG 24.

58. Log of the *Albany,* July 1, 1919, RG 24.

Chapter 23

1. National Archives, College Park, Maryland (NACP), Telegram, Robinson to all commanding officers, June 26, 1919, AEFS, RG 395.

2. Hoover Institution on War, Revolution and Peace (HIWRP), Edith Faulstich Collection, Suchan Mines folder, Eichelberger to his wife "Em," June 27, 1919, Box 14.

3. U.S. Army Military History Institute (USAMHI), Robert L. Eichelberger Papers, "Memoirs," E 85.

4. USAMHI, Robert L. Eichelberger Papers, "Memoirs," E 84.

5. HIWRP, Edith Faulstich Collection, Suchan Mines folder, Pvt. H. Bullard, Memoir, Box 14.

6. HIWRP, Edith Faulstich Collection, Suchan Mines folder, Williams to Vladivostok, "Report of Operation in Suchan Valley, Siberia, June 22–July 5, 1919," 3–4, Box 14.

7. Duke University, Rare Book, Manuscript, and Special Collections Library, Robert Eichelberger Collection, Correspondence from Siberia to wife, July 5, 1919.

8. USAMHI, Joseph B. Longuevan Papers, C. W. Stephenson to Longuevan, December 10, 1969; USAMHI, Robert L. Eichelberger Papers, "Memoirs," E 86.

9. HIWRP, Edith Faulstich Collection, Suchan Mines folder, Williams to Vladivostok, "Report," 4.

10. NACP, Earle Jennings, "History of the Suchan Campaign," August 12, 1919, AEFS, RG 395.

11. HIWRP, Edith Faulstich Collection, George Betz folder, Box 16.

12. NACP, "Troops Engaged and Record of Events," July 9, AEFS, RG 395.

13. National Archives, Washington, D.C. (NADC), Log of the USS *Albany*, July 6–7, 1919, Naval Records, RG 24.

14. HIWRP, Edith Faulstich Collection, Major Robert Eichelberger Letters, Eichelberger to his wife, July 6, 1919, Box 5.

15. NADC, Log of the USS *Albany*, July 7, 1919, Naval Records, RG 24.

16. NACP, "Report of Operation in Suchan Valley, Siberia, June 22–July 5, 1919," AEFS, RG 395.

17. HIWRP, Edith Faulstich Collection, Naval folder, Telegram, Eichelberger to Vlad from the USS *Albany*, July 7, 1919, Box 9.

18. HIWRP, William S. Graves Collection, Personal Communication folder, Box 1.

19. HIWRP, Edith Faulstich Collection, Suchan folder, Vernon I. Basler, "The Evacuation of Suchan," in *Here and There with the 31st*, September 10, 1919, Box 14.

20. NACP, "Operations toward Gordievka," July 15, 1919, AEFS, RG 395.

21. NACP, "Operations Carried Out in This Sector, Shkotovo," n.d., 5, AEFS, RG 395.

22. NACP, "Operations, Shkotovo," n.d., 6–8, AEFS, RG 395.

23. NACP, "Operations, Shkotovo," n.d., 9, AEFS, RG 395.

Chapter 24

1. U.S. Army Military History Institute (USAMHI), U.S. Army, "Order of Battle of the United States Land Forces in the World War: American Expeditionary Forces, Siberia, Command and Staff," (Washington, D.C.: Government Printing Office, 1923), 385.

2. Hoover Institution on War, Revolution and Peace (HIWRP), Fred Bugbee Collection, Faith Bugbee, "American Expeditionary Forces in Siberia," college paper, Stanford University, 1934.

3. Paul Chwlalkowski, *In Caesar's Shadow* (Westport, Conn.: Greenwood Press, 1993), 23.

4. USAMHI, U.S. Army, "Order of Battle," 385.

5. William S. Graves, *America's Siberian Adventure* (New York: Peter Smith, 1941), 162–164.

6. Graves, *Adventure*, 120.

7. Graves, *Adventure*, 121.

8. Graves, *Adventure*, 159.

9. Graves, *Adventure*, 159–160.

10. There is some confusion about the dates and the targets for the two expeditions. Graves reported Company B went to Olga, yet several memoirs reported that the objective was the mines at Tethue. The date of departure varied from July 29 to 31, but July 31 seemed to prevail.

11. HIWRP, Edith Faulstich Collection, V. E. Hockett folder, "Memoir of V. E. Hockett," Box 18.

12. USAMHI, Clifford Catlin, World War I Survey.

13. HIWRP, Edith Faulstich Collection, Naval folder, Eichelberger to his wife July 27, 1919, Box 9.

14. National Archives, College Park, Maryland (NACP), William S. Graves, "Report to the Adjutant General of the Army, Operations to June 30, 1919," May 26, 1920, AEFS, RG 395.

15. Duke University, Rare Book, Manuscript, and Special Collections Library, Robert Eichelberger Collection, Correspondence from Siberia to his wife July 10, 1919.

16. Betty Miller Unterberger, *America's Siberian Expedition, 1918–1920: A Study of National Policy* (Durham, N.C.: Duke University Press, 1956), 160–161.

17. Graves, *Adventure,* 227–242.

18. Max Boot, *The Savage Wars of Peace* (New York: Basic Books, 2002), 228.

19. Graves, *Adventure,* 249.

20. George A. Hunt, *History of the Twenty-Seventh U.S. Infantry* (Honolulu: Honolulu Star Bulletin, 1931), 73–74.

21. Hunt, *History,* 74.

22. U.S. Military Academy Museum (USMAM), Benjamin A. Dickson to his father, August 31, 1919.

23. USMAM, Benjamin A. Dickson to his father, August 31, 1919.

24. NACP, Morrow to chief of staff, "Munition Cars at Chita," November 3, 1919, AEFS, RG 395.

25. NACP, Morrow, "Munition Cars."

26. Graves, *Adventure,* 263.

27. USMAM, Benjamin A. Dickson to his father, December 28, 1919.

28. NACP, Graves, "Report."

29. Graves, *Adventure,* 215.

30. NACP, Graves, "Report."

31. NACP, Graves, "Report."

32. Graves, *Adventure,* 143.

33. Richard Goldhurst, *The Midnight War: The American Intervention in Russia, 1918–1920* (New York: McGraw-Hill, 1978), 216.

34. HIWRP, Benjamin Davis Papers, Summary of events of attempted revolution in Vladivostok.

35. HIWRP, Edith Faulstich Collection, Naval folder, Box 9.

36. NADC, Log of the USS *Brooklyn,* November 17–19, 1919, Naval Records, RG 24.

37. HIWRP, Benjamin Davis Papers, Summary of events of attempted revolution in Vladivostok.

38. HIWRP, Edith Faulstich Collection, Johnson file, "My Recollection of the Rescue of General Romanovsky and Family," Box 8.

39. Major Johnson, Major Graves, 1st Sgt. Marion Roda, Sgt. George Masury, Cpl. Joseph Jerome, and Pfc. Robert Nickovich.

40. Graves, *Adventure,* 285.

41. HIWRP, Edith Faulstich Collection, Eichelberger to his wife, November 18, 1919, Box 5.

42. HIWRP, Edith Faulstich Collection, Gaida's folder, Box 6.

43. HIWRP, Edith Faulstich Collection, Eichelberger to his wife, November 18, 1919, Box 5.

44. Christopher Dobson and John Miller, *The Day They Almost Bombed Moscow* (New York: Atheneum, 1986), 265.

45. National Archives, Pacific Alaska Region, General Court-martial of Anton Karachun, March 22, 1920.

46. Graves, *Adventure,* 302–303.

47. Robert J. Maddox, *The Unknown War with Russia* (San Rafael, Calif.: Presidio Press, 1977), 126.

Chapter 25

1. George F. Kennan, *The Decision to Intervene.* Vol. 2, *Soviet-American Relations, 1917–1920* (Princeton, N.J.: Princeton University Press, 1958), 168.

2. Henry Davison, *The American Red Cross in the Great War* (New York: MacMillan Co., 1919), 270.

3. Davison, *Red Cross,* 274.

4. Hoover Institution on War, Revolution and Peace (HIWRP), Grace Bungey file.

5. National Archives, College Park, Maryland (NACP), ARC report on Typhus train, May 15, 1919, Box 918, RG 200.

6. Jesse A. Anderson, *A Doughboy in the AEF Siberia* (Berkeley, Calif.: Jesse A. Anderson, 1983), n.p.

7. Anderson, *Doughboy,* n.p.

8. Anderson, *Doughboy,* xvii.

9. NACP, Gertrude Pardee Carter, "The Omsk Hospital," RG 200, Box 918.

10. NACP, "Memo from Central and Western Divisions to Washington," October 16, 1919, RG 200, Box 918.

11. HIWRP, E. Alfred Davies file, Diary.

12. NACP, "Memo from Western Division to Finance Committee, Central Division," January 7, 1920, RG 200, Box 918.

13. Wisconsin Historical Society (WHS), Stacey M. Snow, "'Mother' Campbell of the Smile and Great Big Heart," *Red Cross Courier,* January 2, 1928, 6–8, 24–26.

14. William S. Graves, *America's Siberian Adventure* (New York: Peter Smith, 1941), 330–331.

15. WHS, "It's a Dream,"*Seattle Times,* July 28, 1973.

16. Francis D. Connor, Arthur B. Grinell, Willard C. Howry, James J. Johnson, Raymond A. Watson, Edith Barnett, and Mrs. McBride.

17. Graves, *Adventure,* 330.

Chapter 26

1. John Albert White, *The Siberian Intervention* (Princeton, N.J.: Princeton University Press, 1950), 351.

2. Hoover Institution on War, Peace and Revolution (HIWRP), Fred W. Bugbee Collection, Bugbee to his wife, January 22, 1920.

3. HIWRP, Edith Faulstich Collection, Bugbee report on incidents, January 23, 1919, Combat Action folder, Box 3.

4. U.S. Army Military History Institute (USAMHI), Gillem Papers, A. C. Gillem, "Report of Expedition to Mukheeve, January 7, 1920."

5. USAMHI, Gillem Papers, A. C. Gillem, "Report."

6. U.S. Military Academy Museum (USMAM), Lieutenant Dixon to his father and Tracey, January 4, 1919.

7. HIWRP, Virginia Westall Taylor Papers, "Bull Kendall in Siberia," *The Blue Devil Magazine* (May 1987): 6.

8. HIWRP, Taylor Papers, "Bull Kendall," 6.

9. William S. Graves, *America's Siberian Adventure* (New York: Peter Smith, 1941), 313.

10. Graves, *Adventure*, 312.

11. HIWRP, Harris Papers, McCroskey file, Graves to Washington, December 14, 1919, Box 2.

12. HIWRP, Harris Papers, McCroskey file, Harris to Washington, January 14, 1920, Box 2.

13. HIWRP, Harris Papers, McCroskey file, Harris to Washington, February 17, 1920, Box 2.

14. Graves, *Adventure*, 314.

15. Graves, *Adventure*, 315.

16. USAMHI, World War I Survey, Joseph Loughran questionnaire.

17. HIWRP, Edith Faulstich Collection, Admiral Kolchak folder, Box 8; and Herman Bernstein, "Kolchak's Own Story," *Chicago Herald and Examiner*, November 21, 1921.

18. Graves, *Adventure*, 321–323.

19. HIWRP, Edith Faulstich Collection, 31st Infantry file, Special Orders #43, March 8, 1920, Box 13.

20. USAMHI, "History of the 27th Infantry Regiment," unpublished, 1922.

21. Graves, *Adventure*, 328.

22. HIWRP, Edith Faulstich Collection, Military folder, "Dates of Arrival in and Departure from Siberia," Box 9.

23. John Albert White, *The Siberian Intervention* (Princeton, N.J: Princeton University Press, 1950), 361–369.

24. USAMHI, Robert L. Eichelberger Papers, "Memoirs," E 53–54.

25. USAMHI, Joseph B. Longuevan Papers, David R. Opperman, "Army Transports and Navy Warships Participating in the Siberian Intervention," January 5, 1984, 15.

26. Gen. Peyton C. March, *The Nation at War* (Garden City, N.J.: Doubleday, Doran and Co., 1932), 139–140.

Chapter 27

1. George F. Kennan, *Soviet-America Relations, 1917–1920: Volume II. The Decision to Intervene* (Princeton, N.J.: Princeton University Press, 1958), 470.

2. Kennan, *Decision,* 459–460.

3. National Archives, College Park, Maryland (NACP), "Memo from Rear Adm. N. A. McCully to the Secretary of the Navy," August 9, 1919, AEFS, RG 395.

4. Sylvian G. Kindall, *American Soldiers in Siberia* (New York: Richard R. Smith, 1945), 251.

SELECTED BIBLIOGRAPHY

PRIMARY SOURCES

Public Records

American Monuments Battle Commission, Washington D.C., Selected List of WWI Burials.

National Archives, Washington, D.C., Naval Records, Record Group 45.

National Archives, College Park, Maryland, Records of American Expeditionary Force North Russia, Microfilm Reels 1–2, Record Group 120.

National Archives, College Park, Maryland, Records of American Expeditionary Force Siberia, Microfilm Reels 1–12, Record Group 395.

National Archives, College Park, Maryland, Records of the American Red Cross, Record Group 200.

National Archives, Washington, D.C., Naval Records, Record Group 24.

Unpublished

Anderson, Godfrey Manuscript. Michigan's Own Museum (MOM). Frankenmuth, Michigan.

Arkins, Edwin. Journal. University of Michigan, Bentley Historical Library (UMBHL). Ann Arbor, Michigan.

Bahr, Golden. Papers. UMBHL. Ann Arbor, Michigan.

Bahr, Golden. Red Cross Records. Manistee Historical Museum. Manistee, Michigan.

Ballensinger, Richard W. Edward Flaherty Collection. UMBHL. Ann Arbor, Michigan.

Bonnell, Jay. Reminiscence. UMBHL. Ann Arbor, Michigan.

Brock, Edward. Diary. UMBHL. Ann Arbor, Michigan.

Clark, Roger Sherman. Letters. UMBHL. Ann Arbor, Michigan.

Coburn, Cleo. Diary. UMBHL. Ann Arbor, Michigan.

Crissman, John Sherman. Diary. UMBHL. Ann Arbor, Michigan.

Duoma, Frank. Journal. UMBHL. Ann Arbor, Michigan.

Funk, Forest J. Papers. Hoover Institution of War, Revolution and Peace (HIWRP). Stanford, California.

Grace, Charles. Journal. Joint Archives, Hope College (JAHC). Holland, Michigan.

Hall, John. Diary. Wisconsin State Library (WSL). Madison, Wisconsin.

Hancock, Thomas. Diary. MOM. Frankenmuth, Michigan.

Harold Weimeister. World War I Survey. U.S. Army Military History Institute (USAMHI). Carlisle, Pennsylvania.

Hershberger, Russell. Memoirs. JAHC. Holland, Michigan.

James, G. T. Diary. UMBHL. Ann Arbor, Michigan.

Johnson, Godfrey. Collection. Grand Rapids Public Library. Grand Rapids, Michigan.

Knoll, Gerrit. Journal. JAHC. Holland, Michigan.

Krooyer, Fred. George Albers Papers. UMBHL. Ann Arbor, Michigan.

Lawes, A. L. From A. L. Lawes to Mr. W. A. H. Hulton, July 18, 1918. Olga Melikoff Collection. Montreal, Quebec, Canada.

MacMorland, E. E. Letters. USAMHI. Carlisle, Pennsylvania.

McCurdy, Ray. Diary. MOM. Frankenmuth, Michigan.

Oudemuller, John. Diary. JAHC. Holland, Michigan.

Parrish, Silver. Diary. UMBHL. Ann Arbor, Michigan.

Rademacher, Paul. Diary. www.execpc.com/~jpayne/diary21.htm. Internet website.

Rasmussen, Raymond. Diary. UMBHL. Ann Arbor, Michigan.

Ray, Robert. Diary. MOM. Frankenmuth, Michigan.

Report. Conduct of Company I, George E. Stewart Papers. U.S. Military Academy Museum (USMAM). West Point, New York.

Roster of Company K. Percy Walker Papers. MOM. Frankenmuth, Michigan.

Ryan, Charles Brady Diary. UMBHL. Ann Arbor, Michigan.

Salchow, Hugo. Reminiscences. UMBHL. Ann Arbor, Michigan.

Simpson, Charles. Diary. UMBHL. Ann Arbor, Michigan.

Siplon, James. Diary. JAHC. Holland, Michigan.

Smith, Gordon. Diary. UMBHL. Ann Arbor, Michigan.

Stewart, George E. Report of Expedition to the Murman Coast. USMAM. West Point, New York.

Totten, Paul. Memoirs. UMBHL. Ann Arbor, Michigan.

Trombley, Edward. Diary. UMBHL. Ann Arbor, Michigan.

Weeks, Glenn. Diary. Wisconsin Historical Society (WHS). Madison, Wisconsin.

Books

A Chronicler (John Cudahy). 1924. *Archangel: The American War with Russia.* Chicago: A. C. McClurg and Co.

Ackerman, Carl W. 1919. *Trailing the Bolshevik.* New York: Scribner.

Albertson, Ralph. 1920. *Fighting without a War.* New York: Harcourt, Brace and Howe.

Anderson, Jesse A. 1983. *A Doughboy in the American Expeditionary Forces—Siberia.* Berkeley, Calif: William A. Anderson.

Becvar, Gustaf. 1939. *The Lost Legion.* London: Stanley Paul and Co.

Fraser, Eugenie. 1984. *The House by the Dvina.* New York: Walker and Co.

Gordon, Dennis. 1982. *Quartered in Hell.* Missoula, Mont.: Doughboy Historical Society, Inc.

Graves, William S. 1941. *America's Siberian Adventure, 1918–1920.* New York:
Peter Smith.

Hunt, George A. 1931. *History of the Twenty-Seventh U.S. Infantry.* Honolulu:
Honolulu Star Bulletin.

Ironside, Edmund. 1953. *Archangel: 1918–1919.* London: Constable and Co.

Kettle, Michael. 1992. *Churchill and the Archangel Fiasco, November 1918–
July 1920.* London: Routledge.

Kindall, Sylvian G. 1945. *American Soldiers in Siberia.* New York: Richard R.
Smith.

Luvaas, Jay, ed. 1972. *Dear Miss Em: General Eichelberger's War in the Pacific.*
Westport, Conn.: Greenwood Press, Inc.

MacLaren, Roy. 1976. *Canadians in Russia, 1918–1919.* Toronto: McMillan of
Canada.

March, Peyton C. 1932. *The Nation at War.* Garden City, N.J.: Doubleday, Doran
and Co., Inc.

Maynard, Maj. Gen. Sir C. 1928. *The Murmansk Venture.* London: Hodder and
Stoughton.

Medek, Rudolf. 1929. *The Czechoslovak Anabasis across Russia and Siberia.*
London: The Czech Society.

Moore, Joel R. 1920. *'M' Company: 339th Infantry in North Russia.* Jackson,
Mich.: Central City Book Bindery.

Moore, Joel R., Harry Meade, and Lewis Jahns. 1920. *History of the American
Expedition Fighting the Bolsheviki: Campaigning in North Russia.* Detroit:
Polar Bear Publishing Co.

Roberts, Kenneth. 1949. *I Wanted to Write.* Garden City, N.J.: Doubleday and
Co., Inc.

Savinkov, Boris. 1931. *Memoirs of a Terrorist.* New York: Albert and Charles
Boni.

Soutar, Andrew. 1940. *With Ironside in North Russia.* London: Hutchinson and
Co.

York, Dorothea. 1923. *Romance of Company A.* Detroit: McIntyre Printing Co.

SECONDARY SOURCES

Books

Bozich, Stanley J., and Jon R. Bozich. 1985. *Detroit's Own Polar Bears: The
American North Russian Expeditionary Forces.* Frankenmuth, Mich.: Polar
Bear Publishing Co.

Bradley, John. 1968. *Allied Intervention in Russia.* London: Weidenfeld and
Nicolson.

Brandstrom, Elsa. 1929. *Among Prisoners of War in Russia and Siberia.* London: Hutchinson and Co., Ltd.

Carey, Donald E., ed. 1997. *Fighting the Bolsheviks.* Novato, Calif.: Presidio
Press.

Channing, Fairfax. 1923. *Siberia's Untouched Treasure.* New York: G. P. Putnam's Sons.

Chwialkowski, Paul. 1993. *In Caesar's Shadow.* Westport, Conn.: Greenwood Press.

Costello, Harry J. 1920. *Why Did We Go to Russia?.* Detroit: Harry J. Costello.

Davison, Henry P. 1919. *The American Red Cross in the Great War.* New York: The MacMillan Co.

Dobson, Christopher, and John Miller. 1986. *The Day They Almost Bombed Moscow.* New York: Atheneum.

Dupuy, R. Ernest. 1951. *Men of West Point.* New York: William Sloane Associates.

Dupuy, R. Ernest. 1939. *Perish by the Sword.* Harrisburg, Pa.: Military Service Publishing Co.

Encyclopaedia Brittanica, 15th ed. 1968. Vol. 15. Chicago: Encyclopaedia Brittanica, Inc.

Faulstich, Edith. 1972. *Siberian Sojourn.* 2 vols. Yonkers, N.Y.: Edith Faulstich.

Fleming, D. F. 1968. *The Origins and Legacies of World War I.* Garden City, N.J.: Doubleday and Co., Inc.

Fogelsong, David S. 1995. *America's Secret War against Bolshevism.* Chapel Hill, N.C.: University of North Carolina Press.

Goldhurst, Richard. 1978. *The Midnight War: The American Intervention in Russia, 1918–1920.* New York: McGraw Hill.

Halliday, E. M. 1960. *The Ignorant Armies.* New York: Harpers.

Hardman, Ric. 1968. *Fifteen Flags.* Boston: Little, Brown and Co.

Hays, Otis, Jr. 1990. *Home from Siberia.* College Station, Tex.: Texas A&M University Press.

Horne, Charles F., ed. 1931. *Source Records of the Great War.* Vol 6. Indianapolis: The American Legion.

Horowitz, David, ed. 1967. *Containment and Revolution: American Intervention into Russia, 1917–1920.* Boston: Beacon Press.

Hoyt, Edwin P. 1967. *The Army without a Country.* New York–London: The MacMillan Co.

Jackson, Robert. 1972. *At War with the Bolsheviks.* London: Tom Stacey, Ltd.

Kennan, George F. 1958. *The Decision to Intervene.* Vol. 2, *Soviet-American Relations, 1917–1920.* Princeton, N.J.: Princeton University Press.

Kennan, George F. 1960. *Russia and the West under Lenin and Stalin.* Boston: Little, Brown and Co.

Kerensky, Alexander F. 1927. *The Catastrophy: Kerensky's Own Story of the Russian Revolution.* London: D. Appleton and Co.

Lockhart, R. H. Bruce. 1933. *British Agent.* London: G. P. Putnam's Sons.

Longstreet, Stephen. 1970. *The Canvas Falcons.* New York: World Publishing Co.

Melton, Carol W. 2001. *Between War and Peace.* Macon, Ga.: Mercer University Press.

Moorehead, Alan. 1958. *The Russian Revolution.* New York: Harper and Brothers Publishers.

Rhodes, Benjamin D. 1988. *The Anglo-American Winter War with Russia, 1918–1919.* New York: Greenwood Press.

Seaton, Albert, and Joan Seaton. 1986. *The Soviet Army.* New York: New American Library.

Strakhovsky, Leonid. 1972. *The Origins of American Intervention in North Russia (1918).* New York: Howard Fertig.

U.S. Battle Monuments Commission. 1938. *American Armies and Battlefields in Europe.* Washington, D.C.: U.S. Printing Office.

White, John Albert. 1950. *The Siberian Intervention.* Princeton, N.J.: Princeton University Press.

Wilson, John. 1919. *Arctic Antics.* Salina, Kans.: Padgett's Printing House.

Theses

Roe, Murray Oliver. 1969. "American Military Intervention in Russia 1918–1920." Master's thesis, University of San Diego.

Smith, Erik. 1993. "Partisans and Polar Bears." Master's thesis, San Jose State University.

Articles

Clark, Brian. "Russia, 1919." *Sacramento Bee.* February 15, 1980.

Crownover, Roger. "Stranded in Russia." *Michigan History,* January–February 1999.

Goldin, Vladislav. "The Russian Revolution and the North." *International Politics,* December 1996.

Levkin, Gregory, and Serge Savchenko. "The US Military Presence in Russia's Far East." *Far East Review,* April 1998.

Lowe, Karl H. "Americans Defending Vladivostok." *Military History,* October 1997.

MacMorland, E. E. "American Railroading in North Russia." *The Military Engineer,* September–October 1929.

Mason, Herbert M., Jr. "Mission to North Russia." *VFW Magazine,* April 1999.

Stevenson, Charles. "40 Below Zero Campaign." *Army Magazine,* February 1969.

Tolley, Rear Adm. Kemp. "Our Russian War of 1918–1919." *Naval Institute Proceedings,* February 1969.

Wilson, John E. "When Mumansk Went Yank." *American Legion Magazine,* February 1940.

Newspapers

Battle Creek Enquirer. Trench and Camp, July 4, 1918.

Manisteee News Advocate. June 2, 1919.

The American Sentinel. February 15, 1919.

Grand Rapids Press. Undated newspaper clipping.

INDEX

311

ABOUT THE AUTHOR

Robert L. Willett was a banker in Michigan, Florida, and Saipan before joining the Resolution Trust Corporation, charged with cleaning up the S&L situation. Throughout his career, he was fascinated by history, initially with the Civil War period, which prompted him to write two well-received books: *One Day of the Civil War: April 10, 1863,* published by Brassey's, Inc. and *The Lightning Mule Brigade*, published by Guild Press.

After retiring, he undertook volunteer bank-consulting projects in Romania, Poland, Russia, Africa, and Moldova. His time in Russia led him to an interest in America's strange involvement in the Russian civil war. One of his banking clients in Komsomolsk, Russia, who knew of his interest in the American Civil War, suggested that he consider writing about the Russian civil war, known to us as the Russian Revolution. Coupled with his wife Donna's family exposure to that episode through her uncle Golden's participation and death in the American Expeditionary Force North Russia, Willett began the research for *Russian Sideshow*, which took him to both the Russian Far East and North Russia.

In addition to his books, he has published articles in a number of historical publications, including the *Civil War Times, Illustrated; America's Civil War; Chattahoochee Review; MHQ: Quarterly Journal of Military History;* as well as a number of banking and travel periodicals.

He and his wife live in Cocoa Beach, Florida.